On Campaign Against
Fort Duquesne

ALSO BY DOUGLAS R. CUBBISON

The British Defeat of the French in Pennsylvania, 1758:
A Military History of the Forbes Campaign Against Fort Duquesne
(McFarland, 2010)

The American Northern Theater Army in 1776:
The Ruin and Reconstruction of the Continental Force
(McFarland, 2010)

On Campaign Against Fort Duquesne

The Braddock and Forbes
Expeditions, 1755–1758, through
the Experiences of Quartermaster
Sir John St. Clair

Douglas R. Cubbison

McFarland & Company, Inc., Publishers
Jefferson, North Carolina

LIBRARY OF CONGRESS CATALOGUING-IN-PUBLICATION DATA

Cubbison, Douglas.
On campaign against Fort Duquesne : the Braddock and Forbes Expeditions, 1755–1758, through the experiences of quartermaster Sir John St. Clair / Douglas R. Cubbison.
    p.   cm.
Includes bibliographical references and index.

ISBN 978-0-7864-9783-6 (softcover : acid free paper) ∞
ISBN 978-1-4766-2113-5 (ebook)

1. St. Clair, John, –1767.   2. Braddock's Campaign, 1755.
3. Forbes Expedition against Fort Duquesne, Pa., 1758.
4. Braddock's Campaign, 1755—Sources.   5. Forbes Expedition against Fort Duquesne, Pa., 1758—Sources.   6. Quartermasters—Great Britain—Biography.   7. Quartermasters—Great Britain—Correspondence.   8. United States—History—French and Indian War, 1754–1763—Campaigns.   I. Title.   II. Title: Braddock and Forbes Expeditions, 1755–1758, through the experiences of quartermaster Sir John St. Clair.

E199.C9575 2015   973.2'6—dc23   2015008756

BRITISH LIBRARY CATALOGUING DATA ARE AVAILABLE

© 2015 Douglas R. Cubbison. All rights reserved

No part of this book may be reproduced or transmitted in any form or by any means, electronic or mechanical, including photocopying or recording, or by any information storage and retrieval system, without permission in writing from the publisher.

On the cover: *inset* portrait of Sir John St. Clair by Alan Ramsay (Fort Ligonier); lithograph of scene of the battle of the Monongahela: *Life of George Washington—the Soldier* by Régnier, imp. Lemercier, Paris (Library of Congress)

Printed in the United States of America

*McFarland & Company, Inc., Publishers
Box 611, Jefferson, North Carolina 28640
www.mcfarlandpub.com*

Table of Contents

Preface	1
Redcoats in Virginia: Introduction to the Braddock Expedition	3
1. "A mad sort of Fool": Sir John St. Clair, Infantry Officer, Before 1754	9
2. "An officer of distinction, who aids and assists the general": The Staff of Braddock's Expedition	10
3. "I have done every thing in my power to facilitate their march to the Allegany Mountains": Organization of the Movement to Fort Cumberland, January–March 1755	34
4. "The roads begin to be very indifferent": Movement from Alexandria to Fort Cumberland	60
5. "We pursued our route through a desolate country": Movement to Fort Duquesne	72
6. "Amongst the first that were wounded": Battle of Monongahela and Retreat	98
7. Mountains, Wagons and Whiskey: Sir John St. Clair's Participation in the Forbes Campaign, 1758	111
8. "Sir John's long illness": Sir John St. Clair, 1759–1767	123
9. "A Lyon Rampant": Conclusions	129
Appendix A: Sir John St. Clair's Braddock Campaign Letterbook	131
Appendix B: Sir John St. Clair's Chronology, October 1754–September 1755	192
Appendix C: Catalogue of Sir John St. Clair's Letterbook During the Braddock Expedition	197
Chapter Notes	201
Bibliography	215
Index	221

Preface

I grew up in Slippery Rock, Pennsylvania, and my first forays into living history and public education occurred at "The Old Stone House," an early 19th century stagecoach stop and tavern then operated as a historic site by the Pennsylvania Historic and Museum Commission. Located on today's Pennsylvania State Highway #8, a spring at this site had seen a young George Washington pass by on his mission to the Ohio Country in 1753. Western Pennsylvania, to this day, remains influenced by the campaign conducted by British general Edward Braddock against the French-occupied Forks of the Ohio, now Pittsburgh, in 1755. The campaign has always fascinated me, and as my skills and experience as a professional historian and soldier have matured, I increasingly came to believe that this particular campaign is one of the most misunderstood and incorrectly interpreted campaigns in American history. In particular, major tactical questions regarding the Battle of the Monongahela have never been satisfactorily addressed by historians.

Approximately ten years ago, while performing the extensive and exhaustive research necessary to produce my study of the 1758 Forbes Campaign, I encountered the letterbook of a minor Scottish peer, Sir John St. Clair, who served as quartermaster to both Braddock in 1755 and Forbes in 1758, buried in the Headquarters Papers of Brigadier General John Forbes. This discovery served as the catalyst to enable me to develop this study, presenting my interpretation of the Braddock Campaign, told through the letters and participation of Sir John St. Clair in two campaigns across the endless ridges of the Allegheny Mountains.

Unfortunately, in the nearly ten years that I have devoted to this study, I moved through a succession of challenging and productive career positions and residences. During the most recent move to the North Platte River in central Wyoming, my carefully maintained list of acknowledgements was electronically devoured by a recalcitrant computer, a list which cannot now be reconstructed.

I find myself compelled to simply state that I have been assisted in this study by literally dozens of professional associates, archivists, librarians, fellow historians, history buffs, and friends. You all know how you are, and please accept my most sincere and deepest appreciation. I owe all of you a bourbon and cigars...

In particular, throughout the preparation of this manuscript I have regularly attended the annual conference of the Braddock Road Preservation Association, held at the Methodist Retreat at Jumonville, Pennsylvania, the first weekend of November. For anybody interested in the study of the Braddock Campaign, this conference remains the single finest venue in the nation, and I recommend attendance in the strongest possible terms.

Transcription Notes

A. I have made every attempt to preserve capitalization, punctuation and spellings as they are written.

B. Where I have felt it necessary to add punctuation for clarity, I have enclosed the added punctuation in brackets [x].

C. Words that cannot be transcribed for whatever reason are noted within brackets [xxxxx] with a reason and number of presumed words that are illegible.

D. St. Clair uses forward slashes / xxxxxx/, instead of traditional parentheses (xxxxx).

E. Each letter is preceded by page number from letterbook, description of letter with author and recipient, address, and date placed inside brackets [x].

F. A number of letters were placed out of their proper sequence into the letterbook, and I have adjusted their location into the correct chronological sequence as noted.

G. All other notes or comments are included as footnotes.

Redcoats in Virginia
Introduction to the Braddock Expedition

Beginning at the dawn of the 17th century, permanent British settlements began to appear along the western seaboard of the North Atlantic Ocean. By 1752, twelve distinct colonial governments had been organized by Great Britain. Several of these colonies, particularly those in New England and the Middle Colonies such as Pennsylvania, Maryland and Virginia, were comparatively well established. Younger ones such as Georgia were still new and uncertain entities. Although the charters of these colonies extended as far west as the Pacific Ocean, precise boundaries and distances were lacking, and in practice numerous and considerable obstacles stood in the way of such expansion.

The first such obstruction was topographical—the Appalachian Mountains that extended from Georgia in the south to the extreme northern reaches of Massachusetts (today's Maine). This mountain range was among the oldest on the planet, ancient and considerably weathered by the ravages of countless centuries of time. No longer possessing rugged and sharp peaks, its ridges still constituted a formidable impediment to travel and commerce. The slopes and pinnacles were seemingly endless, rolling beyond each other in waves, comprised of badly weathered rock that constituted an obstacle in its own right, featuring steep ascents and precipitous descents, grim bogs and swamps atop and between the ridges, the whole covered with a dense and nearly impenetrable carpet of brush, vines, understory and towering old growth trees. In many places, the canopies of this ancient forest were so dense that sunlight could scarcely penetrate. In Pennsylvania, Maryland and Virginia, the Appalachian Mountains were better known by a local colloquialism as the Allegheny Mountains.

From its western slopes, a series of streams and rivulets continuously gathered forces to become increasingly deep, swift and wide. In turn, creeks became small rivers, and then joined with others to become major waterways, all draining west into another great river that dominated the center of the continent—the Mississippi River.

Two of these great watercourses, the Allegheny and Monongahela rivers, combined at a strategic location to create the Ohio River, which would eventually lend its flow of water to swell the Mississippi River. From the Eastern Continental Divide astride the Allegheny Mountains, it was possible to travel by water far into the continent, to the Rocky Mountains, an almost unimaginable and unknown distance to the west, or into the Gulf of Mexico far to the south. West of the Alleghenies the land gradually flattened to transform into the great seas of grass of the Illinois Country, where the rich plains had soil so fertile that it was black as pudding.

The entirety of the region immediately west of the mountains became known as the Ohio Country, inhabited for centuries by the Native Americans, eager to embrace mutually beneficial commerce with European traders. The Ohio Country was rich land, blessed with natural resources, and teeming with fur bearing animals of considerable wealth that were highly prized in Europe.

It was inevitable that the Ohio Country would become the scene of conflict between three nations. To the north in Canada, the French colony of New France was attempting to expand down the Allegheny and Ohio rivers to reach both the Illinois Country, and the wealthy Spanish settlements at the mouth of the Gulf of Mexico, and it laid early ownership to the Ohio Country. The British similarly claimed title, and politically prominent and wealthy British and Virginia land speculators and investors formed a corporation chartered as "The Ohio Company" to exploit it. They obtained development and settlement rights to millions of acres, ignoring both the interests of the Native Americans who actually lived on that land, and the imperial claims of the French. Inevitably caught in the middle were the various Native American communities, tribes and nations, who eagerly embraced European trade goods and manufactured items, but not at the price of their sovereignty or homeland. These Natives, well versed in diplomatic negotiation and political manipulations, were also formidable warriors. Nevertheless, they were always few, and their villages far apart. Their best tactic, which they had employed with impressive success for decades, was to play the two European powers against each other, to their own considerable benefit, and to the mutual detriment of both French and English.

This long-standing détente began to become unraveled in 1753, when the French dispatched a strong military column to occupy the Allegheny Valley as far as the Forks of the Ohio. Lieutenant Governor Robert Dinwiddie of Virginia, the resident governor of the colony, viewed this development with consternation and alarm.[1] He determined to notify the French intruders in unmistakable, but of course courteous, diplomatic and polite language, that they had occupied land that belonged properly to His Brittanic Majesty, King George II. To deliver his communique across the Allegheny Mountains and far north up the Allegheny River, Dinwiddie required a young, vigorous and determined messenger. He discovered just such a man in an ambitious, eager 21-year-old Virginian named George Washington. It did not hurt that this youth was well-placed politically in Virginian society, was comfortable with Tidewater aristocrats who wholeheartedly recommended him, and was also a minor stock holder in the Ohio Company. It was an added bonus that the young Virginian had actually surveyed beyond the Alleghenies in the Shenandoah Valley.

Washington journeyed west at the beginning of the winter of 1753, enduring a demanding, rigorous, dangerous transit of the Allegheny Mountains by horse, raft and foot to successfully deliver Dinwiddie's missive in the throes of a heavy snow storm to the bemused French officers. They received the packet with polite, courteous and charming diplomacy that was simultaneously entirely dismissive. They knew that they possessed both the strength, and the initiative.

That spring, early in 1754, utterly devoid of any hesitation in response to Dinwiddie's pronouncements, they seized the Forks of the Ohio, ejecting a tiny company of ragged Virginia militia who were attempting to establish a fortified post for their colony at the strategic location.

Immediately, the French began constructing their own defensive stockade, ludicrously small and weak by European standards, but still the strongest fortification west of the Allegheny Mountains. The new French fortification was sufficiently designed and constructed to be secure from any infantry assault, such that only artillery would be capable of driving its garrison away. They christened it "Fort Duquesne" and with this act they secured the Forks of the Ohio as French territory, in fact if not in law.

Dinwiddie initiated what proved to be a feeble effort to regain the Ohio Country, executed by a haphazard, poorly disciplined, miserably supplied contingent of Virginia militia, augmented by a single unhappy independent company of British regulars who wanted to be nearly anywhere else than mired in the midst of the wooded frontier. Through a set of either fortunate or unfortunate circumstances depending upon one's perspective, the young George Washington became Colonel Washington, and he assumed command of the expedition. The youthful officer was entirely untrained, inexperienced, and ill-prepared to actually conduct any military mission, but he was nevertheless aggressive, determined and hard working, traits that went far in the wilderness. Washington drew first blood when he defeated a small part-diplomatic, part-military and part-spy French party at Jumonville Glen, atop Chestnut Ridge about forty miles east of Fort Duquesne. It was a hollow victory, for in short order an overwhelming force of angry French regulars, Canadian militia and Native American warriors surrounded Washington at a crude fortification named "Fort Necessity" in the middle of the Great Meadows. For long hours they poured unremitting gunfire from the protection of a woods, eventually crushing the woeful Virginia "army" and forcing Washington to surrender under humiliating circumstances.

With the best military efforts that his colony could muster on its own having failed miserably, Dinwiddie (and not coincidentally the numerous politically prominent and wealthy stockholders of the Ohio Company, now facing the demoralizing prospect of seeing their investments literally evaporating before their very eyes) clamored for formal British military and naval intervention. King George II and his ministers, under intense and effective lobbying from some of their closest and most influential associates, and viewing with dismay the loss of the entire interior of North America, were all too happy to view such a request in a favorable light.

In the fall of 1754, King George II and the captain-general of his army, his younger son Prince William, the Duke of Cumberland, made a momentous decision. In September of that year they determined to dispatch a British army brigade, supported by ships of the royal navy, to Virginia with explicit instructions to expel through force of arms those annoying, arrogant and abrasive French intruders who had displayed the audacity to seize British territory in the Ohio Valley. They had, after all, been warned.

This represented the first significant deployment of British regulars to North America in the history of these colonies. Accordingly, the Duke of Cumberland assembled Colonel Sir John Halkett's (44th) and Colonel Thomas Dunbars' (48th) Regiments of Foot, then on the Irish establishment, powerful supporting forces such as a general hospital, royal artillery and engineers, and designated a distinguished officer who held his confidence, Major General Edward Braddock of the Guards, to command the whole.[2] Braddock was supported by a complete staff of officers to expedite this Expedition.

Braddock received his appointment as general captain for North America on September 24, 1754. Following frantic preparations, he embarked for Virginia with Lieutenant Robert Orme, his aide-de-camp, and William Shirley, Jr., his military secretary on December 21,

1754. Braddock arrived at Hampton Roads, Virginia, on February 20, 1755. The two regiments and other forces such as the royal artillery sailed from England on January 14, 1755, and arrived at Alexandria, Virginia, on March 15, 1755.[3]

Sir John St. Clair served as the deputy quartermaster general for General Edward Braddock during this campaign to capture Fort Duquesne at the Forks of the Ohio in 1755. In any English army of the mid 18th century, the deputy quartermaster general was a position of immense importance. St. Clair had great responsibilities for the Braddock Campaign, and he was the first British deputy quartermaster general to serve in North America in its history.

St. Clair had been appointed to this post in October 1754, and was the first soldier of Braddock's expedition to be dispatched to North America, departing in early November 1754. As Braddock's quartermaster, it was St. Clair's responsibility to insure that all of the necessary logistical arrangements were established in Virginia so that Braddock and his army could launch the expedition immediately upon their arrival in the colony in early spring 1755. In this capacity, St. Clair was responsible for closely coordinating with the colonies of Virginia, Maryland and Pennsylvania.

Historians have frequently criticized Braddock for the organization and conduct of his campaign. However, the logistic and administrative details of the Braddock Campaign have never been adequately studied. Most histories of the Braddock Campaign have chosen to highlight the military strategy and tactics employed by Braddock, and have focused upon the unfortunate and bloody debacle at Turtle Creek on July 9, 1755, that resulted in the destruction of Braddock's advanced column and his own death.

As was typical for most gentlemen of the 18th century, as quartermaster during the Braddock Campaign and throughout his term in North America, Sir John St. Clair maintained a letterbook for all of his correspondence, both letters dispatched and received. This provided him with a permanent record of his correspondence. One of Sir John St. Clair's letterbooks can be found in the headquarters papers of Brigadier General John Forbes, located at the University of Virginia Library, Charlottesville. When Brigadier General John Forbes was appointed to command a second expedition destined for the Forks of the Ohio in the spring of 1758, among Forbes's first activities was to gather all available information on the Braddock Campaign, and on the terrain and topography between Philadelphia (his logistical base) and the Forks of the Ohio. Among his efforts was to peruse St. Clair's letterbook, as it would provide him considerable information on the logistical challenges that Braddock had faced. Forbes would have had little difficulty in obtaining St. Clair's correspondence, as he was serving in the winter of 1757–1758 as the adjutant general for Lord Loudon, the British military commander in North America. Upon Forbes' death from disease in March 1759 this letterbook was retained in Forbes' headquarters papers, where it resides to this day.

A previous transcription of portions of this letterbook can be found in Andrew J. Wahll, *Braddock Road Chronicles, 1755* (Bowie, MD: Heritage Books, 1999). However, a careful perusal of this transcription revealed numerous errors. Additionally, several letters were placed out of sequence in the letterbook, mistakes that can almost certainly be traced to St. Clair himself, doubtless a result of haste due to the exigencies of the campaign. The previous transcriber failed to detect this error, and as a result several of these letters are not in their proper sequence. Finally, this previous effort performed no efforts at editing, or placing the letters within the context of the overall Braddock Campaign or British army activities of the mid-18th century. This new transcription and editing is intended to resolve these shortcomings.

This new transcription of St. Clair's correspondence offers, for the first time, the possibility to perform a comprehensive study of the logistics that facilitated the Braddock Campaign. Unfortunately, much of St. Clair's correspondence for the movement from Fort Cumberland to the Monongahela River was lost in the engagement of July 9. Still, the complete correspondence from his arrival in Virginia, during the organization of the first stage of the campaign to Fort Cumberland and through the crossing of the Allegheny Mountains, survived the defeat on the Monongahela. This provides an opportunity to understand how the campaign was organized and implemented from a logistical standpoint, to identify critical logistical decision factors that St. Clair and Burgoyne had to face, and the logistical and terrain challenges that they had to overcome to enable the expedition to move forward.

The traditional interpretation of the campaign is that Braddock was old, slow, conservative, a martinet, focused upon discipline of his soldiers, poorly versed in tactics, uninterested in his soldiers or their welfare, logistically naïve, unwilling to cooperate with the colonists, and disdainful of the specific conditions on the Virginia frontier.[4] A virtual litany of logistical, military and leadership crimes has been laid at Braddock's feet. The St. Clair correspondence that comprises the core of this study of the Braddock Campaign presents a radically different interpretation of General Braddock.

1

"A mad sort of Fool"
Sir John St. Clair, Infantry Officer, Before 1754

Prior to his assignment to the Braddock Campaign in the late fall of 1754, little is known of Sir John St. Clair's life.[1] The only extant biography of St. Clair is a brief journal article published in 1885.[2] Unfortunately this short biography is both relatively limited and badly outdated.

John St. Clair was born in Scotland to Sir George St. Clair and Margaret Crawford St. Clair, but the year and date cannot be ascertained. When he died in 1767, one obituary in a New Jersey newspaper mentioned that "he was between 50 and 60 Years of age."[3] If correct, this means that John St. Clair would have been born between 1707 and 1717, and was approximately 40–50 years old during the Braddock and Forbes campaigns.

In November 1726 he succeeded as third baronet upon his father's death and inherited a small landed estate near Tarbet, Argyleshire, Scotland. Although some sources have suggested that his title may have been spurious, St. Clair was certainly a member of the Scottish peerage.[4] However, his landed estate was incapable of solely supporting him, and St. Clair entered the king's service as an officer. In doing so, St. Clair followed a course pursued by numerous minor peers, who possessed a title but whose estate was relatively modest, and who were in military service for both salary and prestige. St. Clair had served with the British army throughout the War of Austrian Succession. In particular, St. Clair served as a subordinate under the fabled Marshal von Browne during his campaigns in the Apennines in northern Italy in 1746–1747. His experience in the mountains would serve as an excellent preparation a decade later in western Virginia in North America. By the end of the conflict, St. Clair was an experienced officer with considerable military service on the continent.[5]

Still, St. Clair did not enjoy a particularly good reputation in the British army. When Colonel John Forbes, a highly experienced and well regarded officer who had served as quartermaster in Flanders during the War of Austrian Succession and was commander of the 17th Regiment of Foot, heard in October 1754 that St. Clair had been appointed to be quartermaster for Braddock, he wrote his brother that he knew St. Clair to be "a mad sort of Fool."[6]

St. Clair was promoted to major in the 22nd Foot on October 7, 1754, and nearly concurrently he was appointed as quartermaster to Braddock on October 15, 1754. The best-known portrait of Sir John St. Clair, one of only two known to exist, is by the noted Scottish portrait artist Alan Ramsey and currently owned and on display at the Fort Ligonier Museum, Ligonier, Pennsylvania. It reveals a rigid, determined, blue-eyed man who appears fiery, argumentative and opinionated even on canvas. This portrait, taken from life, serves as the single best testimony of the man's mercurial personality.

2

"An officer of distinction, who aids and assists the general"
The Staff of Braddock's Expedition

Since the later stages of the 19th century, and in today's contemporary armed forces, a number of key subordinate officers are dedicated to assist a military commander. Each of these officers is a subject matter expert in a range of various specialties—military intelligence, personnel and human resources management, fire support, tactical operations and training, logistics and sustainment, communications technology, information operations, engineering, military planning, information operations, civil affairs and resource management. In turn, a well-established staff of trained, experienced subordinate officers supports each of these individual officers. These staff officers are in turn assisted by a number of non-commissioned officers, enlisted soldiers and civil servants who are specialists in their respective fields. However, this is a relatively recent development in military history. In the middle of the 18th century, a military commander was not provided with such a formalized staff.

Yet although he lacked the formal staff organization of today's armies, in the British army of 1755, a commanding officer was still provided with a rudimentary staff of subordinates who facilitated his operations. Unlike today's military staffs, of which the majority are soldiers, an 18th century staff contained numerous civilians (the equivalent of today's civil servants) and a few commissioned officers. This chapter will discuss the responsibilities of these various offices and will then discuss the individuals who were assigned these responsibilities during the Braddock campaign.

General's Personal Staff

A general's aides-de-camp and his military secretary provided the first level of assistance. Because of the close personal relationship that these men enjoyed, this team was frequently referred to as a general's "family."

AIDE-DE-CAMP

A 1780 military treatise described the aide's duties:

An officer always following the generals ... to receive and carry their orders, as occasion requires. When the king is in the field, he appoints young gentlemen of note to carry his orders, and they are called the king's Aids de Camp. They ought to be alert in comprehending, and punctual and distinct in delivering all orders.¹

The 1779 *Universal Military Dictionary* similarly noted

> an aid-de-camp is an officer appointed to attend a general officer ... he receives and carries their orders, as occasion requires. He is seldom under the degree of a captain.²

The aide-de-camp was essentially an assistant to the commanding officer. During the majority of a campaign, the aide-de-camp would attend to the personal requirements of the commander, so that the general in turn could concentrate upon directing and maneuvering the army. During an engagement or extended march, the aide-de-camp became particularly important as they carried the general's communications and orders across the countryside or battlefield. Thus, the general had to implicitly trust his aides, as these instructions were frequently verbal, and he had to possess confidence that the aide would faithfully transmit his demands. Additionally, the aide also had to understand the commander's intentions, in case there were questions regarding the orders, or in case the tactical situation had changed before the orders arrived. A 1760 military treatise noted of the aide's responsibilities and importance:

> The Words of an Aid-de-Camp, the movement of the Colours, the sound of Trumpets, and the beat of Drums, are so many Echoes, which explain and extend the Orders of supreme Authority, to which every Inferior owes an immediate Submission, even without the delay of a Moment.³

Needless to say, this was a dangerous and exposed position on the battlefield. At the Battle of Bunker Hill in July 1775, all of General William Howe's staff members were killed or wounded. Similarly, at Waterloo in 1815, the entirety of Wellington's staff was killed or wounded during the daylong battle.

Braddock had three aides, two that accompanied him from Britain, and one volunteer from Virginia. The two British aides were Captain Robert Morris and Lieutenant Robert Orme. Captain Morris was a member of Dunbar's 48th Regiment of Foot. Robert Orme (1732–1790) entered the 34th Foot as an ensign and transferred to the Coldstream Guard in 1745. In 1751 he was raised to lieutenant. As a lieutenant of the Guards, Orme ranked as a captain among officers of line regiments, and was generally referred to as "Captain Orme" throughout the campaign.⁴ Braddock's third aide was a provincial volunteer, George Washington. Washington had earned his reputation from his winter 1753 journey carrying dispatches from the lieutenant governor of Virginia to the French officers occupying the Ohio Country, and his role in the unsuccessful 1754 campaign to seize the Forks of the Ohio, where he had gained a minor although controversial victory at Jumoville Glen, and then been forced to surrender to an overwhelming French force at Fort Necessity in Great Meadows. Washington had served during the 1754 campaign as a colonel of Virginia militia. However, at the time a British regular captain outranked even a provincial colonel. Washington had no intention of subordinating himself in such a manner. Braddock tactfully resolved this situation by asking Washington to serve as a volunteer aide on his private staff, an offer that Washington readily acceded to.⁵ Washington had traveled the identical route that Braddock intended to follow in 1753 and 1754, so he was extremely familiar with the topographical and military aspects from the Virginia backcountry to the Forks of the Ohio. Washington's skills as a surveyor would also contribute to Braddock's campaign.

Military Secretary

As the name implies, this was a junior member of the staff who was responsible for taking dictation from the general, turning these notes into draft correspondence which the general would review and modify, and then incorporating these corrections into a final letter for the general's signature. In addition to the original, the secretary copied the letter precisely into what was known as a "letterbook" that contained, arranged by date, duplicates of all correspondence that a general received or transmitted. Since in the 18th century communications, particularly in the wilds of North America, were often uncertain, the secretary would routinely prepare numerous identical copies of important correspondence that would be sent by different means, or delivered by separate couriers. The secretary also maintained and arranged the general's personal papers to include all of his correspondence. Needless to say, a secretary had to possess superlative penmanship and proven written communications skills, had to have training in establishing and maintaining a proper filing system, and had to be capable of working independently with a minimum of guidance from the general officer. Because a secretary was privy to the general's personal and professional correspondence, it was also important that a secretary was reliable and discreet. Typically, a secretary would be a young man who could tolerate a heavy workload that included considerable time at a writing desk, and who at the same time had sufficient social and economic connections that a general could entrust him with important communications. A secretary had to be entirely reliable, since he commonly worked with little or no supervision. Finally, he had to be absolutely precise, since any error in correspondence could cause serious difficulties. A Secretary essentially worked upon what was considered to be a commanding officer's personal correspondence, rather than formal military orders and reports. Braddock's military secretary was William Shirley, Jr., the eldest son of Governor William Shirley of Massachusetts. Shirley fulfilled all of these responsibilities, although being 34 years old he was relatively senior to serve as a secretary.

Besides the aides-de-camp and military secretary that comprised General Braddock's "personal family," he was assisted by a number of other officers and civilians, comprising what would be recognized as a general staff in today's armed forces. Positions within this category included administrative officers, logistical officers, subordinate commanding officers, officers from the Board of Ordnance, and a range of similar specialized staff officers.

Administrative Staff

The first set of officers performed primarily administrative duties, managing the personnel and paperwork of the army. These included the adjutant general, a single individual and the highest-ranking administrator in an army who remained in London; deputy adjutant generals and brigade majors below the adjutant general; and individual regimental and separate company adjutants.

Deputy Adjutant General

At higher command levels, a deputy adjutant general was appointed as the commander's senior adjutant to direct the activities of the individual regimental adjutants. The 1779 *Universal Military Dictionary* addressed the responsibilities of an adjutant general:

an officer of distinction, who aids and assists the general in his laborious duty ... and keeps an exact state of each brigade and regiment.... He every day at headquarters receives orders from the general officer of the day, and distributes them to the majors of brigade, from whom he receives the number of men they are to furnish for the duty of the army, and informs them of any detail which may concern them.[6]

An effective deputy adjutant general had to be an extremely efficient administrator, meticulously well organized, and capable of managing the correspondence for the entire army. The deputy adjutant general was also responsible for the establishment and execution of various military orders, regulations and policies such as the British army's Articles of War. The deputy adjutant general was authorized to give orders and instructions to the several majors of brigade. The deputy adjutant general and regimental adjutants were always commissioned officers. Braddock chose to not fill this position during his campaign. Rather, the single brigade major, Captain Halkett, fulfilled these duties for Braddock.

Brigade Major

The officer assigned as brigade major was detailed from his usual position with the line, and was to receive greater pay and allowances for the significantly increased workload and responsibilities that the position entailed. The brigade major was responsible for all of the administrative duties and functions of the brigade headquarters, including but not limited to the preparation and dissemination of orders, compilation of reports, maintenance of official brigade papers, and organizing and preparing the correspondence of the commanding officer of the brigade. While the military secretary was responsible for maintaining a general's "private correspondence," a brigade major was responsible for managing the general's military papers. The brigade major was also directed to assist a brigade commander, however it was deemed to be appropriate and necessary. Because Braddock's army was in fact a brigade with two Regiments of Foot, a royal artillery detachment, engineers, independent companies of the British army from North America, and various provincial detachments, a single brigade major was appointed for the campaign. This was Captain Francis Halkett of his father's regiment. As brigade major, Captain Francis Halkett was the senior administrative officer in Braddock's army.

Halkett was the middle of three sons of Colonel Sir Peter Halkett, of Pitfirrane, Scotland, the commanding officer of his (44th) Regiment of Foot. Halkett's oldest son, Peter, remained at home to manage the family estate in Pitfirrane, Fife, Scotland, located a short distance north of Edinburgh. Halkett's youngest son, James, was also a lieutenant in the 44th Foot. Although Captain Halkett played a pivotal role in the campaign as Braddock's brigade major, almost nothing is known of the man. Most information on Halkett is derived from a memorial that he prepared during the Forbes campaign in 1758, in an attempt to gain a promotion into another regiment. This memorial stated that he had purchased both his commissions, as lieutenant and captain; that he was the second most senior captain in the 44th Foot; and that he had participated in several campaigns previously, presumably to include service in the 1745 Jacobite Rebellion with then Colonel John Lee's (44th) Regiment of Foot.[7] The limited information available in this document, and the fact that he was appointed by Braddock to a position with significant responsibilities on the campaign, suggests that Captain Halkett was a senior, experienced, and well respected officer. Among his responsibilities as brigade major, Captain Halkett maintained an orderly book throughout the campaign, which remains one of the core primary sources for study and comprehension of the Braddock expedition.[8]

Regimental Adjutant

Each regiment in the British army was assigned an adjutant. This was a permanent assigned duty for a commissioned officer. Numerous military treatises provide descriptions of the duties and responsibilities of a regimental adjutant. The 1780 *Military Dictionary* specified

> an officer who eases the Major of part of the burden of his duty, and performs it all in his absence. He receives the orders every night from the brigade major; which after carrying them to the colonel, he delivers them out to the sergeants. When detachments are to be made, he gives the number to be furnished by each company, and assigns the hour and place of the rendezvous. He also places the guards, distributes ammunition, etc.[9]

Major General James Wolfe, killed at the Siege of Quebec in 1759, provided extremely detailed and comprehensive instructions for a regimental adjutant:

> Adjutant's Duty of the British Foot. Adjutants are to see all detachments before they be sent to the parade; that their arms be clean, their ammunition, accoutrements, etc. in good order, and that a sergeant be sent with them to the parade. That they always choose three or four good sergeants that can write well, to wait orderly, and if occasion happens, to carry verbal messages. That they keep an exact journal of the duty of every one in their respective regiments; viz. all detachments, all sick, gone to or returned from the hospital, deserted, dead, entertained from year to year, discharged, or absent by leave; and they give in a weekly return every Friday morning to the major of brigade in the usual method, to be given to the general of foot on Saturday morning. That they always take care to send their sick to the hospital, and take measures for carrying the arms and accoutrements of the sick. That all the adjutants of the British corps keep an exact list of duty with the majors of brigade that they may see justice performed, and be able to tell every body when they are near duty, in order to keep in camp, and provide accordingly. That all adjutants keep constantly to all the rules and forms of discipline and exercise, now used in the British Foot, and on no pretence whatsoever to change or let fall any of the said customs till farther orders.[10]

The regimental adjutant was also responsible for maintaining a regimental orderly book, which contained all orders issued by higher headquarters by the brigade major on a daily basis, along with any supplemental orders issued by the regimental commander. Typically, a regimental adjutant was a lieutenant, and the adjutant had to be a young officer with some experience, quite energetic, and entirely reliable as his endeavors represented the regiment to higher headquarters on a daily basis. Additionally, if an adjutant were remiss or sloppy in the performance of his duties, the regiment would be unable to fulfill the orders issued by the commanding general.

The regimental adjutant of Halkett's Regiment was Lieutenant Daniel Disney, wounded at the Monongahela.[11] The adjutant of Dunbar's Regiment was Lieutenant John Gordon, who remained at Rock Fort Camp with his regiment.[12] In Disney's orderly book it was ordered that

> the adjutants of the two Regiments and artillery, and also the adjutant of the [Virginia] Rangers to be at the Major of Brigades Tent, every day at eleven o'clock to receive Orders.[13]

Additional orders also instructed that

> the Adjutant who does not send in his return to the Major of Brigade, by seven o'clock in the morning will be ordered under arrest.[14]

At the independent company, provincial company, or detachment level, the adjutant would not have been a full-time position. Instead, a subaltern officer would have been given this assignment as an "additional duty." The other officers who were assigned as temporary, part-time adjutants for the various independent companies, provincial units and the royal artillery during Braddock's expedition have not been identified.

Commissary of Musters

During the 17th century and earlier, regiments in the British army were owned by their colonels, and they were responsible for recruiting of their subordinate officers and soldiers, and for arming, equipping, training, and clothing their soldiers. Before a colonel could be reimbursed by the king for his regiment, the king's appointed officials or officers had to confirm that the regiment contained the number of specified men, that they were fit for service, and that they were adequately clothed, armed and equipped. This procedure was formalized as a "muster." Mustering was thus a standardized process in which all soldiers were verified, inspected, and formally entered into military service for pay purposes. To perform this function, a commissary of musters was appointed, sometimes referred to as a "muster master." The commissary of musters could be either a civilian or a commissioned officer. The commissary of musters was "an officer appointed to muster the army, as often as the general thinks proper, in order to know the strength of each regiment, and company, to receive and inspect the muster rolls, and to keep an exact state of the strength of the army."[15] A 1780 military dictionary noted of these various positions:

> Muster Rolls—The rolls or lists of the companies or troops, which are delivered to the commissary by the captains. Muster—A narrow review of troops under arms to see if they are compleat, and in good condition; that their arms and acoutrements be in good order; thereby to know the strength of an army. The general may order ... as often as he pleases.[16]

James Pitcher served as commissary of musters in North America under Braddock. Pitcher had been appointed to this service on October 25, 1754, by Secretary Sir Thomas Robinson.[17] Pitcher was an Englishman, the equivalent of a modern "civil servant." He served in this role throughout the Seven Years War in North America.

Pitcher initially traveled to Boston, Massachusetts Colony to assist in mustering provincial troops and inspecting those independent companies of regulars who were intended for a proposed invasion of Beauséjour in Novia Scotia. Pitcher reached Boston on this duty on December 10, 1754.[18] This task accomplished, colonial newspapers subsequently recorded Pitcher's arrival in Philadelphia and his immediate departure for Wills's Creek on February 4, 1755. St. Clair noted that he arrived at Fort Cumberland by mid–February.

Pitcher arrived in North America early enough to have fulfilled his responsibilities on the campaign. However, for whatever reason, as numerous letters in his letterbook attested, Sir John St. Clair fulfilled the role of commissary of musters for Braddock's army, inspecting and accepting into service numerous provincial organizations, and the New York and South Carolina independent companies of Regulars. Given that St. Clair already had considerable demands placed upon him as deputy quartermaster general, appointing St. Clair to this additional responsibility seems to have placed an unacceptable burden upon St. Clair, and why these tasks did not naturally devolve upon Pitcher cannot now be verified.

Logistical Staff

These officers performed the full range of logistical activities, necessary for the sustainment and support of Braddock's expedition.

Deputy Quartermaster General

In the English army of 1758, the deputy quartermaster general was a position of immense importance. A 1780 *Treatise on Science Military* confirmed the significance of this position: "The staff properly exists only in the time of war: the Quarter-Master General may be looked upon as the first person belonging to it."[19] The quartermaster general was actually an extremely senior officer that remained in England. The deputy quartermaster general was rather the quartermaster general of an army or column. The deputy quartermaster general for Braddock in 1755, and Forbes in 1758, was Sir John St. Clair. The deputy quartermaster general was responsible for receiving provision, stores and fodder from the commissary; managing and issuing all food for the soldiers; managing and issuing all forage for the animals; contracting for and coordinating wagons and carts, with drovers to drive them, and horses and/or oxen to pull them; contracting for and controlling other transportation such as pontoons or ferries to cross water obstructions, and bateaux and canoes to utilize waterways; determining the precise routes and organization of the daily marches of an army within the General's guidance: selecting camp sites for an army; laying out and organizing these campgrounds; and acquiring and issuing clothing and military equipment (except for arms, ammunition and accouterments which were handled by artillery officers for the Board of Ordnance).[20] In short, the deputy quartermaster general had a myriad of duties that were primarily logistical, supply and transportation in nature. If the deputy quartermaster general was remiss in his duties, an army could not be fed, clothed or even moved. The majority of this treatise will deal with St. Clair's experience as deputy quartermaster general, will document how he performed his duties, and how his efforts contributed to the success and failure of the Braddock Expedition.

Assistant Deputy Quartermaster General

Obviously, the responsibilities of the deputy quartermaster general were extensive. In the case of a campaign in North America, where supplies were being drawn from Philadelphia, eastern Pennsylvania, Maryland and Virginia and other southern colonies, and the army was campaigning from Alexandria, Virginia, to Fort Duquesne on the western side of the Allegheny Mountains, it would be impossible for a single individual, no matter how hard working, well organized and motivated, to fulfill all of these myriad duties. A 1780 military compilation specifically noted of the deputy quartermaster general, "He has commonly three or four assistants, to ease him in his function."[21] Accordingly, the deputy quartermaster general would appoint several assistant deputy quartermaster generals to assist him. The only documented assistant deputy quartermaster general to St. Clair was Lieutenant Matthew Leslie of the 44th Foot. He would be present with St. Clair at the Monongahela, where he was reported as being wounded.[22] Documentary evidence is limited, but it appears that Leslie performed the responsibilities of the deputy quartermaster general in camp, while St. Clair spent most of his time forward with the road construction parties, for the majority of the campaign.

Renowned historian Stanley Pargellis intimated that Captain Gabriel Christie also served St. Clair as assistant deputy quartermaster general, but failed to document his assertion.[23] Captain Christie does not appear in St. Clair's letterbook in this guise, and most likely Pargellis was mistaken. St. Clair's other assistants are unknown.

Quartermaster

Each regiment was authorized a quartermaster. This was a commissioned officer's post. Quite frequently, a particularly experienced and reliable sergeant would be promoted to officer rank to hold this position, as the quartermaster office was extremely important to the regiment, and it required an exhaustive knowledge of British army rules, regulations and administration that a junior subaltern officer would be unlikely to possess. The regimental quartermaster's duties were clearly enumerated in a 1776 military treatise:

> The Quarter-master, though he should have another commission, is to do no duty but that of Quarter-master. He should be an honest careful man, exact at his pen, and a good accountant; very well skilled in the detail of a regiment, and perfectly acquainted with every individual circumstance of its duty and finances. In garrison, he is always to be employed in seeing the quarters kept clean, and receive all things belonging to the wives, infirmary or hospital; provide all the camp equipage; and on all distributions of carriages, provisions, and materials for work, receive and distribute them according to order. He must keep exact accounts, and return what is necessary or ordered, that the regiment may not be answerable for what is missing. He must be very careful in inspecting the bread and provisions, that no unwholesome food be received, and no deliveries made but in just time.[24]

The quartermaster of Halkett's 44th Foot was Ensign Henry Verrant, present but not wounded at the Battle of the Monongahela.[25] The quartermaster for Dunbar's 48th Foot was Ensign Thomas Webb. As was typical for a regimental quartermaster, Thomas Webb was a former enlisted soldier, born in England on May 31, 1725. Webb entered the British army in 1744, at the age of nineteen. He demonstrated abilities and responsibility as an enlisted soldier, and rose to the rank of sergeant. Webb was also sufficiently educated to read, write, interpret regulations and perform mathematics, for he was commissioned as a quartermaster in his regiment on October 29, 1754. Quartermaster Webb remained with Colonel Dunbar at his advanced camp near Jumonville Glen, did not accompany Braddock's column on its movement to Fort Duquesne, and thus was not present at the Battle of Monongahela.[26]

In the case of an independent company or similar detachment, a quartermaster would also be assigned, although this might be a sergeant, or a subaltern officer assigned this as an "extra duty." The temporary, part-time quartermasters for the independent companies, royal artillery and various provincial units remain unknown.

Deputy Paymaster General

Another extremely important civilian appointment was that of deputy paymaster general. The paymaster general was responsible for managing the purse of the entire British army, and as a senior officer remained in London. Deputy paymaster generals were appointed for specific armies and expeditions. The duties of the paymaster, at whatever level, were the same.

> The duty of the Paymaster was to act as sole domestic banker of the army. He received, mainly from the exchequer, the sums voted by parliament for military expenditure, and from other quarters he received fortuitous sums such as those realized by the sale of old stores. He disbursed these sums, by his own hands or by Deputy Paymasters; such disbursements being made under the authority of sign manual warrants as far as related to the ordinary expenses of the army, and under Treasury warrants in the case of the extraordinaries, that is to say the expenses unforeseen and unprovided for by parliament. During the whole time in which public money was in his hands, from the day of receipt until the issue of his final discharge ... his private estate was liable for the money in his hands.[27]

Given a little bit of good luck, and a general absence of morals and ethics, serving as the deputy paymaster general offered considerable opportunities for enrichment. One modern study has noted that

> the common methods of gaining personal profit from government sources were by taking advantage of different rates of exchange, buying up coin at a cheap rate and paying the army at a higher rate, getting percentages from agents for prompt payment, withholding money, or speculation with balances.[28]

The deputy paymaster general for the Braddock expedition was William Johnson, not to be confused with the more famous General William Johnson, baronet, of the Mohawk Valley in New York Colony.[29] Paymaster Johnson arrived in Virginia sometime after March 20, 1755, for on that date Braddock wrote to England, "I have heard nothing yet of the Deputy Paymaster General."[30] Johnson wrote to a correspondent in England confirming that he arrived in Virginia sometime between March 20 and April 1: "I did myself the pleasure of writing to you soon after my arrival at Williamsburgh in Virginia, the latter end of March last. I likewise wrote to you from Fort Cumberland the beginning of June last." Johnson accompanied the army during its movement from Alexandria to Fort Cumberland, and from Fort Cumberland forward. During the final movement to Fort Duquesne, he would remain behind with Dunbar's Column at the advanced camp near Jumonville Glen, safeguarding the military chest of Braddock.[31] As a result, the military chest was not lost at the Monongahela. Thomas Penn, Proprietary Governor of Pennsylvania, wrote to Secretary Richard Peters on November 14, 1755: "I am well pleased to find the Military Chest did not fall into the Enemy's hands."[32]

In addition to the deputy paymaster general, commissioned officers were also appointed to act as regimental paymasters. Unfortunately, the names of the 44th and 48th Foot regimental paymasters are unknown. This would not have been a full-time assignment, and would be considered to be what commissioned officers in the modern armed forces know (and loathe) as an "additional duty." This is confirmed through Halkett's orderly book in the entry for March 27, 1755:

> As the good of the Service renders the Presence of all the Officers absolutely Necessary His Excellence [General Braddock] Cannot suffer any officer to Act as paymaster. The Genl Therefore desires the Colos [Colonels] & Capts will fix upon a proper Person as soon as posoble for that purpose.[33]

Agent for the Money Contractor

Throughout the campaign, the deputy paymaster general was assisted by Mr. John Hunter of Hampton, Virginia. Hunter served as the southern agent for the North American colonies for the London firm of Hanbury and Thomlinson, who were the money contractors to the royal army. In this role Hunter was responsible for providing Johnson the gold, silver and copper specie for his pay chest.[34] Specimens of coins recovered from Braddock associated campsites are a combination of silver Spanish 2-reale coins cut neatly and precisely into quarters, and English copper half pennies.

Since a 2-reale Spanish pistareen was worth approximately 1 shilling, such cut silver coins were valued at approximately 3 pence, a reasonable sum given a soldier's pay. Given British pay rates of the times, and because British soldiers were issued their rations free while

Cut Spanish 2-reale coin recovered from Bare Camp, Braddock Road (Douglas R. Cubbison collection, photograph by Johanna Wickman).

they were serving in North American, a typical enlisted soldier would have been paid approximately six pence per a typical week. Thus, the British regulars needed to be paid in coins of relatively small denomination, particularly as the items that they were likely to purchase from citizens and merchants in Virginia were relatively inexpensive (such as tobacco, spare stockings, needles and thread, alcoholic drinks), and given that coins were scarce in Virginia and thus change for large coins would have not typically been available.[35]

Typically, the money contractor provided specie to the paymaster by obtaining coinage in England, and would then make arrangements to have them transported by royal navy warship to Virginia. This technique was used for the initial shipment of specie that accompanied Johnson and Braddock. Johnson arrived with approximately 14,000 pounds in gold and comparatively large denomination silver coins.[36] Given that Virginia Colony, and indeed all of the North American colonies, had an incessant shortage of specie, Braddock and Johnson rapidly realized that they had been given the modern equivalent of $100 bills, such that it was nearly impossible to spend the more valuable coins. Once in North America, Braddock rapidly realized that he required coins in smaller denominations, and Hunter attempted to obtain this additional specie in Virginia. On March 20, 1755, Braddock wrote to Newcastle from Williamsburgh:

> As small coined silver will be greatly wanted for the payment of the Troops, and as no considerable Quantity of it can be got in this Province; I must beg of your Grace to direct the Contractors, Mr. Hanbury & Mr. Thomlinson, to send over as soon as possible, if they have not already done it, four or five Thousand pounds, in Piastrines & Half Piastrines: which is the more necessary, as all the Money already brought over by the Regimental Paymasters is in Spanish Gold and Dollars.[37]

As a result of Braddock's pleas, additional specie were shipped to him by Hanbury & Thomlinson. Just over £5,000 were sent onboard the *Betsey* on 11 January 1755. This shipment of coins reached Braddock in time to support his campaign against the Forks of the Ohio. A further £19,000 were shipped aboard the *Sphinx* and *Nancy* in May 1755. This latter shipment almost certainly did not reach Braddock in time to be placed into his military chest during the movement forward from Fort Cumberland.

Hunter also attempted to raise specie in Williamsburg, although his best and most vigorous actions could only raise £4,000, which was apparently the maximum available coinage that could be obtained in the capitol city of Virginia. Acting on Braddock's instructions, volunteer Aide-de-Camp George Washington carried this money to Fort Cumberland from Williamsburg.[38] Braddock issued orders to Washington at Fort Cumberland on May 15, 1755: "You will repair to Hampton in Virginia with as much expedition as may be, and immediately upon your Arrival there you will apply to John Hunter Esquire for the Sum of Four thousand pounds Sterling." Washington was also instructed: "You will acquaint Mr. Hunter from me that His Majesty's Service under my direction, requires the further Sum of ten thousand pounds Sterling, to be sent to Fort Cumberland at this place, within the Space of two Months at farthest from this date."[39] Washington reached Williamsburg about May 23, and met with Mr. James Balfour of Hampton, who served as an assistant to Hunter. Balfour had gathered the available specie for Braddock, and he turned this money over to Washington, who immediately departed Williamsburg, returning to Winchester on May 27. Here he delayed for two days while awaiting an escort, eventually receiving a guard from a small party of the Winchester militia, reaching Fort Cumberland by May 30.[40] This augmentation of hard currency, predominantly in low denominations in circulation in the colony, was absolutely critical to facilitating Braddock's operations.

Commissary

The commissary was responsible for furnishing the army with provisions (rations and food) and forage for its draft animals (oxen and horses). A 1776 set of instructions articulated the full range of responsibilities and duties that the commissary was expected to perform:

> You are therefore carefully and diligently to discharge the Duty of Commissary General of Stores, Provisions and Forage for our said Forces, by doing and performing all and all manner of things thereunto belonging. And we do hereby authorize and impower you to inspect the buying & delivering of Stores, Provisions and Forage for the use of Our said Forces.
>
> You are from time to time to appoint any one, or more of Deputy Commissaries, or Assistants whom you shall think fit to preside over, take care of, superintend, aid & assist in the securing and management of Magazines and Depots of Provisions and Forage for the use of the said Army, and also the conduct and Establishment of the Bakery, as the exigency of the Service may require. You are to take charge of all Provisions which shall arrive in Canada for the use of our Army there and superintend the distribution thereof to the Troops. And you are to follow all such Rules and Orders touching the Providing and distribution of Fresh Provisions as you shall receive.[41]

The commissary regularly received the strength of the army from the commissary general of musters as the campaign was planned and organized, and would then receive on a weekly basis the strength of the army updated and current in the field from the deputy quartermaster general. The commissary would enter into a range of contracts with private vendors (businessmen or farmers as appropriate) in England, Scotland or Ireland to purchase the necessary provisions. The commissary would then coordinate with the Treasury Department to ship supplies from the United Kingdom to North America. Within the colonies, the commissary coordinated with the storekeeper of stores and provisions to temporarily store and safeguard the provisions, and then with the deputy quartermaster general and wagon master to arrange for transportation of these provisions. The commissary would then deliver the necessary stores, provisions and forage to the deputy quartermaster general, who would in turn distribute the food to individual regimental or company quartermasters for issue to the soldiers and draft animals of the army.

Almost exclusively, the commissaries were civilians. The Braddock Expedition was unique in that it was supported by two "joint" commissaries—Mr. Thomas Walker and Mr. Charles Dick, appointed by Governor Dinwiddie of Virginia Colony.[42] Both were respected, experienced and well-established Virginia businessmen. Walker was from Albermarle County, which he would later represent in the House of Burgesses.[43] Dick was an Alexandria merchant and trustee of the original town of Alexandria.

The commissary were assisted by a range of deputy commissaries or assistant commissaries. Sometimes these would be appointed for different regions—that is, they would make purchases from a specific region, colony, county or community. At other times, the post might be appointed for different classes of supplies. Thus, a deputy commissary of forage might specifically and exclusively purchase fodder for animals. At one point during the campaign, Assistant Deputy Quartermaster General Matthew Leslie was dispatched to Philadelphia to purchase forage, a responsibility more commonly performed by the commissary.[44] Another member of the commissary, identified only as "Mr. Lake," served as commissary of provisions, principally at Fort Cumberland although he apparently accompanied the army for a portion of its forward movement.[45] A cousin of George Washington's, Townsend Washington, was appointed assistant commissary, presumably for purchasing provisions in Tidewater Virginia where he resided.[46]

The commissary further contained a number of experienced bakers who cooked the soldier's flour into bread or hard biscuit. None of these bakers have been identified by name, the orderly books suggest that they may have simply been skilled soldiers who were detached for this duty.[47] Normally, the work of the commissaries was done in the rear of the army, they did not accompany the military column into the field, and the Braddock Expedition followed this precedent.

STOREKEEPER OF STORES AND PROVISIONS

One of the civilian officials that assisted the commissary was the storekeeper of stores and provisions. The storekeeper was responsible for receiving supplies intended for the commissary, and storing and safeguarding them until the commissary transported them forward to the army. The storekeeper for the Braddock Expedition was John Carlyle, a well-established, wealthy Scottish merchant of Alexandria. Braddock appointed him on April 10, 1755.

> I hereby appoint you Storekeeper of all the Provisions, Arms, Ammunition, Baggage of all other kinds whatever belonging to the forces under my Command which are now in Alexandria or Shall at any time hereafter be brought thither. You are therefore to take the same under your Care and Direction, and to be Accountable for them, keeping them safe and in good condition & Giving Proper Receipts for all that by Virtue of this Warrant shall be entrusted to you, as well for the Stores that are now in Alexandria as for those that shall hereafter be brought thither.[48]

Besides his extensive mercantile connections and experience, Carlyle had previously served as commissary for the Virginia Expedition against the Forks of the Ohio commanded by George Washington in 1754. Thus, Carlyle had a campaign's experience with the requirements and responsibilities of commissary, and with the types of supplies that he would be responsible for receiving, storing and disbursing. Obviously, Carlyle remained in Alexandria in charge of the king's storehouse there.

Wagon Master

Once a quartermaster had obtained through contract, purchase, or impressment the various wagon teams and draft animals necessary to transport the army, a wagon master was appointed to provide daily management, direction, and supervision of the army's wagon trains and baggage trains.[49] The wagon master was nearly exclusively a civilian appointee. Needless to say, this was an extremely demanding job, and required that the wagon master be familiar with loading of wagons, instructions to teamsters, organization of convoys, care and feeding of animals, negotiations of obstacles, repair of wagons and harness, and most importantly overcoming a range of obstacles and difficulties that were certain to introduce themselves. If the wagon master failed in his responsibility the transportation of the army would collapse, wagons would be destroyed or demolished, teamsters would desert or become surly, and animals would be injured or killed. The June 14, 1755, orderly book maintained by Halkett provides a hint of the duties of the wagon master:

> In case any wagon should break down in such a manner as to be unable to keep with the Line it is immediately to be drawn out on one side of the road and a report of it with what it is loaded to be sent to Mr. Scott Wagon master general who is to order it to be repaired, or see that the load is divided among the rest of the wagons as he shall think proper.[50]

During the Braddock Expedition, the wagon master general was Thomas Scott of Pennsylvania, as the majority of the wagons, teams and teamsters were provided from that colony.[51]

Normally the wagon master would be assisted by a number of deputies or assistants. In this case, the senior wagon master would be referred to as the "wagon master general."[52] When a number of wagons came from a discrete geographic source, such as a single county in a colony, the deputy wagon master would be from that community, and acted as wagon master for those wagons, under the supervision of the army's wagon master general. The majority of these men, appointed as such deputies for the campaign, are unknown. The only identified deputy wagon master was John Read (appointed on May 9, 1755) of Pennsylvania, a brother of Benjamin Franklin's wife, Deborah Franklin.[53]

Board of Ordnance

In the British system of 1755, the Board of Ordnance was responsible for the engineers and royal artillery. It was also a distinctive entity from the British army, and functioned independently and autonomously. The Board of Ordnance controlled promotion, pay and assignments of all artillery and engineer officers, personnel, organizations, and equipment including artillery, firearms, ordnance materials, siege materials, ammunition, and military accouterments. Accordingly, the Board of Ordnance maintained a separate staff that supported the Braddock Expedition.

Unlike the infantry and cavalry officers of the British army, who could simply purchase their commission, engineer and royal artillery officers were required to be classically trained at the Royal Military Academy at Woolwich, on the Thames River in London. Woolwich also served as the royal foundry, the home of the Board of Ordnance, and provided barracks and training grounds for the artillery companies. The Royal Military Academy had been established by King George II in 1741, in recognition that the artillery and engineering corps were becoming increasingly sophisticated, and that technical competence required a sound mathematical foundation accompanied by a well-established military education, subsequently expanded by continuing professional study and experience. Woolwich was among the first military academies in Europe. To qualify for admission to Woolwich, in addition to being a gentleman of social standing, a candidate had to pass a mathematics and Latin examination.[54] Once admitted to Woolwich as a "gentleman cadet" he was required to spend one to three years engaged in a course of study that was heavy in mathematics and gunnery, and provided increased leadership responsibilities over junior cadets. The faculty included a drawing master responsible for teaching the gentleman-cadets in "Sketching Ground, the taking of Views, the drawing of Civil Architecture and the Practice of Perspective." Students were expected to perform the majority of their study at their own pace. More significantly, mathematician John Muller had been serving as head master and professor of fortification and artillery of the Royal Military Academy since 1741. Muller was the foremost military scholar in England, and his exhaustive knowledge of military art and science, most particularly engineering, artillery and siegecraft had been imparted to every engineer and artillery officer in Braddock's army.

Engineers

Braddock's expedition was supported by three formally trained engineering officers. Military treatises of the mid–18th century addressed the duties of an engineer:

> Engineer is an Officer of the military branch, who, assisted by geometry, delineates upon paper or marks upon the ground all sorts of forts, and other works proper for offense and defense; who understands the art of fortification; can discover the defects of a place; find proper remedies, and knows how to make an attack on a place, or defend it when attacked.
> Engineers are necessary for both these purposes, and should not only be ingenious, but brave in proportion to their knowledge ... both expert and bold men. ... Their business is to take all advantage of ground, delineate the lines of circumvention and contravention, mark out the trenches, places of arms, batteries and lodgements, taking great care that none of their works be flanked.... An engineer should be an adept in arithmetic, to project the plots of places, and calculate the expenses of the siege, in geometry, to measure his work and raise plans in military architecture; in civil architecture to know how to conduct buildings, and works of places; in mechanics, to make sluices, march cannon, and use al sorts of machines; in perspective, to express his works on paper in their just proportions; for without design, he can neither make charts or plans. These sciences are called the genius, in which consists the whole spirit of war and fortification.[55]

Although this was a grandiose job description, the engineer's duties actually extended far beyond the art of sieges and fortifications. The engineers also had to design and construct roads, bridges, fords and ferries; supervise laborers; design and construct military structures such as barracks, guardhouses, storehouses, magazines and offices; design and construct field fortifications to protect an army column while on the march or in temporary camp; and maintain financial accounts and records to documents expenditures. Engineers approved additional cash payments, or issues of rum or whiskey, to soldiers performing labor on roads, structures or fortifications.[56] Although carrying commissions, engineers were not permitted to command infantry or cavalry in the field, and were only authorized to perform technical supervision of soldiers while serving as laborers.

Braddock was to have been supported by a chief engineer in North America, the highly experienced and renowned James Montresor, who unfortunately arrived in Virginia too late to participate in the campaign. Braddock's principal engineer was thus Patrick Mackellar (born in 1717), another seasoned engineer who was quite well regarded, having previously supervised the fortifications of the important post of Minorca. Another comparatively senior engineer, Harry Gordon, had been commissioned in 1742, had served in Flanders during the War of Austrian Succession, and was particularly renowned for his road building expertise, skills and talents that would prove crucial to the Braddock Expedition. Gordon was the most skilled of the three, and his road building talents in particular would prove to be of inestimable service to both Braddock and St. Clair. Subsequently, Gordon would go on to an illustrious career as a senior engineer in North America, with his most renowned accomplishment being the design and construction of Fort Pitt in 1759.[57] The junior engineer was Lieutenant Adam Williamson, 44th Foot (born in 1736). He had only graduated the Royal Military Academy in 1753, so unlike Mackellar and Gordon, he was a comparatively inexperienced engineer on his first active campaign.[58]

The engineers were supported by a complete suite of necessary technical and engineering equipment:

For Service of the Engineers

Theodolite compleate with Tellescope Sights	1
Plain Tables compleat with Indexes	2
Surveying Chains, 100 Feet	2
Surveying Chains, 50 Feet	1
Cases of Pocket Instruments compleat	4
Parallel Rules from 12 to 18 Inches	4
Drawing Pens	6
Pocket Compasses with a Spare Needle to each	4
Armor, Backs	3
Armor, Breasts	3
Armor, Head pieces	3
Camp Colours	12.[59]

The armor was intended for the engineers to wear during active siege operations, when they would be relatively vulnerable and exposed, because the loss of an engineer during a siege would endanger the success of the entire army and campaign. The camp colors were used to mark the camps in advance, so that the regimental quartermasters would know where they were to encamp their soldiers upon arrival in the evening's encampment.

Artillery Commander

Among the most important components of Braddock's army was a formidable artillery detachment. Without this artillery, Braddock could not reduce the defenses at Fort Duquesne and force the French to yield the Forks of the Ohio, nor could he subsequently establish an effective garrison to defend the Forks once captured. The senior artillery officer was responsible for advising Braddock in the employment of that branch of the service, and was responsible for supervising the training and readiness of this extremely technical branch. Captain

Thomas Orde (variously spelled as Ord) was the senior artillery officer present with the Braddock expedition. By 1755 Captain Orde was a veteran artilleryman, who had been on active duty at least since 1741, and had been ranked as a captain since 1746.[60]

The composite royal artillery detachment that Captain Orde commanded included himself, his immediate subordinate Captain-Lieutenant Robert Hind, Lieutenant Robert Smith, Lieutenant William MacLeod, Lieutenant James Buchanan, Lieutenant Jonathan McCulloch, one sergeant, two corporals, 57 other ranks artillerymen, and one drummer for a total of 67 men, from no less than six different companies of the royal artillery.[61] This force departed the royal arsenal at Woolwich, London, on November 15, 1754, and arrived at Hampton, Virginia, on the 8th and 10th March, 1755, following a lengthy voyage. The artillery contained four light 12-pounders, six 6-pounders, four 8" howitzers, and twenty 4⅖" (Coehorn) mortars. Although Burgoyne has been criticized for carrying an extraordinarily large train of artillery to Virginia, such criticisms are entirely unwarranted, and only the 8" howitzers can be considered to be siege artillery. The 12-pounders were specifically the lightest model of this cannon, well suited for service in North America. The 6-pounders were lightweight, highly-mobile guns intended for service directly with the battalions of infantry. The smaller coehorn mortars in particular were considerably well suited for service in North America.[62] In fact, this train of artillery was the smallest conceivable that could besiege Fort Duquesne, defend a new garrison at the Forks of the Ohio, and then support a continued attack against Fort Niagara.

Commissary of Stores and Paymaster to the Royal Artillery

As noted, the royal artillery was not a component of the army. Rather, it responded to the Board of Ordnance, as did the engineers. To assist the senior artillery officer in performing his range of duties, the Board of Ordnance dispatched an important civil servant who accompanied the army, Mr. James Furnis, commissary of stores and paymaster to the royal artillery. In this capacity, Furnis was responsible for the disposition and accountability of all artillery, engineering, and any other Board of Ordnance equipment inclusive, and he carried a separate military pay chest for the exclusive use of the engineers and artillery.[63]

Other Board of Ordnance Positions

As a separate entity, the Board of Ordnance maintained its own staff, that essentially mirrored that of Braddock's army. These positions were filled by either royal artillery officers or civilian employees from the Board of Ordnance. Identified officials included:

Adjutant—Lieutenant Robert Smith, Royal Artillery
Commissary of Horses—Lieutenant William MacLeod, Royal Artillery
Quarter Master—Lieutenant James Buchanan, Royal Artillery
Waggon Master—Lieutenant Jonathan McCulloch, Royal Artillery
Surgeon—Thomas Blair
Clerk of Stores and Assistant Paymaster (essentially assistant to Mr. Furnis)—William Marsh
First Conductor—James Hocket
Second Conductor—John Hawkins

Third Conductor—Thomas Scott
Fourth Conductor—John Defever.[64]

Lieutenants Smith, MacLeod, Buchanan and McCulloch performed these responsibilities as "additional duties" in addition to their artillery specific duties. The "conductor" was responsible for receiving, accounting for, safeguarding, issuing, and keeping in good order and repair all equipment of the Board of Ordnance, including but not limited to the artillery pieces.

Artificers

These were craftsmen with a wide range of talents such as blacksmiths, carpenters, tinsmiths (then referred to as whitesmiths), shipwrights, masons, harness makers, leather workers, etc. who would help the artillery with a wide and diverse range of repair, fabrication and construction projects. The Board of Ordnance dispatched a contingent of artificers to participate in the Braddock expedition. These artificers were all civilians:

First Carpenter—William Hardy
Carpenter—John Tyrrett
Carpenter—Francis Edwards
First Smith—Robert Harragad
Smith—Edward Smith
Smith—Janes Notlage
First Wheeler—Barnaby Chettle
Wheeler—Hugh Lewis
Armorer—Stephen Pullen
Armorer—Joseph Russell
Collarmaker [Horse Collars]—Samuel Special
Cooper—John Ward.[65]

Collectively, this was a robust artillery detachment, specifically configured to maintain an appropriately sized train of artillery under hard service.

Other Staff Officers

The remainder of the staff officers and civilians that supported Braddock provided specialty services.

Provost Marshal

The provost was essentially the military police of the 18th century, and the provost marshal was the officer in charge of the provost. A 1780 military treatise defined his duties and responsibilities:

> an officer appointed to seize and secure deserters, and all other criminals. He is to hinder soldiers from pillaging, to indict offenders, and to see the sentence passed on them executed. He also regulates the weights and measures and the price of provisions, etc. in the army.[66]

The provost operated the jail, received all prisoners, and maintained strict records of the same. As soon as a prisoner was remanded to jail the provost marshal was responsible for informing his regiment, and documented the charges against him and the arresting officer. The provost also had less glorious duties, such as "burying all dead horses and carrion" in camp.[67]

Surviving orderly books from Braddock's expedition provide additional insight into the activities of his provost guard. On March 28, 1755, at Alexandria the provost guard was established with Robert Webbster of Halkett's 44th Foot as the provost marshal, and "1 Serjt 1 Corpl & 12 men to mount as a Guard in ye Provoe [provost] And to be Relieved every Forty Eight Hours."[68] Among their duties on April 1 was to "send a Corpl & a file of men every Night at 9 oClock and to see all lights are Extinguished in the Soldiers Tents, And is frequiny [frequently] to send Patroles Round the Regts as fare as his Centrys Are Posted, to see that everything is quiet. And the Patrol is to take up all soldiers That are making any Noise or Any way disorderly & to releive all Centrys that Suffer any Disturbence near their post or otherways [are] negligent ... at the same time to take Caer that all Fires ... [are] Extinguished." During the march from Alexandria on April 10, it was specified that "the Provoe Marshal is to March with Col Dunbars regt And to have a Guard of 1 Serjt & ten men who is to make the Rear of the whole." This was a common practice, to pick up stragglers so that they could be treated and returned to their proper commands, and to prevent desertion and plundering. Once arrived at Fort Cumberland, the provost marshal was ordered on May 21: "to go his rounds ever day through all the Roads leading to the Camp. Every Soldiers or woman he shall meet with on the other side of the Rivers or beyond the Guard of the piquet's without a pass from the Regt or the Officer Commanding the Company They belong to he is to order [the Provost Guard] Immediately to Tye them up & give them fifty Lashes and to March them prisoners through the Camp to expose Them."[69]

Provost Marshal Webbster was the only permanent member of the provost guard, the other soldiers were detached from the British regiments and temporarily assigned as provost guards for a period of 48 hours. Webbster is not listed as being at the Battle of the Monongahela, he remained with Dunbar's column at the camp near Jumonville Glen at the rear of the army, as his orders mandated.

Chaplain

In the British army, each regiment was permitted to commission a chaplain, who was appointed directly by the colonel of the regiment. Two chaplains accompanied Braddock's regiments from Ireland. Philip Hughes was chaplain of Halkett's 44th Regiment of Foot, having been appointed to that regiment on January 4, 1752. John Hamilton was chaplain of Dunbar's 48th Regiment of Foot, appointed on November 13, 1754. A 1760 military treatise observed that

> nothing will contribute more to the Reformation of a Corps than the choice of a good Chaplain, who is universally known to be a Man of Worth and Probity [integrity, honesty], and who, by his Preaching and Example, is capable of inspiring the Men with solid Sentiments of Religion, which is the only true Foundation of military Honour. Such a Person will have it in his Power to become a principal Instrument towards maintaining a proper Harmony and Regularity throughout the whole.[70]

Unfortunately, this lofty and greatly to be desired ideal was often not realized. The chaplain position was more frequently a patronage post for the colonel, and although always filled, many chaplains were habitually absent from their regiments, preferring to draw their pay while remaining in comfort and ease at their homes rather than sharing in the rigors and dangers of an active campaign.

Apparently Chaplain Philip Hughes of the 44th Foot fell into this category at least once during the Seven Years War. In September 1760 Hughes was chastised by General Jeffery Amherst:

> The bad Choice that has been Made of Persons to Officiate for the Chaplains of the Army, Which has made it necessary to Discharge one latterly for imbibing Seditious principles into the Soldiers & the Other Your Deputy having Seldom Appeared during the Campaign, added to the few Chaplains that have come out to Attend their Duty; rendering it of Absolute Necessity, in Order to Convince his Majesty's new Acquired Subjects [in Canada] that their Brethren have a Sense of the Duty they owe to God; that all those Who are Appointed to have the Care of their Souls Should Attend to Discharge that trust; and the Regiment to Which You belong being to Winter in these Parts. I can no longer Admit of your Absence from the Same; You will therefore immediately upon the receipt hereof Set out for, and with all possible Diligence, repair to this place, in Order to remain with them & duly to Discharge the Office, You have taken upon You by the Acceptance of the Commission You Enjoy.[71]

As discussed by General Amherst, these chaplains would commonly hire an "assistant" to fulfill their duties in their absence. The inevitable result of this state of affairs was to seriously degrade the status and honor of this position.[72] A 1783 satire on "Officers of the British Army" observed:

> The chaplain is a character of no small importance in a regiment, though many gentlemen of the army think otherwise. If you are ambitious of being thought a good preacher by your scarlet flock, you must take care that your sermons be very short. Never preach any practical morality to the regiment. That would be only throwing away your time. To a man they all know, as well as you do, that they ought nought not to get drunk or commit adultery. You may indulge yourself in swearing and talking bawdy as much as you please; this will show you are not a stiff high priest.[73]

There is reason to believe that at least one of the two regimental chaplains failed to demonstrate the demeanor and conduct expected from a truly devout chaplain. On March 2, 1755, Mrs. Charlotte Browne, matron of Braddock's general hospital, complained in her journal: "Sunday but had no Prayers till Aftern-Noon our Parson being indispos'd by drinking too much Grog the Night before."[74] Another piece of evidence that suggests that the chaplains were remiss in the fulfillment of their responsibilities was noted by Captain Robert Cholmley's batman following the Battle of the Monongahela, after his arrival at Fort Cumberland during the retreat:

> Friday July the 25th. The men dying so fast daily that they [the survivors] digg holes and throw them in without Reading any service Over them, Altho we having two Ministers with us.[75]

While in camp at Alexandria, Virginia, on March 29, Braddock issued orders that "on Sunday every Regiment in Camp, is to have divine service at the Head of their Colours."[76] Chaplain Hughes of Halkett's 44th Foot is documented to have been at Fort Cumberland on May 18, when he performed a funeral service for Captain Bromley of Halkett's 44th Regiment of Foot.[77] Chaplain Hughes would be reported as "not wounded" but present at the Battle of the Monogahela.[78] Chaplain Hamilton remained with Colonel Dunbar at Jumonville and was not present at the engagement.

Chaplain Hughes would write a letter dated July 23, 1755, from Fort Cumberland to a correspondent in England, which was reprinted in the *Public Advertiser* newspaper on

October 31, 1755. In this letter, Chaplain Hughes documented his participation in the fight at the Monongahela, without falling into the vice of being overly modest:

> I believe I am the first Chaplain who ever saved a Pair of Colors which I took within fifty Yards of the Cannon, when the Enemy were Masters of them. The French and Indians crept about in small Parties so that the Fire was quite round us, and in all the Time I never saw one, nor could I on Enquiry find any one who saw ten together. The Loss killed and wounded 864. The French had 2000 Men, besides Indians, we had six Indians, they at least as many hundreds. We marched near 400 Miles in three Months, cut 350 thro' Woods, and for the last 200 saw no House but this dirty Fort. Rum 20 s [shillings] a Gallon, the worst brown Sugar 4s 6d [pence] a Pound, a Year old Calf sold to Sir Peter Halket and our Mess at 3 Pounds. After the 25th of June a Dollar for a Pint of Rum, so you may judge of our Distress. The whole Country is a Wood.[79]

The chaplains were intended to provide spiritual guidance and comfort to the officers and soldiers of Braddock's army. Unfortunately, insufficient primary sources exist to positively determine whether or not chaplains Hughes and Hamilton fulfilled this important role for Braddock, or to document their daily activities upon the campaign. However, what limited evidence does survive strongly intimates that both regimental chaplains came up far short in fulfilling the responsibilities of their office.

SURGEON AND MATES

Each regiment in the British army was assigned a surgeon and surgeon's mate, who was responsible for the soldier's health and welfare. A 1787 manual and autobiography by a British army surgeon noted of his duties:

> Each regiment, regular as well as Militia, is allowed a surgeon as he is termed and a surgeon's mate. Their business is to attend to the disease of the men at all times when-ever it is judged necessary. For this service the surgeon is allowed four shillings a day; the mate three and sixpence.[80]

The surgeon and mate were exempted from all regimental duties except caring for the sick. Although they carried military commissions, the surgeon and mate ranked below the youngest ensign.

Braddock, as will be seen from his correspondence with St. Clair, was extremely concerned with the health and well being of his soldiers. He carried with him from England a well-manned and fully-functional hospital, which was provided with a considerable augmentation of medical personnel besides the two regimental surgeons and mates that would have been expected. Dr. James Napier was director of this hospital. A highly accomplished surgeon, Napier had previously served as master surgeon of the hospitals in Flanders on the European continent during the War of Austrian Succession.[81] The two regimental surgeons were Dr. Robert McKinley of Hackett's 44th Foot and Dr. Robert Murdoch of Dunbar's 48th Foot.[82] Dr. Napier was assisted in the general hospital by doctors John Adair and John Cherrington. Adair had previously served as a surgeon on an expedition to Brittany during the War of Austrian Succession in 1746. Dr. Cherrington was accompanied by a surgeon's mate, apothecary Robert Bristowe, and his sister Mrs. Charlotte Browne, who was matron of the general hospital. All five of them had served on the garrison staff at Louisburg between 1745 and 1749.[83] Surgeon James Craik served as surgeon for the various provincial (mostly Virginia) Companies.[84] Craik had previously served as a British army surgeon in the West Indies, and functioned as surgeon to Washington's Virginia provincials during the 1754 Fort

Necessity campaign. Craik was an established physician in the small frontier town of Winchester, Virginia Colony. Thus, Braddock's medical staff was extremely experienced, containing veteran and seasoned medical practitioners, with considerable prior military service on active campaigns. An additional apothecary with the general hospital was identified as William Couch. The various surgeon's mates were identified as Matthew Leslie, Jonathan Lee, Charles Swainton (or Swinton), William Congleton, Robert Bass, George Tuting, Joseph Williams, and James Campbell.[85]

An extremely large list of necessaries was prepared for the hospital, including "eight hundred flock beds and bolsters, each bed six by three feet, along with one pair each blankets and sheets, eight marquees, eight troopers tents, and other necessary equipage."[86] When Mrs. Browne departed England on November 17, she recorded she "embark'd on Board the Ship London, Captain Browne, Laden with Stores for the Hospital."[87]

This was, by the standard of 18th century armies, an incredibly well equipped hospital. When Mrs. Browne departed Alexandria for Fort Cumberland, she noted that her party included "2 Nurses, 2 Cooks."[88] During the campaign, two hospitals would be established, the general hospital at Fort Cumberland, and a field (or regimental) hospital with Dunbar's column. Some medical staff accompanied Braddock's lead column marching upon Fort Duquesne, for surgeon's mate Charles Swainton was killed at the Battle of the Monongahela.[89]

Summary

Braddock was provided with a completely manned military staff by George II's and his son the Duke of Cumberland's standards. In fact, particularly as regards the hospital, Braddock's supporting staff was augmented well beyond the standards of the mid–18th century British army.

COMMANDING GENERAL
Major General Edward Braddock

PERSONAL STAFF

Aide-de-Camp	Lieutenant Robert Orme, Coldstream Guards
Aide-de-Camp	Captain Robert Moore, 48th Foot
Volunteer Aide-de-Camp	Mr. George Washington, Alexandria, Virginia
Military Secretary	Mr. William Shirley, Jr.

This was a sufficient personal staff to permit Braddock to fulfill his role as commanding general of the expedition.

ADMINISTRATIVE STAFF (EQUIVALENT TO A MODERN G-1 PERSONNEL AND ADMINISTRATIVE SECTION)

Brigade Major	Captain Francis Halkett, 44th Foot
Regimental Adjutant, 44th Foot	Lieutenant Daniel Disney
Regimental Adjutant, 48th Foot	Lieutenant John Gordon
Adjutant of Virginia Rangers	Simon Frazer
Other Appointed Adjutants	Various Unknown
Commissary of Musters	Mr. James Pitcher

This was an adequate personnel and administrative staff to enable Braddock to successfully manage the army as a commanding general.

INTELLIGENCE SECTION (EQUIVALENT TO A MODERN G-2 INTELLIGENCE SECTION)

During the era of George II, the British army had no such staff element. A commanding general was expected to operate his own intelligence operation.[90] For example, it is well documented that George Washington, as the patriot commander in chief of the Continental army, operated his own highly effective intelligence network during the War of American Independence.[91] Accordingly, Braddock was expected to manage his own intelligence operations entirely by himself.

OPERATIONS STAFF (EQUIVALENT TO A MODERN G-3 PLANS, TRAINING AND OPERATIONS STAFF)

During the era of George II, the British army had no such staff element. A commanding general, ably supported by his subordinate commanders, was believed to possess sufficient military experience and knowledge to supervise his own planning, training, and operations. Accordingly, Braddock was assisted by the commanding officers and field officers from his two Regiments of Foot.

Braddock was accompanied by the 44th Foot commanded by an extremely able and experienced Scottish officer, Colonel Sir Peter Halket, and the 48th Foot commanded by a considerably less able English officer, Colonel Thomas Dunbar. Halket, a Scottish lowlander from near Edinburgh, has seen considerable active experience during the 1745 Jacobite Rebellion, had been captured after heavy fighting at the Battle of Prestonpans, and had proven himself to possess considerable morale courage and honor following his parole. Dunbar had considerable less experience on actual field service.

Colonel, 44th Foot	Colonel Sir Peter Halkett
Lieutenant Colonel, 44th Foot	Lieutenant Colonel Thomas Gage
Major, 44th Foot	Major William Sparke
Colonel, 48th Foot	Colonel Thomas Dunbar
Lieutenant Colonel, 48th Foot	Lieutenant Colonel Ralph Barton
Major, 48th Foot	Major Russel Chapman

BOARD OF ORDNANCE

As previously discussed, the engineers and royal artillery operated using a different system than that of the regular British army, and were considered to be upon a different establishment.

Commander, Royal Artillery	Captain Thomas Orde [or Ord], Royal Artillery
Commissary of Stores & Paymaster to the Royal Artillery	Mr. James Furnis
Engineer	Engineer Patrick Mackellar
Engineer	Engineer Harry Gordon
Junior Engineer	Lieutenant Adam Williamson, 44th Foot

Of the three engineers, two were highly experienced; Lieutenant Williamson was a relatively young engineer. By mid–18th century standards these three engineers were supported by a complete engineering ensemble that enabled them to perform all necessary surveying and drawing tasks. Braddock's expedition was supported by an entirely adequate engineering detachment.

Logistics Staff (equivalent to a modern G-4, support and sustainment staff)

Deputy Quartermaster General	Sir John St. Clair
Assistant Deputy Quartermaster General	Lieutenant Matthew Leslie, 44th Foot
Joint Commissary	Mr. Thomas Walker (Merchant, Albemarle County, Virginia)
Joint Commissary	Mr. Charles Dick (Merchant, Alexandria, Virginia)
Commissary for Provisions	Mr. [unknown] Lake
Assistant Commissary	Mr. Townsend Washington
Other Assistant Commissaries	Unknown (presumably several)
Storekeeper for Stores and Provisions	Mr. John Carlyle (Merchant, Alexandria, Virginia)
Baker(s)	Unknown
44th Foot Regimental Quartermaster	Ensign Henry Verrant
48th Foot Regimental Quartermaster	Ensign Thomas Webb
Appointed Quartermasters	Several Unknown
Deputy Paymaster General	Mr. William Johnson
44th Foot Regimental Paymaster	Unknown
48th Foot Regimental Paymaster	Unknown
Agent for the Money Contractor	Mr. John Hunter (Merchant, Hampton, Virginia
Assistant Agent for the Money Contractor	Mr. James Balfour (Merchant, Hampton, Virginia)
Wagon Master General	Mr. Thomas Scott (Pennsylvania)
Wagon Master	Mr. William Reed (Pennsylvania)
Wagon Masters	[Others Unknown]

This was a sufficient logistical staff to maintain Braddock's army in the field.

Other Staff Officers

Provost Marshal	Robert Webbster, 44th Foot (rank unknown)
Chaplain, 44th Foot	Reverend Phillip Hughes
Chaplain, 48th Foot	Reverend John Hamilton

That Braddock was concerned with his soldier's morale and welfare is evidenced that both his regimental chaplains accompanied his expedition from England to Virginia, at a time when it was quite common for regimental chaplains to be entirely absent from their duties. This concern would be demonstrated during the campaign, for when Braddock divided his army into two columns, Chaplain Philip Hughes of Halkett's regiment accompanied the forward column marching upon Fort Duquesne, while Chaplain John Hamilton of the 48th Regiment of Foot remained with Colonel Dunbar's supporting column.

General Hospital

Director, General Hospital	Dr. James Napier
Surgeon, 44th Foot	Dr. Robert McKinley
Surgeon, 48th Foot	Dr. Robert Murdoch
Surgeon, Virginia Provincials	Dr. James Craik (Physician, Winchester, Virginia)
Additional Surgeon, General Hospital	Dr. John Adair
Additional Surgeon, General Hospital	Dr. John Cherrington
Matron, General Hospital	Mrs. Charlotte Brown
Apothecary, General Hospital	Apothecary Robert Bristowe
Apothecary, General Hospital	Apothecary William Couch
Surgeon's Mates	Matthew Leslie
	Jonathan Lee
	Charles Swainton [or Swinton]
	William Congleton
	Robert Bass
	George Tuting
	Joseph Williams
	James Campbell.

This was, by the standards of the middle of the 18th century, an extremely robust and capable medical staff.

Taken collectively, Braddock's army was extremely well equipped by the standards of George II's British army, and was intended to operate in the remote and difficult wilderness conditions of North America for an extended period of time, while caring for the health and well-being of the soldiers to the maximum extent possible.

3

"I have done every thing in my power to facilitate their march to the Allegany Mountains"

Organization of the Movement to Fort Cumberland, January–March 1755

There were five distinct phases of the campaign in which St. Clair as deputy quartermaster general was intimately involved. The first phase, detailed planning for the expedition to the Forks of the Ohio, occurred in London in the fall of 1754, before the embarkation for Virginia. Surprisingly, this phase of the campaign has received scant interest from historians. Unfortunately, how extensive St. Clair's involvement in this planning phase was cannot be documented through extant sources, but it must have been relatively brief.

Since 1749 the 22nd Regiment of Foot had been stationed on the Irish establishment, and in the late summer of 1754 St. Clair was a captain with this regiment when he was informed that the Braddock expedition was being planned. St. Clair then used his influence as a member of the Scottish peerage to obtain the position of deputy quartermaster general.[1] It is known that the position of deputy quartermaster general was viewed as a lucrative position, and that a number of officers, including Lieutenant Colonel John Forbes of the Royal Scots Grays who possessed considerable experience as quartermaster in Flanders a decade earlier, lobbied for the position. Colonel Forbes would be disappointed in his efforts, as Forbes wrote a letter on October 19 noting that St. Clair's selection had been announced "in the papers."[2] St. Clair became a major in the 22nd Foot on October 7, 1754. Nearly simultaneously, St. Clair was appointed as deputy quartermaster general to Braddock on October 15, 1754. Assuming that St. Clair was either with his regiment in Ireland, or in Scotland visiting his family and estate, October would have been extremely hectic for him as he would have had to return to London, settle his personal affairs, receive his instructions for the campaign, and obtain clothing and personal equipment necessary for an extended deployment to North America. Because St. Clair arrived in Virginia on January 9, 1755, he would have had to embark aboard a transport in early November, and accordingly his involvement in the planning phase was necessarily limited.

The second phase of the campaign occurred between January and early April, and involved preparations for the movement forward. This phase will be comprehensively discussed in this chapter. The third phase of the campaign occurred between April and May, and moved Braddock's army from the Virginia tidewater at Alexandria to Fort Cumberland, which would serve as the advanced depot for the expedition. St. Clair's contributions to this movement forward will be comprehensively discussed in Chapter 6. The fourth phase of the campaign occurred between June and July, and was the movement of the army from Fort Cumberland to Fort Duquesne. St. Clair's participation in this movement will be comprehensively discussed in Chapter 7.

The fifth phase of the campaign would never be executed, because of the defeat at the Monongahela. However, all of St. Clair's logistical plans had to be formulated with this phase in mind, as it was the objective of the entire campaign. Specifically, the year's campaign was devoted to placing a sizeable military force in front of Fort Duquesne at the Forks of the Ohio, augmented by provincial forces to perform necessary labor of siegeworks and construction of artillery platforms, and carrying a sufficient force of artillery supplied with adequate ammunition to force Fort Duquesne to yield. St. Clair's logistical plans would have to support this siege, or all the efforts of the spring and summer would be for nothing. Once Fort Duquesne was captured, St. Clair would have to support the construction and/or repair of fortifications at the Forks of the Ohio, and establish and maintain a permanent defensive garrison at this location. St. Clair would also have to construct bateaux, barges and other watercraft at the Forks of the Ohio to perform an exploitation of Braddock's victory, traveling up the Allegheny River in the direction of the other French forts in the Ohio Valley and eventually Fort Niagara, and logistically support such a movement. The implications of the subsequent steps of the campaign upon Braddock's and St. Clair's plans and actions have been entirely ignored by historians.

Upon his arrival in Virginia early in January 1755, St. Clair had the following major responsibilities:

- establish a logistical system, including appropriate commissaries and other support staff, in Virginia;
- prepare for the arrival of the British soldiers in Virginia, to include establishing a general hospital, barracks and/or campsites. The preliminary plan, formulated in London by the Duke of Cumberland, Braddock and St. Clair, was for Braddock's two regiments to initially disembark in Hampton, Virginia;
- prepare for the arrival of various supplies (including military material and provisions) from England, to include overseeing the acquisition and/or construction of necessary warehouses and storehouses;
- arrange for the acquisition of a transportation system consisting of qualified wagon masters, wagons with teams and drivers, additional teams to transport the royal artillery guns and wagons, and supplemental horses to carry the officer's baggage;
- facilitate the recruitment of an additional 200 recruits for each British Regiment of Foot;
- Muster, inspect, and prepare for active service the two New York and one South Carolina independent companies of the British army then stationed in North America, that had been assigned to join Braddock's expedition;
- recruit, muster, arm, equip and train the various provincial companies intended to augment the two Regiments of Foot;
- prepare for the water transportation of the army and its supplies from Hampton, Virginia, up the Potomac River to Fort Cumberland;

- establish Fort Cumberland as the forward logistical base to support the movement of the army across the Allegheny Mountains; and
- identify and improve the route that Washington had traversed the previous year (1754) in his campaign against the Forks of the Ohio, to permit Braddock's Army to reach Fort Duquesne. In London, it was believed that only fifteen miles of additional road would have to be constructed.

Having embarked aboard *HMS Gibraltar*, a spanking new 20-gun sixth-rate frigate that had just entered service with the royal navy that year, in early November, Sir John St. Clair arrived at Hampton, Virginia, on January 9, 1755.[3] St. Clair almost immediately traveled to Williamsburg, the capitol of Virginia. His first letter in North America was written on January 12 from Williamsburg.

Lieutenant Governor Dinwiddie of Virginia and Governor Horatio Sharpe of Maryland had done much to organize the logistical support for the expedition before St. Clair arrived.[4] Most importantly, the joint commissaries and storekeeper for stores and provisions had already been appointed and started their efforts. As early as January 15, St. Clair reported to Braddock: "The Governour [Dinwiddie] has been extremely active and diligent on gathering together all kinds of provisions for Willis's Creek, and to make a Deposite at Fredericksbourgh [Fredericksburg], and Winchester to be near at hand." St. Clair regularly communicated with his commissaries and storekeeper to monitor their progress.

It is obvious that St. Clair also routinely coordinated with Dinwiddie and Sharpe regarding these logistics. St. Clair wrote to the commissaries in early February: "I shall be glad you will let his Excellency Gover Dinwidee, know from time to time what Success you have had, and what Provisions you have in View." When the exigencies of his numerous commitments permitted, St. Clair met with these officers personally. On March 12 St. Clair wrote to Braddock from the crossing of the Great Cacecapon River: "I shou'd have wrote this Letter from Winchester but I was willing to see Mr Commissary Dick, who I met at this house; I herewith Transmit to your Excellency what he tells me of Mr Commissary Walker's Success at Pennsylvania." During this stage of the campaign, St. Clair depended upon his two joint commissaries and John Carlyle to fulfill their responsibilities. He expended relatively few efforts upon altering or revising the logistical arrangements that they had entered into, instead he spent most of his efforts upon raising soldiers (particularly provincials) for the campaign, and arranging for the campaign's transportation needs and routes from Alexandria to Fort Cumberland.

As a component of these early efforts, St. Clair immediately attempted to expand his knowledge of North America. He wrote all the various governors requesting accurate maps and information regarding their colonies. St. Clair also conducted various meetings with knowledgeable individuals who had served on or visited the frontier. Although it appears that maps and detailed information were relatively scarce, St. Clair made every effort to obtain what was available, and spent considerable time in the saddle to verify the intelligence that he gathered.

St. Clair's initial assignment from Braddock was to prepare Hampton to receive the British regiments: "Ye 1st[:] To provide an hospital at Hampton or Williamsburgh for 150 Sick with the Director, 2 Surgeons, 2 Apothecarys and six Mates." St. Clair reported to Braddock as early as January 15, almost immediately after his arrival:

The 12th I went with the Governour [Governor Dinwiddie] to Hampton in order to provide an Hospital and Lodgings for the proper Officers. Next day I went and examined the whole Town of Hampton, but Cou'd [could] not find any one place Sufficient to Contain any number of Sick, all I could get was two very small warehouses, But there are no houses in town which will be shut to us on this Occasion, So how disagreeable it may be to the Surgeons to have their sick Separate there is a Necessity for it at present. There are numbers of indigent people who will take the sick into their houses, and least bedsteads may be wanting I have given directions for 100 Cradles to be built, I have provided two Extreme good lodgings at the Town Clerk's house for two of the principal Officers of the hospital, the others may lodge with those people who keep publick houses until Mr [Mister] Graham leaves his dwelling house, which will be towards the end of February. I should not have hesitated one moment in running up a large hospital of boards, if I cou'd have got a Sufficient Quantity of Deal and Artificiers but both are wanting.[5] I gave directions to Mr. Hunter / who delivers you this / concerning Stock of Fire wood for the Hospitals and to get as much fresh provisions Collected together for the sick as possible, as likewise to throw on board of the Transports some sheep and fresh pork / and some Beefes if they are to be had/.

St. Clair also consulted with Governor Dinwiddie regarding the future movement of Braddock's men from Hampton to Alexandria, and following discussions he recommended to Braddock that the regiments be transported directly by water to Alexandria, rather than landing at Hampton as initially planned in London: "I have been talking to the Govr Concerning the properest Method of landing the troops, he is of opinion that they should proceed to Alexra in their Transports and march as soon as possible to Willis's Creek, for if they were to land at Hampton and be dispersed about the Country they would have a long march by land, that all the horses and carriages which will be wanted to carry provisions to the deposites wou'd be wanted to attend the Troops on their march to Alexria: and that if they were to march by land they have ferrys to cross which might be attended with a long delay, after examining the Situation of the Country maturely and the quick dispatch that Affairs require, I am of the above opinion with the Governour for we shall at least gain 3 Weeks by going up directly by water." This was the course adopted by Braddock upon the arrival of the British regiments in mid–March. When hospital matron Mrs. Brown arrived off Hampton on March 11 she noted, "The Captain ... received his Orders to sail up the River Potomac" and her transport sailed directly with a "fair wind" on March 13 "for Potomack" without her disembarking at Hampton.[6]

Having made this recommendation, St. Clair expended few further efforts in Hampton, after early January his only such work being the establishment of hospital facilities in Hampton. This was a recognition that some soldiers would have been taken ill upon the long, cramped, damp and cold winter voyage from North America, and that they would need to be landed expeditiously for their care and recovery. St. Clair wrote on January 15 to Commissary Hunter to ensure that this hospital was established in Hampton: "I must beg of you to have an Eye to what is doing about the hospital and the making of the Cradles [hospital beds] and erecting stoves with a provision of Wood." St. Clair also reiterated in early February that "I will carry this letter down to Hampton with my other letters on the 14th ... and shall see the hospitals and every thing in order for the sick." Mrs. Brown recorded that Dr. John Cherrington landed at Hampton, presumably to attend the general hospital temporarily established there, upon their arrival on the shores of Virginia.[7] Surprisingly, the transports arrived from Ireland with "not a sick man among them, which is pretty extraordinary considering the length of the passage."[8] The general hospital at Hampton was accordingly disbanded, and all of its medical practioners, facilities and equipment transferred to Alexandria.

Braddock's second instruction to St. Clair was "Ye 2[:] To provide provisions against the landing of the troops[,] and during their stay at Willis's Creek." As previously mentioned, the preliminary plan had been to land the regiments at Hampton and Fredericksburg and to march overland across Virginia to Alexandria. The stockpiling of supplies at Fredericksburg was intended to feed the army during this movement. St. Clair provided Braddock a detailed proposal to support this initial scheme on February 9:

> That the Transports which have on board one Regiment may Stop in the River Potomack as near Fredericksburgh as they can, that Regt [Regiment] may be Quartered in the following manner.
>
> 3½ Companys at Winchester 6 days march from Fredericksburgh
> ½ Company at Conogogee 8 days by Winchester
> 6 Companys at Fredericksburgh and Falmouth
>
> ---
>
> 10 Companys
>
> The other Regt
>
> 5 Companys at Alexandria, with the Complt [complement] of Artillery and Stores of all kind
> 1 Compy [Company] at Dumfries 2 days March from Alexa.
> 1 Compy at Upper Marlbro 2 days March in Maryland
> 1 Compy at Blandensburgh 1 day March in Maryland
> 2 at Frederick, 2 days March in Maryland
>
> By this disposition the other Companys which are quartered at Winchester, Conagogoee and Fredrick [Frederick, Maryland] form the Chain to Cover our Magazines, and will be near at hand to advance either to Willis's Creek or Savage River as you shall judge most proper.

This dispersed approach would be overruled by Braddock, who followed an alternative approach recommended by Governor Dinwiddie and St. Clair. Braddock was particularly concerned with keeping the two regiments together upon their landing in Virginia. Because of the numerous drafts from several regiments to bring the 44th and 48th Foot up to strength that had been received shortly before their departure from Ireland, and the numerous new (and entirely untrained) provincial enlistees that he anticipated adding to the regiment in Virginia, Braddock was determined to retain his brigade's integrity so that it could be drilled to a high standard, and that normal discipline could be established within the newly expanded regiments.

Once in Alexandria, the two regiments had sufficient time available to incorporate the Irish draftees received in the 44th and 48th Regiments of Foot shortly before they embarked for Virginia. Newly forwarded to these two regiments, they were trained soldiers experienced in the British army drill, although there were minor discrepancies between each regiment. A month of drill at Alexandria should have been more than sufficient to accustom the draftees to their new regiment's idiosyncrasies in military evolutions.

On his first meeting with St. Clair, Governor Dinwiddie recommended that Braddock's men be transported by water directly to Alexandria. St. Clair forwarded this suggestion to Braddock in a letter dated February 17: "Shou'd you think it more Adviseable to encamp the 2 Troops than to Quarter them in the manner I proposed in my last there is a good Camp Close to the Town of Alexandria, all I can say of the encamping the Troops is that I have felt no Weather in this Country since my arrival but what a Soldier might be very comfortable in his Tent[.] if you approve of this method it will get our new men easily disciplined[,] and detachments may be sent up to Cover our Magazines." This is the alternative that Braddock actually utilized, and accordingly St. Clair would have to make arrangements in Alexandria for the arrival and lodging of Braddock's two regiments and royal artillery detachment. The February 17 letter also indicates that in his guise as quartermaster St. Clair selected the actual campsites that Braddock's regiments used in Alexandria.

St. Clair depended upon a well-established Alexandria merchant with extensive business contacts, John Carlyle, storekeeper for stores and provisions, to provide the construction of a warehouse and stockpiling of provisions in Alexandria. St. Clair noted in a February 22 letter to Carlyle, "As Genl Braddock, with the British Forces is arrived. You are hereby ordered to get together all the Fresh provisions you possibly can and compleat every thing in the best manner for their reception as soon as may be, if any Carpenters should be wanting I have directed Captain Mercer to give you what number may be necessary." When St. Clair ordered a company of Virginia carpenters to march forward from Alexandria on March 5, he wrote to Captain William Polson, "During your stay at this place Mr. Carlile [sic] will furnish you with provisions for your Effective men, and will furnish you with 5 days Provisions which your men are to Carry with them for their March." St. Clair elaborated the next day: "I must desire that you will take Receipts from the Commanding officer of Companys and Detachments for the Quantity of Provis [provisions]: you deliver out to them those Receipts are to be signed every Monday for the weeks provision before, and will serve you for your proper Vouchers." Identical instructions were issued to other Virginia provincial companies on March 7 and 12. Carlyle supervised the construction of a large warehouse directly on the Potomac River at Alexandria's Lumley Point, at the northeast head of Duke Street (one of the main roads in the town), specifically to hold Braddock's supplies.[9]

St. Clair also ordered the construction of other storehouses at Conococheague in Maryland. This was a strategic location, as the Conococheague Creek flowed from a rich agricultural area in Pennsylvania into the Potomac River here. The Conococheague Valley would be an important source of provisions and forage for St. Clair and Braddock's army. Today the Conococheague Creek flows from Franklin County, Pennsylvania, to Williamsport, Maryland.

Among the most important of St. Clair's duties was to establish the transportation system for the expedition. In the British army of George II, horses and wagons were not furnished by the crown. The Board of Ordnance did provide some specialized equipment such as artillery tumbrels and ammunition wagons, but the majority of an army's transportation needs had to be contracted for. And even the Board of Ordnance did not provide draft animals for their carriages, these still had to be acquired for the train of artillery. St. Clair had to obtain wagons with teamsters and teams, baggage horses for the officers with drivers, riding horses for the officers, and horses for the Board of Ordnance. Since St. Clair had been instructed to raise a Virginia company of light horse, a comparatively large number of riding horses also needed to be purchased for this troop.

Among St. Clair's specific instructions from Braddock was "Ye 3[:] Bats Horses to be provided for the Officers when they arrive." The use of pack horses was routine in the British army. Such horses were formally referred to as "bat horses" from the French "cheval de bât" which literally means "horses of baggage," a "bât" being a pack saddle. In the British army of the Seven Years War their use was authorized by officers to transport their personnel gear, and officers were provided with an allowance to pay for bat horses when on campaign. During the later Forbes campaign of 1758 Colonel Henry Bouquet estimated that each bat horse should be capable of carrying two hundred pounds of baggage, which appears to have been a standard load that would also have been used in 1755.[10]

St. Clair reported to Braddock of his efforts to obtain horses:

> [January] 10th I went to Williamsburgh and delivered my Dispatches to the Governour, the next day I consulted with his Excellency the properest methods of going to work on this urgent piece of service. That day one hundred horses were contracted for, 40 of which were to be delivered the first week in February and the Remaining part the first day of March, each of these horses are to bring with them 200 Weight of Flour to Willis's Creek.

St. Clair expended considerable efforts in obtaining horses and wagons. On January 14 he documented, "I saw some more horses bought for the use of the troops." St. Clair instructed the joint Commissaries on February 2, telling Walker, "By the 18th day of March the 100 Waggons employ'd for that Service are to proceed to Winchester if Required, and are to be paid for by the Government: 40 Horses are to be at the Fort with 200 Weight of Flour if these horses are according to Contract they are to be sent to Mr. Dick at Winchester to be employ'd in the Governmt Service[.] you are to apprise Mr. Dick of this[,] and let him know that he is to lay in at Winchester provender of all kinds For horses as much as he can." St. Clair instructed Dick in separate correspondence, "I have desired Mr. Walker to send to you to Winchester the 40 horses Contracted for, which were to be delivered at the Fort the first week of Feb: with 200 Weight of Flour on each: These horses you are to Employ in Carrying up provisions to the Camp, and it will be Necessary to have a man hired for each four horses."

St. Clair told Braddock on February 9, "I expect 100 Waggons from Pensylvania with flour at Winchester by the 15th of March which Waggons will serve for Carrying the Ammunition and Stores up from Alexandria." St. Clair believed that the wagons could carry 2,000 pounds apiece, a reasonable estimate for the flat coastal plain of Flanders, but wildly optimistic for the mountainous and primitive roads of western Virginia and Pennsylvania. On February 18 St. Clair asked Governor Dinwiddie to "write Mr Carlyle to press Waggons agreeable to Act of Assembly to carry up 400 brls [barrels] of pork that will very soon be sent to Alexandria." A barrel of salt pork weighed approximately 233 pounds, so four hundred barrels would weigh 93,200 pounds. At 2,000 pounds per wagon, St. Clair would have needed approximately 47 wagons for this job. However, eight barrels would have been carried by one wagon (1,864 pounds) because half barrels cannot logically be carried, so fifty wagons were requisitioned.

St. Clair was confident that he had adequately addressed the challenge of acquiring sufficient wagons and horses, as he reported to General Braddock: "As the Army will be able to take the field by the 10th day of May, the Commissaries are directed to Assemble two Hundred Waggons, and two Thousand Horses, at the Camp of the British Army at Willis's Creek by that day, that they are to take all Necessary precaution in providing pack saddles and halters for the Horses."

St. Clair's belief that he had made adequate arrangements to obtain wagons and horses was rapidly shattered, as it became apparent that the wagons and horses stipulated by the various contracts that St. Clair and his commissaries had issued would never materialize. By early April, it was obvious that all of his meticulous plans had fallen apart. St. Clair wrote frantically on April 13:

> I have this moment Received an Express from his Excellency General Braddock Complaining that the Country people are very Dilatory in sending their Waggons and Teams of horses for our Artillery & Stores which are lying at Alexandria[.] this is the only thing that Retards all our Operations. I hope you have sent down the Waggons for their 2d Loading but I am very sorry to Acquaint you that the numbers which were to bring down last week are far short of what I expected.
>
> I am now to Acquaint you that 58 Waggons are immediately Wanted to be at Alexandria and 24 Teams of horses with their Harness besides the 34 Teams of Horses I Ordered Mr Dick to send down[.] I wou'd not have the Country people Plead that they have their ground to plough, the Service of the King and Country must be first done, and the People who have the Waggons employ'd will soon earn money enough to purchase horses for Labour. You are therefore to warn all the Waggons in the Country for his Majesty's Service, the numbers mentioned above to be sent to Alexandria and the others are to load stores at Winchester for the Fort taking the Road by H. Enoch's and Crossing the Potomack at the mouth of the south Branch. Shou'd any of the Inhabitants Refuse to go on this Service, You are to let me know their names that I may apply to Sir Peter Halkett for a Detachment of our Soldiers to be Quartered on them; and you may take my word for it, that if those people do not go on this service with their Waggons and horses, I shall Convince them that they had better draw up our Artillery gratis from Alexandria, and been Yoked in place of their horses.

This was an extremely hot-tempered and injudicious letter, unlikely to produce beneficial results, and it reveals much of St. Clair's personality and the great stress that he was under.

Fortunately, in response to St. Clair's efforts to insure that an effective system of messengers was established between the army and the colonies to the east, Benjamin Franklin, postmaster general for the colonies, traveled to Frederick in early April to meet with Braddock and St. Clair. Franklin recounted he and his son

> found the General at Frederic Town, waiting impatiently of those he had sent thro' the back Parts of Maryland and Virginia to collect Waggons.... When I was about to depart, the Returns of Waggons to be obtain'd were brought in, by which it appear'd that they amounted to only twenty-five, and not all of those were in serviceable Condition. The General and all the Officers were surpriz'd, declar'd the Expedition was then at an End, being impossible, and exclaim'd against the Ministers for ignorantly landing them in a Country destitute of the Means of conveying their Stores, Baggage, &c. not less than 150 Waggons being necessary.

Franklin's rendition is borne out by Braddock's correspondence, for he wrote Colonel Napier (and through him the Duke of Cumberland) on June 8:

> It would take up too much of your Time were I to tell you particularly the Difficulties and Disapointments I have met with from the want of Honesty and Inclination to forward the Service in all Orders of people in these Colonies, which have occasion'd the great Delays in getting hither, as well as my being detain'd here a Month longer than I intended. I was assur'd at Williamsburg [by St. Clair] that two hundred wagons and two thousand five hundred Horses would be there by the 10th of May, as also great Quantities of Forage at proper distances upon the Road, where the Artillery and Waggons were to pass, and that proper persons and such as could be depended upon were emplo'd for that purpose; but I soon found that there was hardly any Forage in the Country and that the promises of the people of Virginia and Maryland were not to be depended upon: if we press'd Waggons, as we were oblig'd to let the Horses go into the Woods to feed, they went off directly, the pack Horses the same.[11]

Franklin continued his narrative of his discussions with Braddock:

> I happened'd to say, I thought it was a pity they had not been landed rather in Pennsylvania, as in that Country almost every Farmer had his Waggon. The General eagerly laid hold of my Words, and said "Then you, Sir, who are a Man of Intereste there, can probably procure them for us; and I beg you will undertake it."[12]

Braddock immediately issued Franklin with a warrant on April 22 authorizing him to obtain wagons from Pennsylvania.[13] Franklin moved swiftly, and on April 26 he published a broadside advertising for 150 wagons, and delineating the terms under which the wagons would be contracted. Franklin's broadside concluded with this ominous pronouncement:

> If this Method of obtaining the Waggons and Horses is not like to succeed, I am oblig'd to send Word to the General in fourteen Days; and I suppose Sir John St. Clair the Hussar, with a Body of Soldiers, will immediately enter the Province, for the purpose aforesaid, of which I shall be sorry to hear.[14]

Shortly thereafter, a copy of Franklin's wagon broadside was delivered by Franklin's newly established express postal service to Braddock's headquarters. Its perusal occasioned great merriment, as reported by Franklin's son, William Franklin:

> By what I hear from all the Officers your advertisement afforded them a great deal of Diversion. Mr. Orme told me, that the General laughed for an hour together at it. And Sir John himself looked on it as a king of Compliment, till he heard, that the officers made themselves merry with it; and even now he seems rather to be angry with them than you.[15]

Franklin's transformation of St. Clair into becoming a hussar was found to be particularly hilarious by Braddock and his British officers. They well knew that St. Clair had never been a hussar; that there was not a single hussar in the entire British army; that St. Clair was currently serving as a mundane quartermaster officer at the head of a slow moving convoy of baggage wagons and road construction instead of leading a band of dashing, wicked, mustachioed swashbucklers; and that western Virginia contained no hussars available for any potential foraging foray into Pennsylvania even if St. Clair was so inclined. But the predominantly German Pennsylvanians were well familiar with the European hussar (particularly the Russian, Polish and Hungarian variations of the same) and their propensity for terrorizing the local population, plundering, looting, stealing, drinking, absconding with local women, and frightening innocent farm animals was both terrible and devoutly to be feared. Franklin's threat of turning "St. Clair the Hussar" loose upon their farm villages was sufficient to encourage even the most stingy, tight-fisted Pennsylvania farmer to divest himself of his cherished wagon and team for the duration of Braddock's campaign.

The common description of Braddock as a boring, pompous, rigid British aristocrat is entirely altered by the vision of him and his fellow officers in the officers' mess at Frederick, laughing uproariously at Franklin's creativity on their behalf. It also reveals that Sir John St. Clair was devoid of much of a sense of humor, particularly when the joke was at his expense. But through Franklin's intervention, the wagon and horse problem had been, if not entirely resolved, considerably ameliorated. Braddock would be grateful to Franklin, writing Colonel Napier in London: "Mr. Franklin undertook and perform'd his Engagements with the greatest readiness and punctuality."[16]

When the expedition had been planned in London, a version of a recently produced map not yet published was utilized. This cartography of "North America from the French of Mr. D'Anville Improved with the Back Settlements of Virginia and Course of Ohio Illustrated with Geographical and Historical Remarks" would be published in London by Thomas Jefferys in 1755. St. Clair wrote to Colonel Napier, the Duke of Cumberland's chief of staff, on 10 February 1755, from Williamsburg: "In Jeffereys map Winchester is marked Frederick. Willis's Creek marked Caicuchick Creek. The Road to Savage River I mention

Frederic James (1915–1985), "Braddock and Franklin" offers a considerably different, more human view of both Braddock and Franklin at Frederick, 1755 (courtesy Braddock's Battlefield History Center, Braddock, Pennsylvania; photograph by Mr. David Kissell).

runs from a small River which Runs in from the West into the South Branch." Clearly St. Clair had seen and utilized a version (or the original) of this map in England in 1754, a year before it was formally published in London. The map is generally accurate for the Atlantic seaboard, but becomes increasingly inaccurate the further away from the Atlantic Ocean that it ventures. Still, it is significant that Braddock and St. Clair were using the most current map available in 1754 to plan the campaign.

Unfortunately, although this map notes the "Great Falls" of the Potomac, it fails to indicate that the Potomac is not navigable past the Great Falls. In fact, from Alexandria to nearly the Forks of the Ohio a dotted line seems to suggest the existence of an established route to "English Fort Taken by the French 1754" at the Forks. Thus, St. Clair and Braddock were misled into believing that they could use the Potomac River for water transportation from Hampton to Fort Cumberland.

On January 15, 1755, St. Clair prepared a memorandum on his activities, to update Braddock once he arrived in Virginia. In this, he specifically noted among his tasks "Ye 5[:] Floates or Battoes for the Transporting the Artillery and baggage from the falls of the Potomack River to Willis's Creek." St. Clair then noted of these plans "that part of my Instructions which Regards the building of battoes or Floats on the Potomack at the Falls of Alexa [Alexandria], I am oblig'd to delay executing as I am informed the doing of it would be in vain, for that in winter the Stream is so Raised that there is no Rowing heavy boats against the Current; and that in summer there are many flatts and shoals which will render the Navigation almost impracticable." In fact, no less than four major obstructions prevented the movement of artillery and baggage up the Potomac. The Little Falls, three miles above Alexandra, was the first obstacle. This was the first series of rapids that did not appear on Jefferys' map. A significant obstacle was the Great Falls, properly marked on the 1755 map, another six miles further up, which dropped no less than 76 feet in a quarter mile and contained extensive rapids. Apparently, nobody in England realized the extent and significance of the obstacle that the Great Falls presented. Seneca Falls was farther up with another large drop and series of rapids. And finally Shenandoah Falls, about seventy miles above Alexandria, dropped 30 feet in three miles. These latter two falls were also absent from Jefferys' map. These rapids all prevented the use of the Potomac River for water transport.[17]

St. Clair, upon his first visit to Fort Cumberland with Governor Sharpe of Maryland, was severely disappointed. He complained to Braddock on February 9: "I cannot learn what cou'd [could] induce people ever to think of making a Fort or a Deposite for provisions at Willis's Creek; It covers no Country, nor has it the Communication open behind it either by Land or Water, the River not Navigable." St. Clair continued gloomily: "In my last letter to you I acquainted you that Govr Dinwiddie told me that the Navigation of the Potomack is impracticable, this I can now Affirm from Experience[,] because Govr Sharp and I found this for all other Vessels but Canoes cut out of a Single Tree, we attempted to go down the River in this sort of boat, but were obliged to get ashore and walk on foot especially at the Shannondoe Falls: So that the getting of Floats or Battoes made for the transport of the Artillery and the baggage of the Regiments, cou'd serve for no other thing but to throw away the Governments money to no purpose and lose a great deal of Time." St. Clair was describing the use of a dug-out canoe, an expedient Native American canoe burned and hollowed from a large tree trunk. Such a canoe, although not particularly maneuverable, is sturdy and easily made, and requires almost no water to be floated. If even a dug-out canoe could not utilize the Potomac River, St. Clair well understood that it was not navigable for military purposes.

This was a demoralizing discovery, for it meant that Braddock's army would have to travel by poor roads from the shores of the Chesapeake Bay to Fort Cumberland, which rendered logistics considerably more difficult and challenging. Thus, by early February, St. Clair realized that the logistical framework for the entire expedition prepared in London was not viable, and that all of the campaign plans would have to be entirely revised, to include the construction and improvement of numerous roads, the construction of additional storehouses and warehouses along the route to Fort Cumberland, the crossings of numerous immense ridges to be negotiated, and either fords or ferries established over the numerous water courses in the way. This was a serious constraint, not foreseen in London, which considerably complicated Braddock's and St. Clair's planning and efforts. To make matters worse, St. Clair would have to improvise swiftly, for Braddock and his regiments were anticipated to arrive at any time, and the opening of the campaign season would be upon him within a matter of weeks rather than months. This would become one of St. Clair's most vexing challenges during the first three months of 1755.

Braddock was accompanied from Ireland by the 44th and 48th Regiments of Foot, two regiments that had been maintained on the "Irish establishment" for a number of years. Regiments on the Irish establishment were not maintained at full strength, although the 44th and 48th Foot were reputedly well drilled, disciplined and equipped upon notification that they would be moving to Virginia. It should be noted, however, that the Irish establishment was notorious for having poorly drilled, poorly disciplined, and badly under-manned regiments. One historian has noted of regiments on the Irish establishment, "The wide dispersal of regiments, the poor attendance of subaltern officers at quarters, the customary absence of one of the two field officers in Dublin, and the enormous desertion which was a result of the common failure of officers to account justly with their men, combined to produce an army very dissimilar in its appearance and abilities." A contemporary officer remarked upon "A Whole Army Absolutely Ruined in Ireland."[18]

As with all regiments on the Irish establishment, in September 1754 both regiments consisted of ten companies, each company consisting of one captain, one lieutenant, one ensign, two sergeants, two corporals, a drummer, and twenty-nine other ranks (soldiers). The total strength of each regiment was 374 officers and men. Upon receipt of orders for North America in October 1754 they had been hastily filled to just over five hundred men with drafts from other regiments on the Irish establishment, and certainly these drafts were not of the highest quality. It is a long established army tradition to use a draft to eliminate trouble makers, malcreants, "awkward" men, slackards, drunkards, weak, or habitually sick by sending them to another regiment. If by some miracle those men received were of good material, the two regiments had no opportunity to integrate these men into their ranks before they embarked for Virginia.[19]

Even with these drafts, both regiments remained under strength when they departed Ireland. The intention was for these two regiments to be recruited to their full strength of 700 men upon arrival in Virginia. This was one of St. Clair's principal tasks as assigned by Braddock: "Ye 6[:] To settle with the Govr [Governor] the best and speediest manner to Compleat the two Battns [Battalions] with 200 good men each." Therefore, immediately upon his arrival, on January 12, St. Clair would write Governor Sharpe of Maryland: "It will be of the greatest Consequence to have the proportion of men from your Province in Readiness for Compleat'g [completing] the two Regiments from 500 men each to 700."

This was yet another unrealistically optimistic approach, as the colonies were renowned for a shortage of labor that resulted in extremely low unemployment and high wages. Accordingly, it was unlikely that the British army would be particularly successful in recruiting in the North American colonies. By early in February, it must have been apparent to St. Clair that he would encounter significant obstacles obtaining men from Virginia or Maryland for the British regular regiments. St. Clair was able to recruit only a few men in Virginia, and these recruits proved to be of extremely poor quality (run-away apprentices, indentured servants deserting to avoid their obligations, financial failures fleeing from debtors prison, and the sick, lame or lazy) as could well be anticipated. The only other viable solution in the limited time available was drafting provincial soldiers for service in the regulars, a resolution hugely unpopular with both the provincials drafted, and the regulars who received these less than enthusiastic draftees.

St. Clair was obviously considering this solution as early as February 12, for on that date he wrote Governor Sharpe, enquiring, "If I am to see which men of the Maryland detachments will do for our Troops." St. Clair reiterated on February 22, "As the Maryland

Forces will be wanted to Compleat the English Regiments I have sent an Order by Mr. Pitcher to Willis's Creek, that the detachment of Maryland Forces now at that place may forthwith march to Frederick to join the rest, they will be then at home to be incorporated with the British Regts." Sharpe responded favorably, formally instructing St. Clair on February 17 to muster the Maryland provincials, and continuing, "You are likewise to mark down such men as you shall think proper for Compleating the two British Regiments daily expected, that they may be in readiness for them on their Landing, and to order them with proper officers forthwith to repair to Alexandria and Fredericksbourg, and to remain there till further orders." Governor Dinwiddie followed with a nearly identical response on February 18.

St. Clair also wrote to Colonel Napier in London on February 15: "Let me have your opinion about the New York independent Companys enlisting men for a term of Years, had they any Toleration for it?" In the British army at this time, enlistments were for life. Therefore, St. Clair was ascertaining if enlistments for "terms of years" rather than life was having any effect on recruitment, suggesting that St. Clair was considering adopting such a course to encourage additional recruits for the regulars from the colonies.[20]

St. Clair was successful in drafting provincials for the British regiments, as he documented on March 6: "I have given Capt Hog the care of 21 Men that I have draughted for the British Batts and they march to Fredericksburgh on Saturday where he will be joined by the others as soon as I Review them. I have destin'd Alexandria for the Maryland Draughts, you are greatly Oblig'd to Lt Savage for the good Recruits he has rais'd that Officer has done his duty and deserves your countenance." He concluded, "[I] hope to have half a dozn [dozen] of men for the British Regiments." Eventually, as estimated by historian Franklin T. Nichols, Virginia would provide 350 and Maryland 120 draftees to the two regular regiments.[21] This would have been sufficient to increase both regiments to their full strength. Unfortunately, the records are not adequate to determine how these provincial draftees were assimilated into these largely English and Irish regiments, how successfully they were drilled and trained in the relatively brief period available to Braddock (from March/April to early July 1755), how they were accepted by the British regular officers, NCOs and soldiers, and their performance on campaign. Most of these men remained at Rocky Fort Camp with Colonel Dunbar and were not present at the Battle of the Monongahela.

When the expedition was being planned and organized in London, it was specified that three of the independent companies of the British regulars stationed in North America would join Braddock's two regiments once they arrived in Virginia. There were actually five of these independent companies of British regulars, four stationed in New York City and one in South Carolina. The four independent companies stationed in New York City had been established in 1701. A fifth company had been established in South Carolina in 1720. These independent companies were the only British regulars located in the North American colonies in 1754. Abandoned for all practical purposes by the British government for decades, these independent companies were in a woeful state of readiness. In the ensuing decades since their establishment, these independent companies had seen no active campaigns, or engaged in any other duties than routine guard mounting in garrison. They were never inspected by the British army, and had rarely if ever performed company drill. Certainly, they had never functioned in any formation larger than a company. They received insufficient funding from England, and as a result most of their enlisted men took additional employment from civilian firms to earn extra pay simply to survive. Their officers were renowned for maintaining false or inflated rolls to draw pay for men that didn't exist or were incapacitated, simply to obtain extra compensation. The South Carolina independent company under the command of Captain James Mackay had participated in the 1754 Fort Necessity campaign, in which their performance had been less than stellar.

During the Braddock campaign, two New York independent companies, one commanded by Captain John Rutherford and the other by Captain Thomas Clark, and the South Carolina independent company, now commanded by Captain Paul Demeré, participated. Clark was extremely ill, and he would never join Braddock's expedition past Fort Cumberland. Clark sold his commission and the command of his independent company to Captain Horatio Gates, who arrived at the end of March in Frederick to assume its command.[22]

Among St. Clair's assigned duties were to inspect and muster these three independent companies, and ensure they were prepared for the campaign against Fort Duquesne. Suggesting the importance of this task, St. Clair wrote to Muster Master Pitcher as early as January 14: "I must entreat of you to send me the State of the independent Companys you have Muster'd, [mustered] that I may have it ready to lay before General Braddock on his Landing, as you have been formerly employ'd [employed] as Commissary [of Musters] you will be better able to Judge how necessary it will be that the Genl [General] should know their numbers in case they should be immediately wanted for Service."

St. Clair first saw these three independent companies in late January at Fort Cumberland, and he was not favorably impressed. He documented his initial glimpse of these soldiers in a letter to Braddock written February 9:

> I found the Governour of Maryland at Willis's Creek.... He had with him at the fort three Independent Companys, the one of South Carolina and the other two of New York, the latter seem to be Draughted out of Chelsea, the excuse they make for having so many old men does very little honour to those Companys that are left behind at New York, for they say that they are draughted from them. The Carolina Company is in much better order and Discipline.

"Chelsea" refers to the royal hospital at Chelsea, London, England. Established by King Charles II late in the 17th century, this hospital served as the 18th century equivalent of a retirement home for soldiers discharged for wounds, or retired with disabilities after years of service. Thus, St. Clair is saying that the independent companies appear to have been filled with invalids.[23] St. Clair expanded his derision of the New York independent companies, further noting that "the Comg Officer at the Fort [Cumberland] has orders to be on the defensive, but that is not Necessary for 2 of his Companys have neither Legs to get upon the heights nor to run away thro [through] the Valleys."

Alarmed at St. Clair's assessment of the three independent companies, Braddock in late February ordered St. Clair to perform a complete inspection and muster of them (a duty which muster master Pitcher should have properly performed rather than St. Clair):

> As the good of his Majestys Service Requires that a Review should be made of the three Independent Companys now at Willis's Creek, as well as of the Forces newly raised in the Provinces of Virginia and Maryland, and as the Circumstances of Affairs puts it out of my power to make that whole Review myself. I therefore order you to make the Review of such troops as you shall find at Winchester, Willis's Creek, Frederick, or else where, and to make a report to me of the State you find them in you are likewise required and directed to order all such men of the Independent Companies from Carolina and New York ... as you shall find unfitt for his Majestys Service / giving the Reasons why they are so / to be forthwith discharged.

Apparently St. Clair's inspection of the South Carolina company and Rutherford's New York company proved satisfactory, but Captain Clark's independent company was found to be so deficient that it was ordered to the rear to reorganize, recruit, and re-equip.

St. Clair ordered Captain Clark on March 18, following this audit:

> Whereas, in making the Review of the two independent Companys of for service, on account of a deficiency in their Numbers, and a great number of old men so that the Company wants more than half to Compleat it. That his Majesty's service may suffer as Little as Possible by this great Neglect, I hereby order that the independent Company Comand'd by Capt Clarke do march from this to Frederick in Maryland and then the Subaltern Officers, are to go from thence on the Recruiting Service so that the Company may be Completed with good able Bodied men, to Its Establishment by the 25 day of April. Capt Clarke is hereby Ordered to provide his Company with Camp Equippage and all other Necessarys According to the annexed List to be ready to take the Field by the 25 of April.

One modern historian has said of these independent companies: "They were in wretched shape, overaged, low in morale, and poorly provisioned."[24] Braddock would write Colonel Napier in London on March 17 about the "Independent Companies of New York ... which two ... are good for nothing."[25]

Captain Horatio Gates arrived at Frederick in late March and assumed command of the company. Although both Captain Gates' efforts and St. Clair's role in assisting Gates are not documented, it is apparent that Gates rapidly returned his independent company to an adequate state such that it could participate in the campaign. In a return dated June 8 from Fort Cumberland, Braddock reported the strength of this company to possess 84 rank and file for duty. The other New York company had 82 fit for duty, and the South Carolina company had 96 soldiers fit for duty. Both New York companies were intended to contain 91 soldiers, and the South Carolina company required 100 soldiers, "to compleat the Establishment."[26] This suggests that Gates had entirely recovered his company by this date, a significant accomplishment for which the young captain deserved considerable commendation.

A major focus of St. Clair's efforts was to recruit a number of provincial companies to participate in the campaign, and to ensure that these soldiers were properly enlisted, mustered, armed and equipped, and trained in time to join Braddock's two British regiments of foot. Although several hundred provincial soldiers from Virginia had been enlisted for the 1754 Fort Necessity campaign, these soldiers were all discharged by the time that St. Clair arrived in Virginia. Fortunately, governors Dinwiddie and Sharpe had already initiated efforts to enlist replacement Virginia and Maryland provincials to support Braddock.

St. Clair's efforts in this direction began on February 1, when he determined to form a Virginia company of carpenters and artisans. St. Clair made this decision upon realizing that Braddock's army would have to move from Alexandria to Fort Cumberland by land rather than the Potomac River, and that the entire expedition would have to be logistically supported by these same overland routes. This alteration to the campaign would require that considerably more improvements be done to these extremely crude roads than St. Clair had originally foreseen. Accordingly he determined to form "Twenty Sawyers and Sixty men that understand the use of Carpenters Tools to be Commandd by a Captain, Two Subalterns, Three Serjeants, Three Corporals, and one Drummer. You are hereby ordered to draught [draft] from the detachment under your Command all men that are Carpenters by Trade and Sawyers, Boat or Ship Builders and to appoint a Subaltern, or Non Commissioned Offi-

44th Regiment of Foot, Battalion Company, 1755 (courtesy Company of Military Historians, © 1961).

cers in proportion to the Number of Draughts with directions to proceed to the next Detachment accordg [according] to their Route till the Number Required shall be Completed, or such a Number as shall be found amongst the Troops, and to proceed after passing the Several detachments to Alexandria where they are to wait for further Orders. Captain Mercer is appointed to this Command."[27]

Captain George Mercer was a native twenty-two-year-old Virginian. Born June 23, 1733, at Marlborough Plantation, Virginia, Mercer had attended William and Mary College in Williamsburg, Virginia, was a trained surveyor, and was a member of one of Virginia's leading families. He had been wounded while serving under Washington at Fort Necessity

Major, 44th Regiment of Foot, 1755 (courtesy Company of Military Historians, © 1995).

in 1754, and was one of the few Virginians with legitimate military experience. He was an excellent choice for this important and arduous service that would require considerable independent action.

By early February recruiting was progressing in both Maryland and Virginia. St. Clair and Braddock were particularly interested in attracting provincial soldiers for operations on the Virginia frontier. St. Clair was subsequently ordered to raise "four Companies of Rangers, Company of Carpenters, and the Troop of light horse" from Virginia. The rangers were intended to be American born soldiers used to frontier conditions, to assist Braddock's column with scouting, patrolling and reconnaissance duties. The two companies of carpenters eventually established contained besides skilled carpenters, a quantity of trained artificers, similar to those with the royal artillery.

Two additional companies of Maryland provincials were raised. The Maryland soldiers would be used to garrison Fort Cumberland, legally on the western frontier of that state. To ensure that trained British officers would not be diverted from the movement against Fort Duquesne, provincial colonel John Innes of North Carolina was appointed commanding officer at Fort Cumberland. Colonel Innes had commanded the North Carolina troops in George Washington's 1754 Fort Necessity campaign.

By the end of February, Braddock determined to slightly expand his Virginia forces to two companies of carpenters, and established the organization and pay of the various companies. The second company of carpenters was to be commanded by Captain William Polson, another veteran as a lieutenant of Washington's 1754 Fort Necessity campaign. The four companies of Virginia rangers were to be commanded by captains Adam Stephens, Andrew Lewis, Thomas Waggoner, and William Peyronie (also spelled "Perrony" or "Péronie"). The troop of light horse would be commanded by Captain Robert Stewart.

Andrew Lewis (1720–1781) had come to Virginia from Ireland in 1732 and had served as a company commander under Washington in 1754. Thomas Waggoner (d. 1760) had also served as a lieutenant under Washington in the 1754 Fort Necessity campaign. Peyronie was a Frenchman with prior military experience who arrived in Virginia about 1750 and had been wounded at Fort Necessity. These Virginia officers had served throughout the previous year's campaign and were well-seasoned officers. By early March, these various provincial companies were in relatively good order and were beginning their movement forward to Fort Cumberland, improving the roads as they marched. These provincial companies would provide exceptional service to St. Clair and Braddock throughout the campaign.

As with the independent companies and British regular recruits, St. Clair was ordered by Braddock to inspect and muster these companies into service. Occurring at a time when St. Clair was fully occupied with planning the land movement of the British regiments from Alexandria, and since Muster Master Pitcher was present by this time in Virginia, it does not seem that this increase in St. Clair's duties was warranted. Why St. Clair had this responsibility placed upon him by the general cannot now be ascertained.

St. Clair travelled regularly to Fort Cumberland, at the junction of Wills Creek and the Potomac River. Wills Creek is a tributary of the north branch of the Potomac River that is located in Pennsylvania and Maryland. Its headwaters are located in modern Somerset County, Pennsylvania, in the Allegheny Mountains. It flows generally south until entering the north branch of the Potomac at modern Cumberland, Maryland. This strategic location was selected in London as the site for the advanced or forward logistical depot to support Braddock's final movement upon Fort Duquesne. St. Clair as early as his first letter from Williamsburg on February 7 would write to Maryland's Governor Sharpe: "I should have thought myself extremely happy if I had any prospects of finding you at Willis's Creek for which place I propose setting out from here by the middle of the week, in order to set people to work for Erecting Log houses for the quarters of the two Regiments which are daily expected." This was in accordance with Braddock's instructions to St. Clair: "Ye 4[:] To Consult with the Governour the proper measures for Erecting Loghouses or Barrics [barracks] at Wills's Creek for the following Numbers Vizt. 2 Regts. of 530 men Rank & File each one Sub Director of Ingeniers [Engineers] one Ingenier in Ordinary 12 Ingeniers Extraordinary and 2 Practitioner Ingenier a Detachm't of 110 of the Artillery."

The Ohio company had constructed a storehouse on the south shore of the Potomac River in 1753, to support their planned settlement of the Ohio Country. During the 1754 Fort Necessity campaign, the site for Fort Cumberland had been selected on a prominent, large flattened bluff to the north of the Potomac River, and that overlooked Wills Creek to the east. In 1754 the fort consisted of a small, four-bastioned fortification that contained a number of barracks, a commandant's headquarters, guardhouse, and several storehouses. The four bastions consisted of horizontal logs filled with dirt, and the curtain walls were simple vertical palisades. Against European artillery the fort would be helpless, but it was more than adequate to safeguard the supplies for the movement upon the Forks of the Ohio, and to repulse any conceivable Native American attack. The fort was approximately 120 feet on a side. Underneath the fort a magazine was excavated into the limestone to safeguard the ammunition stored at the site, and a tunnel was excavated leading to Wills Creek that provided protected access to water.[28] A stout log house that served as the commissary's quarters and storehouse was located outside and north of the fort, and another solid log structure that served as a hospital was constructed on the southern exterior of the fort.

In the spring of 1755, in anticipation of Braddock's arrival and in accordance with his instructions, St. Clair had Fort Cumberland considerably expanded. He did this by enclosing the fort's large parade ground to the east with what was technically referred to as a "horn work," essentially a rectangular protrusion constructed of vertical palisades that extended from the east curtain wall of the fort. The horn work contained a large number of long, crude log structures that served as officers' quarters and soldiers' barracks for Braddock's army. When Matron Brown of the general hospital arrived at Fort Cumberland, being one of the few ladies accompanying Braddock's army, she was assigned quarters within the fort, which she found less than comfortable. "June the 13th. At 6 we came to Fort Cumberland the most desolate Place I ever saw ... went to the Governor to apply for Quarters I was put into a Hole that I could see day light through every Log and 1 port Hole for a Window which was as good a Room as any in the Fort."[29]

Fort Cumberland had been sited, designed, and constructed with no real military skills, and certainly without the benefit of a qualified, trained military engineer. Topographically and tactically, Fort Cumberland's location was badly flawed. It was overlooked by a number of ridges and knolls, which enabled Native American scouts to easily monitor activities within its walls, and warriors regularly harassed soldiers going about their business in and around the fort. St. Clair assessed the fort in detail following his first visit, and he was not impressed with what he saw, as he reported to Braddock on February 9:

> I cannot learn what cou'd [could] induce people ever to think of making a Fort or a Deposite for provisions at Willis's Creek; It covers no Country, nor has it the Communication open behind it either by Land or Water.... I found the Governour of Maryland at Willis's Creek, who had been at that place but a few days, not long enough to make any considerable Alteration nor to Reconoitre the Country. He had with him at the fort / or more properly a small piece of ground inclosed with a Strong Palisade joined pretty close / ...Least it should still be more adviseable to pass the Mountains at Willis's Creek, there are a number of Trees cut ready for Erecting Logg houses, and I gave directions for Palisading a house near the Fort for a powder Magazine.

Engineer Gordon professionally evaluated the fort on May 11, shortly after he arrived at Will's Creek.

> Fort Cumberland is situated within 200 yards of Will's Creek on a Hill 400 yards from the Potomack. Its greatest length from East to West is 200 yards, and breadth about 40. It is built with Loggs drove into the Ground and 12 feet above it. Embrazures are cut out for 12 guns, which are 4 Poundrs, though 10 are only mounted, with loop holes for small arms.[30]

Gordon subsequently observed "three pieces of 6-pound cannon, with the advantage the ground would naturally give them, could knock the fort to pieces."[31] Of course, since the French were unlikely to transport three 6-pounders to the fort, Gordon's observations were technically accurate but unrealistic.

St. Clair complained bitterly about the pace of progress at Fort Cumberland. He wrote to Sir Peter Halkett on April 17: "Last night I arrived at this place after having been on the Roads a Week to make them passable[.] on my coming to this Place I found every thing in the Situation I left it, that is to say not any one thing done which I had Ordered."

Still, considerable improvements were made at Fort Cumberland throughout the spring of 1755. Upon the arrival of the 44th and 48th Foot at Fort Cumberland in early May they found wooden barracks, no matter how rudimentary Mrs. Brown believed them to be. Engineer Gordon wrote in his journal for May 10: "March'd to Will's Creek; and Encamp'd on a Hill to the Eastward of the Fort."[32] Captain Cholmley's batman similarly recorded, "Saturday May the 10th. We marched to Willses Creek. Close By the Creek is the Portwomack River.... We passed the foart and Incamped upon the hill above the Fort which his Called Fort Cumberland."[33]

During the planning for the first phase of the expedition, St. Clair had to face two great crises. The first one was forced upon him, by the decision in London that the expedition would proceed from Virginia. This decision was not based upon logistical or tactical considerations, but rather political considerations. Specifically, it was heavily influenced by Lieutenant Governor Robert Dinwiddie of Virginia, and the numerous prominent members of the Ohio Company. Unfortunately, Virginia's economic and transportation system was water based because of the numerous waterways that flowed into Chesapeake Bay. Accordingly, wagons and draft animals, particularly horses, were a comparatively scarce commodity. Dr. Alexander Hamilton, a Virginia physician, wrote to his brother in Scotland that Braddock's army "mett abundance of difficulty in procuring Waggons & Horses for their Baggage and Ammuntion, which were [not] to look for, after the Forces had been two Months in the Country. This they might well expect in a Country Such as this, where the Breed of Horses is small and degenerate, and Few can afford to keep any better, than such as will barely answer for the Drudgery of the Plough."[34]

Hamilton somewhat exaggerated, as many of the wealthy Tidewater planters were wildly enthusiastic horse breeders, but these thoroughbreds were extremely expensive animals, used to a grain rich diet, bred and raised specifically for the racetrack. They were scarcely suitable to drag carts, wagons and cannon through the wilderness. In any event, without the specialized diet they had been raised upon for the entire lives, these horses would have provided service for only a short duration.[35]

Although Virginia possessed numerous river ports, and many of these such as York, Hampton and Alexandria were well-established mercantile centers, Virginia did not possess a single large harbor, or a significant trading and manufacturing city. Notwithstanding all of St. Clair's earnest efforts, Virginia simply could not provide sufficient logistical and transportation support for a campaign the size of Braddock's expedition. This was also the case for Maryland. Exacerbating the problem, Virginia's logistical and transportation resources capable of supporting a military operation had been seriously depleted during the 1754 Fort Necessity Campaign. St. Clair, or anybody for that matter, was simply incapable of ameliorating these challenges.

It is instructive that three years later, when Brigadier General John Forbes was selected to lead another expedition against the Forks of the Ohio, he determined to establish the logistical base for his campaign in Philadelphia, and route his approach march through Pennsylvania. Philadelphia was the largest city and harbor in North America in the 1750s. It was a sufficiently robust mercantile center that Forbes could draw all of his Native American gifts from Philadelphia, and significantly augment his logistical requirements such as shoes and blankets from the city's manufacturers and vendors. Philadelphia was at the hub of an economic and transportation system that was predominantly dependent upon land transportation, and thus a comparatively greater number of wagons and draft animals, particularly horses, were available in Pennsylvania.[36] One historian has estimated that "by 1776 there were more than 10,000 wagons in the countryside west of Philadelphia."[37] Additionally, Pennsylvania's resources had not been depleted by a recent military operation.

The wagon and horse situation in Virginia was so severe that by early April at Frederick, Braddock, St. Clair and the other British officers recognized that the expedition could not progress any further. Only the fortuitous arrival of Benjamin Franklin, with his ability to tap into the horses and wagons of Pennsylvania, saved the campaign and enabled it to resume its movement west.

The second great crisis was occasioned by the realization that water transportation of the army and its supply train from Alexandria to Fort Cumberland by the Potomac River was not practicable. This was a major calamity, and represented a change in plans of staggering magnitude. Most of St. Clair's efforts between early February, when he made this realization, and early April would be focused upon addressing this sweeping alteration of the expedition's entire logistical approach.

Once St. Clair realized that the water route was unfeasible, he rapidly began efforts to establish an alternate land route. As early as January 26 he wrote to Lord Fairfax for assistance with road construction. Thomas Fairfax, 6th Lord Fairfax of Cameron (October 22, 1693– December 9, 1781), was one of the greatest landed proprietors in the colonies, and the only English peer then resident in the colonies. Lord Fairfax was an early benefactor of George Washington, and at one time owned all of Virginia between the Rappahannock and Potomac rivers. As such, he possessed immense power and influence, and assumed much of the responsibility for improving the roads west of Alexandria. Of course, improving the roads to his properties would benefit nobody but Lord Fairfax, as it would make his large landholdings west of Alexandria that much more accessible, and that much more valuable. St. Clair wrote to Fairfax:

> It is My duty to Acquaint you on what State I found the Roads in my way hither. The float on the Shanondoe [Shenandoah River] is now amaking by a Carpenter sent by Your Lop [Your Lordship] e promised me to have it finished by the 4th Feb. but as I gave him two guineas to employ more hands to work under him I imagine it will be finished by the end of the month. The Roads near the

River are very narrow over the Mountains which makes it impossible for Waggons to pass one another and at present a number of Trees lying a cross the Roads[.] there are many small runns of water which requires Trees to be laid over them for the Conveniency of Foot passengers. The Road from Fort Edwards[38] to the North River is very bad, that River has neither canoes nor floats on it tho' the Ford is deep and at bottom very Stony, the Ford of the Little Capeapon is not near so bad, there is neither canoes nor float over it[.] I shou'd have been glad to have found the new Road marked out, which was only done at the further end 5 miles from Jos. Pearceall's[.]

Your Lords Carpenter is to go to the south branch by the first of the month to build a float over the River which is greatly wanted, it will be likewise good to have a float made over Patterson's Creek in the flow where the new Road that is to be cut is to cross it, I should likewise have been glad to have seen that Road; but no part of it was mark'd. I could pretty well guess where it joined to the Road in the Valley.

When I was two miles on this side of the South branch I had a good view of the ground that runs along the Savage River it seems good for a carriage Road and might be of great Service if your Ldp would order it to be marked out as I shall soon be obliged to visit all that ground.

I must Recommend it to your Lop to give directions that all the new Roads which are to be Cut may be made at least 30 or 35 feet wide and carries along the Ridges of the Mountains as much as possible to avoid the valleys Shou'd the expence of this be too great for the Countys to bear which are only in their Infancy, I shall do my duty to Recommend it to the Governour to have a General Charge made of it[.]

Road construction was an extremely important component of a quartermaster's duties. In 1755, roads were not constructed to any recurring standard. The widest documented carriage that Braddock's army employed was the British Board of Ordnance's ammunition wagon, which was seven feet or eighty-four inches wide. Accordingly, the absolute minimum width that a road could be was eight feet. Typical roads of the period were one rod, or 16½ feet, wide. A road constructed to this width would have permitted two ammunition wagons to pass each other, with their teams in harness. A road associated with the Thomas Ellison grist mill, New Windsor, Orange County, New York (in the Hudson Highlands), constructed in 1741 was "at least seventeen" feet wide when archaeologically excavated. Why St. Clair was mandating roads to be constructed to a nearly two-rod width cannot be determined, and such a standard seems excessive.[39]

On February 9 St. Clair prepared a letter for Braddock

from the 23d to the 26th. I was on the Road to Willis's Creek this is 85 miles of the worst Road I ever travelled, and greatly Lengthened by the Roads being in the Channels of the Rivers, when they might be shorten'd by Cutting them along the Ridges of the Mountains, which Lord Fairfax promised me shou'd be done about this time, this will shorten that Road about 15 Miles, and avoid the bad Road by Patterson's Creek. When I had got about two miles on the other side of the South branch I had a full view of the mountains on each side of the Potomack above Willis's Creek, and from what I could see there is a Road easily to be made across the Country to the mouth of Savage River, which will be gaining 30 Miles. If I am not more deceived than I have been of late with Regards to ground, the mouth of Savage River is the place where we ought to cross the Allegany Mountains. I have only been able to find one Woodsman who can give me any distinct Account of that ground, which gives me a great satisfaction. I wrote Lord Fairfax to have the Road mark'd [marked] out to the mouth of Savage River.

Recognizing that a single route to Fort Cumberland would be vulnerable to being easily cut by weather, accident, or French intervention, St. Clair wrote to Deputy Governor Robert Morris of Pennsylvania on February 14, asking him to open an additional road through Pennsylvania.[40]

> The B. [British] Troops are daily expected and as the Season is far advanced, they have no time to Loose before they begin their opperations, I have done every thing in my power to facilitate their march from their landing place to the Allegany Mountains which will be a very great trouble and Expence as I make no doubt, but that the French will unite all their Strength together to make a Stand before we can get on the Ohio which will Oblige us to have the assistance of and all of the regiments now Raising in the Northern provinces, this Step must confuse the French a good deal as they will expect an Attack from all quarters. You must be very sensible what a great detour these Troops must make by marchg thro' Philad [Philadelphia] Frederick in Myld [Maryland]. Crossing the Potomack at the mouth of the Monocasey and joining us at Wincher [Winchester]. This wou'd restrain all our Motions. For this reason I must press your Excly in the most earnest Manner to open a Communication by Cutting or repairing the Roads towards the head of the Yougheagany or any other way that is nearer to the French Forts, by the Map I have of yr province there appears to me to be a Road from Phila which Crosses the Susquena a little below the junctn [junction] of the River Juniata, and that there are two paths from your place leading to the black log [sic] which is at no very great distance from the Youghangany / called the Turkeys Foot / where we are to Cross. Shd the Roads not be wanted for this purpose I may venture to assure your Excy that no General will Advance with an Army without having a Communication open to the provinces in his Rear both for the Security of his Retreat and to facilitate the transport of Provisions the Supplying of which we must greatly depend on your province.... Shou'd any small Rivers be to Cross when the Roads are amaking, I must Recommend to have Floats made on them for the Crossing a waggon, and that the Roads be made wide at Least 30 Feet and Carryd along the Ridges of the Mountns to avoid the Channel of the Runns of Water.

As a result of St. Clair's request, James Burd of Pennsylvania began constructing a road from Carlisle to the west to Ray's Town, then southwest to the Great Crossing of the Youghougany River to join Braddock's Road to Fort Duquesne, thus connecting Braddock with Pennsylvania. This road, which would become known as "Burd's Road," was initiated in April of 1755. It followed the "Old Trading Path," a long established Indian trading route across the Allegheny Mountains. This trading path had been used for centuries as the overland route by Native Americans traveling between the Atlantic coast and the Ohio Valley. Before Burd worked on the road in 1755, the only Europeans who had used it were a few Indian traders, leading strings of packhorses across the mountains.[41] St. Clair requested that this new road be constructed thirty feet wide, further evidence that St. Clair considered this to be the normal width for a road.

St. Clair was extremely anxious that these roads be constructed as rapidly as possible. In fact, he wrote Lord Fairfax an extremely curt letter on February 26, less than a month after he had asked for construction to be initiated, demanding that more positive progress be made.

> The Reporting My Lord, at home that the Roads are not finish'd by any frivolous disputes that may happen at your Courts of the Diffirent Countys can be of no excuse to me no excuse to me in doing my duty, I shou'd with Regret be oblig'd to Report to my Royal Master that it wou'd be <u>much</u>[42] easier to Carry on War from an Enemys Country than to protect his just Rights to one of <u>his</u> most Loyal provinces in America.

And, this in February, when the snow still lay heavily on many of the ridges, and the various creeks and rivers were in freshet! The simple fact that St. Clair wrote such a terse letter to one of the most powerful and prominent men in the Colonies is indicative of St. Clair's temperament, his response to the great stress that he was under, and the absence of wise judgment.

By late March, St. Clair had a number of the provincial companies that he had raised already at work on improving the roads, ordering on February 26,

> You are hereby Required and Directed to March with the first Company of Rangers under your Command, and make the Roads passable for all kind of Carriages from Winchester to Enoch Enoch's[43] on the Capecapon, when you have cut the Roads that far, You are to Consult with Henry Enoch the proper place for crossing on a Flatt. You are to Cut the Roads down to that place, and Level the banks of the River for that purpose, Shou'd I not be able to join you before you have Cut the Roads this far, you are to pass the River and Cut the Road blaz'd out by Henry Enoch to the Mouth of the South Branch, he will attend you on this service[.] and has directions from me that all the inhabitants within Eight Miles of the Road that is to be Cut shall attend on this important piece of service for the good of their Country. You are to march from hence so soon as you can get Tools, and you are to work with 20 men of your Company each Day who shall be paid six pence British Sterling for their Work which the Commissary shall have my Orders to pay. The Commissary has my directions to furnish you with provisions. If this work can be finish'd before my Return, You are to pass the Potomack to Col. Crisip's and march from that to the Fort at Willis's Creek, You are on your March and when Encamp'd to Observe good Order and Discipline and Conform yourself in every Respect to the Rules and Articles of War.

As regards the payment of soldiers for their work on the roads, in 1755 it was not considered part of the British soldier's normal duties to perform road construction. Because this was considered to be exceptional service, soldiers were paid an additional six pence a day until 1778, when the rate was raised to nine pence a day. St. Clair was adhering to standard procedures for the British army.[44]

By April 3 St. Clair recommended, and Braddock approved, that the British army would move forward from Alexandria in two separate columns. St. Clair's plan was that the first column would follow a southern route through Virginia, comprised of the 44th Regiment of Colonel Sir Peter Halkett, and the Board of Ordnance including the royal artillery, that would proceed along the southern side of the Potomac River to Winchester. Colonel Dunbar's 48th Regiment would form the second column, employing a more northern route predominantly through Maryland. Dunbar's column would cross the Potomac River at Alexandria, pass through Maryland on the northern side of the Potomac River, through Frederick, turn south once past South Mountain, re-cross the Potomac River at William's Ferry near Conococheague, and then proceed south on the Great Philadelphia Wagon Road.

From Alexandria to the Great Philadelphia Wagon Road existing roads were available, and a number of established communities were also in place to support the march. However, west of the Wagon Road no true roads existed, only Indian trading paths. St. Clair had to construct a new road for the army west from this point to Fort Cumberland. Both columns would re-unite on the Great Philadelphia Wagon Road several miles to the north of Winchester, and join St. Clair's new road from there forward. This new road would cross the Potomac River, for Dunbar's Column a third time, before Fort Cumberland could be reached.

The young George Washington, a proponent for his home colony of Virginia and a loyal member of the Ohio Company, strongly criticized this decision in a letter to his mentor, Lord Fairfax, on May 5:

> You will naturally conclude [that] to pass through Maryld (when no business required it) was an uncommon & extraordinary rout for the Genl, and Colo. Dunbarr's Regiment to this place; but at the same time the reason, however, was obvious to say that those who promoted it had rather have the communication that way, than through Virginia, but I now believe the Imposition has too evidently appeared, for the Imposer's to subject us to the same Inconveniences again.[45]

Washington reiterated his opinions to another prominent Virginian merchant and his friend,

John Carlyle, in a letter written from Fort Cumberland on May 14: "I overtook the General at Frederick Town in Maryld and proceeded with him by way of Winchester to this place; which gave him a good opportunity to see the absurdity of the Rout, and of Damning it very heartily."[46]

St. Clair, as quartermaster responsible for the roads and route that Braddock's army would follow, had made this recommendation to Braddock. Captain Orme recorded in his journal:

> The General enquired of Sir John St Clair the nature and condition of the roads through which the troops and artillery were to march, and also if he had provided the wagons for the Ohio. Sir John informed the General that a new road was near completed from Winchester to Fort Cumberland, the old one being impassable, and that another was cutting from Conegogee to the same place, and that if the General approved of making two divisions of the troops and train, he might reach Will's Creek with more ease and expedition. He proposed that one regiment with all the powder and ordnance should go by Winchester, and the other regiment with the ammunition, military and hospital stores by Frederick in Maryland. That these should be carried ten miles up the Potomack to Rock Creek, and then up the Potomoack to Fort Cumberland. Sr John assured the General that boats, bateaux, canoes and wagons were prepared for the service, and also that provisions were laid in at Frederick for the troops. A return was called for of the wagons and teams wanted to remove the train from Alexandria, which Sir John went up the country to provide. He told the General two men had undertaken to furnish two hundred waggons and fifteen hundred carrying horses at Fort Cumberland early in May.[47]

As St. Clair recommended, employing dual columns had a number of advantages, and relatively few disadvantages, notwithstanding Washington's vigorous denunciations. First, the conditions of the roads west of the relatively well established and long settled tidewater were atrocious, and dividing the large British army (considerably larger than any organization which used these roads previously) would significantly reduce the wear and damage incurred upon a single route. Additionally, by employing two routes the corresponding congestion on a single road would be reduced. Restricting Braddock to a single road meant that a simple wagon accident, much less damage to a bridge, or heavy rains and accompanying erosion at a single location, would constrict his entire logistical approach. Utilizing routes through both Maryland and Virginia enabled the army to draw supplies from both colonies, effectively doubling the quantity of local provisions and transportation available to Braddock. Splitting the column doubled the amount of forage available to the army's draft animals, and ensured that sufficient fodder remained along the route of march to support subsequent supply trains moving towards Braddock's advanced columns. The availability of forage for the army's draft animals was a major factor when moving so early in the year, for grass and vegetation were just beginning to grow for the season, and if the forage was entirely devoured at the opening of the campaign, future travel along the lines of communication would become difficult if not impossible. Finally, by initially employing two divergent routes, any French spies or allied Native American scouts would not have known which final route Braddock was actually going to take, thus inserting some element of military deception into the early stages of the campaign. The only detriment of St. Clair's plan was that Dunbar's column would have to cross the Potomac River twice. However, the impact of this decision was somewhat reduced by directing that the artillery and ordnance trains accompany Halkett through Virginia without having to make such a passage. Washington's parochial interests aside, St. Clair had recommended the most militarily viable alternative.

St. Clair established detailed provisions for the movement of the heavy artillery, writing to Braddock on March 28,

That a proper person of the Artillery shou'd be sent to Rock Creek to Receive the Stores sent thither by water, and lodge them in the Storehouse provided by Mr. Beal, that he is to see these stores loaded on Waggons for Conogagee, for which he is to take Receipts from the Waggoners, for the Quantity loaded, and that he is to give a ticket Specifying their load which the Waggoner is to deliver to the person who is appointed to Receive the Stores at said place, and on that persons signing a Receipt for the load, the Waggoner will be paid by the Comy of Stores at the Rate of 16 pence of Maryland money a mile, as the law of Maryland directs, Care is to be taken that they load 2000 Weight. Mr. Cresap will provide Storehouses at Conogagee.

That a Proper Person of the Artillery shou'd be sent to Conogagee to Receive the Stores sent thither by land from Rock Creek, he is to see that the stores are according to the List sent him from Rock Creek, and give the Waggoner a Receipt on the back of their Ticketts, for their payment. He is to see the Stores put on board Cannoes, and sent to the Fort at Willis's Creek, and to Consign them to the Officer at the Fort, who will Receive them, and Mr. Commissary Walker will pay the Water Carriage. That an Officer of the Artillery shou'd be sent Eight days hence to Willis's Creek, to Receive all stores sent thither, for which there are proper Magazines.[48] That a proper Person of the Artillery shou'd be sent to Winchester, to Receive and forward all Stores by land in the same manner as the one at Rock Creek.

It is recommended that the Commissary of Stores for the Artillery shou'd Consult with Mr Commissary Dick, that he may know what Waggonage he is to state to him for the Ordnance of Stores.

St. Clair truly worked miracles in the first three months of 1755. Arriving by himself, his plans were almost immediately altered by the realization that the Potomac River was not navigable past the Little Falls approximately three miles west of Alexandria. St. Clair ascertained that Virginia was an extremely poor choice as a starting point for the largest army ever deployed in the North American colonies. This selection, made in London, nearly prevented the expedition from proceeding for lack of wagons and draft animals. Only the perfectly timed arrival of Benjamin Franklin at the crisis of the campaign salvaged Braddock's plans. During these three months St. Clair traveled several thousand miles on horseback, held scores of meetings with a range of individuals from royal governors to commissaries to frontiersmen, and he generated a formidable amount of correspondence, all without any appreciable assistance. And he was able to organize the campaign with no previous experience in North America, and only a vague and imperfect comprehension of the geography of Virginia when he first arrived. By the time that the 44th and 48th Regiments of Foot arrived in Virginia in early March, the campaign was well along in its preparations, due entirely to John St. Clair's herculean efforts.

Although transportation was a serious issue (and would remain so throughout the campaign), an effective quartermaster system was put in place, the general hospital at Hampton was successfully established, adequate provisions were obtained to feed Braddock's two thousand men, the three independent companies were readied for campaign (in the case of the New York companies this requiring no small effort), a strong and capable force of provincials were raised, sufficient men were located to increase the two British regiments to full campaign strength, and two adequate land routes were surveyed and work begun to make them passable for a large military force, considerably larger and heavier than had ever previously traveled in Virginia and Maryland. And all of this had to be accomplished before Braddock's force could ever stir from the banks of the Potomac River. This first phase of the campaign was a remarkable, even incredible, accomplishment for which Quartermaster St. Clair deserved great reward and recognition.

4

"The roads begin to be very indifferent"
Movement from Alexandria to Fort Cumberland

Halkett's 44th Foot began his overland march from Alexandria to Fort Cumberland first, nearly a week before Dumbar's northern column would begin its march. This separation in time and distance ensured that both regiments would not congest St. Clair's new wagon road west of Winchester.

Colonel Sir Peter Halkett led six companies of the 44th Regiment of Foot west from Alexandria on April 9, 1755. Lieutenant Colonel Thomas Gage shortly followed with the other four companies of the regiment escorting the heavy guns. Gage (1719/1720–1787) was the senior field officer of Halkett's 44th Foot. He entered the British army as an ensign sometime between 1736 and 1740. Gage had served in Flanders in the War of Austrian Succession to include being present at the Battle of Fontenroy (1744–1745), been in the field for the Jacobite Rebellion (1745–1746) to include serving at the Battle of Culloden, and then returned to Flanders for the remainder of the War of Austrian Succession (1747–1748). Although he had considerable active campaign experience, all of his service had been as aide-de-camp to Lord Albemarle, and he had not exercised any independent troop command or field leadership. Gage had been lieutenant colonel of the 44th Foot in Ireland since 1751. Gage was thus a long-serving officer, who unfortunately lacked much actual leadership experience. In fact, he was on his first active campaign with troops.[1]

Before this march began, Braddock's brigade remained in the encampment established by St. Clair in Alexandria. Although the precise location of this encampment is today unknown, it was on a hill or ridge west of the 1755 town's limits, most likely in the vicinity of the modern Masonic George Washington Memorial. Braddock established his headquarters in Alexandria at the residence of one of the community's founding fathers and a prominent Scottish merchant, John Carlyle. He would later complain of Braddock's occupation of his house, writing his brother after Braddock's death in August,

> The Generall & his Aid de Camps, Secretary & Servants Lodged with Me. He took everything he wanted, abused my home & furniture, and made me little or No Satisfaction- tho Expressed a Great deal of Friendship for me & Gave me a Commission as Keeper of the Kings Store houses, which he assured Me Should be worth 100 Pounds per Anno to me, and paid me 50 Pounds for the use of my house for a Month.[2]

To use the vernacular, Carlyle doth complained too much. Certainly, the establishment of a military headquarters in any private residence was a great inconvenience, with a large military contingent to provide services for; activities at all hours of day and night; messengers coming in dirty, muddy and wet from the road; officers reporting in all kinds of weather;

and a host of similar intrusions and loss of privacy. However, being paid £50, almost certainly in gold coins, for a month's use of the house was a magnificent amount of rent as compensation for the hardships that the Carlyle household doubtless experienced. For any Virginia merchant, receiving this quantity of hard specie in the chronically coin-poor colonial economy was a financial windfall of epic proportions.

As a component of his assigned responsibilities, Braddock had been charged with consulting with the royal governors of the colonies, and in the process to "cultivate the best Harmony & Friendship possible with the several Governors of our Colonies & Provinces."[3] Initially, Braddock had attempted to meet with a number of the governors at Annapolis, Maryland, but the event had to be scrubbed due to a heavy spring snowstorm that rendered travel impossible. Finally, on April 13, 1755, a grand conference was held with Braddock and numerous governors and Colonel William Johnson, superintendent to the Six Nations of the Iroquois Confederation. Both of Braddock's colonels were already moving forward with their regiments, but all of Braddock's military family was present, and presumably several other of his staff officers.[4] For two individuals this meeting was particularly poignant, as Governor William Shirley of Massachusetts had the opportunity to meet at length with his eldest son, William Shirley, Jr., who was Braddock's military secretary. Sadly enough, it would be the last time that father and son would ever meet upon this earth.

The complete details of this conference are outside the scope of this study, but one decision that would directly effect St. Clair's actions as quartermaster was that Braddock determined to coordinate the three principal columns moving upon Fort Niagara, Fort St. Frederick at Crown Point, and of course the column under his direct command moving against Fort Duquesne.[5] Braddock committed himself to arrive before the French fortification at the Forks of the Ohio "upon the end of June, nearly in July."[6] Braddock, who was entirely committed to fulfilling this timetable, would subsequently perform all of his planning and efforts in this direction. In turn, this would have a substantive effect upon St. Clair's duties as quartermaster as he attempted to fulfill Braddock's commitment.

Immediately following this conference, Braddock departed Alexandria along the Maryland route, passing through Frederick. Once he left Alexandria the general traveled in style and comfort, for Braddock had purchased from Governor Horatio Sharpe of Maryland a magnificent and handsome carriage, a six-horse English chariot.[7] This was properly known as a "half coach" because it only had one double seat enclosed behind the coachman's box. Such a "chariot" or "half coach" was extremely popular with English gentlemen of the 18th century. Colonial Williamsburg has documented that in 1768 George Wythe of Williamsburg ordered a "well built handsome post chariot" from London.[8] Braddock utilized this carriage for his journey west as far as Fort Cumberland, beyond which it was simply impossible, and in any case it would have been irresponsible, for the General to further enjoy its use.

Doubtless much to his chagrin, Sir John St. Clair missed the grand conference in Alexandria, as he was otherwise engaged in constructing a new road from the Great Philadelphia Wagon Road to Fort Cumberland. This was a particularly demanding piece of construction, and came entirely as a surprise to St. Clair. When the planned water route down the Potomac River proved impossible, St. Clair felt confident that a land route already existed to Fort Cumberland that could be employed as an alternative. St. Clair based his assumption upon a 1754 intelligence report on the "Different Routes in North America" that stated without equivocation, "From Winchester to Will's Creek, 50 Miles, Thus far the Road is very good, and passable with all sorts of Carriages."[9] St. Clair was appalled to discover upon his first journey to Fort Cumberland that in fact there was no passable road of any kind west of Winchester, and that what few trails existed were passable for *no* sorts of carriages, only packhorses. St. Clair would report, aghast, "I was on the Road to Willis's Creek this is 85 miles of the worst Road I ever travelled." Coming from a man who had grown up traveling the notoriously horrid paths and trails of the Scottish Highlands, this was a grim assessment indeed.

Numerous significant obstacles had to be traversed by St. Clair's new road. First, two long, gradual and incessant but not insurmountable ascents of the North Mountain and Bear Garden Mountain, then the Cacapon River crossing at the Forks of the Cacapon through Henry Enoch's Plantation, followed by the precipitous, brutal Spring Gap Mountain that comprised one of the most difficult ridge ascents of the entire route, followed by a large number of crossings of the Little Cacapon River immediately south of the Potomac River, and then a major river crossing of the Potomac River again. Once across the Potomac River, the north bank of the river to Fort Cumberland went through the flood plain and was relatively smooth and flat. St. Clair initially believed that local residents under the urging of Lord Fairfax would improve this road, but he was to be sorely disappointed in this expectation, as there were few residents west of Winchester, and in early Spring they were entirely committed to spring planting.

Despairing that the Virginians would ever complete the necessary improvements to this road, St. Clair took it upon himself to initiate construction of this stretch of road on March 21, when he ordered a company of Virginia rangers then at Winchester to commence work upon it. According to Aide-de-Camp Orme, St. Clair informed Braddock on March 27 that "a new road was near completed from Winchester to Fort Cumberland."[10] Since he had only ordered a Company of men to work on this road beginning on March 21, and given the mercurial weather spring weather which St. Clair had already experienced in this part of Virginia, this appears to have been an extraordinarily optimistic statement on the part of St. Clair, probably based upon his erroneous assumption that the local Virginians would have completed this work as he had specified to Lord Fairfax. Still, it appears that once St. Clair set the Virginian provincials to this task that they performed yeoman's work on this road, for St. Clair reported the road open and passable "in 2 or 3 days" on April 13. Another letter written by St. Clair on April 17 from Fort Cumberland suggests that at this date some work still remained to be accomplished: "I am able to do but little without some of Your Regt. at this place. I have now Ordered 100 men to Cut the Road which I expected wou'd have been finish'd before now, and shall want a great many men to work on the two Bridges that are to be Laid[,] and must have a Strong detachment to go with the Ingeneers to Reconoiter the Road to Fort Duquesne. All this I cannot Affect without a Strong detachment from you." Still, by early May when Halkett's and Dunbar's columns turned onto it from the Great Philadelphia Wagon Road, the new "Braddock's Road" was completed and ready for their transit. This was a remarkable achievement on St. Clair's part.

However, at the same time that St. Clair was accomplishing this great feat of constructing a new road from Winchester to Fort Cumberland, he caused serious harm to his relationship with Braddock. In early April while he was at Fort Cumberland, probably on or around April 16, St. Clair was visited by George Croghan, and four other official representatives, from Pennsylvania. St. Clair had just arrived at the fort, having that day ridden over the road from Winchester and been both alarmed at its poor condition recognizing that the army's movement was impending, fatigued and exhausted by the labor of traveling over and carefully examining the fledgling road. Croghan and the Pennsylvanians were then engaged in surveying the course of a road that St. Clair had requested be constructed from Carlisle, Pennsylvania (then the effective beginning of the Pennsylvania Colony's frontier), to Fort Cumberland. St. Clair exploded upon being advised that the road had not yet been finished, and that it had barely been surveyed. St. Clair lost his temper, his decorum, and his professionalism. Croghan reported to Governor Morris that St. Clair "is extremely warm and angry at our province. He would not look at our draughts [road surveys] nor suffer any representation to be made to him in regard to the province but stormed like a Lyon Rampant":

> He [St. Clair] threatened that instead of marching to the Ohio, he would in nine days march his army into Cumberland County [Pennsylvania] to cut the Roads, press Horses, Wagons, etc. that he would not suffer a Soldier to handle an Axe, but by fire and Sword, oblige the Inhabitants to do it, and take away every Man that refused to the Ohio, as he had, yesterday, some of the Virginians; that he would kill all kind of Cattle and carry away the Horses, burn the Houses, etc. and that if the French defeated them by the Delays of this Province he would with his Sword drawn pass through the Province and treat the Inhabitants as a parcel of Traitors to his Master; that he would to-morrow write to England by a Man-of-war; shake Mr. Penn's proprietaryship, and represent Pennsylvania as a disaffected province; that he would not stop to impress our Assembly; his hands were not tyed, and that We should find: ordering Us to take these Precautions and instantly publish them to our Governor and Assembly, telling Us he did not value anything they did or resolved, seeing they were dilatory and retarded the March of the Troops, and [expletives delted] on this occasion; and told Us to go to the General, if We pleased, who would give us ten bad Words for one that he had given us. He would do our Duty himself, and never trust to Us; but we should dearly pay for it. To every sentence he solemnly sore, and desired we might belive him to be in earnest.[11]

Within this context, St. Clair would write to Colonel Sir Peter Halkett on April 17, and he was clearly still furious with Pennsylvania: "Last night I arrived at this place after having been on the Roads a Week to make them passable[.] On my coming to this Place I found every thing in the Situation I left it, that is to say not any one thing done which I had Ordered, and what is worse the Pennsylvanians have disappointed us in Cutting their Roads and sending in their flour."

St. Clair was entirely in the wrong. By mid–April, spring had barely begun in western Pennsylvania. Winters in the Allegheny Mountains are brutal with frigid temperatures, deep snow and cutting winds. Snow remains in the ravines and ditches in the mountains even in mid–April, and the spring rains and snowmelt inevitably cause flooding and mudslides. No surveying, much less road construction, could conceivably begin across those mountains until this time of year. Such work was simply impossible in winter and spring, and Pennsylvania was starting the project as early as conceivably possible. John St. Clair, from the Scottish Highlands, should have well realized this, but he was totally self-absorbed with supporting the crushing schedule that Braddock had committed him to.

Furthermore, Pennsylvania was already proving considerably more supportive of the expedition than Virginia or Maryland, and St. Clair had now insulted the official representatives of the Colony that was to supply the majority of the provisions and transportation to Braddock's army. In any event, St. Clair had no legal authority to impress either wagons or citizens into the army, or to interfere in the management or administration of a colony. Finally, Croghan had valuable relationships with the Native Americans of the Ohio Country, and Croghan's contacts and participation in the campaign was absolutely critical to obtaining Native American support. Insulting and humiliating Croghan would accomplish little towards moving Braddock's expedition forward.

St. Clair's loss of control and self discipline, his absence of common courtesy and respect, and his actions in insulting official representatives of the colony of Pennsylvania, were not appreciated by Braddock, and clearly diminished St. Clair's standing in the eyes of his commanding general. General Braddock was not amused, and felt himself obliged to issue a formal apology to Governor Morris and the colony, reprimanding St. Clair at the same time.[12] From this date forward, a perceptible "cooling" in the relationship between Braddock and St. Clair is discernable, particularly since the Pennsylvania incident came at the same that the wagon and horse fiasco was manifesting itself. Most likely, only the absence of any other qualified officer for the Quartermaster post saved St. Clair from relief.

While St. Clair was arguing with Pennsylvania, Halkett's column was alerted for their march west on April 11, with the following route specified:

	Miles
To the Old Court House	18
To Mr. Colemans on Sugar Land Run were there is Indian Corn, &c.	12
To Mr. Miners	15
To Mr. Thompson the Quakers where There is 3000 weight corn	12
To Mr. They's Ferry of Shann	17
From Mr. Theys to Winchester	23
[Total]	97.[13]

Halkett's Regiment simply had to depart their camps and begin marching west. Essentially their route generally followed the modern Leesburg Pike (Virginia Route 7). The first day's march is today entirely taken over by suburbs of Washington, D.C., including Falls Church, Vienna, Tyson's Corner, Reston and Herndon. The first night's encampment was at the Old Fairfax County Courthouse. Although Braddock's columns are frequently derided for dilatory movement, it must be noted that Halkett's regiment, moving over generally good roads that were well established, marched no less than eighteen miles in their first day's march, a commendable effort. The site of the Old Fairfax County Courthouse is now lost, and was in the modern vicinity of Tyson's Corner.[14] Just west of Dranesville the historic road diverges from the Leesburg Pike and follows Sugarland Drive, Juniper Avenue and Maries Road through modern residential and commercial neighborhoods that have removed all historic integrity and context of the route.

The only section of Braddock's Road that retains any sense of historic place and presence is a 9/10 mile section of Vestal's Gap Road through Claude Moore Colonial Pike, just west of Sugar Land Run. This road remains dirt today, proceeds through light woodlands and farm fields, passes by an 18th century tavern, and for one brief glimpse retains the appearance and feeling that the roads and landscapes possessed as Halkett's soldiers slogged along and through it in April 1755.

Coleman's was located near Sugar Land Run, and that historic site is also now lost. Returning to the modern Leesburg Pike, Goose Creek was forded at the general location of the "Old Route 7 Bridge." "Mr. Minor's" was then reached, an inn owned by Nicholas Minor where the Days Inn now stands on East Market Street in Leesburg. Once past that city, the rural character of Braddock's Road emerges, which will be generally maintained all the way to the modern city of Braddock, Pennsylvania. From modern Leesburg this road, then known as Vestal's Gap Road, diverged.

This was typical of the 18th century, for when all roads were dirt and relatively poorly maintained, it was common for a road to split, with each portion of the road in use seasonally as drainage and weather permitted. The first branch of the road headed nearly due west on Dry Mill Road and then Highway 9. The second branch of the road headed north-northwest on the Old Waterford and the Old Wheatfield Road. Along this route a segment of historic forest remains, the Morvan Park, a spectacular grove of hickory and oak. These two branches converged again near the modern hamlet of Wheatland. From here, the course followed the modern Highway 9 and ascended the first ridge of the Allegheny Mountains, Blue Ridge at Key's or Vestal's Gap, then rapidly descended to the Shenandoah River to They's Ferry. This is in the vicinity of the modern Bloomery Bridge. Once across the Shenandoah River Halkett's Route briefly passed through the modern state of West Virginia. Progressing through modern Charles Town, Braddock's Route followed Highway 51, before turning left to the crossroads town of Middleway. Here, along the property that belonged to a Mr. John Evans, Halkett's regiments marched briefly south along the Great Philadelphia Wagon Road. It was at this point that the corridor of the two columns of Braddock converged for the remainder of the campaign.

The Great Philadelphia Wagon Road was a well-established transportation and commercial route that led from the Port of Philadelphia west through the farmlands of Pennsylvania, entered the Cumberland Valley, traveled south through the valley to cross the Potomac River at William's Ferry. It then followed the Shenandoah Valley due south, providing a good road connecting the frontier to Philadelphia, with immigrants and manufactured goods flowing west, and raw materials (particularly agricultural) traveling east. The road was in use from early in the 18th century, and was first documented by the "Map of the Inhabited part of Virginia, containing the whole province of Maryland with Part of Pensilvania, New Jersey and North Carolina, 1751" drawn by Thomas Fry and Peter Jefferson. Regrettably, all of the soldiers and officers whose written accounts are known to have survived traveled with Dunbar's northern column through Maryland, and as a result no written accounts of Halkett's march are extant. Halkett corresponded with St. Clair from Winchester, but unfortunately he failed to provide any details of his march west from Alexandria.

Because of Braddock's concern that the two columns not converge on the same road at the same time, Halkett's column proceeded Dunbar in march sequence, so that his regiment accompanied by the artillery could arrive first at Fort Cumberland. St. Clair's timing of Halkett's and Dunbar's march ensured that there was never more than one regimental column at any given place and time on the road, thus precluding congestion from two separate columns attempting to share the same route, sparing the road from additional damage, and offering an opportunity for the road to be repaired as each regiment moved ahead in turn.

Most likely because of the three crossings of the Potomac River that Colonel Dunbar's 48th Regiment of Foot would have to perform, the Naval detachment and Engineer Gordon accompanied him. Dunbar's column had initially been alerted for the march forward on Monday, April 7: "Col. Dunbar's Regimt is to march on Saturday.... March Rout of Col. Dunbars Regiment from the camp at Alexandria to Frederick in Maryland."

	Miles
To Rock Creek	—
To Owens Ordinary	15
To Dowden's Ordinary	15
To Frederick	45
[Total]	45.

Saturday was April 12, but Dunbar's departure was delayed until Monday, April 14. Dunbar's regiment had to briefly retrace its steps, marching east back through Alexandria to the banks of the river. Dunbar's column first crossed the Potomac River near the confluence of Rock Creek to the west of the modern Theodore Roosevelt Memorial Bridge but actually closer to the Francis Scott Key Bridge, taking advantage of the presence of an island (now Theodore Roosevelt Island) to facilitate the crossing of the river.[15] This crossing could only be achieved with the assistance of the transports, specifically the *Sea Horse* and *Nightingale* that provided all small boats for the passage.[16]

Once across the Potomac, Dunbar's men followed the Great Road west (modern Wisconsin Avenue to the old Rockville Pike or Highway 355). This first day's march, to a tavern known as Owen's Ordinary, has now been entirely absorbed by metropolitan growth from the City of Washington and District of Columbia. Lawrence Owen's Ordinary was apparently not much of an establishment, the unidentified servant of Captain Robert Cholmley recording in his journal, "Munday April the 14th. We Marched to larance Owings or Owings Oardianary, a Single House, it being 18 Miles and very dirty."[17] A midshipman with the Naval Detachment recalled, "April 14th. Detachment of Seamen was order'd to March in the Front; arrived at Mr. Lawrence Owen's, 15 Miles from Rock's Creek, and encamped upon good Ground, 8 Miles from the Upper Falls of Potomack."[18] Owens Ordinary is in the modern town limits of Rockville, Maryland, at the intersection of the Rockville Pike and Highway 28. It was destroyed early in the 20th Century. Its first day this column traversed fifteen miles, a respectable daily march.

On April 15 Dunbar continued along the Great Road to Dowden's Ordinary, in miserable weather as a cold front swept through, producing rain followed by heavy snow. Cholmley's servant wrote, "We marched to Dowdans Oardianary, it Beeing 16 Miles, the Night being very wet and bad with Thunder and Rain and the Next Morning a great Quantity of Snow Oblig'd us to halt their. The day following being Wedensday April the 16th, the Snow Being so Vialent [violent] that we where Oblig'd to Beat if of the Tents several times for fear it should Breck the Tent Pools."[19] The naval midshipman gave a similar account: "April 15th. Encamped on the side of a Hill near Mr. Michael Dowden's, 15 Miles from Mr. Owen's in very bad ground and in 1 ½ foot Snow."[20] The location of Dowden's Ordinary is ½ mile west of Clarksburg, Maryland on Maryland, Highway 355. The tavern foundation has recently been confirmed by archaeology performed by Montgomery County, Maryland. However, although the immediate tavern site is now a small county park and contains a stone commemorative marker, the site of Braddock's two-day encampment has been entirely developed by townhouses and homes.[21]

The snow having relented, the march continued on April 17, and late that afternoon Dunbar's men reached Frederick. The most significant event of that day occurred as the Great Road crossed the Monocacy River, where there was no bridge, and the ford was washed out by a freshet caused by the heavy rain and snow runoff. The young naval officer recalled of this difficult and time consuming traverse, "April 17th. Marched to Frederick's Town, 15 Miles from Dowden's the road very Mountainous, Marched 11 Miles, when we came to a River called Monsklso [Monocacy River], which emplies itself into the Potomack, it runs very rapid, and is after hard rain, 13 feet deep, we ferried over a Flat for that Purpose."[22] Cholmley's batman wrote, "Thursday April the 17th. We marched to Frederick. 4 miles this side of Frederick we crossed the River Menercus [Monocacy River], it being a hundred yards Over and only one flat made the Baggage so late before it got Over that we was Oblig'd to lay in Quarters that Night, it being 16 miles in a Pleasant fine Cuntry."[23] The historic 1746 trace of the Georgetown Road and Middle Ford Ferry crossing of the Monocacy River remain extant within the boundaries of Monocacy National Battlefield, a National Park Service entity. Here is the first opportunity to gain an impression of the historic appearance of Dunbar's route along the Braddock Road through Maryland.[24]

The Naval subaltern recalled of the Frederick campground, "Encamped ... at the North End of the Town, upon very good Ground." He recorded his impressions of Frederick: "This Town has not been settled Above 7 years, there are 200 Houses & 2 Churches, 1 Dutch, 1 English; the inhabitants chiefly Dutch, Industrious, but imposing people; Provisions & Forage in plenty."[25] Braddock's encampment is believed to have been along modern Washington Street (US Highway 40) in Frederick, west of the Washington Street School.[26] This area is now crowded with sub-divisions and commercial growth, and the historic sense of Dunbar's campground is entirely lost.

His "Grand Conference" in Alexandria concluded, Braddock arrived at Frederick on April 21, 1755, riding in splendor in Governor Sharpe's spectacular chariot, accompanied by his military family. The engineer's journal recorded of the event: "The General attended by Captains Orme, Morris and Secretary Shirley; with Sr John St Clair; arrived at Head Quarters."[27] St. Clair had written to Sir Peter Halkett from Fort Cumberland on April 17, noting, "I am under a Necessity of going to Frederick in Maryland to General Braddock to see if he will march a party of the 2d Brigade into that province to press Wagons loaded with Flour, otherwise our expedition must be at a stop." St. Clair wrote another letter from Winchester on April 21, probably quite early in the morning, and he must have spent the entirety of that day riding from Winchester to Frederick. Unfortunately, the location of Braddock's headquarters in Frederick is not documented, and it has almost certainly long since vanished. It was here that the devastating news regarding the utter absence of wagons and horses obtained from Maryland was received, and Benjamin Franklin's fortuitous intervention on behalf of John St. Clair and Braddock salvaged the campaign.

Colonel Dunbar's column spent nearly two weeks tarrying at Frederick while the various logistical and transportation arrangements were sorted out. Finally, on April 29, Dunbar's regiment departed their camps and marched due west, almost immediately ascending South Mountain, the first true ridge of the Allegheny Mountains that they would encounter. This climb is not particularly difficult, but it is long and unrelenting. Dunbar crossed South Mountain at Fox's Gap, which just over a century later would serve as a battleground in 1862 during the American Civil War. Even with the ascent of South Mountain, Dunbar's column still marched 18 miles in a single day, a formidable march. Descending South Mountain, the regiment crossed Antietam Creek at a ford at Pry's Mill. That night Dunbar's regiment encamped at Chapman's Ordinary, actually owned by a Mr. Walker, located about ½ mile east of the modern crossroads hamlet of Bakersville, Maryland. Captain Robert Cholmley's batman recorded, "We marched to Chapmans Ordinary, it being Nigh 18 Miles."[28] Surprisingly, he failed to even record the crossing of South Mountain. The engineer's journal was a bit more comprehensive: "March'd to Mr. Walkers, 18 miles from Frederick's Town, pass'd the South Ridge, commonly called the Blue Ridge, very easy Ascent and a fine Prospect; no kind of Refreshments."[29]

Braddock tarried in Frederick a few additional days completing his logistical and transportation arrangements. He would be joined here on May 1 by Mr. George Washington, who would serve as his aide-de-camp for the remainder of the campaign.[30] The next day Braddock, and his military family including Washington, departed Frederick, also crossing over South Mountain at Fox's Gap. Just east of Mr. Walker's, Braddock and his personal staff turned south, departing the route of his infantry column, and riding through Sharpsburg to cross the Potomac River at Thomas Swearingen's ferry (modern Maryland Highway 34) at Shepherdstown, West Virginia. Braddock hurried south for Winchester, where he had scheduled a conference with various Native Americans. He reached Winchester on March 3, after what Washington, an experienced and seasoned traveler, referred to as "a very fatiguing ride."[31] Braddock was not accompanied by St. Clair, who departed after a brief visit at Frederick to proceed immediately to Fort Cumberland to insure that the road west of Winchester to Wills' Creek was satisfactory. St. Clair wrote to Braddock from Fort Cumberland on May 2, regarding several contracts for pack horses.

From Mr. Walker's, Dunbar's column proceeded to Conococheague in another day's march, traversing sixteen miles on April 30. The youthful midshipman was impressed with Conococheague: "April 30th. Marched to Connecochiag, 16 Miles from Mr. Walker's, close by the Potomack, a very fine Situation, where we found all the Artillery Stores preparing to go by Water to Will's Creek."[32] Chomley's servant concurred: "We marched to Cunneceojeg where we Incamped by the River Portwomack, it being 18 miles and a plesent Cuntry."[33] The route that Dunbar followed subsequently became known as the Old Sharpsburg Road. At Conococheague the regiment camped immediately to the southwest of the modern Williamsport, Maryland, close to Conococheague Creek.

The next day, May 1, the 48th Regiment of Foot crossed the Potomac River at Evan Watkins' ferry, which had been established in 1744 across the Potomac River just south of Conococheague Creek, and marched past Watkins' spectacular stone home constructed in 1741. And with this movement, Braddock's army departed Maryland, having been in the colony about two weeks. The Great Philadelphia Wagon Road crossed the river here, and for the next several days the marches would be along this road, Dunbar's column proceeded due south from here. Again, this was another lengthy day's march, although it was following the well-established wagon road (modern US Highway 11). The captain's servant recorded, "Thursday May ye 1st. We marched Cross the River Portwomack into Virginia to Widow Evens and Carried three days provisions along with us it being 18 miles."[34] The youthful midshipman was more verbose: "Employed in ferrying (over the Potomack) the Army Baggage into Virginia in 2 Flats and 5 Batteaux. The Army March'd to Mr. John Evans, 16 Miles from ye Potomack and 20 miles from Winchester, where we encamped, and had tolerable good living with Forrage; the roads begin to be very indifferent."[35] He noted succinctly, "Halted and sent the Horses to Grass."[36]

John Evans' 1755 limestone residence is located in the southern portion of the modern community of Martinsburg, West Virginia. The historic structure survives on a single acre, although nearby farmland retains some historic appearance of Braddock's campgrounds. It was also known as Big Springs in 1755, hinting at the reason why its location was attractive for a two night layover. The next day, May 2, Dunbar's column paused at Evans to rest the soldiers and draft animals, as was standard procedure for the British army. On May 3, Dunbar's 48th Regiment of Foot continued south on the Great Philadelphia Wagon Road. About five miles north of Winchester, the column turned west onto St. Clair's new road, marching another few miles to the west to the Widow Barringer's place. From here, the army would follow a single route. The observant naval officer recorded the day's efforts: "May 3rd. Marched to Widdow Barringer's, 18 Miles from Mr. Evans, the day was so excessive hot that many Officers and Men could not arrive at their Ground until Evening; this is 5 Miles from Winchester and a fine Situation."[37] The captain's servant didn't consider the weather hot enough to mention, but apparently his attention was focused upon a spectacle of a different nature: "We marched to Widow Billingers about 19 miles and Rec'd two days Provisions and drumed a woman out of the Camp."[38] Here, just west of the modern crossroads of Brucetown, an 18th century spring house remains to mark the site of the Widow Barringer's. Braddock's campground was located in close proximity to the spring. Mrs. Brown, who moved along the road several days behind the main column of the army, spent the evening of June 8 at "my Friend Bellingers who bid me wellcome," documenting that Bellinger was a member of the large Quaker community in the vicinity.[39]

St. Clair's new road departed from the Great Philadelphia Wagon Road approximately five miles north of Winchester. St. Clair specified that his new route avoid Winchester, apparently because St. Clair perceived the city as a bottle neck. Additionally, the new route eliminated about ten miles of travel by skirting Winchester to the north. St. Clair described it to Sir Peter Halkett in a letter written April 17, while the road's construction was well underway: "The Route is to Henry Enoch's 2 days March as before. From Henry Enoch's to the Spring 2 Miles. From the Spring to Col. Cresops 18 Miles, at the mould of the South branch you pass the Potomack. From Col. Cressop's to the Camp at Will's Creek 14 Miles."

From "Friend Barringer's" house and spring, the new road proceeded generally due west on rolling and then gently ascending ground to "Mr. Potts." This campsite's precise location is now lost, but it was approximately in the vicinity of the small modern community of Gainsboro on Virginia Route 522. The midshipman briefly reported on this day's march: "May 4th. Marched to Mr. Pots 9 Miles from the Widdows where we were refresht with Venison and wild Turkeys; the Roads excessive bad."[40] The captain's batman succinctly journaled, "Sunday May the 4th We marched to Potses Camp, it Beeing 9 Miles."[41] This day's route is significant in that a portion of the road is now flooded by an artificial lake and road named in Sir John St. Clair's honor: "Lake St. Clair" and "St. Clair Road"!

The next day the march continued, trending towards the northwest, following the general route of the modern Virginia Highway 522 and West Virginia Highway 127 to Henry Enoch's house at the Forks of the Cacapon River. Here a well-established ford, that in fact remains in use today, crossed the river. Although the previous day's march had been short, this day's march was a full one. The youthful naval subaltern recorded: "March'd to Mr. Henry Enock's a Place called 'The Forks of Cape Capon' 16 Miles from Mr. Pots, over prodigious mountains and between the same we crossed a Run of Water in 3 Miles distance, 20 times. After marching 15 Miles we came to a River called 'Kahepatin' where the Army ferried over. We found a Company of Sir Peter Halket's Regiment, waiting to escort the

Train of Artillery to Will's Creek."[42] The captain's servant, obviously accompanying his master's baggage with the regimental train, wrote, "Munday May the 5th. We marched to Kennets [Henry Enoch's] Camp after a very Rainy Night and Morning. The tents being very wet made the Baggage very heavy, it being 18 miles."[43] The next day, May 6, Dunbar's column halted according to tradition, to rest the soldiers and draft animals, perform necessary repairs to animal harness and wagons, and maintain the soldiers' equipment, accouterments and shoes. The young naval officer apparently enjoyed his time here, recalling with pleasure "the Officers for passing away the time, made Horse Races and agreed that no Horse should Run over 11 Hands and carry 14 stones."[44] The enlisted soldier serving as Captain Cholmley's servant had more mundane interests in mind: "We halted and Rec'd five days provisions but no forige for our horses nor any thing to be sold. We should be starved if it was not for the Kings Allowance."[45] The midshipman would shortly discover that the easy marches were finished.

Here, shortly after crossing the Opequon Creek (referred to by St. Clair as the North River of Cacapehon), the original Braddock Road follows the modern "Sir Johns Road" named for Sir John St. Clair, for about five miles, one of only two segments of the modern Braddock Road so named.

The next day was a brutal march, starting with a long, gradual but unrelenting climb up Bear Garden Mountain, and then ascended the horrific obstacle of Spring Gap Mountain, the most severe ridge that Braddock's men had crossed to date, and one of the worst in western Virginia. In western Pennsylvania, this ridge is known as Sideling Hill. Once past the ridge, the road endured numerous crossings of the Little Cacapon River. The naval officer was impressed: "we crossed another Run of Water 19 times in 2 Miles, Roads bad."[46] When Matron Browne traversed the same route a month later, on June 11, she wrote, "The Roads were so bad that the poor Horses were not able to Keep on their Legs ... 2 of the Waggons broke down, halted till they were mended, I walked till my [feet] were blister'd." The next day she added that "there is no describing the badness of the Roads I walked as far as I was Able. The Poor Horses no longer regard the Smack of the Whip or beat of the Drum and as to Black [a horse] she could go no further[,] 2 of the Waggons broke down."[47] The captain's servant recorded the day's march as "12 miles."[48] One anonymous British officer commented upon the picturesque Virginia countryside, probably written as he negotiated Bear Garden Mountain: "There is nothing round us but trees, swamps and thickets. I cannot conceieve how war can be made in such a country. There has not been ground to form a battalion since we left the settlements."[49]

The campground was on the south bank of the Potomac River, and at the junction of this river and the Little Cacapon a ferry had been established by St. Clair. The young naval subaltern recalled for May 8,

> Ferried over the River into Maryland and March'd to a Mr. Jackson's 8 Miles from Mr. Cox's where we found a Maryland Company encamp'd in a fine Situation on the Banks of the Potomack; with clear'd ground about it; there lives a Colonel Cressop, a Rattle Snake Colonel, and a D[amned] Rascal; calls himself a Frontiersman, being nearest the Ohio; he had a Summons some time since from French to retire from his Settlement, which they claim'd as their Property, but he refused it like a Man of Spririt. This place is the Track of Indian Warriors, when going to War either to the No[rth]ward or So[uth]ward. He hath built a little Fort round his House; and is resolved to keep his Ground. We got plenty of Provisions etc. The General arrived with Captains Orme and Morris, with Secretary Shirley and a Company of light Horse for his Guard, under the Command of Capt. Steward; the General lay at the Colonel's.[50]

The term "rattlesnake colonel" is an intriguing one. The specific qualifications and job requirements for a "rattlesnake colonel" were and are relatively ill defined.[51] However, nearly every single soldier and officer who passed through noted "a Rattle Snake Colonel nam'd Crisop."[52] Colonel Thomas Cresap and his son Michael Cresap had gained notoriety by supplying St. Clair with unpickled beef which had to be condemned and buried, and his son had failed to fulfill a pre-paid contract for flour.[53] Conceivably, reprehensible conduct such as this was sufficient to earn infamy as a "rattlesnake colonel." Possibly the promiscuous slaying of dangerous reptiles contributed to the reputation. Just as likely, Cresap's personal demeanor and conduct may have earned him this approbation. Braddock's campground and the site of Cresap's 1755 residence where Braddock stayed overnight are carefully maintained and protected by the National Park Service as a component of the Chesapeake and Ohio Canal National Historic Park just south of Oldtown, Maryland. Michael Cresap later served as the captain of a rifle company in the War for American Independence. His circa 1764 brick house also survives today in Oldtown, Maryland, where it is operated as the Irvin Allen/Michael Cresap Museum.

From Colonel Cresap's, the columns marched due west on comparatively good ground on the north bank of the Potomac River to Fort Cumberland. St. Clair's road generally follows the route of modern Maryland Highway 51 from Oldtown to Cumberland. The captain's batman reported of the march, "Satterday May the 10th. We marched to Willses Creek Close by the Creek is the Portwomack River, it Being 15 Miles."[54]

Fort Cumberland had been reached. The easy portion of the campaign had been concluded. Worse awaited. Much worse.

5

"We pursued our route through a desolate country"
Movement to Fort Duquesne

Braddock's brigade now paused for a brief interlude at Fort Cumberland, while various logistical arrangements were finalized, and critically important military drill and discipline could be performed. As regards to training, the American draftees transferred into the 44th and 48th Foot needed to perform exhaustive drill and training so that they could be incorporated into the two regiments. The American draftees did not share the advantage of the previous British military training that the Irish draftees possessed, and in any event they had arrived too late at Alexandria to be taught much more than rudimentary movements sufficient to enable them to stay in ranks during the march through Maryland and Virginia. Accordingly, the British sergeants and corporals certainly had their work cut out for them at Fort Cumberland, as they had less than two weeks available to perform necessary instructions in the full range of military drill and evolution that the American draftees would require on the battlefield.

But this instruction was left to the two regiments of foot, and it was logistical arrangements that absorbed St. Clair's time. The majority of this work was routine, mundane and ordinary. Continuous efforts were made to obtain additional pack horses, draft animals, wagons and teamsters, all with minimal success. Wagon trains rotated between Fort Cumberland and Connocheague and Alexandria, transporting the stockpile of supplies necessary to enable Braddock to move forward. Storehouses were organized, and filled as swiftly as convoys struggled up the hill from Wills Creek and the Potomac River. Barrels of flour, salt pork and salt beef had to be received, inspected, either accepted or condemned, and then rolled into the storehouses. Returns were regularly received by St. Clair, to ensure that proper quantities of provisions were on hand and being issued.[1] Equipment had to inspected, approved, improved, repaired or replaced. Provisions had to continuously be distributed to the regimental and company quartermasters. Simple mud and wood ovens were constructed by the bakers, who then struggled through the hot May weather to bake loaves of bread for immediate consumption, and hard biscuit for the march. This work was, in a word, boring. And it went, for the most part, unrecorded. But it was vitally important work, and the success of the entire campaign entirely relied upon it.

On May 26, 1755, Halkett's orderly book documented St. Clair's activities in regards to one of a quartermaster's most important responsibilities, specifically regarding the acquisition, transportation, storage, and issuing of provisions for the Army. On this date, it was noted a return to be given in to Sr John St. Clear by the Qr Masters of each Brigade And Artillery of the Quantity of provisions drawn from the Commissary And a Return to be given in to Sr John St Clear every Monday of the Quantity of provisions drawn the proceeding Week.[2]

This order was necessary because rations were issued based upon the daily, reported strength of a regiment, independent company or detachment. This strength would vary, as soldiers died or were killed, were detached, or were transferred sick, injured or wounded to the hospital. Thus, the quartermaster general was receiving accurate records of precisely how many rations the army was daily consuming at Fort Cumberland.

At about this time, one of the more bureaucratic regulations regarding the rights, authority and responsibility of a quartermaster in the British army was addressed in orders. Specifically, the quartermaster was not to be issued paroles and countersigns. Rather, he was to report to the commanding officer to obtain it. This rather arcane procedure was documented by Captain Thomas Simes, a British army officer who prepared a range of military manuals and treatises that chronicled the various procedures and policies then in general practice in the army. Simes noted regarding the limitations upon a Quartermaster's authority:

- he works with the General on whatever regards the marches of the army;
- he has no direct authority over the troops; and
- he goes to receive the parole from the Major General of the day; but when necessarily employed, he sends one of his assistants to fetch it to him.[3]

On March 27, 1755, a very lengthy and extremely precise set of orders was issued to the army by Braddock, which regulated and directed its conduct. Among this involved set of procedures it was specifically noted that "the Adjt of the day to send a Serjt to Sir John St Clear with the Orders."[4] Thus, Braddock was somewhat deviating from standard practice, by proactively ensuring that St. Clair was issued with orders directly from headquarters. Theoretically, this would serve to somewhat streamline the operations of Braddock's quartermaster.

St. Clair's most visible effort during the month of May 1755 at Fort Cumberland was scouting and patrolling the route from the gates of Fort Cumberland west to the Forks of the Ohio. Although Washington's Fort Necessity campaign had traversed this precise route only the year before, he had sustained his considerably smaller "army" (less than the size of a British battalion) exclusively using packhorses. Braddock's considerably larger brigade required several score wagons, and carried with it a sufficient train of artillery to both reduce Fort Duquesne, and then garrison the Forks of the Ohio against any possible French resurgence. St. Clair had to assume that at least a rudimentary siege of Fort Duquesne would have to be sustained, in addition to constructing and continuously maintaining a new British garrison at the Forks of the Ohio, and moving sufficient supplies forward to enable Braddock to then move north up the Allegheny River and then Lake Erie against Fort Niagara. Accordingly, the horse paths that Washington had used were insufficient, and these trails had to be turned into a functional road. St. Clair's first step before he could begin work on the roads was to simply ascertain where the roads needed to proceed, or more accurately, where the terrain dictated they would be placed.

In his previous visits to Fort Cumberland, St. Clair had little time or opportunity available to him to scout much west of Wills Creek. At his first journey there in late January he had noted to Lord Fairfax: "When I was two miles on this side of the South branch [of the

Potomac River] I had a good view of the ground that runs along the Savage River it seems good for a carriage Road and might be of great Service if your Ldp would order it to be marked out as I shall soon be obliged to visit all that ground." St. Clair would reiterate to Braddock in early February: "When I had got about two miles on the other side of the South branch I had a full view of the mountains on each side of the Potomack above Willis's Creek, and from what I could see there is a Road easily to be made across the Country to the mouth of Savage River, which will be gaining 30 Miles. If I am not more deceived than I have been of late with Regards to ground, the mouth of Savage River is the place where we ought to cross the Allegany Mountains. I have only been able to find one Woodsman who can give me any distinct Account of that ground, which gives me a great satisfaction. I wrote Lord Fairfax to have the Road mark'd [marked] out to the mouth of Savage River." St. Clair was extremely optimistic regarding his views of the terrain, as two miles west of Fort Cumberland would have offered him little actual knowledge of the rugged endless ridges of the Allegheny Mountains that he would have to cross, and the topography made it impossible for St. Clair to have seen anything west of the Savage Mountain, a mere twelve miles west of Fort Cumberland.

In the middle of March St. Clair had told Braddock, "I am now making a Disposition for my seeing Youghangany River before I Return to Alexandria[,] this may take me up three days, but it will put me past all doubts with Regard to our passing the Potomack." By early April St. Clair had been unable to escape from the other exigencies of his responsibilities to perform this reconnaissance.

> When the Troops are Assembled, and the whole got together in Readiness to March from Willis's Creek to Fort Duquesne; the march must be Fixed for one of the two following Routes, viz. One through the Meadows, and Across the River Yohiogane, being the Route taken by Col. Washington last Year, and the other must be by turning the head of that River, if found practicable, the latter seems most Eligible, since by taking the Former, the French may dispute our passage, in crossing the River, and give us the trouble of laying Bridges, and making Works to Cover them. The Reconoitring of the latter Route, shall be set about with the utmost Expedition, and if Found practicable, the Troops now at Willis's Creek, may be employ'd in Cutting the Road Open. They may venture to Cut the length of 25 Miles before the other Troops arrive. The disposition of marching the Army from Willis's Creek, may be better deferred until the above Route Round the head of the Yohoganie is Reconoitred, then a disposition shall be made, and sent with the Report of that Route.

St. Clair reported to Braddock in early April that since he was unable himself to make this reconnaissance, he would have the engineering officers fulfill this task: "Mr Mackellar and Gordon will undertake to Recoinoitre that Road; and I shall order them a proper Party for their Escort on the Road to Fort Duquesne, which I meant to Reconoitre before; and save our Crossing the Monongahela and Yohogany."

Once at Fort Cumberland, the engineers initiated surveying for the precise route of the new Braddock Road to Fort Duquesne. On May 18 general orders were issued: "1 Corpl & 8 men of the Line to Attend the Engineears in Surveying. They are to parade at 9 oClock."[5] There are a number of other orders calling for company sized details of soldiers to report to St. Clair on various dates (May 18, 20, 25) but the orderly books do not indicate if they were accompanying St. Clair on scouting expeditions, or for some other purpose associated with his other duties and responsibilities as quartermaster.

The naval midshipman supervised additional work in the vicinity of Fort Cumberland, beginning on May 21: "100 Carpenters were employed in making a flat, building a magazine & squaring timber to make a bridge over Will's Creek, the Smiths were making Miners' Tools."[6] When Braddock arrived, there was only a Ford across Will's Creek, and since he had to spend time at Fort Cumberland anyway, Braddock determined to expend the time wisely and to construct a bridge to facilitate communications across the watercourse.

Although St. Clair's scouting efforts are poorly documented, it is apparent that by late May his efforts had proceeded sufficiently that at least the beginning of the route to the Forks of the Ohio was identified. Late that month a Council of War was called by Braddock at Fort Cumberland, attended by the following officers:

- Colonel Sir Peter Halkett, 44th Foot;
- Colonel Dunbar, 48th Foot;
- Lieutenant Colonel Thomas Gage, 44th Foot;
- Lieutenant Colonel Ralph Burton, 48th Foot;
- Major Russel Chapman, 44th Foot;
- Major William Sparks, 48th Foot;
- Major Sir John St. Clair, Deputy Quartermaster General.[7]

A Council of War was, as defined by a British officer in 1776, "when a commander in chief of an army, or governor of a garrison, assembles the principal officers for their advice, upon some affairs of importance."[8] Braddock routinely called for Councils of War to guide the conduct of his expedition, and typically assembled his field grade officers for this purpose, along with Major St. Clair as deputy quartermaster general. The relatively junior officers who served a general as his military family did not attend a Council of War, although it was not uncommon for an aide-de-camp to serve as a secretary to strictly document the discussions and findings of the Council of War.

At this Council of War the decision was made to send forward a strong advanced guard, consisting of six hundred men under the nominal command of Major Chapman of the 44th Foot, but actually under the direction of Sir John St. Clair and the engineering officers, to begin construction along the general route of Nemacolin's Path, a long existing Indian trail that had been used by Washington during his journeys west in 1753 and 1754. This trail, for it could scarcely be called a road, would require significant improvement and expansion before it could accommodate an army of several thousand soldiers, scores of wagons, and heavy artillery pieces. Other decisions were made that St. Clair would have contributed to, such as the standard organization that would guide the nightly establishment of the army's camps, and for which St. Clair as quartermaster would have been responsible. This camp arrangement is only documented in Orme's Journal, which provides no provenance for it. However, it was St. Clair's responsibility as quartermaster to establish the layouts of the army's encampments, and he was the only officer attending the Council of War who had actually proceeded past Fort Cumberland. Although it cannot be confirmed, it is conceivable that this was St. Clair's creation.

Each column was to march in two columns upon the road, with strong advanced parties, flanking parties, and a rearguard. Such precautions were well documented in numerous military treatises of the time, constituted standard British army procedures, and were scarcely innovative. The advanced party typically consisted of the sturdiest soldiers in Braddock's army, the two grenadier companies of the 44th and 48th Regiments of Foot. Upon arriving in camp for the evening, "the Grenadiers were to encamp across the road," presumably in company front. At the same time the wagons remained in line on the road, "drawn up in close order." Each company was to halt on either the right of left side of the wagon train, face right or left as appropriate into company front, and encamp there. The rear guard would close up the column, and similarly form company front to safeguard the back of the rectangle. Thus, the valuable baggage train and train of artillery was always safeguarded at the center of the army, halted along the road, with the grenadiers and regiments forming the four sides of a giant rectangle around them.

The various flank parties were in turn to form a number of picket posts around the encampment, and a series of sentries and strong picket posts entirely surrounded the camp. Once these sentry positions has been established, they were to open "a free communication by cutting down saplings and underwood." These avenues of communication were to be created directly from the wagons to the picket posts, and laterally between the various posts. The result was a secure encampment with the main army and wagon train at the hub of a wheel, the various picket posts and sentries around the rim of the wheel, connected by paths like the spokes of the wheel. Any post on the perimeter that was threatened could be expeditiously reinforced, and the army could effectively and rapidly maneuver along interior lines. It was an effective plan that was perfectly adapted for a camp in the wilderness. The fact that it was efficient can be validated by the fact that the French and their Native American allies never launched any type of probe, much less a deliberate attack, upon any of Braddock's encampments during the entire expedition.[9]

A careful examination of the transportation capacity of the army was conducted at a second Council of War held at Fort Cumberland, at which St. Clair revealed that he only possessed 190 wagons, 150 provided by Franklin's endeavors in Pennsylvania, and a mere forty contributed from the entirety of Virginia and Maryland. Augmenting these wagons were six hundred pack horses. St. Clair estimated that the transportation available "were insufficient to carry seventy days flour and fifty days meat, which he was of opinion was the least he could march with without running great risques of being reduced to the utmost distress before the Convoy could be brought to him."[10] Assuming that the wagons could carry the full planning weight of 2,000 pounds, and that the pack horses could transport their full load of 200 pounds (both hopelessly optimistic planning estimates), St. Clair could carry at any given time in the wagons 380,000 pounds (190 tons), and on the pack horses an additional 120,000 pounds (60 tons). Given the army's bare minimum requirements of three pounds a day for daily rations per man (6,000 pounds daily), this consisted of approximately ninety days' rations for the army. In the event, the load that the wagons and horses carried were far too generous, and would have to be drastically reduced. St. Clair's letter suggests that the army could transport approximately 360,000 pounds total (180 tons). And the wagons and horses also had to carry baggage and ordnance supplies. It appears that St. Clair was accurately estimating the transportation capacity of his supply train.

Accordingly, on May 28 Braddock issued St. Clair detailed orders:

Instructions to Sir John St. Clair Deputy Quarter Master General

1. You will proceed with a detachment of Six Hundred men, Order'd for that purpose under the Command of Major Russell Chapman, to Open & Repair a Road over the Allegany Mountains, towards the great meadows to a distance not exceeding forty Miles.

2. You will Acquaint Major Chapman, whom I have directed to Consult You in the execution of

his Orders, what part of the detachment you Shall think necessary to be employ'd in Opening and Repairing the Road, and you will also give him your opinion with Regard to the disposition of the Remainder, for the defense of the Working party, and the Convoy under his Escort.

3. You will cease opening and Repairing the Road, at the end of seven days, or sooner if it shall be thought Adviseable, and fix upon such a Spot as shall appear proper to yourself, and the Engineers Order'd upon this Service for Constructing a place of Defence for the party, and the provision order'd to be lodged there.

4. Upon Major Champman's leaving you, You will employ the Remaining part of the detachment, which will be left under your Command, in Compleatg the place of defence, and you will make such dispositions, and preserve such discipline as the service shall Require.

At daybreak of May 29, 1755, St. Clair and Major Chapman of the 44th Foot led forward the advanced party from Fort Cumberland in compliance with these orders. The third and most important phase of the campaign had begun, the direct movement upon Fort Duquesne at the Forks of the Ohio.

St. Clair's advanced detachment was initially commanded by Major Russel Chapman, the junior field officer of Halkett's 44th Foot. Chapman had served with the 44th Foot from its establishment in 1741. He was a captain in 1741, and had been promoted to major in 1750. Most likely, he had served with the 44th Foot at the Battle of Prestonpans against the Jacobites in 1745.[11] Accordingly, he was an experienced and a well seasoned field officer. This detachment was recorded by Engineer Gordon in his journal: "Major Chapman, with a Detachment of 600 Soldiers March'd with 2 Field Pieces and 50 Waggons full of Provisions, when Sir John St. Clair, 2 Engineers, Lieut. Spendelow & 6 Seamen with Some Indians were ordered to clear the Roads for them."[12] Although St. Clair was the nominal commander of this large work party as quartermaster, Major Chapman was the actual commander. Under British army procedures, Sir John St. Clair as quartermaster did not possess the authority to actually command soldiers, or issue them orders or instructions. Only a regimental infantry or cavalry officer could perform such a function. This was also the case for officers from the Board of Ordnance such as royal artillery and royal engineers, who were not authorized to command troops of the line. St. Clair's authority was rather limited to identifying the route intended for the road, and the actual labor that had to be performed. Major Chapman, as commanding officer of the detachment supporting St. Clair, would actually issue orders to his soldiers, and supervise their work.

Captain Cholmley of the 44th Foot and his servant were assigned to this working party. His servant wrote, "Thursday May the 29th. This day we marched about seven miles and 8 hours of marching it, it being very Bad Roads that we Where Oblig'd to halt Every hundred yards and mend them. As soon as we Came to our [encampment] ground there was a working party sent out to Cut the Roads, and a Covering party to guide them, the Working party Being 200 men, the Covering party 100 men." A day later he would note: "We marched at 6 oClock. We marched till Eight at Night and only marched three miles ... the roads Being all to Cut and make passable." The work continued unrelenting on June 1, "sent a party of men to Cut the Road Over Halligany Mountains," and on June 2, "the Rocks being so large that we where Obliged to Blast them several times before we Came to our ground."[13]

This working party was inadequate to the task, and additional parties were moved forward from Fort Cumberland. On June 2 the following instructions were received: "The Hatchett men of the Two regts & 1man per Compy of the rest of the Line to parade this Afternoon at 3 oClock at Mr. Gordons Engineers Tent. 4 Serjts 2 Corpls & 100 men without

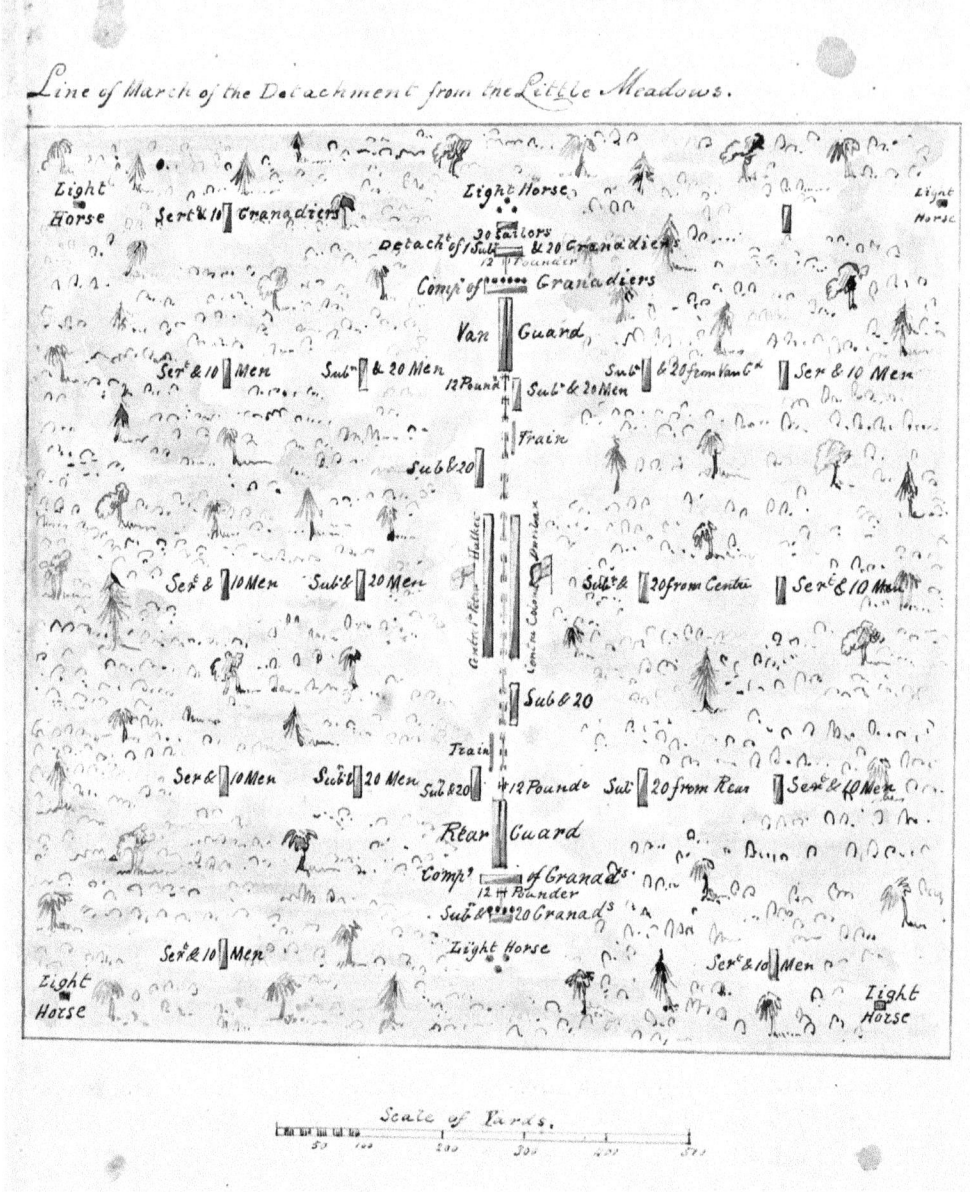

"Line of March of the Detachment from the Little Meadows." This diagram, drawn from the Journal of the campaign maintained by Captain Orme (published 1852), depicts the daily line of march adhered to by Braddock's Army. This effective line of march afforded effective security to Braddock's column on the march. Alterations performed during the final march on Fort Duquesne across the Monongahela River rendered it vulnerable (courtesy Historical Society of Pennsylvania).

Opposite: "Encampment of the Detachment from the Little Meadows." This diagram, based upon Captain Orme's Journal of the campaign (published in 1852), provides the meticulous defensive position established by Braddock's Army at the end of every day's march. The numerous picket posts around the perimeter of the encampment, and the lines of communication cut between each detachment, prevented the French and their Indian allies from launching a single attack upon Braddock's camp (courtesy Historical Society of Pennsylvania).

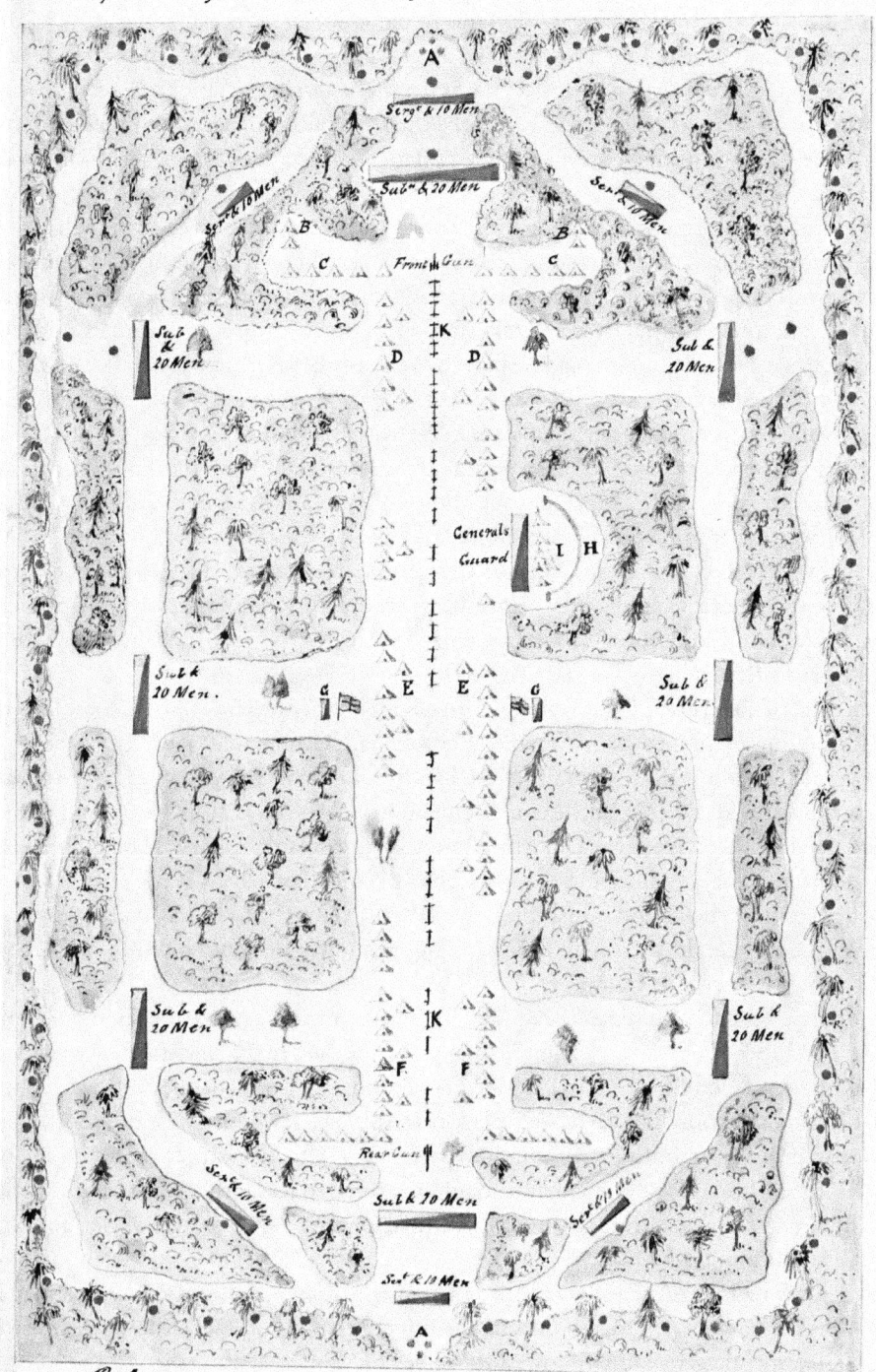

Encampment of the Detachment from the Little Meadows

References.
A. Vuidet of Light Horse.
B. Party of Sailors.
C. Compy of Granadiers.
D. Van Guard.
E. Main Body.

Scale of yards.
50 100 150

N.B. The Red Dots by the Trees are Sentrys.

References.
F. Rear Guard.
G. Color Guard.
H. One Company of Light Horse.
I. General's Tent.
K. Line of Baggage.

Arms 1 Sub 1 Serjt 1 Corpl & 30 men with Arms to parade to morrow Morning at Revalley beating Att the Head of the Line & to receive Their Orders from Mr Gordon Engineer." Another augmentation consisting of 150 men was detailed on June 3. Captain Mercer's company of Virginia carpenters marched to reinforce the road building party on June 4.[14] This was an extremely large working party, and by this date nearly half of Braddock's army was employed upon the roads.

The route that St. Clair initially surveyed and constructed went directly over the precipitous Wills Mountain (actually its southern extension now known as Haystack Mountain) immediately west of Fort Cumberland. St. Clair had simply followed the existing course of Nemacolin's Indian path, which was entirely suited for Native Americans, Indian traders, and pack horses such as Washington had employed the previous year, but was catastrophically bad for heavily laden wagons and artillery.[15] In fact, it was not even a passable route. When the road was finally completed with considerable effort by Major Chapman's large work party, the wagons began crossing Wills Mountain. It was an unmitigated disaster. Captain Orme wrote of the debacle: "The ascent and descent were almost a perpendicular rock; three wagons were entirely destroyed, which were replaced from the camp; and many more were extremely shattered."[16] Braddock personally examined the road, and determined it to be impassable by howitzers, and in desperation ordered additional men to work upon it. The army, quite simply, did not have sufficient wagons to absorb the loss of any more, and it had no spare artillery whatsoever.

At this critical juncture, Lieutenant Charles Spendelow of the royal navy accomplished a task that Braddock's engineers and St. Clair himself had been unable to perform. He discovered a detour around Wills Mountain. With barely discernable pride, on June 2 the naval midshipman attested in his journal, "Lieut Spendelow ... reported that he had found a tolerable Road which might avoid the bad Mountain that they would otherwise be obliged to pass; and accordingly it was determined to March the Army that way, it being only 2 Miles about." The next day the young midshipman personally led a party of "100 pioneers" to construct the new route. It took them four days, but on June 6 he could brag: "Completed the New Road & Return'd to Camp."[17]

Once again, St. Clair had failed Braddock in the performance of his duties as quartermaster. His inability to perform an adequate survey of the road's route, immediately adjacent to Fort Cumberland, certainly did little to impress Braddock. The general must have wondered that if St. Clair could not accurately perform a survey a few miles west of a post that he had been visiting for months, how could he perform an effective survey scores of miles into the wilderness? Braddock knew that he could ill afford to lose either wagons or time if he was to maintain the aggressive schedule that he had committed to at Alexandria, and St. Clair had just cost him both.

Spendelow's revised route followed the cut that the waters of Wills Creek had made through Wills Mountain, looping around to the northwest until a small tributary entered from the south. Spendelow's route followed the valley of this small watershed to the south, until it in turn eventually twisted to the west. At this point Spendelow's detour re-joined St. Clair's original course along Nemacolin's Path. At the junction of these small creeks the first night's encampment was established, designated "Spendelow's Camp" in honor of the officer whose accomplishments had made it possible.

Because of commercial and residential growth of the City of Cumberland, the initial portion of the historic road track has been lost. It is believed that Braddock's Road generally followed modern Green Street out of Cumberland (a Maryland historical marker attests to this). The Braddock Road roughly paralleled the route of the modern Alternate 40, the National Pike, although the Braddock Road took numerous meanders to exploit the vagaries of the terrain, and only in a few spots does it actually occupy the modern right of way. The Braddock Road passed through the narrows, turned south, and followed the valley of what is today known as "Braddock Run." Spendelow's Camp was located at the modern location of the village of Allegheny Grove. A Maryland state historic marker is the only commemoration of the camp. The marker is currently located at Vocke Road (Maryland Route 53) south of Exit 40 from Interstate 68, although it was moved by the Maryland Department of Transportation to this site which is not historically accurate. The original Spendelow's Camp would have been located in close proximity to Braddock Run in Allegheny Grove.[18]

The custom of military road construction of the time was to follow high ground, and the crests of ridges, to avoid water crossings and low, marshy ground while fostering military security and reconnaissance. When possible, civilian roads ran around hills or knolls, rather than over top of them as military roads were wont to do. However, St. Clair and his engineers shortly discovered that this was not practicable in western Maryland and Virginia, where the ridges generally coursed from north to south and the army was moving in a perpendicular direction (west for Fort Duquesne). Additionally, as the experiment on Wills Mountain had proven, simply ascending and descending these steep, rocky ridges was a near impossibility. Accordingly, throughout the campaign the army's route would instead adhere to civilian road construction principles of the time, constructing roads to generally follow the upper slopes of valleys to avoid difficult terrain as much as feasible.[19] Civilian and military roads alike would be placed as high up a slope as possible, so that crossings of the inevitable gullies and ravines would be simplified. Additionally, by the course of a road being placed high up on the natural terraces, the marshy, boggy, wet ground of the floodplains would be avoided.

The most difficult problem that St. Clair faced was traversing the numerous water courses of western Maryland and western Pennsylvania. When possible, the preferred approach would be to simply ford the creek. If banks needed to be lowered to accomplish this, a few hours' or days' work with picks, shovels and spades would be necessary. If the water was only a foot or so deep, the obstacle could simply be forded. If the water was deep enough that fording was difficult or dangerous, or the approaches passed through swampy or marshy ground, a causeway would have to be constructed. Most commonly, fascines and logs would be used. Fascines were a military engineering device that could be manufactured by soldiers with little supervision. Essentially, they were tight bundles of sticks, twigs, and branches of less than thumb size. Soldiers constructed a wooden X-shaped cradle, and then filled it with the wood. Once filled to capacity, a simple chain or rope tool would tighten the bundle, which would then be tied with vines, green saplings, or rope. So long as sufficient materials are available, fascines can be manufactured rapidly and simply, and a lack of materials in the wilderness of western Maryland and Virginia was never an issue. The fascines were tight enough that the hooves of draft animals could cross over them without particular difficulty, so long as the fascines were laid perpendicular to the line of travel (that is, lying across the road), but loose enough that water could naturally flow through them. When

Reproduction facscines at Fort Ligonier Museum (author's photograph).

fascines were not used, logs could be cut to size and laid perpendicular to construct a simple corduroyed road.

John Kennedy Lacock, a Pennsylvania native and graduate of Harvard, was a lifelong professor of history at that institution. His particular interest was the construction and route of the Braddock Road, and he devoted most of his summers and vacations from 1908 until his death in 1933 to investigating and documenting a number of historic roads across the Allegheny Mountains, particularly in western Pennsylvania.[20]

Lacock devoted numerous summers attempting to trace and personally walk the entirety of Braddock's Road from Fort Cumberland to Turtle Creek, and Lacock proved successful in identifying a significant portion of the historic road. He made an intriguing discovery regarding how St. Clair placed his fords along the course:

> It is an interesting fact that throughout the route the fording of a stream was in every case at or slightly below the mouth of a tributary. At such a place there is usually a riffle caused by the formation of a bar of sand, gravel, and mud, the crest of which offers a very practical opportunity for fording. Some of the apparent deviations of the road from what would seem to have been the natural course may have been made for the sake of avoiding a depth of water which might have rendered the streams impassable except by bridging. In other instances a circuitous route may have been the most practicable way of passing a swamp or a bog.[21]

As Lackock adroitly noted, bridging was avoided whenever feasible. However, when a simple ford or causeway was not sufficient, a bridge would have to be contemplated. This was a serious proposition, as a bridge had to be designed and its construction supervised by a professionally qualified engineering officer, and be built by trained carpenters. Bridges also required a quantity of iron fasteners, which had to be manufactured by blacksmiths serving as artificers, and transported to the site. As a final drawback, bridge construction was time consuming. Still, bridges had to be constructed when a watercourse could not be readily forded.

For those rivers too wide to be bridged, ferries consisting of bateaux, floats and/or pontoons would have to be constructed. Again, this could be a time consuming chore, and soldiers trained in their operation would have to be permanently stationed at each ferry to operate them continuously as wagons, animals and soldiers moved back and forth from the rear to the front of the advance on a daily if not hourly basis.

A serious, and naturally occurring, concern along the hastily constructed Braddock's Road was water drainage. If this was not accounted for during road design and construction, during the incessant heavy rains all too common in the Allegheny Mountains the rushing water would either (or both) erode the road, or pool against the road creating marshy or swampy conditions that could bog down wagons or artillery pieces. Inadequate or poorly considered water drainage was the greatest enemy of the expedient roads whose construction St. Clair supervised. The hooves of the animals, and the narrow iron wheels of the wagons and artillery pieces, served to absolutely slice a road to pieces if it was the least bit wet or muddy. Often in the 18th century, a wagon road would be made quite wide, one or two rods in width, and once a boggy area became impassable the road simply shifted around it. However, in the wilderness, this required a considerably wider road to be constructed through trees and rocks, requiring not only additional labor, but most crucially, additional time. A common approach was to use expeditiously placed fascines to permit water to drain through a road, while stabilizing the road. Alternately, a simple French drain could be constructed of gravel, small rocks, rock rubble and any other available miscellaneous debris. In western Maryland and Virginia there was scarcely a shortage of such materials. When circumstances permitted, adequately planned water drainage had the potential to save or considerably extend the lifetime and utility of a road, even though as George Washington would complain, it required both time and effort to construct it.

Throughout the campaign, road construction followed a generally established sequence that rarely varied. First, the engineers or St. Clair surveyed the route of the road. This frequently entailed the use of a small axe or fascine knife (a heavy, sturdy knife used to chop through branches and saplings) to clear sufficient brush that an adequate line of sight could be obtained. The selection of the road course was absolutely critical. As noted, terrain would be selected to minimize water crossings, or to simplify water crossings when necessary. Low or wet ground would be avoided, and the road detoured around large rock obstacles or boulders whenever feasible. Once the road course was chosen it was marked with distinctive slashes or cuts in the trees or rocks so that the working party following behind could identify the construction corridor. During this phase in the campaign St. Clair wrote to the Duke of Cumberland in England documenting the challenges that adequate surveying presented past Winchester:

> I am not at all surprized that we are ignorant of the Situation of this Country in England, when no one except a few Hunters knows it on the Spot; and their Knowledge extends no further than in following their Game. It is certain that the ground is not easy to be reconoitred for one may go twenty Miles without seeing before him ten yards.

Once St. Clair's working party arrived, the most crucial step in the process was for the covering party, well armed with muskets, to clear the road corridor of any hostiles that might be lurking in the vicinity, and then to establish guard posts on high ground or likely avenues of approach to protect the working party who were inevitably not armed, and focused upon their tasks at hand. Once the construction corridor was cleared and safeguarded, the working party could then begin their labors. Moving through the wilderness, the single greatest obstacle that St. Clair faced was simply clearing the trees and rocks to create a road. Using axes and saws, trees would be cut and removed. Given severe time constraints, the stumps were not grubbed out or removed, rather the trees were cut as close to the ground as possible and permitted to naturally rot over time. Because cutting a tree directly at ground level is more laborious than cutting it higher, inadequate or absent supervision would result in a plethora of stumps of varying heights plaguing the road. When possible, the road simply detoured around rocks and boulders. Only when there was no other possible recourse would rocks be excavated, for this was arduous, back breaking labor with levers (crowbars), hammers and chisels. When rocks could not be simply pried out of the way, they would have to be removed by using sharpened steel chisels which were in turn struck with smaller hand-held hammers, or with heavy hammers using one man to hold the chisel, and one man to pound the hammer. Obviously, a considerable amount of expertise and trust was necessary to employ this more effective technique. Only when even these techniques proved inadequate would the expenditure of valuable black powder (which had to be transported from the tidewater ports where it had been landed) to blast the offending material out of the way be authorized by the engineering officers. Typically, the road was not leveled, unless a severe impediment was identified that could not simply be avoided. Brush and trees would be removed to the side, used for fascines or corduroying roads, saved for firewood at the evening's campsite, or piled into heaps and burned. As can well be imagined, a tangle of brush close by the side of the road constituted natural cover and concealment for hostile scouts and Indians, and could not be permitted to remain.

All of this effort, with the exception of the occasional and spectacular black powder detonations to remove stone, had to be done by manual labor. Certainly the men of the

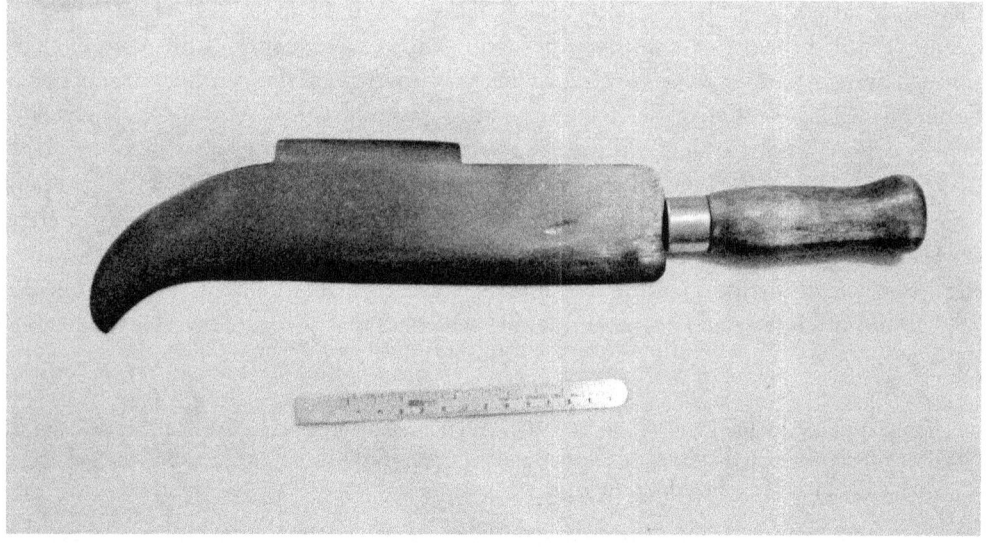

Reproduction fascine knife (author's photograph).

working party were well inured to long hours of such work. Still, it was exhausting, arduous, and dangerous. And finally, all of this labor in and of itself caused another problem, as tools were quite literally eradicated by the incessant hard use. Handles were shattered or broken every day, and carpenters would spend every moment of their spare time re-helving tools. When not working, the laborers used hand files and grind stones to continuously re-sharpen their instruments, as they were incessantly ground down and dulled through continuous rough employment. Assignment to a working party was financially lucrative, as soldiers were compensated an additional six pence a day, and also awarded additional rum or whiskey, both of which were a considerable inducement. However, a modern historian has to sincerely wonder if an extra six pence and a cup of rum really was adequate compensation for the long, demanding, and dangerous hours that road construction demanded of the soldiers.

As a result of Lieutenant Spendelow's accomplishment, and the unremitting labors of the soldiers of his working party, a decent road had eventually been completed west of Fort Cumberland. Halkett's 44th Foot finally departed Fort Cumberland on June 7. The seaman's journal reported "Sir P. Halket's Brigade Marched with 2 Field pieces and some Waggons with Provisions, 1 Midshipman & 12 Seamen were ordered to assist the train."[22]

Braddock's plan was for St. Clair to construct the new road as far forward as Little Meadows, where he was to construct a small defensive fortification and establish a forward depot for supplies. Aide-de-Camp George Washington reported upon his return to Fort Cumberland on June 7 with additional hard specie for Braddock, "I found that Sir John St. Clair had Marched with 500 Men to amend the Roads, that the main body might move with the greater ease" and "Sir John St. Clair with a body of 500 Men had Marchd to prepare the Roads, lay a deposit of Provisions at the little Meadows, and to erect some kind of defensive work there."[23]

Braddock's army travelled in three separate columns to avoid overwhelming the rudimentary road through the wilderness, with Halkett in the lead, Dunbar comprising the middle, and the heavier wagons and more cumbersome artillery train in the rear. St. Clair would be forward of these three columns with a smaller advanced detachment consisting of the engineers, the two companies of Virginia provincial carpenters, the royal navy detachment under Lieutenant Spendelow, and a working and covering party initially drawn from the two British regiments, to construct the road forward. Braddock cautioned St. Clair not to move more than seven days in advance of his main body, writing in this vein as early as May 31:

> It was very far from my intention that your Detachment shou'd be seven day march from me. I propos'd that the Road you shou'd make in seven days. I might be able to March it in three or Four at Farthest, but According to the Account I hear of it I must be much longer marching it than you as my Carriages are heavier and more Numerous which is by no means what I propos'd[.] I must therefore desire you to make no more haste than good Speed.

St. Clair replied, doubtless with bitter wisdom and grim humor already acquired through a series of hard knocks and rough experience acquired along the road, "Your Excellency need not be Apprehensive of us getting too far ahead, I wish with all my Heart that the Ground wou'd permit it."

From the Spendelow encampment, St. Clair continued to labor on the road to Little Meadows. The route generally proceeded west-northwest through western Maryland. It initially followed the north slopes of Braddock Run, and then negotiated the upper waters of Georges

Creek. The historic route followed the approximate alignment of modern US Highway Alternate 40, although Braddock's road trace was generally a mile to the south. St. Clair reached Georges Creek by June 1, where he established a second encampment at what was known as "Martin's Plantation" south of the modern town of Frostburg, Maryland. A Maryland state historic marker south of Frostburg is the only commemoration of it. The marker is currently located at Maryland Highway 36 at Highway 40, although it was again transferred to this site that is not historically correct but more visible.

At Martin's Plantation St. Clair received the second in a series of letters containing instructions from Braddock: "The General ... does not Choose to have you advance more than the seven days as he is very desirous of getting from this place as soon as possible and that his Excellency intends a junction of the whole Convoy at Georges Creek, instead of the Little Meadows." Braddock then issued instructions that St. Clair doubtless found unwarranted: "[His Excellency General Braddock] would have the Road Repair'd as much as it will Admit of."

It was at approximately this point of the march from Fort Cumberland that Washington would complain in a private letter to his brother: "I found, that instead of pushing on with vigour, without regarding a little rough Road, they were halting to Level every Mold [mole] Hill & to erect Bridges over every brook, by which means we were 4 Days getting 12 Miles."[24] Washington was still a very young and inexperienced officer. He could not perceive that there was a difference between moving packhorses over a wilderness trail as he had done in 1753 and 1754, and maneuvering a heavy train of artillery and wagons with sufficient ordnance and provisions to sustain 2,000 soldiers through a wilderness, to conduct a siege upon arrival, to establish a permanent garrison, and then to continue the campaign. In fact, just such a military road, with all the "molehills leveled" and streams bridged, was what Braddock required, and it was precisely this sort of road that St. Clair was constructing.

The surviving primary source accounts fail to pay justice to the brutally hard work that St. Clair's soldiers performed on a daily basis, for St. Clair and his working parties consistently made good progress, reaching an interim camp at the Savage River on June 2, from which St. Clair reported to Braddock: "Our present Convoy has this day got over the hill on this side George's Creek, and with as little trouble as we cou'd hope for. We have taken a great deal of pains upon the Road over it, but some Parts of it cannot be made very good in so short a time, we shall likewise Continue to make it from here to the Little Meadows, as well as the Nature of the ground, and the time will Admit off. I hope we shall get there on Wednesday Night for there is no nearer place to encamp at."

St. Clair passed through a gap in the formidable Savage Mountain, and the modern Old Beall School Road follows the trace of Braddock's Road through this pass. The Savage River camp was located just west of this gap, directly on the Savage River which could be forded in 1755, on the historic Henry Blocher farm. On June 3 St. Clair continued his progress west, establishing an interim camp at Mudlick Run by June 4. The next day St. Clair reached the Little Meadows. Captain Cholmley's batman noted the difficulties posed by this day's march: "Thursday June the 5th We marched to the little Meadows, it being 4 miles, very Bad Roads Over Rocks and Mountains almost unpassable We was ten hours in marching it."[25] The western slope of the Meadow Mountain is the Kuykendall Estate of Little Meadows, which marks the "Little Meadows" camp of Braddock, located about one mile north of modern US Highway Alternate 40 and immediately east of Maryland Highway 219.

It was during the march of June 5 that St. Clair traversed the infamous and dreaded "Shades of Death," an area marked by a towering and thick mature forest whose canopy was dense enough to preclude sunlight from striking the ground. The result was a dismal, dark and depressing location, perpetually damp because it never dried out. St. Clair constructed an excellent segment of road here, for when Braddock's main column marched through it, his aide-de-camp Orme noted that "a great part of this day's march was over a bogg which had been very well repaired by Sir John St. Clair's advanced party with infinite labour."[26]

Braddock had instructed St. Clair to remain at Little Meadows to construct a small fortification, establish storehouses to comprise an advanced depot, and then create an advanced depot. Captain Cholmley's servant was primarily focused upon culinary interests here, noting in his journal, "This day our hunter Shot us two Elks and one Bear and a Dear and Wounded two more To day we dined on Bear and Rattle Snake." He noted St. Clair's initial efforts at moving supplies forward to the Little Meadows: "Fryday June the 6th. We halted and unloaded all the Wagons and sent them to Fort Cumberland where we came from." This observant servant continued to note the continued work at the Little Meadows: "Satterday June the 7th The working party went a Clearing the Camp, and some to Build a house Over the Provisions." The work continued "Munday June the 9th. The men went to work a Clearing the wood out of the place from where they fel'd it and to lay it Round the Camp for a Brest work Against the Enemy."[27] This work continued through June 15, when the lead two companies of Halkett's regiment arrived, followed by the remainder of Braddock's main element the next day. Captain Cholmley's batman recorded work on the breastworks and storehouse at Little Meadows continuing from June 7 through June 16, suggesting the work was carried on in a somewhat dilatory manner. St. Clair had a large enough working party at his discretion that such labor should have been completed much more expeditiously.

While St. Clair waited at Little Meadows for Braddock's columns to catch up, he continued surveying and then constructing the road to the west. The next immediate obstacle was a long-established ford of the Casselman River, approximately eight miles west of the Little Meadows, known as the Little Crossings. Captain Cholmley's servant recorded that the first working party departed Little Meadows to extend the road through Little Crossings beginning on Friday, June 13.[28] The general vicinity where Braddock's Road crossed the Casselman River has remained the traditional National Road crossing. Early in the 19th century the Casselman Arch Bridge was constructed at what was allegedly the precise crossing of the Braddock Road, although this claim does not appear to be particularly well documented. Casselman Arch is today maintained as a Maryland state park.

While his three main columns were moving from Fort Cumberland, on June 11 Braddock held another Council of War at Spendelow Camp. St. Clair was not present, as he remained working forward at Little Meadows on this date.[29] Braddock's infantry and wagon columns were not making favorable progress. Lieutenant Colonel Burton of the 48th Foot, presumably with the rear column containing the majority of the artillery and wagons, complained to Braddock, "that he had been two days in marching about five miles on a better road than we were to expect afterwards, occasioned by the extreme faintness and deficiency of the horses." Accordingly, Braddock called together his officers, and requested that they reduce their baggage to a bare minimum, and then provide the horses thus spared to become pack horses. Braddock and his military family set the example, providing no less than twenty horses through a reduction in their own baggage. As a result of Braddock's initiative, one

Modern view of Little Crossings with 19th century Casselman Arch Bridge on left (author's photograph).

hundred additional pack horses were so obtained. As a recurring theme, although Braddock is often portrayed as a military martinet, obsessed with military customs and prerogatives of his rank, and unwilling to adopt to frontier conditions, his personal sacrifice at jettisoning his own baggage, and thus setting the example to encourage a concomitant reduction in his officers' baggage, presents a radically different perspective of the general.

Braddock's decision provided an additional 20,000 pounds (ten tons) of transport capability, but he realized that this would still be insufficient as the army progressed further into the Maryland and Virginia wilderness. Accordingly, he also reduced his artillery train by two six-pounders and four coehorn mortars (small 4⅖" mortars), thus freeing up an additional twenty wagons (or 40,000 pounds) of capacity. Finally, he also sent back to Fort Cumberland the British ammunition wagons which had been dispatched from England by the Board of Ordnance. These wagons were simply too large, too heavy, and required too many horses for the Allegheny Mountains' terrain, and the road that St. Clair had been able to construct across it west of Fort Cumberland. Braddock made other alterations to his transport arrangements. He reduced the load of each wagon from 2,000 pounds to 1,400 pounds, and increased the number of horses hauling the heavy artillery.[30] Thus, although Braddock had significantly decreased the load that his wagon train was carrying, by reducing the capacity in each wagon his overall logistical capacity remained the same. Still, with lighter wagons he could theoretically move more expeditiously. All of these actions are indicative of a flexible military officer, who was actively adjusting his plans based upon the actual conditions that he was encountering.

Braddock was concerned with the relatively slow progress that his army was making, considerably when viewed against the "late June" arrival at Fort Duquesne that he had committed to while standing in John Carlyle's parlor. Accordingly, Braddock called another Council of War upon his arrival at the Little Meadows. No attendance roster for this Council of War was recorded, but almost certainly John St. Clair would have been a principal member.[31] Braddock's biographer, Lee McCardell, believed that St. Clair's opinions influenced the General at this Council.[32] Braddock's Virginia Aide, Mr. George Washington, recommended to Braddock before the formal council convened:

> The Genl before they met in Council askd my prive Opin concerng the Expn; I urgd it in the warmest terms I was able, to push forward; if we even did it with a small but chosn Band with such Artillery and light Stores as were absolutely necessary; leavg the heavy Artilly Baggage &c. with the rear division of the Army, to follow by slow and easy Marches, which they might do safely while we were advanced in Front.... This was a Scheme that took & it was detd that the Genl, with 1200 Chosen Men and Officers from all the differt Corps, under the following Field Officers vizt Sir Peter Halkett who acts as Brigadier.[33]

Braddock followed the young Washington's advice (most likely because it mirrored his own inclinations), although it is probable that he received identical recommendations from St. Clair, and split his army into two wings. For the remainder of the advance upon Fort

Reproduction British ordnance department artillery wagon at Fort Ligonier Museum (author's photograph).

Duquesne Braddock would personally accompany a lead advanced column marching as lightly and as unencumbered as possible, and a heavier rear column that would follow behind with the major logistical and support elements. Colonel Sir Peter Halkett would command the advanced column, Colonel Dunbar had the challenging duty of bringing up the supplies. Sir John St. Clair accompanied Halkett's advanced column, and continued to march forward of it with the advanced guard consisting of the working and covering parties. It was noted that Halkett's advanced column contained the most reliable and experienced men of the 44th and 48th Regiments of Foot, primarily composed of those soldiers who had traveled with the regiments from Ireland, and Captain Gates' independent New York company. It was accompanied by a considerably reduced train of artillery, four 12-pounder cannon, two 6-pounder cannon, four 8" howitzers, and three Coehorn (4⅖") mortars.[34]

Unfortunately, all of St. Clair's correspondence after June 12 was lost at the Battle of the Monongahela. Apparently St. Clair left his letterbook completed prior to that date with the baggage carried forward by Dunbar's column, and all his subsequent correspondence he carried with him on the movement forward to Fort Duquesne where it would be subsequently abandoned during the engagement. Another of St. Clair's letters to Colonel Napier and thus the Duke of Cumberland, written from the Little Meadows on June 13, has also survived and is provided at the end of this chapter in its proper chronological sequence. Still, although over three weeks of St. Clair's detailed letters are regrettably absent (from June 14 to the Battle of the Monongahela on June 9), we can obtain a few glimmers regarding the deputy quartermaster general's activities past Little Meadows from other sources.

From this point forward, St. Clair essentially worked forward of Braddock's main column, surveying the road a minimum of two days ahead of Braddock, while a large working party protected by a strong covering party constructed the road. Where St. Clair's survey identified a need for particularly time consuming work such as constructing a bridge, Braddock slowed or delayed his march. This is revealed by Captain Orme, who noted in his journal:

> Therefore a detachment of one field-officer with four hundred men, and the deputy quarter master general marched on the 18th [June 18th] to cut and make the road to the little crossing of the Yoxhi Geni (Youghaghany River] taking with them two six pounders with their ammunition, three waggons of tools, and thirty five days provisions- all on carrying horses. And on the 19th the General marched with a detachment of one Colonel [Halkett], one Lieutenant Colonel, one Major, the two eldest Grenadier Companies, and five hundred rank and file. The party of Seamen and eighteen light horse, and four howitzers with fifty rounds each, and one hundred rounds of ammunition for each man, and one waggon of Indian presents; the whol number of carriages being about thirty. The Howitzers each had nine horses, the twelve pounders seven, and the waggons six. There was also thirty five days provision carried on horses.[35]

Although this method of advance continuously moved the road forward, it was still slow going. Washington complained, "We were 4 Days getg 12 Miles."[36] Given the condition of the horses at this time, a reduced rate of progress was for the best. Captain Orme recalled, "The horses grew every day fainter, and many died."[37] And constructing four new miles of road every day over the brutal, challenging terrain of the Allegheny Mountains was no mean accomplishment.

Once past Little Crossings, St. Clair was faced by another significant obstacle, that of Negro Mountain. The next encampment, known as Laurel Camp, was established just west of the Casselman River, at the eastern foot of Negro Mountain. Here, Braddock cautioned his teamsters: "When the troops come to Savage River the servants, bat men Waggoners and horse drivers must take particular care to prevent their horses from eating of laurel, as it is certain death to them."[38] The Negro Mountain was another difficult ascent, and just as terrible a descent. From this point forward, St. Clair was challenged by terrain that was either mountainous and rocky, or in low ground, swampy and muddy. When Captain Orme and his general finally reached the western bank of the Youghiogheny River on June 19 he recorded, "We halted here two days, having a road to cut in the side of a mountain, and some swamps to make passable."[39] Captain Orme could have written this for any date for the remainder of the journey forward.

Historian Winthrop Sargent has vividly described of St. Clair's incessant labor to move the army forward:

> The advanced party under St. Clair was constantly engaged in cutting the road; but its progression was necessarily slow, and the rest of the army had to encamp at their heels and march within sound of their axes. Steep, rugged hills were to be clomb [climbed], to whose summits the artillery and baggage were with cruel labor drawn; headlong declivities to be descended, down which the cannon and wagons were lowered with blocks and tackle; or deep morasses to be threaded, where the troops sunk ankle or knee-deep in the clinging mire.[40]

St. Clair himself complained of the route being "either Rocky or full of Boggs."[41] Mr. William Johnson, the deputy paymaster general with the army, remembered, "We pursued our route throgh a desolate country, uninhabited by anything but wild Indians, bears, and rattlesnakes."[42]

From Laurel Camp the route continued generally west-northwest, crossing Negro Mountain, looping around to facilitate crossings of small rivulets, and proceeding to what was known as "Bear Camp" located approximately one mile east of the modern crossroads village of Oakton, Maryland. Actually, this camp was first christened "Bare Camp" because it was located atop a barren hill. However, in short order the name was corrupted into "Bear Camp." Captain Cholmley's batman recorded of this day's march, "Fryday June the 20th. This day we Marched to a place they Call Bears Camp, it being 8 miles, very Hilly, but the Camp leavel." From here, St. Clair contemplated the next great challenge to the expedition, the crossing of the Youghiogheny River at what was traditionally known as the Great Crossings. To prepare this ford, Halkett's advanced column remained at "Bare" or "Bear Camp" for two days while the advanced guard moved forward to construct the road. On June 21 the good captain's servant wrote, "We halted and sent out a working party to Cut the Road up a large hill and the Covering party along with them to guarde them" and for the next day, "This day we halted here and the Advance party Marched to the great Crosins."[43] On June 23 Braddock's main column marched a further eight miles to the east bank of the Youghiogheny River where they established Squaw's Fort Camp.[44]

Finally, on June 24, St. Clair's advanced party completed their labors and the river could be crossed. Captain Orme reported, "we marched at five in the morning, and passed the second branch of the Yoxhio Geni, which is about one hundred yards wide, about three feet deep, with a very strong current."[45] Unfortunately, because of the impoundment of the Youghiogheny River at this location, the actual Great Crossings site is now inundated. The ford that St. Clair selected is just to the south of the modern US Highway 40 bridge, and no longer possesses any relationship to its historic appearance.

From the Great Crossings the road proceeded generally northwest, the historic trace located approximately one to two miles south of the modern US Highway 40 (National Road) in this vicinity. In this portion of the Braddock Road good road traces remain, and a substantial portion of the original roadbed continues in use.[46] Once past the Great Crossings of the Youghiogheny River the terrain is extremely difficult, featuring a succession of nearly continuous precipitous ridges that have to be ascended and then descended with considerable labor and difficulty. On June 24 the army marched approximately five miles to the east side of the Great Meadows, to a camp simply designated by Captain Orme as "the camp on the east side the Great Meadows."[47]

On the next day's journey the army passed through the Great Meadows, site of George Washington's defeat and ensuing surrender to the French the previous season. An anonymous British officer recorded his impressions:

> There are about 150 Acres of Meadow-land entirely clear. In ye middle of this spot is Fort Necessity; built by Mr. Washington last Year when he retreated from the French; it was a small foursided figure, with a trench dug round it; they had some very good Swivels which when they retreated from thence, the french entirely disabled, but left them in the ditch. There are many human bones all round ye spott; but at present every thing is entirely pulled down.[48]

Captain Cholmley's batman paid no mind to the abandoned fortifications, but he did take note of the large meadows: "June the 25th. This day we marched Eight miles and Marched a Cross the large Meadows, it being a Mile long and two hundred yards Broad."[49] The entirety of this day's march route is today preserved through the Great Meadows and Fort Necessity National Battlefield. What was known as the "Orchard Camp" was established approximately another five miles from the previous night's encampment, a total of ten miles west of the Youghiogheny River, on rising ground near good water, just across a small, unnamed tributary of Sandy Creek. According to local lore, the camp was named "because of the large numbers of wild crab apples which grow in the area."[50] This camp was also known as "Camp on the West Side of Great Meadows" or simply "Camp Beyond the Great Meadows."[51]

From Orchard Camp the army faced a difficult ascent of the Chestnut Ridge. Once that climb was completed, the army's course temporarily turned north following the crest of the broad ridge. The next night's camp was established just past the scene of Washington's skirmish where a French party under the command of Ensign Joseph Coulon de Villiers de Jumonville had been destroyed in 1754. Because of the extremely rocky situation, numerous rock outcrops, and large boulders of this encampment site it was dubbed "Rock Fort Camp." This camp would be established on what would become the grounds of the post–Civil War Pennsylvania Orphans School and modern Jumonville Methodist Camp and Retreat Center, and the camp and surviving road traces in its vicinity are well marked. A superb archaeological collection belonging to the Braddock Road Preservation Association, and interpretation of this camp and the Braddock Road, is located in a small museum on the grounds of the Jumonville Methodist Camp.

Somewhere about the time, some level of animosity manifested itself in the relationships between the senior officers of the expedition. Evidence for this, and what role St. Clair might have played in it, is somewhat murky. In his letter to Colonel Napier on June 13, St. Clair previously noted, "The Commanding General pursues his Schemes with a great deal of vigour and Vivacity."[52] However, an alternate view was forwarded by Dr. Alexander Hamilton of Maryland, who most likely treated and accordingly conversed with St. Clair following the termination of the campaign: "Sir John St. Clair, the Quarter Master General, he [Braddock] show'd no more respect to, than if he had been his Lacquai [lackey]."⁵³ Historian Stanley Pargellis concluded "there was obviously a feud in Braddock's little army, with Burton, the aides and their friends on one side, and the ranking field officers on the other." Pargellis assessed that the first faction was informally led by Aide-de-Camp Captain Robert Orme and contained Braddock's close personal friend Lieutenant Colonel Burton of the 48th Foot, his other aide-de-camp, Captain Roger Morris, and another Braddock friend, Captain Robert Dobson of the 48th Foot, while the second faction consisted of Colonel Sir Peter Halkett, Colonel Thomas Dunbar and Sir John St. Clair.⁵⁴ An anonymous British officer who participated in the campaign recorded a heated argument between Captain Orme and Colonel Dunbar in which General Braddock had to personally intervene, chiding the participants: "Gentlemen, you are hot."⁵⁵ Braddock's sole biographer, veteran newspaperman Lee McCardell, concurred with Pargellis.⁵⁶ Sir John St. Clair in his letters after the campaign made several relatively mild, indirect complaints regarding the course of the campaign, but none of these are strong enough to support Pargellis's contention. The evidence for this claim seems to be less than conclusive, and most likely whatever difference of opinion existed has been overstated.

On June 27 the army marched north and dropped down from Chestnut Ridge on a difficult descent, marching nine miles to the plantation of Christoper Gist astride the modern Gist Run.⁵⁷ Captain Orme complained that "the road still mountainous and rocky."⁵⁸ The site of Gist's Plantation is in the general vicinity of the contemporary Connellsville Airport, located in the Gist Run valley.⁵⁹ Once off Chestnut Ridge, the Braddock's Road followed the corridor of the modern Old Braddock Road and then the modern Pennsylvania Highway 119. The descent from Chestnut Ridge was a significant milestone for the campaign. With Chestnut Ridge behind St. Clair and Braddock, the last major mountain obstacle of the Allegheny Mountains had been negotiated. With discernable relief, an anonymous British officer recorded, "Here ye mountains begin to diminish & a fine pleasant rich Soil is seen."⁶⁰

While at Gist's Plantation the working and covering party laboring on the roads for John St. Clair was relieved and replaced by different, and presumably fresher, soldiers. Orders were formally placed into the regimental orderly books for two days regarding this transition:

> June 26th: 1755. The Officers and Soldrs of the Two Regts upon Detacht with Sir John St Clair to be relieved to Morrow upon the Troops Coming to their Ground.
> Camp at Guest [Gist's] house June 27th: 1755. Capt Waggoners & Capt Perrnes Compy of Rangers to parade to Morrow Morning at day break At the head of the Front Gun to March of[f to] Sir John St Clairs Camp & put themselves Under his Command. The Whole detach of the Two Regts now Under the Command of Sir John St Clair to Join their Respective Corps to Morrow morning at 5 oClock.⁶¹

With Braddock's army closing in on Fort Duquesne, it was Braddock's intention to return the Irish veterans of the 44th and 48th Foot to their regiments, while providing St. Clair's advanced detachment with the two companies of Virginia provincials commanded by Captains Thomas Waggoner and William Peyronie. From this point forward in the campaign, St. Clair's working and covering parties would be provided by these two provincial companies.

From Gist's Plantation the course ran generally north in the direction of the Youghiogheny River, which would now have to be crossed a second time. Marching on June

28, Captain Cholmley's batman recorded succinctly of this day's efforts: "We marched 7 miles, the terable Rain that ever hapnd."[62] To facilitate the river crossing, the next encampment was established at Robinson's Falls, approximately half a mile south of the river. Captain Orme inaccurately stated that this camp was located "on the east side of the Yoxhio Geni." Here the column paused for two days, while St. Clair's advanced party continued their unremitting labor on the road north of the Youghiogheny. The anonymous British Officer documented in his journal: "The 30th. Remained in Camp, the working party only advancing to clear ye road for ye next days march."[63] On June 30 Braddock's columns waded across the river at what was known as Stewart's Crossing, Captain Orme noting, "We crossed the main body of the Yoxhio Geni, which was about two hundred yards broad and about three feet deep."[64] Here, the river remains fordable, and in 2005 during the 250th anniversary of the Braddock expedition a large contingent of living historians similarly crossed the river at this exact location, again fording the obstacle.

Stewart's Crossing was described early in the 20th century as being "below the mouth of Opossum Creek, to a point on the opposite side of the river above the mount of Mounts Creek, half a mile below Connellsville."[65] Apparently, although the living historians reported that the crossing was relatively easy, there must have been some delays in bringing the wagons and artillery across the ford, for the next night's encampment was only half a mile beyond Stewart's Crossing. Although he does not clearly state such challenges, Captain Orme's journal intimates this.[66]

The movement forward resumed on July 1. The anonymous British officer remembered, "We marched early over a very long & high ridge, the Yaughyaughgany runing on each side of us. There was frequently found pieces of coal which when trid burned like pitch; this days march we went 8 or 9 Mile, ye soil good & tollerably level; our course Northerly."[67] St. Clair's working party was apparently quite busy on this date, as Captain Orme reported: "could advance no further by reason of a great swamp which required much work to make it passable."[68] This day's march followed modern Narrows Road north of Connellsville.[69]

The next day the army advanced six miles to Jacob's cabin, a local landmark, and on July 3 the army progressed another six miles to Salt Lick Creek.[70] From here, as the anonymous British officer noted, the course of travel changed from northward to northwest.[71] Surviving accounts are not distinct regarding where these two camps were located.[72] Upon arrival at this camp, on July 3 a Council of War was held by General Braddock at the Jacob's cabin camp at Salt Lick Creek (now known as Jacob's Creek). Besides Braddock, this Council of War was comprised of Colonel Sir Peter Halkett, Lieutenant Colonel Gage, Lieutenant Colonel Burton, Major Sparks and Sir John St. Clair. At this Council of War, according to Captain Orme: "Sir John St. Clair proposed to the General to halt at this Camp, and to send back all our horses to bring up Colonel Dunbar's detachment. Captain Orme devoted no less than three pages of his journal to a summation of this Council of War, suggesting that the conversation that St. Clair's recommendation generated was intense and heated. However, the sense of the Council appears to have been to not accept any further delays, and to push on for the Forks of the Ohio. Accordingly, Captain Orme concluded: "...the council were unanimously of opinion not to halt there for Colonel Dunbar, but to proceed the next morning." Given what little we know of St. Clair's ego and temperament, he could not have been pleased. This was the fourth, and final, Council of War that Braddock called during the campaign.[73]

5. "We pursued our route through a desolate country" 95

Modern view of Stewart's Crossing (author's photograph).

July 4, 1755, was the first anniversary of Washington's surrender at Fort Necessity, although it is likely that this event went unrecorded with Braddock's column. Of this day's travels, Captain Orme recorded: "We marched about six miles to Thicketty-run."[74] On the next day, St. Clair was continuing to perform one of the most important duties of a quartermaster, specifically establishing the direction of the route of march, and supervising the construction and operations of the army's routes of transportation (roads). The unknown British officer noted, "[July] the 5th. We remained in Camp except a reconnoitering party with Sir John St. Clair & an Engineer who returned ye same Evening."[75]

During the march on July 6, an unfortunate friendly fire incident occurred, during which one of the few friendly Native American fighters still accompanying Braddock's army was killed in a case of mistaken identity. He was subsequently buried with full military honors, and Braddock personally expressed his condolences (and presumably presented bereavement gifts) to his father to assuage his grief. The day's march was variously reported as between six and ten miles to the northwest, and the camp was named in honor of the deceased warrior, Monacatootha.[76]

On July 7, St. Clair again proceeded the army, departing early in the morning from Monacatootha's Camp. St. Clair's mission was to scout a ridge that was rumored to avoid the deep defile of Turtle Creek, and lead directly to Fort Duquesne. In fact, just such a ridge existed to the north of Braddock's Route, and three years later Brigadier General John Forbes would utilize this same ridge to approach the French fort. Captain Orme recalled of St. Clair's instructions:

> The General ordered Sir John St Clair to take a captain and one hundred men, with the Indians, guides and some light horse, to reconnoitre very well the country. In about two hours he returned and informed the General that he had found the ridge which led the whole way to Fort Duquesne, and avoided the narrows and Frazier's, but that some work which was to be done would make it impossible to move further that day. We therefore encamped here, and marched the next morning about eight miles to the camp near the Monogahela.[77]

However, the distance that St. Clair had to traverse has been estimated as eight to ten miles, too far to reach and return, much less perform any reconnaissance, within two hours. An anonymous British officer's journal provides a different estimate of the time that St. Clair required for his scout: "Advanced both parties. After we had marched 5 Miles along a very fine ridge, we were obliged to halt at least four hours, the Guides having lost their Way; we kept to ye right of ye Old Indian path to avoid some bad Swamps which put the Guides entirely out."[78]

Historian Paul Wallace believed that St. Clair's report that this ridge route required a considerable detour to the north convinced Braddock to instead select a more direct route to the Forks.[79] Apparently this decision was not made lightly. Captain Orme recounted that St. Clair also made an additional recommendation to Braddock upon returning from his reconnaissance:

> When we arrived ... Sir John St. Clair mentioned the sending a detachment that night to invest the fort; but being asked whether the distance was not too great to reinforce that detachment in case of an attack, and whether it would not be more advisable to make the pass of the Monongahela or the narrows ... with our whole force, and then to send the detachment from the next camp, which would be six or seven miles from the fort, Sir John immediately acquiesced, and was of opinion that would be a much more prudent measure. The guides were sent for, who described the Narrows to be a narrow pass of about two miles, with a river on the left and a very high mountain on the right, and that it would require much repair to make it passable by carriages. They said the Monongahela had two extreme good fords, which were very shallow, and the banks not steep. It was therefore resolved to pass this river the next morning.[80]

Thus, the ridge route north of Turtle Creek was abandoned.

Because so much time had been expended in St. Clair's scouting, Braddock was able to advance only about two miles this day, Captain Cholmley's servant recalled. "We marched about two Miles and Incamped Near Turtals [Turtle] Creek."[81] The camp was nicknamed "Blunder Camp" because of St. Clair's unsuccessful reconnaissance.[82] Given St. Clair's absence of a sense of humor as previously discussed, it is doubtful that he approved of this nomenclature for the evening's respite. And, to be fair to St. Clair, no blunder was actually committed on his or anybody else's part. St. Clair had successfully located the ridge that did avoid Turtle Creek and led directly to Fort Duquesne. Braddock had simply determined to employ a more expeditious route.

From Connellsville, the Braddock's Road route follows rolling terrain to the northwest through modern Westmoreland County. The route follows a number of rural roads, and has been well documented by local Westmoreland County historians.[83] This night's camp was located at the intersection of the modern Lincoln Way and Foster Street, just east of the modern City of McKeesport. A Pennsylvania state historic marker has unfortunately been adjusted from its correct location to the more visible White Oak Borough Swimming Pool.

On July 8, St. Clair was once more upon the roads early, to prepare the road from Turtle Creek to the Monogahela River. According to Captain Orme, "Sir John St. Clair was ordered to march at 4 of the clock with a detachment of two hundred and fifty men to make the roads for the artillery and baggage, which was to march with the remainder of the troops at five."[84] Captain Cholmely's batman with the main body of the 44th Foot remembered of this day's travails, "We marched 7 miles and as soon as we Came to our ground my Master went upon the Advance party to Cover the working party, it being Eight O clock before we came to our Ground." St. Clair had to perform considerable work on this segment of the road, as the army moved extremely slowly.

Even with their late arrival in camp the night before, St. Clair and Braddock's army arose the next morning while it was still dark. It was a beautiful starry night, and shortly the skies were illuminated by the first blood red rays of dawn.[85] That morning, July 9, Braddock intended to cross the Monogahela and execute his penultimate march against Fort Duquesne.

Although Burgoyne and St. Clair have often been accused by historians of moving quite slowly, entirely based upon Washington's contemporary criticism, the British brigade traversed 95 miles between Fort Cumberland and the Monongahela River in a mere five weeks, through for all practical purposes virgin wilderness, and having to construct a new road the entire way. Rather than moving slowly, this was an impressive accomplishment. Of the various British and provincial columns then operating in North America, only Braddock's was able to maintain the aggressive schedule that he had committed to in Alexandria. Braddock carried with him not only 2,000 infantry, but a complete wagon train, and of greatest significance an adequate train of artillery to besiege Fort Duquesne, and then to garrison the Forks of the Ohio once captured. To the British officers, it seemed that the most challenging and difficult portion of the campaign, simply reaching the Ohio Country from Virginia, had been accomplished. Now all that remained to do was to invest Fort Duquesne, and its fall would be preordained.

6

"Amongst the first that were wounded"
Battle of Monongahela and Retreat

For the final approach march to Fort Duquesne, Braddock divided his brigade into three detachments. The first was under the command of Lieutenant Colonel Thomas Gage of Halkett's 44th Foot, and was comprised of an advanced guard and working party. The advanced guard, directly under Gage's personal supervision, was in the van. It consisted of approximately three hundred men, the two grenadier companies from the 44th and 48th Foot that had composed the advanced guard during the entire march from Fort Cumberland, augmented by approximately one hundred "battalion" men from the 44th Foot under the command of Captain Robert Cholmley of the same regiment. Following closely behind the advanced guard was the working party, under the guidance of Sir John St. Clair. This working party consisted of approximately two hundred men of the two Virginia provincial companies of captains Wagonner and Peyronie. This working party was immediately followed by two bronze 6-pounder cannon with a small infantry escort, several tumbrels carrying engineering tools for the working party, presumably a pair of powder carts carrying additional gunpowder and projectiles for the two guns, and the engineer officers.

A tumbrel was a small Board of Ordnance cart that could be pulled by a single horse, and that was specifically intended "to carry the pioneers and miners tools." A powder cart was a small artillery cart that could be pulled by a single horse, and was provided with "an oil cloth to prevent dampness from coming to the powder."[1]

The main body of the army followed behind the advanced guard, under the direct control of Braddock, assisted by his close friend Lieutenant Colonel Burton of the 48th Foot. The main body marched in twin columns of companies, most likely in files of two, with the 44th Foot on the left (south) and the 48th Foot on the right (north) side of the road. Finally there was a modest rear guard, protecting the invaluable but vulnerable artillery, wagons and pack horses, under the direction of Colonel Sir John Halkett.

Braddock's plan, as proposed by his guides on July 7, was to cross the Monongahela River twice, and to then march directly upon Fort Duquesne. At dawn of July 9, Braddock's army was upon the east bank of the Monongahela River and the north bank of the Youghiogheny River, approximately five miles to the east of the Monongahela. A brief march of about two hours would bring the army to a good ford of the Monongahela. At this location, where the Monogahela River was joined by Turtle Creek from the north, the river turned and flowed roughly due west to join the Allegheny River at the Forks of the Ohio. Thus, after the first crossing of the river, Braddock would be on the wrong, or southern, bank of the Monongahela. This required Braddock to march north across the straight of

Reproduction tumbrel (left) and powder cart (right) at Fort Ligonier Museum (author's photograph).

the river's bend, and then cross the river a second time where a relatively good ford was located. Braddock's route was dictated by the locations of the two fords across the wide Monongahela River, and his desire to avoid crossing the steep and constrained defile of Turtle Creek. Once upon the northern bank of the river, on the same side as the French Fort Duquesne and with no further topographical obstacles in his army's way, the British columns would turn their faces west and march towards the Forks of the Ohio and glory.

As soon as Braddock's army reached Fort Duquesne, it was St. Clair's intention to erect an artillery battery across the Monongahela River on what is today known as Mount Washington, a commanding promontory within easy range of the 12-pounder cannon and 8" howitzers that the army was carrying. From here, this battery would have been able to pound Fort Duquesne into submission at will, in the event that a formal siege had to be resorted to.[2] All Braddock needed to do was to get St. Clair and his artillery the last few miles to Fort Duquesne, and the French would be all but helpless. Braddock's officers and soldiers anticipated their arrival before Fort Duquesne on the morning of July 10.

St. Clair had surveyed this approach march as far as the eastern bank of the Monongahela River the previous day, and based upon his view up and down the river, he was concerned with this double river crossing. According to St. Clair, he shared his worries with his friend, Colonel Sir Peter Halkett. Both officers then approached Braddock:

> Sir John St. Clair and Sir Peter Halkett were apprehensive that the Enimy would attack them at the passing of this river (which they really intended, but happened to come a little too late) they with some difficulty persuaded the General to form the army into battle order; in this order they marched so.[3]

This particular account, referred to as the "British B Eyewitness Account" by renowned historian Paul Kopperman, is among one of the most complete primary sources of the campaign and engagement, and as it particularly involves Sir John St. Clair it accordingly demands a comprehensive evaluation. As Kopperman has related, a partial copy of this original account resides in the Maryland Historical Society. Kopperman, working from this partial copy, determined that "his wild claims are in most cases overwhelmed by the evidence presented by more reliable reporters."[4]

However, recent scholarship located a complete copy of the original letter in the National Library of Scotland. This information was not available to Kopperman. His "British B Eyewitness Account" is actually a letter written by Scottish physician Dr. Alexander Hamilton, who practiced in Virginia and Maryland in 1755.[5] A careful perusal of this letter strongly suggests that it was in fact the account of Sir John St. Clair of the campaign, as he related it to Dr. Hamilton while receiving treatment from him at Williamsburg, Virginia, in August 1755. St. Clair and Hamilton were both Scottish, and it is natural that St. Clair would have sought care for his extremely serious wound from a well known and professionally trained Scottish physician. It is also known that the Hamilton and Halkett families enjoyed very close relationships, that St. Clair and Halkett were also friends during the campaign, and it was natural that St. Clair confided in Dr. Hamilton.

In his letter Dr. Hamilton mentioned regarding his rendition of the engagement, "It is taken from the mouths of the Principal officers, who were present at that bloody & Tragical action."[6] Dr. Hamilton's letter contained details that were only known by St. Clair, Halkett and Braddock, and since St. Clair was the only one of these three officers to have survived the Battle of the Monongahela, these details had to come from him. Thus, the "British B Eyewitness Account" provided in Kopperman, and the complete letter as written by Dr. Hamilton, is almost certainly Sir John St. Clair's account of the Battle of the Monongahela as St. Clair related it to Dr. Hamilton.

Acting upon St. Clair and Hackett's insistent recommendations, once the army reached the first ford of the Monongahela, Braddock formed his army into line of battle. He maintained this tactical configuration until the second ford was negotiated and the cabin of John Frazier, an early British settler and blacksmith whose home had been destroyed by the French the previous year, was reached. During this advance, the first crossing of the river was in good condition and required little improvement by St. Clair's working party. However, at the second ford the northern bank of the river was both high and precipitous. Gage positioned the two 6-pounders here to cover St. Clair's Virginians, who had several hours hard labor to cut a roadbed through the river channel to permit the army, and particularly its accompanying artillery and wagons, to pass.

The morning's march saw Gage's advanced guard accompanied by St. Clair leaving their camp as early as 2:00 a.m., with the main column about one hour behind. They arrived at the ford about 4:00 a.m., completed the crossing of this first ford by about 5:00 a.m., and then marched in line of battle across the bend of the Monongahela River. Braddock's brigade was in tactical formation and moving cautiously to avoid an ambush, and it required until about 6:00 a.m. to reach the second ford. Here, St. Clair's working party labored about two hours cutting down the steep northern bank of the river into a viable roadway. The crossing of this second ford by the army would have begun about 8:00 a.m.

Captain Cholmley's servant accompanied his captain, who commanded the one hundred "battalion" men of the 44th Foot with Gage's advanced party. He provided an extremely detailed account of the approach march and double crossing of the river:

> Wednesday July the 9th. The Advance Party Marched at two in the Morning, Consisting of two grannadier Companies and a hundred Pattalion. My Master Commanded the Pattalion. We marched to take Possession of a Pass Over the River which is Called Muningahele [Monongahela] River, we having all the morning two pieces of Cannon which was very troublesome to get forward before any Road was Cut, which there was not at that time for the working party b'hind at that time. A Bout Eight in the Morning we Came to the River after Marching Near Seven Miles. When we Came Close to the River some of our men saide they saw great many of the French Indiens on the Other side of the River. Some saide their was not Any but to be Shure Colonel gage who Commanded the Party Ordered the Cannon to be taken off the Carriages and to be drawn Over by the men, Ready to Ingage if accation. The men all marched Over in line of Battle with the Cannon till they Came to the Other side of the River where we had a Bank to Rise Eight yards perpendiquler that we was Oblig'd to Sloape before we Could Rise the hill. The River is betwixt two and three hundred yards Over and not much more than knee deep. After we had Rose the bank we had not a Bove two hundred yards to Frayzors Plantation where we marched and our Command went no further at that time.[7]

An anonymous British officer gave a similar account of what happened:

> Wednesday July the 9th. As we were to cross ye Monagahela that day & so near the Fort as we were drawing, it was found absolutely necessary to detach a party to secure the crossing. Accordingly Lieut: Coll: Gage with 300 Men & the Grenadier Companys with two pieces of Cannon marched before day break and before the road was cleared. At day break the whole detachment marched, tho slowly, having a great deal of trouble with ye road, after 5 Miles march we came to ye first crossing of the river which was extreamly fine having a view of at least 4 Miles up the river & ye breadth about 600 Yards; near this first crossing our advanced party scared some Indians from their holes, finding many spears & their fires newly burning. From this crossing to the other was near two miles & much the finest of the two; on the other side ye second crossing ye advanced party had halted at Fraziers house close to ye bank which was very steep & took us two hours to make it passable for ye cariages.[8]

Once past the second Monongahela ford, during the pause at the ruins of Frazier's Cabin, St. Clair approached Lieutenant Colonel Gage and asked if he should move the two cannon forward to cover the continued progress of the advanced guard. Gage deferred, telling St. Clair, "No Sir I think not, for I do not think we Shall have much Occation for them and they being troublsome to get forwards before the Roads are Cut."[9] This was both a crucial decision, and a significant tactical error, on the part of Thomas Gage, for had the two 6-pounders been at the forefront of the advanced guard the ensuing day's events could have had a radically different ending.

This day's march proceeded from the previous night's camp east of modern McKeesport, along the general route of the modern Pennsylvania Highway 48/148 on the north bank of the Youghiogheny River, to the Monongahela River. There is no modern bridge over the historic first ford site. The river must be crossed on the nearby Duquesne bridge to the modern suburb of Dravosburg. Once in Dravosburg, the approximate two-mile route of Braddock's army across the bend of the Monongahela River followed modern Pennsylvania Highway 837 through Duquesne. At the modern Kennywood Amusement Park, today's visitors will be at the general location of the second ford. A historic marker used to be within the grounds of Kennywood, but its presence has not been reported by recent observers. A Pennsylvania state historic marker does remain here. Again, there is no modern bridge at the second historic ford. To reach the north bank of the Monongahela River, the modern visitor must continue on Highway 837 approximately 1½ miles to the modern Rankin Bridge and then return to downtown Braddock. The last day's march has entirely been occupied by modern industrial, commercial and residential development, and no real historic context or integrity remains.

Braddock permitted the march to halt at Frazier's cabin while the men ate a hasty breakfast from their linen haversacks. It was his intention to march about 2½ more hours, or another five miles, until about 3:00 p.m. and then to establish a camp approximately four miles west of Fort Duquesne. Believing that the most dangerous part of the day's march, the twin crossing of the river, had been successfully completed without opposition, and desiring to expedite his march, Braddock ordered the army to resume marching in column rather than line of battle. St. Clair was alarmed at this decision:

> about a quarter of an hour after they had passed the river ... was ordered again to resume the line of march, and got into their wonted Confusion. Sir John at this appeared uneasy, and solicited the General again to form the army into the line of battle but to no purpose.[10]

Braddock was now confident and in a hurry to move forward. If he pushed the march in the early afternoon of July 9 Fort Duquesne could be reached the next morning.[11] St. Clair remained uneasy as this approach march in column continued.

> Sir John alledged to the General pointing to a valley with a small rising hill upon each side, scarce half a mile distant from the front, that the enimy would attack him there. The General asked him by what Intelligence he knew that. He replied by the same Intelligence as his Excellency had had of the Indian Sachem, which when the General made slight of, Sir John assured him, that were he his enimy and knew his numbers and disposition as well, as he was assured the french knew it, he would himself undoubtedly attack him in that very place, and he judged that the french officer or officers would in common prudence pursue the same scheme. The general still slighted this advice, and Sir John begged that he would only suffer him with an advanced party of two or three hundred men to go and reconnoitre the fort and bring him proper Intelligences, which request was refused, and soon they marched in the same confused manner, with artillery and baggage.[12]

In Gage's advanced guard, the two grenadier companies from each regiment were marching in files of two, with the 44th Foot Grenadier Company on the left (south) side, and the 48th Foot Grenadier Company on the right (north) side of the road. Engineer Gordon confirmed that the advanced guard was deployed in column of march instead of line of battle: "Gage's party march'd By files four Deep."[13] The road that the advanced guard was marching down was "about twelve foot wide."[14]

St. Clair reported of the vegetation along the road past Frazier's cabin: "This wood was so open that Carriages cou'd have been driven in any part of it[.]" Engineer Captain Gordon was able to observe the enemy attack that would shortly transpire: "I saw myself that their whole Numbers did Not exceed 300" supporting St. Clair's assertion.[15] Lieutenant William Dunbar of the 44th Foot similarly reported "the woods open."[16] Obviously, if this were the case, and carriages could be driven through the open woods, Lieutenant Colonel Gage's decision to reposition the two 6-pounder cannon was badly flawed.

However, other participants in the day's events suggest that the woods were somewhat thicker than St. Clair intimated.[17] Major William Sparks recalled, "We were attack'd in a pass surrounded with Hills of wood, that render'd our Enemys invisible to us."[18] A young naval midshipman was afterwards told by participants that "the Trees were excessive thick round them."[19] Captain Orme also remembered "the place of action was covered with large trees, and much underwood upon the left, without any opening but the road."[20]

After the column had proceeded west for half a mile in distance and one hour in time, the advanced guard collided with a French party consisting of approximately three hundred French marines, French Canadian militia and Native American warriors advancing east from Fort Duquesne.[21] The time was variously reported as between 12:30 p.m. and 2:00 p.m.[22] Most likely, the moment was recorded accurately by Mr. James Furnis, the clerk of the Board of Ordnance, a careful, meticulous man, and of perhaps greatest significance not immediately involved in the fighting. Furnis definitively stated that "the Action began about half an hour past One."[23] The French intention had been to ambush Braddock's army at the second crossing of the Monongahela, but they had been delayed by resolving wavering commitments and dissension within the French forces at Fort Duquesne, and particularly by initial hesitations among their Native American allies to participate in the attack. Thus, they had arrived too late to obstruct Braddock at the river ford. Accordingly, the result became a classic meeting engagement, where both commands were surprised by the other's presence, and where circumstances and luck dictated the tactical responses to this chance encounter.

Fortunately for the French, they had struck Gage's advanced party during the only 2½ hour period that day during which it was vulnerable. If they had attacked at any time before 12:30 p.m. Braddock's army was in line of battle, alert, ready, and with two 6-pounder cannon covering its front. Had they attacked at any time after 3:00 p.m. Braddock's army would have been safely ensconced in their effective rectangular encampment, concentrated for their defense. But for the two and half hours timeframe during which Braddock marched his army west from Frazier's cabin in column, at the same time as Gage had withdrawn the two 6-pounder cannon from their forward position covering the front of his advanced guard, the British brigade was exposed and vulnerable.

For the French, it was pure dumb luck that they engaged Braddock's men when they did. The great Prussian military theorist General Carl Von Clausewitz wrote of warfare, "There is an interplay of possibilities, probabilities, good luck and bad that weaves its way throughout the length and breadth of the tapestry. In the whole range of human activities, war most closely resembles a game of cards."[24] On the afternoon of July 9 "lady luck" chose to deal her fortunes entirely on the side of the French.

Following the initial impact, confusion reigned supreme on both sides. The two grenadier companies successfully deployed into line of battle and unleashed at least one devastating volley against the French, which inflicted numerous casualties and disordered the French moving east on the road. In this preliminary British fire the French commander Beaujeau was killed outright, and a number of the Canadian militia fled the field in panic. However, the Native Americans immediately adopted their standard tactic, extending forward to envelop both flanks, placing the British advanced guard into a double enfilading fire.[25]

St. Clair later related to Dr. Hamilton "as Sir John had conjectured, they were surprized with a very hot and heavy fire, both on their front and flanks, from a party of french, concealed in a parcell of high weeds and brush on the left hand, and a great number of Indians from the rising of the hill on every hand. This put them into a terrible confusion and the men dropt very fast."[26] Captain Cholmley's batman, serving alongside his captain at the advanced guard, remembered, "Immediately they began to Ingage us in a half Moon and

48th Regiment of Foot, Grenadier Company, 1755 (courtesy Company of Military Historians © 1961).

still Continued Surrounding us more and more. Before the whole of the Army got up we had about two thirds of our men Cut off that Ingaged at the First. My Master died before we was ten Minuits Ingaged. They Continually made us Retreat."[27] Engineer Harry Gordon with the van similarly reported, "As soon as the Enemys Indians perceiv'd our Grenadiers, they Divided themselves & Run along our right & Left flanks. The Advanc'd party Coll: Gage order'd to form, which Most of them Did with the front Rank upon the Ground & Begun firing, which they continued for several Minutes."[28]

The tactical response of Lieutenant Colonel Gage was hesitant at a moment where any delay proved fatal. St. Clair hastened forward to consult with Gage and quite early in the fight he was seriously wounded: "I was shot through the Body amongst the first that were wounded or Shot dead upon the Spot." Dr. Hamilton, well familiar with the wound as he subsequently treated it, recalled, "Sir John St. Clair had now received a desperate wound from a musket ball that went thro' his shoulder, followed with a large profusion of blood."[29] St. Clair would subsequently record that his shoulder bone and collar bone had been broken, and his arm disabled, by this wound.[30]

St. Clair's participation in the engagement was distinctly limited, but he had given orders for the two companies of his working party to form with the two 6-pounder cannon at the rear of the advanced guard, before he had gone forward to see Gage and subsequently been wounded. St. Clair's working party, caught forward in the most vicious fighting, would suffer severely. It is reasonable that some members of St. Clair's working party carried tools in their hands instead of muskets, and were doubtless struck down before they ever had the opportunity to defend themselves. Braddock's Virginia aide, George Washington, would describe the fight that they made: "The Virginians behavd like Men, and died like Soldiers, for I believe out of 3 Companys that were on the ground that Day, scarce 30 were left alive: Captn Peyrouny and all his Officers down to a Corporal were killd."[31]

While Gage vacillated, the Native American response was perfectly suited to the tactical situation in the woods, and shortly Gage's advanced guard and St. Clair's working party found themselves in a heavy and deadly enfilading fire that seemingly came from every direction. Gage failed to immediately bring up his cannon from the rear of his detachment to the front of the column so as to command the road, and simultaneously failed to reinforce his flanking parties. The result was that the flanking parties were decisively engaged by the Native Americans and driven back onto the advanced guard with heavy casualties and in confusion. Engineer Captain Harry Gordon who was with the advance guard remembered that "the Indians very soon Dispers'd Before their front & fell upon the flank partys, which only consisted of an Officer & 20 men, who were very soon Cut off."[32] An unidentified member of the royal navy or royal artillery reported, "The first Fire the Enemy gave was in front & they likewise gaul'd the Piquets in Flank, so that in few Minutes, the Greanadiers were nearly cut to pieces and drove into the greatest Confusion, as was Capt. Polson's [Peyronie's] company of Carpenters."[33] Lieutenant Colonel Gage himself said in his Official Report of the action, "This fire killed several of our men on the flanking parties, who came running in on the detachment, as did also the vanguard, which completed our confusion. The enemy took advantage of it by coming round us covered by trees, behind which they fired with such success, that most of the officers were in a short time killed or wounded, as also many of the men, and the rest gave way."[34]

Caught in a crossfire, the grenadiers of the advanced party were driven back into St. Clair's working party. Shortly, Gage's entire advanced column was thrown into bewilderment and continued to incur heavy casualties. Gage reported: "We found Sir John Sinclair's working party in the same confusion."[35] The documentary evidence is unclear regarding whether Gage deliberately ordered his advanced guard to withdraw at this point in the engagement, or if they were driven to the rear by the heavy enemy fire. Truthfully, it made little difference, for the result was the same, and just as inevitable.

The accepted response of an advanced guard to enemy action is for it to hold its ground, regardless of casualties, buying time with their blood so that the commanding officer to the rear can develop the situation, and maneuver the main body aggressively forward to defeat the enemy. This tactical guidance was clearly articulated in the standard British Army military treatise of the time, originally prepared by Lieutenant General Humphrey Bland in 1727 and regularly updated since then, *A Treatise of Military Discipline, In Which is Laid down and Explained The Duty of the Officer and Soldier, Through the several Branches of the Service.* Bland stated in two separate locations: "When the van-guard discovers any body of men, it is to halt, and the Officers is to send back immediately and acquaint the commanding Officer with it, and to know what particular commands he has for him, and when he discovers any thing further, he is to do the same, whether it relates to their numbers, quality, movement and disposition that he may take measures accordingly." Bland continued: "As soon as the advanced parties discover any [enemy] troops, they are to acquaint the commanding Officer immediately with it, and whether they appeared to be horse or foot, what number, and which way they were marching; and so from time to time, in case they discover any thing further. Upon such a disovery, the advanced parties are to halt, and to remain there till they are ordered to retire, or forced to it by the enemy; in which case, they are to retire in a regular manner, and not with precipitation, lest they should intimidate the whole by a disorderly light."[36] As an experienced officer with years of service, much of it as a staff officer under senior commanders, Gage was intimately familiar with Bland.

Instead, as Bland specifically cautioned against, on the afternoon of July 9 the British advanced guard retreated under intense pressure, being badly broken and shattered in the process. Whether or not Lieutenant Colonel Gage issued such an order, it was his command responsibility to maintain the advanced guard in their position, resisting the French and Indian attack to buy time for Braddock to advance the main body. He failed in his charge. If the attack upon the advanced guard was so intense that it had no recourse but to yield ground, such a retrograde maneuver must be performed in a disciplined, controlled manner and the retreat had to have been under Lieutenant Colonel Gage's direct supervision and command. He failed miserably in his charge. His leadership failure, and his loss of command and control over his advanced guard, sealed the fate of Braddock's army.[37]

The disordered retreat of Gage's advanced guard ran directly into the British main body under Braddock. An anonymous witness to the engagement wrote: "the advanced guard being between three fires gave way, and was rallied by their officers, gave one fire, and then retreated in the greatest confusion imaginable, till they had thrown Dunbar's regiment [i.e. Braddock's main body] into disorder."[38] Captain Horatio Gates, commanding the New York independent company with Braddock's main body, similarly observed: "the main body of the army instead of being form'd in a line of battle, on the Van Guards being attacked moved up in a line of march were flank'd on both sides by the enemy which caused an immediate confusion."[39]

Gage's advanced guard withdrew in confusion and under intense pressure at the same time as Braddock and Lieutenant Colonel Burton were attempting to deploy the main body from column into line of battle. This maneuvering was misinterpreted by various observers as a movement forward, which it technically was as the two lead companies would have been wheeling forward into line of battle perpendicular across the road. Assuming that Braddock intended to initially deploy his army into the two companies wide rectangle, the identical deployment that Braddock had used for his daily encampments throughout the march forward, the shattered remnants of the advanced guard passed through the two lead companies of the 44th and 48th Foot as they were in the midst of wheeling from column into line of battle, with the remaining length of the army's ranks remaining in column on the road as they waited for the two lead companies to wheel into line of battle so that they could take their proper distance to their respective flanks to establish the two long sides of the rectangular.[40] Nearly simultaneously, the French and Indians unleashed a devastating enfilading fire from both flanks. The result was pandemonium and chaos within the British ranks, and they never recovered against a dangerous, deadly enemy whose standard tactics of double envelopment and autonomous action were perfectly suited to the woodland environment.

John St. Clair staggered to the rear and reported to the commanding general. In St. Clair's own succinct words, "I then went up to General Braddock who was then at the head of his own guns and beg'd of him for God's sake to gain the rising ground on our Right to prevent us being totally surrounded. I know no further of this unlucky Affair to my knowledge being Afterwards insensible." St. Clair, with his eye long practiced at surveying the terrain along the army's route, had observed the promontory to the right that entirely controlled the road and thus Braddock's army.

St. Clair had been critically wounded and was losing blood rapidly and going into shock. However, he retained enough of his senses to observe the panicked and disordered condition of Braddock's army, the hopeless intermingling of the various organizations, the tactical disadvantages that the army faced, and the general confusion reigning on the battlefield. St. Clair recognized that the army was defeated this day, but not catastrophically so. He must have believed that if the army retreated immediately, they could be swiftly and successfully reorganized south of the Monogahela River, and the advance on Fort Duquesne could have been expeditiously resumed either the next day or shortly thereafter. However, St. Clair must have also realized that the window of opportunity to implement this course of action was brief, and that the deadly accurate French fire pouring into the British ranks, and particularly focused on the British officers, would shortly preclude the British from implementing any ordered maneuver.

St. Clair elaborated considerably to Dr. Hamilton, who inadvertently described the same incident twice in his narrative:

> While affairs were in this disorder Sir John St. Clair again awaited the general, and told him that he was certainly being defeated, if he did not speedily make as regular a retreat as possible, and endeavor to save the Remainder of the army; this was not regarded, and Sir John was ordered again to his post.
> ...He [St. Clair] immediately rode up to the general and Speaking to him in Italian, told him that he was defeated, and all was ruined, to whom when the general made some scornful reply, Sir John told him, that by the fresh bleeding of his wound, he did not expect to survive many minutes, and therefore could have no Interest in dissembling, or saying what he really did not think.[41]

St. Clair was presumably speaking in Italian so that he could converse with Braddock in confidence, without contributing to the deteriorating situation, or spreading further demoralization throughout adjacent observers.

His recommendations ignored by Braddock, St. Clair fainted from loss of blood and shock. Dr. Hamilton was told: "Sir John was immediately carried off by his Servant, he having tied him on the horses back, as he was thro loss of blood unable to keep the saddle."[42] St. Clair was fortunate that he was wounded quite early in the action, and his servant, who regrettably remains unidentified, was able to remove him by horseback while retreat was still possible. As he passed the ruins of Frazier's cabin unconscious in his servant's care, Sir John

St. Clair's participation in the Braddock expedition and the Battle of Monongahela came to a cessation.

St. Clair's servant evacuated him east along the road that he had so recently constructed with such arduous and heartbreaking labor. He was not the first survivor to arrive at Colonel Dunbar's encampment at the Rock Fort near Jumonville Bluff, but he was the first officer to arrive. Dunbar himself recorded, "The next Morning by five o'Clock I had the Account by a follower of the Army that was in the Engagment and in a few hours Another Arrived and About One o'Clock Sir John St. Clair who saw the whole."[43] St. Clair, badly wounded as he was, provided Dunbar with the first accurate accounts of the engagement, and confirmed that a debacle had ensued.

The distance of the road was about sixty miles from Frazier's cabin to Dunbar's encampment at the Rock Fort Camp, and assuming that St. Clair left the battlefield about 2:00 p.m. on July 9 he required 23 hours to travel this distance. Thus, St. Clair and his servant had sustained a rate of travel about 2⅔ miles per hour, which given the fact that they had risen before daybreak that day, had eaten but a single meal since then, had been through a battle in which St. Clair had been grievously wounded, and then they had to travel continuously throughout the darkness of the night, was a commendable rate. St. Clair's servant must have been a determined and resourceful man, and it is a shame that his story and identity have been lost to history.

Although how long the engagement was underway before St. Clair left the field of battle is not documented, it must have been quite early, certainly within the first thirty minutes of the fighting. On the banks of the Monongahela behind him, once Gage's advanced party fled in disarray down the road, the Main Body was thrown into such a state of confusion and under such heavy fire that Braddock was never able to regain control of the situation.

Once disordered by the advanced guard retreating through them in disarray, the soldiers who had remained in column along the road turned, per human instinct, towards the perceived threat, that is in the direction that the elite grenadiers were running from (towards the west). Instantly, the British regulars were in a confused, huddled mass facing down the road. An anonymous English officer shortly afterwards recorded: "Such was ye confusion, that ye men were sometimes 20 or 30 deep."[44] Lieutenant William Dunbar of the 44th Foot, with the Main Body, recalled that "men were seized with the same Pannic & went into as much disorder, some Part of them being 20 deep."[45] Engineer Harry Gordon similarly reported, "Nothing afterwards was to Be Seen Amongst the Men But Confusion & Panick. They form'd Altogether, the Advanced & Main Body, in Most Places from 12 to 20 Deep."[46] George Washington, in the thickest part of the battle alongside General Braddock, wrote, "Our numbers consisted of about 1300 well arm'd Men, chiefly Regulars, who were immediately struck with such a deadly Panick, that nothing but confusion and disobedience of orders prevail'd amongst them."[47]

Immediately upon the first general disorganization astride the road, the officers stepped forward to the fronts and flanks of their commands and took measures to regain control of the situation and re-organize their commands. In doing so, they made themselves unmistakable targets with their gold laced coats, distinctive red sashes and gorgets, and bright scarlet jackets. The French and Indians promptly concentrated their fires upon the prominent officers, and they suffered catastrophically heavy casualties. Captain Orme remembered "a vast number of officers were killed, by exposing themselves before the men."[48] Captain Cholmley's

Batman recorded "a great many Officers was killed."[49] Another observer similarly reported, "Most of our Officers were either wounded or killed."[50] Lieutenant William Dunbar noted that by the termination of the engagement there was "scarce an officer left to head them."[51]

Colonel Sir Peter Halkett and his youngest son James Halkett, a lieutenant also in the 44th Foot, were both killed "at the beginning." Colonel Sir Peter Halkett was killed nearly instantaneously as he came forward from the rear guard to lend his assistance, and Braddock thereafter suffered from the absence of Halkett's experienced, combat proven leadership.[52]

The site of the Battle of the Monongahela in the latter part of the 19th century and early 20th century was entirely overgrown by the modern community of Braddock, expanding to serve the steel mills that occupied the site of Frazier's cabin. The wooded hills and ravines over which so much blood was shed are today urban streets and neighborhoods, and almost no historic integrity or context remains. No sense or appreciation of the terrain or fighting can be gained by a visit. The only commemoration and interpretation of the contest is provided by the Braddock's Battlefield History Center, a recently opened and superb museum located nearly where the engagement began on that grim July day.

The British and provincials stayed and fought on ground that they had not selected for the struggle, their situation becoming increasingly more desperate, the majority of the officers killed or wounded, command and control consequently disintegrating, until Braddock himself finally fell. Once Braddock was knocked from his horse with a fatal wound, the British army's discipline disintegrated, and the army to a man fled from the field, leaving nearly half their strength behind them dead, wounded, or prisoners. George Washington himself saw the critically wounded Braddock safely removed from the field. No British soldier would view Fort Duquesne, except as a captive, for another three long years.

Once he arrived at Colonel Dunbar's camp, after rendering a report of what little of the engagement he had witnessed, St. Clair's wounds were treated and dressed for the first time. While he convalesced for several days near the site of Washington's Jumonville skirmish a year earlier, St. Clair was shocked and appalled to observe the ordnance supplies that he had transported with so much difficulty and toil from Alexandria being deliberately destroyed, under absolutely no pressure from the French and Indians whatsoever. This demolition was done under the direct instruction of General Braddock, who wanted to spare room on the wagons for the wounded men so that they could be evacuated to Fort Cumberland. Although Braddock has been severely criticized for his lack of concern for his men's welfare, it is instructive that the last command that he ever uttered upon this earth was for the care and treatment of those soldiers that had been wounded fighting alongside him at Turtle Creek.

Still, St. Clair observed with disdain of this decision, "The second day after the action, we arrived at Colo. Dunbar's Camp, and that evening and the next day were taken up in destroying some of our provisions and almost all our military stores, which I think gave the finishing stroke to all further Attempts for this year, this I believe was one of Mr. Braddock's last orders, and if it had been left to himself I think he wou'd not have give it, the intention of it was to make waggon Room for the wounded, and to facilitate our Retreat, but I think all this might have been effected with great security and the stores saved likewise, with only taking a little more time." St. Clair's rendition is confirmed by Mr. James Furnis, responsible for all Board of Ordnance property, who demanded a written order from Braddock before he would permit property that he was responsible for to be destroyed. Furnis provided a copy of this written order from Braddock to the Board of Ordnance in a letter dated October 7, 1755.[53]

St. Clair reached the Rock Fort Camp at midday on July 10, and he was shortly thereafter evacuated to Fort Cumberland. By mid–August he would return to Williamsburg. His first letter was a brief two paragraph note to Commodore Keppel written from that fort on July 18, suggesting that it was eight days before he was well enough to dictate even this succinct missive. St. Clair would not be able to compose a full length letter until July 22, two full weeks after he had received his wound. He would write as late as September 3 from Williamsburg: "I am extremely sorry that the severe wound I received, which broke my shoulder blade and Collar bone, has hinder'd me from being with General Shirley by this time. The passage of the ball is not quite shut, nor am I able to walk 100 yards nor have I the use of my Arm." Governor Dinwiddie wrote to Commodore Keppel of the Royal Navy on September 6:

> Sir John St. Clair has been here about ten days; he recovers of his wounds pretty fast. He is very silent in regard to the action at Monongahela, but I think he does not approve of the dispositions of the army, and says it was contrary to his opinion.[54]

After striving for seven long months, from January to July, to move Braddock's campaign forward to Fort Duquesne, Sir John St. Clair's participation in the final battle in front of the French fort lasted less than thirty minutes. As St. Clair was being carried in retreat back east, bandaged and drifting in and out of consciousness from loss of blood, the expedition of Major General Edward Braddock was disintegrating in the woods and underbrush along Turtle Creek. St. Clair must have been bitterly distressed and disappointed in the failure that 1755 had turned into, regardless of all his talents, his lifetime of military experience, his months of hard work, meticulous planning, exhaustive travel, and unremitting labor.

Yet although numerous other officers turned the blame for the debacle onto the soldiers who had fought and died under their command, to Sir John St. Clair's great credit he never espoused this view. He would write of the provincial troops of his working party to Virginia's Governor Dinwiddie, "I assure you I have to lay to the Courage of the Forces of your Province, during the few Minutes I was able to stay with them in the Action." And St. Clair stoutly defended the British regulars, writing, "I find since the Attack on our Convoy, that our Miscarriage was laid to the Cowardice of our British Soldiers. I hope never to live to see that Argument made good against our men unless some previous Steps were taken to make them dilatory in doing their duty." He reiterated in another piece of correspondence, "I shall only make this Observation to your Lordship once a Military Man, that something besides Cowardice must be Attributed to a Body of men, who will suffer the one half to be diminished by Fire without being pursued in their Retreat."[55]

Days later, while Edward Braddock lay dying of his wounds he murmured, "We shall know better how to deal with them another time."[56] St. Clair, suffering from his own serious wound, probably never heard these words, but he would have heartily agreed. And unlike Braddock, he would have the opportunity to deal with the French at Fort Duquesne another time, and he would find the affairs of the quartermaster's office arranged considerably differently upon that occasion.

7

Mountains, Wagons and Whiskey
Sir John St. Clair's Participation in the Forbes Campaign of 1758

Interlude

Sir John St. Clair After the Braddock Campaign

Sir John St. Clair remained near Williamsburg through October, convalescing from his wound. Aside from a handful of letters that St. Clair received and logged into his letterbook, and his conversations with Dr. Hamilton, little is documented of his activities during this timeframe. Yet, even grievously wounded, St. Clair still managed to ignite a controversy with Virginia provincial company commander Captain Adam Stephens, generating an acrimonious exchange of letters.[1] Three years later, the dispute that St. Clair created would have grave repercussions upon his career, as articulated in the subsequent chapter.

St. Clair resumed his duties as deputy quartermaster general at Albany in late October. His time in Albany was relatively short, as he had traveled south to New York City for winter quarters by November 27, 1755, according to St. Clair "on Account of the Climate."[2] He had barely settled into his office once more when he single handedly unleashed another controversy. This time, St. Clair spent the better part of November writing venomous letters complaining about the promotion of John Bradstreet to Lieutenant Colonel, "by many years a Younger Officer than I am."[3] As late as late March and early April, 1756 St. Clair was still loudly complaining about Bradstreet's elevation.[4]

St. Clair unleashed a particularly violent response to Shirley after the governor issued Lieutenant Colonel Bradstreet sole responsibility for the bateaux service in late March. His temper clearly became carried away, one correspondent reporting to Sir William Johnson, "Yesterday Sir John St. Clair was in violent wrath, in consequence of a letter from Bradstreet."[5] St. Clair concluded his letter to Shirley, "Therefore Sir [I] must entreat your Excellency will be pleased to order me home to England where probably I may be of some use to my Country." With this letter, St. Clair had finally wore out Governor Shirley's patience, and received a blistering rebuke from the majesty's senior governor in the colonies. "You have business sufficient for the employment of any one Person to discharge the duty of Quarter Master General … I cannot conclude, Sir, without letting you know that I am really extremely concern'd at the Construction you have given to this affair, when upon mature Consideration whatever inconveniences could have arisen from it might have been easily

111

Remedied, without your coming to that Resolution of desiring to be orderd home, which I can by no means comply with."[6]

Not dissuaded, St. Clair continued his bad habits, entering into yet another bitter quarrel, this time with the mayor of Albany regarding winter quarters for the two regiments from Braddock's campaign. St. Clair felt obliged to report to Major General Napier from Albany on August 30, 1756:

> I have Reason to believe a Complaint has been made against me for telling the Mayor of this Town he was an Old disafected Rascal. I own I did tell him so, and his Behavior has plainly shown he is the man I have described him.[7]

St. Clair returned to Albany for the summer campaign in late March, 1756, and he then went back to New York City for the next winter sometime in December 1756. During the campaigns of 1756 and 1757 St. Clair's activities could best be described as routine and mundane, raising several companies of provincial bateaux men for transportation on the interior waterways of New York Colony, and coordinating various logistical details. In particular, St. Clair played a role in the fiasco that became the British efforts to supply the garrison at the various forts at Oswego, which resulted in that garrison nearly starving at one point, and being captured by a French incursion in the summer of 1756.[8] A large portion of St. Clair's energies was also devoted to settling his tangled accounts from the Braddock campaign, an effort that would eventually require years to resolve.

Clearly, St. Clair was still suffering from the effects of his life endangering wound, for on December 22, 1755 he wrote at the end of one letter, "I hope this bad writing will be excused as it is the first time I have been able to use my right hand."[9] In his letters he calls frequent reference to being ill, and debilitated to various degrees. In May 1756 he submitted a memorial to Governor Shirley asking that a clerk be paid to do his writing for him, as he had little or no use of his right arm.[10] As late as November 1756 he wrote, "My arm being still Stiff I am not able to write a page in two hours nor shall I ever be able to draw."[11] In the man's defense, what must still have been a painful and crippling wound may have contributed to his irascible disposition, and tendency to engage in petty disputes with fellow officers.

Although generally St. Clair's correspondence during these two years is without particular interest, still several fascinating logistical details reveal themselves. On March 23, 1756 Colonel John Bradstreet wrote to St. Clair from Albany, articulating "the size of the Battoes are 29 feet long and 29 inches wide which measure I hope those making all the same and well built."

St. Clair also expended some efforts to obtaining an Ensigncy for "the nearest relation I have, his name is James Sinclair." However, St. Clair's most frequent activity was self promotion. St. Clair wrote to Governor Shirley of Massachusetts from New York on March 2, 1756, concluding his letter: "I am much Oblig'd to your Excellency for your mark of Friendship towards me. I have always endeavoured to move your Esteeem by Carrying on to the best of my Capacity the Branches of the Service that are trusted to my Care."[12] A portion of St. Clair's complaints were finally ameliorated in the summer of 1756, when he was promoted to lieutenant colonel in the Royal American Regiment, a position in which he never served, as he remained deputy quartermaster general.[13] It would be in this guise that he finally reentered the field on an active campaign again in the spring of 1758.

Sir John St. Clair Re-Enters the Field, 1758

On March 4, 1758 Colonel John Forbes, commanding officer of the 17th Regiment of Foot and currently serving as adjutant general for British forces in North America with duty at British headquarters in New York City, was promoted to brigadier general and given the responsibility to capture the same Fort Duquesne at the Forks of the Ohio that had stymied General Braddock three years earlier. Forbes, who had previously referred to St. Clair as "a mad sort of Fool" attempted to have British lieutenant colonel John Bradstreet appointed as his quartermaster.

Bradstreet served in the British army in Newfoundland in 1745, and in 1755 and 1756 had served as a deputy quartermaster responsible for supplying Fort Ontario at Oswego. In 1756, he had commanded a detachment of bateaux ambushed along the Mohawk River corridor, fighting off a determined Indian attack. In 1757, he had served a similar function along the Hudson River corridor, responsible for supplying the large British army at Fort William Henry and Fort Edward from the logistical depot at Albany. Thus, by early in 1758, he was one of the most experienced and proficient quartermasters in North America, and had been battle proven. He was Forbes's first choice to manage the critical logistics for his campaign.

However, Bradstreet was recognized as an expert on watercourse logistics, and was renowned at effectively organizing and managing bateaux and whaleboat convoys, a skill that would be absolutely critical for the column of the 1758 campaign that would be operating on the Hudson River/Lake George/Lake Champlain corridor. Accordingly, Bradstreet was assigned to the expedition aimed at Fort Carillon at Ticonderoga. Because Sir John St. Clair possessed direct logistical and quartermaster experience crossing the Allegheny Mountains by a land route during Braddock's previous expedition, he was again assigned to serve as the quartermaster for the Fort Duquesne expedition. This assignment was made directly against Forbes's own desires.

St. Clair wasted little time joining the expedition. St. Clair wrote his first letter to Forbes on April 5, a brief congratulatory missive. Governor Denny of Pennsylvania informed General Forbes on April 5, "I hear [Sir John St. Clair] is upon the Road" to assume his duties as quartermaster for the operation. St. Clair wrote his first official letter to Forbes from Philadelphia the next day, having arrived in Philadelphia. He followed this up with another nearly identical letter three days later, with the only new content some information on the support that Forbes could anticipate to receive from Maryland. St. Clair regularly corresponded with Forbes in early April, until Forbes arrived in Philadelphia on April 17, and they could then meet directly.[14]

Following their face-to-face meetings in the city, Forbes issued the following instructions to St. Clair, which was to guide his actions and activities to facilitate Forbes' advance. These orders provide a record of St. Clair's responsibilities as quartermaster for this campaign, as Forbes assigned them:

> As the Season of the Year advances very fast you are hereby desired to repair to the Provinces of Pennsylvania, Maryland & Virginia, where you will give such orders and directions as shall seem necessary to you, for the accelerating the Military Operations that are to be carried on during the ensuing Campaign.
>
> Giving particular attention to the state of the roads, and ordering provendor of all kinds for horses, at proper places upon those roads and taking care that the bridges be repaired and floats made

where necessary. You will inform yourself how we can be supplyed with carriages of all kinds, and in all bargains or contracts made, that there must be large pecuniary fines in case of failure. You will cause the provinces to establish posts for horses for the special communication of all intelligence. And you will constitute a small number of Guides of the most intelligent people who know the Country that can be found.

And as it will be necessary to have a certain number of waggons attending the army, you will inform yourself whether the gaining of them by contract or purchasing them will be most expedient, and you will take notice that they are to be covered with oil cloathes & numbered and that the horses & drivers are to be able and sufficient. You will hasten the working tools, bespoke by Mr. Howell at Philadelphia, as likewise to provide scythes and sickles with some grinding stones. You will remember to determine if there can be water carriage from Conegocheegee [Creek] to Will's Creek, and to get the roads betwixt them repaired, and forage laid in at different stages. And to get as much as possible laid in at Fort Cumberland [at the intersection of Wills Creek and the Potomac River, in the Colony of Virginia].

You will hasten as much as possible the new Levies, and inforce with all your arguments the forming of ranging companies, and the Governours must be required to send orders to all troops & others under their command to obey your directions, and when you learn where their troops are, you will make a disposition of the Pensilvania and Maryland forces all along those roads leading to Conigockey where a deposite for the provisions should be made, and the Virginia forces may be posted upon the road from thence up to Fort Cumberland. If there be any Cherokee Indians arrived at Winchester or [letter torn and word missing] you will give them all sorts of incouragement in going out upon scouting parties, joining some of the provincials with them, by which our convoys may be kept free of the enemys scouting parties, and our march and designs be kept secret from them. The provincial forces of Pensilvania and Maryland as soon as leveyed are to be ready to march to Conagocheegee, in order to be reviewed, and in the meantime to assist in escorting the provisions stores &c and the men unfit for that service are immediately to be taken notice of and the provinces acquainted that better men may be sent in their place.

The Virginia people are to be employed from Conegocheegee to Fort Cumberland where they must be assembled & reviewed likewise, and as the Kings provisions can not easily be furnished to either upon those routes they will be allowed four pence sterling & Rum. N.B.: Virginia has six months provisions for 1200 men at Winchester. A proper person ought to be appointed to reside with [letter torn word missing] of the provinces in order to solicit what may be wanted and to give intelligence how they proceed.

Enquiry ought to be made immediately about proper people used to deal with the Indians, in order to send two, three or more of them (unknown to one another) up to Fort Duquesne, and the Ohio, to get intelligence and to bring us a state of the enemys strength & situation.

As the magazines for provisions and for forage must be your first and principle [letter torn, word missing] there must be no time lost in getting them ready with all the diligence possible.[15]

It did not take long at all for Forbes to became extremely displeased with how Sir John St. Clair fulfilled these assigned duties.

General Forbes spent most of April and May in Philadelphia, preparing and organizing the campaign. Simultaneously, Sir John St. Clair as his quartermaster operated in eastern Pennsylvania and western Virginia, inspecting the provincials as they were raised and/or arrived, contracting for wagons, teamsters, draft and baggage horses, pack saddles, and forage, making arrangements for provisions for the soldiers, and investigating routes for the road to Fort Duquesne. All of these tasks should have been familiar to St. Clair, for they were identical to how he had spent the early phases of Braddock's expedition three springs ago.

Among the responsibilities that Forbes assigned St. Clair was that of inspecting, and mustering in, the newly raised provincial regiments. Although Braddock had made use of several companies of Virginia provincials in 1755, most of Braddock's brigade were British regulars of the 44th and 48th Regiments of Foot. However, the majority of Forbes's army consisted of provincials with three battalions of Pennsylvanians, two regiments of Virginians, companies of light horse from Virginia and Pennsylvania, an artillery detachment from Pennsylvania, a battalion from Maryland, and small battalions from Delaware (the lower counties of Pennsylvania) and North Carolina. St. Clair wrote to Forbes from Winchester in the middle of May regarding the two regiments from Virginia, and stating his commendation of the condition of these two organizations, and most particularly that of Colonel George Washington's First Virginia. Later in the summer, he performed a similar function for the two companies of North Carolina provincials.

Although St. Clair performed these relatively simple and familiar responsibilities without problems, he soon ran into difficulties with horses, wagons and forage, his old nemesis from three years earlier. Acquisition of sufficient wagons, teamsters and horses; adequate pack horses and pack saddles; and forage for the army's transportation, was absolutely critical. As Braddock and St. Clair had discovered three years earlier, contracting for wagons and horses was a continuous challenge in North America, although Forbes's decision to move through Pennsylvania where wagons and horses were easier to obtain served to ameliorate this issue. However, St. Clair appeared not to have learned his lessons very well.

His first mistake was in accepting hastily and shoddily manufactured pack saddles. When these crude saddles were first used, the fact that their manufacturers had not inserted sufficient padding in order to increase their profits became immediately apparent, when nearly every horse was rubbed sore underneath their loads. This was Sir John St. Clair's responsibility, and he had failed miserably. Forbes was livid, writing his senior General James Abercromby on July 4, "Sir John having served me as he did General Braddock, promising every thing and doing no one Individual thing in the world, except confusing what he undertakes. There are 700 Bats horses and Bats saddles provided by him, the first days tryal of the sadles gauled all the Horses into the bone, so they must every one be refitted & new stuffed."[16] Forbes echoed his complaints to Abercromby five weeks later. "I mentioned ... the Scandolous imposition of the 700 Packsaddles, which after ruining a number of Horses are now useless until I can get fresh Stuffing up from Lancaster."[17]

St. Clair's second mistake was the wagons, to which he apparently paid woefully insufficient attention. When Forbes found the initiation of his campaign delayed by an absence of wagons, he was stunned when he received a letter written in late May from George Stevenson of York County, Pennsylvania, answering Forbes's calls for additional wagons from his county: "Sir John said when here that 70 [wagons] was enough, or there might have been more."[18] St. Clair also failed to establish a rigorous chain of command of a wagon master general, and subordinate wagon masters, to regulate the wagons and supervise the poorly disciplined civilian teamsters. How St. Clair could have ignored this simple leadership principle is hard to imagine, for such a system had been implemented by Braddock's army three years earlier. The inevitable result was utter chaos in Forbes's wagon train. When Forbes arrived at Carlisle on June 6 Forbes reported to his subordinate Bouquet that he "did not find things quite so well as I could have wished particularly the Waggons, which by mixing of Brigades and employing Waggon masters promiscuously, have fallen into the greatest Confusion."[19] Again, this was St. Clair's direct responsibility, and he had failed Forbes a second time within weeks.

St. Clair's third mistake was a failure to adequately gather intelligence on the cross-Allegheny Mountain route from Carlisle, a critical responsibility of the quartermaster of any army. Apparently St. Clair blithely assumed that Forbes would follow the identical route as Braddock has followed, and chose not to perform any reconnaissance for a new route directly west from Pennsylvania. When Forbes consulted with St. Clair regarding this topic, he was astonished to discover that St. Clair was entirely clueless regarding paths across the Allegheny Mountains west of Fort Loudon. Unable to provide an accurate answer, St. Clair attempted to avoid a response, instead telling Forbes that "there were many Indian Traders that knew these roads very well." In exasperation, Forbes "stopt him short by saying if that was the case, that I was sorry he had never found them out, or never thought it worth his while to examine them. In short he knows nothing of the matter." Performing route reconnaissance and selecting the route for an army was one of the most important responsibilities of a quartermaster general, and again, St. Clair had gravely disappointed Forbes.[20]

St. Clair's fourth mistake was that he failed to adequately provide for forage, another key quartermaster responsibility. Over a century later, during the American Civil War period of the 1860s, the United States army based its logistical calculations upon each horse requiring fourteen pounds of hay and twelve pounds of grain (oats, corn or barley) daily.[21] Without at least twenty pounds of forage per day, not only could the valuable animals not move their loads, but they would shortly sicken and founder. Forbes was very displeased with St. Clair's performance as regards forage, as he complained to Bouquet on July 23:

> But not to crowd you or distress you [at Ray's Town] in Provendor, the providing of which has been most terribly neglected, the troops now shall move slowly on, and in place of allowing the Waggon Horses, and Bat horses to make their halting days of refreshment at Raestown, you will order their Waggon Masters to conduct them backwards, and you give them days of refreshment anywhere else, otherwise we might be drove to the necessity of quitting Raestown before we choose it for want of forage and provendor for our horses. I have spoke very roundly upon this subject to Sir John, who was sent up the Country from Philadelphia for no other purpose than to fix the roads and provide forage, both of which I am sorry to say it, are yet to begin.[22]

In the vernacular of the time, to speak "roundly" meant that Forbes was speaking "plain, free, without delicacy or reserve, almost rough."[23] Put simply, Forbes had chewed out St. Clair's ass.

Colonel Bouquet recognized early in the campaign that St. Clair had utterly failed to take adequate measures to locate, obtain, safeguard and stockpile forage. On July 27 he wrote Forbes:

> It was a great Neglect in the Quarter Master General [St. Clair] not to have given directions in time, to make [a] magazine of Hay at Cumberland, having Such facility, and so many Hands to employ. That omission is Sufficient to ruin the Expedition, as I hear that grass is very Scarce in Several Places upon the Road, and we Shall be unable to Support Several Places upon the Road, and we can not carry the whole at once....[24]

Forbes further complained to Governor Sharpe on September 3: "I foresee I shall be in great distress for want of waggons, the Horses of those with me being ruined as they say for want of forage, a neglect that Sir John St. Clair can never answer for, who was sent from Philadelphia by me to make magazines of Forage all along the march route and to have a great Quantity in store at Raestown."[25]

St. Clair also assumed considerably greater authority than he actually possessed as Quartermaster. By this time he held a lieutenant colonel's commission in the Royal American Regiment (60th Regiment of Foot), although when acting as quartermaster, this superseded his line commission. Under the British army system the quartermaster had no authority to command or issue orders to any troops or officers, except in the performance of his official duties, such as road building. However, St. Clair apparently did not believe this, and he wrote Forbes an airy missive on May 21 from Winchester in which he essentially stated that he was serving on this campaign as an independent commander with full authority to directly command soldiers and subordinate officers:

> I am concerned that you should put me under his Orders [Colonel Bouquet] / after giving me yours in writing / as if he were able and in a condition to relieve me from the many difficulties I labour under, nor do I apprehend it is in your Power at the distance you are, so as to remedy the Evils, I must now lay before you. I shall correspond with Colonel Bouquett and advise him of every motion I make, and you may depend on my never assuming to order anything when I am in his Neighborhood. Until I have your answers I shall act as my Honour directs me, and consult the good of the Service, in following your Intentions, but if I am totally to act under Colonel Bouquett's Orders please to let me know it, and your commands shall be punctually obey'd and with pleasure.[26]

St. Clair rapidly discovered what Forbes's pleasure was. Forbes, who possessed years of experience as a quartermaster in Flanders during the War of Austrian Succession, had a reputation of being a consummate professional intimately familiar with British army regulations, policies and procedures. These rules, of long standing and certainly fully comprehended (if not adhered to) by Sir John, were unarguable. A British military manual of the time specifically noted regarding the duties of the quartermaster general that "he has no direct authority over the troops."[27] The general reigned in his troublesome subordinate in a blistering reproach:

> I did not understand your <u>paragraph with regard to your acting under Colonel Bouquet's orders totally: when you have any orders in writing; or at your being concerned for being put under his orders</u> [highlighted in original]. You know very well that Colonel Bouquet is named by the Government the second in this command, and consequently commands ever where in my absence; And you may easily believe I shall give no orders without acquainting of him, and therefore fancy he knows the service too well, and will have better manners, than to alter any of my orders in my absence; without very good cause; and what fresh orders he gives according to circumstances in my absence, are most certainly as valid, as if they came from me. And as you very well observed that one at a distance cannot judge of circumstances, so well as those present, I have therefore always thought that affairs of moment trusted to proper officers ought in most cases to have discretionary power in the execution, according to the exigencies of things. So I cannot see that you will find any difficulty in carrying on the service, as it is scarce to be supposed that I am to order one thing, and Colonel Bouquet another, or that he present is to order one thing, and I absent to order the contrary.[28]

Once again, Forbes was speaking "roundly" to St. Clair, but it appears that his Quartermaster failed to take the lesson to heart, as his conduct continued to deteriorate.

St. Clair, during the Braddock expedition, had earned a reputation of being prickly, humorless, short-tempered, and ill-mannered. Three years later, it did not take him long to demonstrate that his argumentative personality had not improved with age. Colonel John Armstrong, an experienced commander of the 1st Battalion of the Pennsylvania provincials, reported to Bouquet:

> You desire the reasons of [his brother, Major George Armstrong] George's sending down his Commission; it was owing to Sir John St. Clair's ordering him in Arrest, on the Complaint of a Serjeant

(to whom George had given a Box on the Side of the head for Some neglect or other) without hearing George, together with sundry blustering threats out of the Usual mode of treating an Officer- this, tho' a matter which Sir John Shou'd not have trouble have troubled him Self before I had heard it, I put up with, but found that Gentleman's rash and extraordinary manner of treating the new Levys under my particular Care & Command, together with his ingrossing the detail of the Troops which belongs to every Colonel or Commander of a Core [corps], that I was Oblig'd to resent the Conduct, upon which a Quarrel ensu'd betwixt us.... I hear the General has made all this matter Square ... Sir John is now very Polite.[29]

Forbes was also concerned with St. Clair's relatively poor financial management skills, which he considered to be woefully deficient, and he felt that Sir John was both reckless and irresponsible with public funds. Forbes wrote Abercromby as early as June 15, as the campaign was just opening: "For I see my friend Sir Jno. St. Clair does not value what expence he runs into, which I must moderate as much as possible."[30]

Sir John St. Clair's sole productive contribution to the Forbes campaign was introducing Forbes and Bouquet to the beneficial properties to be derived from the liberal distribution of corn and rye whiskey to the Provincial soldiers laboring along the roads. Inexperienced with the propensities of the provincials, initially Bouquet believed that a mere twenty hogsheads (or 1,260 gallons) of whiskey would be adequate for the entire campaign. St. Clair, who had worked with these same men three years previously, knew better. He informed Forbes on June 17, "I have directed all the whiskey I can get to be brought up."[31] He further advised Bouquet on August 12 from the foot of Allegheny Mountain, "The work to be done on this Road is immence ... the work I have to do is all digging, pick Axes Crows & Shovells is what is most wanted. Likewise more Whiskey." St. Clair repeated the ominous concern that whiskey was running low with the hard-working road building parties in the mountains: "Send me as many men as you can with digging Tools, this is a most diabolical work, and whiskey must be had."[32] Forbes and Bouquet took St. Clair's hints to heart, and in short order Bouquet was requesting no less than 100 hogsheads (or over 6,000 gallons) of whiskey for the expedition.[33]

Once the campaign began moving forward in early June, Sir John spent the majority of his time as he had the Braddock campaign, working with the advance upon the Forbes Road corridor, cooperating with Forbes's engineers to identify the precise road route, and then supervising the soldiers detailed on work parties to actually construct the road. Although St. Clair was well practiced in this role, he neglected other elements of his quartermaster's duties, particularly including fiscal management and transportation issues. And Bouquet and Forbes were not pleased even with St. Clair's management of road construction, a field in which he possessed more experience than anybody else with the army. The roads were not constructed to Bouquet's satisfaction, for he reported to Forbes from Loyalhanna on September 11: "After the fine description which had been given of the roads [by Sir John St. Clair], I was greatly surprised to find them abominable. The way has been opened by cutting down trees, but that is all. No trouble has been taken to go around the hills, to remove or break the stones, and the bridges are worthless. To my great regret it is a job which must be done over."[34]

At times, St. Clair's performance as quartermaster went beyond being simply incompetent and unprofessional, and bordered upon the bizarre. In the midst of constructing the new route traversing Allegheny Mountain, the most critical piece of road construction along the entire Forbes Road, St. Clair wrote to Bouquet: "Send me turnup Seed to sow my Garden." Just how, when and where St. Clair was going to sow a garden, atop a mountain, in the midst of an active campaign, was a great question, and it rendered such a request to the second in command of the entire expedition to be absolutely ludicrous.[35] Forbes' cousin, Governor Glen, recounted from Ray's Town in early August that St. Clair had "returned yesterday from Loyal Hanning, his appearance was somewhat grotesque, a long beard, a blanket coat, and trousers to the ground. A masterly hand would have found matter sufficient for a curious caricature."[36] Definitive primary source evidence is lacking, but there is considerable reason to suggest that Sir John St. Clair was suffering from some psychological issue by the summer of 1758, beyond simply poor decision making and interpersonal relationships.

Forbes, in exasperation, reported to Abercromby on August 4, "Sir John having served me as he did General Braddock, promising every thing and doing no one Individual thing in the world, except confusing what he undertakes."[37] The final straw that would break the camel's back descended in short order.

During the Braddock campaign, St. Clair had fallen into a dispute with one of the Virginia provincial officers, Captain Adam Stephen, commander of one of the ranger companies raised in that colony. During the Forbes campaign, now lieutenant colonel Adam Stephen was a senior provincial field grade officer who served as Washington's second-in-command for the 1st Virginia Regiment. This would be Stephen's fifth consecutive year on active campaign, and previous to that he had served as a surgeon with the Royal Navy during the War of Austrian Succession. By 1758, Stephen was a well-seasoned officer with considerable military experience. But none of this mattered to St. Clair, and in short order he renewed his vehement argument with Lieutenant Colonel Stephen, a controversy that this time become so serious that it threatened the unity of the entire army.

Besides his conflict with Major George Armstrong, Sir John had earlier tangled with Colonel Burd, who was sufficiently wise, politically astute and socially prominent enough to avoid falling into any such trap. However, ominously, Colonel Burd reported to Bouquet that the bad blood between St. Clair and Stephen had been rekindled:

> I am sorry to see matters here in such state as Cannot Conduce to the good of the service. Sir John St. Clair & Colonel Stephens has no doubt inform'd you of their Affairs & disputes, something of the same Nature had like to have happen'd to me, but I have Carefully avoided every thing that should have the least tendency to Retard the service, Sir John & I form Different camps & I Command in my own to prevent disputes.[38]

St. Clair reported to Bouquet on August 27 that he had taken the momentous step of placing Lieutenant Colonel Stephen under arrest upon his own authority. Authority that, as quartermaster, he did not possess:

> Lt. Col. Stephen's behaviour is the most extraordinary, I ever saw or hear'd of, I have confined him for Mutiny in the camp, so that the Virginians are now under Major Lewis.... As I had not sufficient Strength to take him by the neck from amongst his own Men, I was obliged to let him have his own way, that I might not be the Occasion of Blood Shed. The Reason I confined that Lt. Col. was that he told me he had given out his Parole and that rather than receive any Orders from me he would break his sword in pieces.[39]

As can well be imagined, Lieutenant Colonel Stephen had a rather different view of the affair, as he had already reported to Bouquet one day earlier, in a letter that in retrospect appears considerably calmer and more reasoned. Stephen claimed St. Clair had previously insulted him by intimating:

> that the Road [that Stephen was building] was impassable which I had pretented to Open, after Waggons had pass'd it, because he had no hand in Making it. His imperious & insulting manner of communicating his Intention making no difference; giving the Same orders to ensign under my Command as my Self. His assuming the Authority of Ordering troops or Work in an arbitrary manner without regard to Detail. Upon receiving a genteel Letter from me Informing him of the officers Sentiments of that Affair- He bellow'd out Mutiny & appearing to be in the greatest dilemma roard out what shall I do; shall I fire upon them!

Stephen then described the incident that occurred late in the evening of August 24:

> I walked up to him in a respectful manner with my hat off, and Whispered softly to him that as I had sent over the Serjeant for Orders, and likewise spoke to him myself I thought that he had a mind to leave us to Order our selves; and According I had given out the Parole. Upon Which he flew in a passsion & ordered me in an imperious manner To Alter it! Alter it! I told him that He had Usd me extreamly ill in Not sending his Orders by the Serjeant in a proper maner & Seasonable hour, nor mentioned any thing of them to me when I arrived on the Road ... and as I looked upon him as Quarter Master general then I imagin'd I should not be Obliged to Alter the Parole. As to the Number of men he wanted, or where they were to be employed &c. If he would inform us of it, They should be ready at any hour; but as to any Other Orders I would not receive them from him; untill I was better informed & that the Gentlemen under my Command thought themselves so ill Used, that they complained to me of the Affair & that I could not bear his insults nor would I allow them under my Command to be emposed upon. He asked me if I bullied him in my Own Camp, I told him I was the same at any place & upon roaring out some thing about his Orders he Orderd me in Arrest.... I had no Orders & Saw no Order about obeying him other than as Quarter Master General about the Roads....

Most damning to the hard-working Virginia provincials, Stephen also noted, "His not supplying my Detachment with Rum."[40]

Bouquet's patience with St. Clair had finally reached its end, for without hesitation he immediately dispatched a stinging rebuke to St. Clair, who was in swift order acquiring quite a collection of such letters from his superior officers:

> I am afraid, My dear Sir, that there has been Some heat in this affair, and that you will have a good deal to do to justify the necessity of Such a violent measure against an officer of his Rank, Commanding a Corps. I am not So thoroughly informed of all the Rules of the English army.... But I know that in all other Services, They have no right to command as such: You do not act in this Expedition as Colonel, but at Q.M.G. only, and the Parole being the Ensign [symbol] of Command, I doubt that you can pretend to give it and if by usage you have exerted [exercised] that right it was left to you by the Commanding Officers as a Compliment and not an obligation.... His [General Forbes'] Intentions and repeated order to me are to establish and preserve a good harmony with the Provincial Troops, and you may be Sure that he will find this measure & you both precipitate and unseasonable. If you think proper to have him informed of it I think you should State the Case to him your Self.[41]

Bouquet re-instated Stephen in command on September 13, following a careful investigation into the actual circumstances that entirely vindicated Stephen, and determined the quarrelsome quartermaster to be completely at fault.[42] Sir John had exceeded his authority as quartermaster, and of greatest significance, he had openly violated the express orders and instructions of his commanding General, who was absolutely committed to maintaining a smooth working relationship between the various contingents of his army. Forbes had previously been aware of St. Clair's propensity to tangle himself up in personal arguments, and he had informed Abercromby regarding St. Clair's performance along these lines on June 27: "My friend Sir John having almost disobligded the whole Virginians with their new Governour [Francis Fauquier] in to the bargain."[43] Sir John had just worn out his welcome within the army, a feat he had accomplished in less than five months of active campaigning.

Forbes wanted nothing so much as to remove Sir John from his army. With a regiment of Highlanders, a contingent of British artillerymen, a battalion of Royal Americans commanded by international officers, Native Americans from two nations, and provincials from five colonies serving on this expedition, Forbes had absolutely no intention that internal discord would erupt within his expedition. He wanted his subordinates and officers entirely focused upon moving the army forward against the French, rather than supporting either St. Clair or Stephen.

However, Forbes well understood that formally relieving St. Clair would be a drastic step which would encompass serious repercussions including detailed letters of explanation to Abercromby, painful compilations of witness statements, and officers being withdrawn from his campaign to furnish evidence. St. Clair had his patrons who would certainly become involved with all of the resulting political implications, and inevitably a series of protracted, time-consuming and messy court martials would ensue. Thus, simply relieving St. Clair as quartermaster was not a viable option.

Forbes's solution to this conundrum was absolutely brilliant. By late August, shortages of wagons, teamsters, horses and pack horses were severely constraining the campaign. Forbes desperately needed more transportation, and the Pennsylvania farmers and counties were not forthcoming. Accordingly, Forbes ordered St. Clair to return to eastern Pennsylvania, and to obtain the wagons, horses and forage that he so desperately needed. Forbes blamed St. Clair for this situation, and he had angrily fumed to Bouquet on July 10 from Carlisle:

> The Waggons have been the plague of my life, as I found them here in the greatest degree of Confusion, nor indeed had Sir John taken the smallest pains, or had made the least inquiry how to sett those matters to rights.... Wee likewise have been and were like to be at ane Intire stop for want of provender for our horses as Sir John has only made ane Imagineary provision, for in reality wee have not one pound of Hay.[44]

Forbes doubtless figured who better to put things to right than the man that had created the mess in the first place.

Simultaneously, Forbes issued what must have been a truly hideous and horrifying threat to the inhabitants of the colony of Pennsylvania. Only a threat of this magnitude would be sufficient to break loose the recalcitrant Pennsylvanians from their valuable wagons and horses. John Forbes threatened to turn Quartermaster John St. Clair loose upon them:

> I have sent to Philadelphia the Quarter Master General, who will explain to you fully the Situation of the Army. I should be sorry to employ him in executing any Violent Measures, which the Exigency of Affairs I am in at present must Compel me to do, if I am not relieved by a Speedy Law for the Providing the Army with Carriages, or a general Concurrence of Magistrates and People of power in those Provinces in assisting, to their utmost, to provide the Same, and that with the greatest Diligence. Everything is ready for the Army's Advancing, but that I cannot do unless I have a Sufficient Quantity of Provisions in the Magazines at Ray's Town. The Road that Leads from the advanced Posts to the French Fort may be opened as fast as a Convoy can march it. Therefore my movement depends on his Majesty's Subjects entering cheerfully in carrying up the necessary Provisions.[45]

The vision of argumentative and hot-headed Sir John St. Clair being unleashed with uninhibited martial powers in their countryside was enough to break even the most vacillating Pennsylvania politicians loose from their lethargy. Shortly, large numbers of Pennsylvania wagons and horses started to reach Forbes at Ray's Town and Loyal Hannon, arriving at precisely the moment that the General required them.

Thus, Forbes removed Sir John St. Clair from his army, without having to formally relieve him of his responsibilities, ensuring that St. Clair would not turn Forbes' army against itself. At the same time, Forbes stroked St. Clair's ego by telling him that he was on an important and crucial mission, which in fact he was.[46]

St. Clair remained in eastern Pennsylvania throughout September and October, dutifully dispatching wagons and horses over the Forbes Road, and did not rejoin the army until the second week in November. He was reported to be present with Forbes for a council of War at the Loyalhanna encampment on November 11, 1758, although it appears that he did not accompany Forbes's army on its final approach to Fort Duquesne that started on November 13.[47] Forbes probably did not trust St. Clair, and relegated him to routine logistical and administrative duties at the Loyalhanna encampment.

Sir John St. Clair's participation in the Forbes Campaign had proven to be a dismal, utter and complete fiasco. Typical was Forbes's letter that he had written following his arrival at Carlisle on July 9, when he reported, "Gott here July the 4th. Where (God grant I may keep my temper) I found everything a heap of Confusion, and Sir John St. Clair at Variance with every mortall."[48] Forbes, as the commanding General of the Expedition who had achieved a great victory for Britain, had the final word: "He is a very odd Man, and I am sorry it has been my fate to have any Concerns with him."[49]

8

"Sir John's long illness"
Sir John St. Clair, 1759–1767

Still, even with the 1758 Forbes campaign brought to a successful conclusion with the capture of Fort Duquesne in late November, St. Clair remained a thorn in Forbes' side. Almost immediately upon his return over the mountains, St. Clair rushed for British army headquarters in New York, to complain of his treatment during the campaign to British commander in chief General Jefferey Amherst. Wearily and terminally ill, Forbes wrote to Amherst:

> Sir John Sinclair being gone to York will attack you upon a subject upon which I must put you on your guard. He has taken it in his Noble mind, that as Quartermaster General he commands in the army wherever he comes, outposts, Detachments &c. are instantaneously to obey his sovereign will, and even Garrisons have been threatened with pains & penaltys for not attending him immediately on his arrival and receiving the parole & report of the State of their Garrison. This fancy tho never so absurd is not to be removed by me altho I told him that I had a longer experience than him in that office of Quartermaster General, and never lookt upon myself in the active military Capacity- but only as a person employed to take care of the Police of the Army. This has not hindered him from interfering with military command & putting several field officers in arrest for not complying with his immediate orders ... I beg if he talks to you, that you will set him right as to this affair.[1]

Colonel Bouquet had not been impressed by St. Clair's performance on this campaign, for he dispatched a long missive to Forbes on February 14, 1759, when he heard about St. Clair's heading to New York:

> Sir John's maneuvers do not surprise me. I have heard reports of so many deeds of this sort, and have seen so many myself, that there is nothing so low that I do not think him capable of.... General Amherst, not knowing him, may have let himself be imposed on by his audacity, but if he wants to cast his eye on the innumerable proofs which can be given of his incapacity and of his character, I do not think he would be much inclined to risk the success of an expedition with such a quartermaster general. He brought us within a hair's breadth of disaster by a total lack of forage, and he involved the government in very great expenses by the number of horses which perished and the wagons abandoned on this occasion. But on that important point he should be condemned ... with the whole army I can certify to the fact, which is that we had no other stores of forage than those you yourself established in September, and that no one knows him ever to have taken any trouble or step about this. As to the roads, and the part he had in finding and opening them, I can furnish convincing proofs that this man's sole talent is to bring disorder and confusion wherever he is, and to delay and ruin the service as soon as he is given the slightest authority. At the time of his difference with Colonel Stephen, although I believed him in the wrong, I treated him with all possible consideration ... he has not ceased to malign me secretly ever since, wherever he found people willing to listen to him. I abhor such infamous practices, and I spoke plainly enough to him at Ligonier to reduce to silence any man who had a trace of deceny and honesty left. He has spread his underhanded defamations too long. It is time to snatch away the mask and reveal the man as he is.[2]

Unfortunately for Sir John, he was unaware that Brigadier General John Forbes and General Jeffery Amherst were close personal friends, having served together on the staff of General Ligonier throughout the War of Austrian Succession in Flanders. When Amherst was informed of Forbes's death in March 1759, he wrote to Bouquet: "This moment I receive your Letter ... with the account of the death of poor Forbes, whose loss I feel and condole with you, as I had the pleasure of being intimately acquainted with him, and I lament his death from my heart."[3]

Furthermore, Forbes had just gained a monumental victory for Great Britain, and it was widely understood that he had sacrificed his own health and life to achieve this victory for his nation. Forbes had served directly under Lord Ligonier for several years, fighting by his side, and had earned his patronage. Ligonier, in turn, enjoyed a close working relationship and the personal respect of William Pitt. Thus, in the spring of 1759, Forbes was as well politically placed as any general officer in the British empire.

The interview between Sir John St. Clair and General Jeffery Amherst at Amherst's headquarters in New York City was not recorded by either officer, and even what precise date it occurred cannot be documented. However, it can be inferred that this interview did not proceed as Sir John intended, for Amherst did not entrust Sir John St. Clair with any responsibilities during the campaigns of 1759 and 1760 against Canada, in the West Indies between 1761 and 1763, or even during the response to Pontiac's Rebellion in 1763 and 1764. For all practical purposes, Amherst relegated Sir John to reviewing financial accounts, and approving invoices for payment. Sir John St. Clair never again commanded soldiers in any capacity, or exercised his functions as quartermaster general in North America. In the vernacular, Amherst benched Sir John St. Clair.

Following his abortive interview with Amherst, St. Clair returned to Philadelphia, for all practical purposes in military exile. He spent the next four years reviewing and approving accounts.[4] There is also compelling evidence that St. Clair had failed to maintain acceptable financial records of his service as quartermaster during the Braddock and Forbes campaigns, for he was still attempting to clear his accounts as late as 1762.

St. Clair was clearly frustrated by his enforced inactivity, for he wrote Amherst on August 1761, pitifully pleading for active employment:

> I have taken the liberty of applying to Your Excellent to request being employed this Autumn, should any Troops be sent on Service; it would be presumption in me to point out to Your Excellency in what manner I should be imployed; it is equal to me provided I can serve my Country. I have had some very disagreeable Campaigns since I have been in America, occassioned by the Death of two of my Generals; but should think my self amply compensated by making one on Service this Campaign as my Constitution is so much mended that am able to undergo any fatigue.[5]

Unfortunately, St. Clair could not shake his old propensity for engaging in disputes with other officers, which had caused him so many prior difficulties. Clearing accounts in 1762, St. Clair could not resist taking a swipe at Colonel Henry Bouquet, one of the most successful and popular British officers serving in the colonies: "Colonel Bouquest woud think I did it on purpose to distress him, as our Foreigners are very susceptible of such Jealousies."[6] Such snide comments did little to move St. Clair's agenda forward.

St. Clair's opportunity finally presented itself with the onset of "Pontiac's Rebellion" in 1763. Colonel Henry Bouquet was dispatched from Philadelphia west along the Forbes Road to relieve Fort Pitt and counterattack the Native Americans in the Ohio country. With the situation desperate and limited manpower reserves available to him, Amherst was forced to call upon St. Clair to serve as the quartermaster for Bouquet's expedition. On June 25, 1763, Amherst ordered St. Clair:

> I think it Necessary you should Set out for & proceed to the Communication between Philadelphia & Fort Pitt, in Order to Forward Every thing in that Department as much as possible, on this Critical Occasion ... you will Station Yourself Either in the most Centrical place, for Forwarding the Provisions, or Hastening any Provincials that may be raised ... or proceed to Fort Pitt, as Circumstances may Require & as Colonel Bouquet may think necessary.[7]

Yet once again an all too familiar story repeated itself, as St. Clair foundered. He never moved forward past Carlisle, which he reached on July 10. He remained there less than one week, and was back in more comfortable quarters in Philadelphia by July 24, even while Bouquet's command was moving vigorously west towards active combat. St. Clair immediately claimed illness, and retired from the campaign.[8] In frustration, Amherst wrote St. Clair on September 7, 1763: "Should you Continue of the mind of going to England in the Fall for the Recovery of your Health, I shall Readily Grant your Request."[9] One suspects that Amherst considered this to be good riddance. And with this debacle, St. Clair's final active service, brief as it had been, was concluded.

By now, Sir John St. Clair had other interests. While auditing accounts in Philadelphia, he had the opportunity to discover the active social life in that city. St. Clair made the acquaintance of Miss Elizabeth "Betsey" Moland, the eldest daughter of John Moland, a wealthy Philadelphia landowner and large property owner who maintained an expansive country estate known as "Moland House" in Warwick Township, Bucks County.

St. Clair was eager to marry into a prosperous family, and the young and attractive Miss Morland was equally enthralled with becoming "Lady St. Clair." They were married on March 17, 1762, at St. Mary's Episcopal Church, Wood and West Broad streets, Burlington, New Jersey.[10] In 1763 Sir John was placed on half pay when two of the four battalions of the Royal American Regiment were disbanded, until February 1766 when he was appointed Lieutenant Colonel of the 28th Regiment of Foot, then a garrison regiment in New York City and New Jersey.[11] Most likely, this was primarily a sinecure, doubtless awarded to St. Clair in recognition of his years of prior service, effectively serving as a retirement pension.

Sir John and Lady St. Clair established their residence at Belleville, his newly purchased country estate outside of Trenton. By this time St. Clair had finally achieved financial prosperity through his marriage, as he established a second property outside of Elizabethton (modern Elizabeth), just across the Hudson River from New York City, and more accessible to British army headquarters in that city. With the exception of his short-lived participation in Pontiac's Rebellion, St. Clair spent the rest of his life in military retirement in New Jersey.

Not surprisingly, St. Clair's tendency for interpersonal conflict and controversy soon manifested itself in his new family life, as St. Clair quarreled with both his mother-in-law and sister-in-law. In February 1763 Lady St. Clair wrote a chilly note to her sister:

> I am sorry to tell you that I have been Obliged to make youse of all my prevailing arguments before I could get Sr John to send for you again, if you do not cum now you Certainly may Stay all together for him & for me tue [too], as it has cost me some disagreeable reflections already, Sr John cannot forgive you for making him send his old Chariot horse to bring you Safe home & you to refuse Cuming I think almost unpardonable. Sr John desired me just now to tell you that if you do

Top and above: The John Moland House was constructed by John Moland west of Philadelphia in the mid–1700s. It is the only surviving structure that remembers Sir John St. Clair's footsteps, as he regularly visited the future Lady St. Clair and her family here. The house has been preserved and is interpreted by the Warwick Township Historical Society (author's photographs).

not cum with he never will Concern himself more about you. Believe me to be your Affectionate Sister Eliza St Clair.[12]

Catherine Moland, John Moland's widow and Lady St. Clair's mother, frequently complained to attorney John Dickinson, the executor of John Moland's estate, regarding Sir John St. Clair's treatment of her. On July 26, 1765, she typically commented, "Sir John has ruined me...."[13]

Even living the life of a prosperous country gentry, Sir John and Lady St. Clair faced some adversity. Their first child, John St. Clair, died as an infant. A second child, also John St. Clair, was happily born. The date of his birth is not recorded, but it was sometime between 1764 and 1765. In 1764, St. Clair had to return to his native Scotland, his first and only trip back home since he arrived in Virginia early in 1755, to settle the affairs of his Scottish estate.[14] Details of this trip are lacking, but he had definitely returned to America by December 1765.[15]

By that year, St. Clair's health had begun to deteriorate markedly. Apparently his old Monongahela wound had never completely healed, and likely his journey across the North Atlantic Ocean had exacerbated the infection. St. Clair's December 1765 letter to John Dickinson was written in an extremely weak and poor hand, quite dissimilar from his previous penmanship. An authorization for payment was signed by Sir John St. Clair in June 1766 in a shaky and hesitant pen. On February 7, 1767, Lady St. Clair wrote to John Dickinson, "I have been much longer in Answering your Obliging Letter; than I ought to have been, on Account of Sir John's long illness, which still Continues."[16] St. Clair must have known that the end was drawing near, for on October 26, 1767, he drew up his will.[17] Sir John passed away at Belleville, his estate in Elizabethton, on November 26, 1767. He was buried with full military honors at St. John's Episcopal Church, Broad Street, Elizabeth, New Jersey.[18] Sadly enough, his gravesite has subsequently been lost.

In his will, St. Clair left his estate to his wife, Lady St. Clair, until his son attained legal age. His widow was enamored with her married title, and never abandoned it, remaining "Lady St. Clair" her entire life, although she subsequently remarried. One of her childhood friends from Pennsylvania, having met Sir John and his wife during their brief stay in London while he was settling the affairs of his Scottish estate, recalled, "I saw faint traces of the once agreeable Miss Moreland in Lady St. Clair, a title empty as that of a Knight's wife, seems to have obscured those qualities which alone can render wealth and grandeur truly respectable."[19] Enjoying the prestige afforded to the wife of a senior office in the British army, she married Lieutenant Colonel Dudley Templer of the 26th Regiment of Foot, following an appropriate mourning period, on March 14, 1769.[20]

Not surprisingly, the St. Clair and Moland families remained Loyalist as the American War of Independence approached. Hannah Moland, Lady St. Clair's younger sister, was married to Captain David Hay of the Royal Artillery. Her younger brother, Joseph Moland, was an ensign in the 29th Regiment of Foot, eventually rising to the rank of captain during the American Revolution. Sometime in 1776 they fled to New York City as members of the flood of Loyalists joining the British army in that city. With their estate in the hands of John Dickinson, an avowed and ardent patriot, the Moland and St. Clair families lost the entirety of their estates, including buildings, lands and investments. Lady St. Clair filed for a loyalist claim in London in 1778, eventually receiving a grant of £100 annually. Shortly thereafter her son, even though he was only 15 years old, received a commission as an ensign in the 61st Regiment of Foot (South Glouchestshire Regiment), a garrison regiment stationed at the fortress of Minorca, on October 22, 1779. He served throughout and survived the arduous siege of Minorca in 1782, and must have distinguished himself, for he became a lieutenant on November 5, 1783. Lady St. Clair died in London on October 29, 1783. Sir John St. Clair appeared on British army lists as a lieutenant through 1784, and his last surviving record was correspondence from London regarding his loyalist claim in 1790.[21] Thereafter, he vanishes, and with him the legacy of his father's devotion and service to Great Britain.

9

"A Lyon Rampant"
Conclusions

Sir John St. Clair played a prominent role as the quartermaster for two campaigns of the Seven Years War in North America, that of General Edward Braddock in 1755, and that of General John Forbes in 1758, both directed against the French Fort Duquesne at the Forks of the Ohio. Behind General Braddock himself, Sir John St. Clair was arguably the second most important officer on Braddock's expedition. The responsibilities that Sir John St. Clair faced during the Braddock campaign were immense. The success or failure of the entire campaign rested upon his shoulders. He was dispatched to Virginia by himself, the very first British soldier to be sent across the North Atlantic. Once landed in Hampton, he had to depend entirely upon provincial appointed officials and merchants, none of whom he had ever met or corresponded with before. St. Clair had no meaningful assistance, although he was certainly accompanied by a servant there is no evidence that he even brought a clerk with him from London. Upon stepping ashore in Virginia, St. Clair realized that he lacked such a rudimentary tool as a reliable map of the terrain that his campaign had to traverse. Planning assumptions for the campaign made in London proved to be so horribly erroneous that, without any assistance, Sir John St. Clair had to create an entirely new operational and logistical approach for the campaign shortly after his arrival. Once he began his labors in Virginia and Maryland, the travel required was extensive and exhaustive, particularly given the abysmal conditions of the roads in Virginia and Maryland. St. Clair travelled hundreds if not thousands of miles by horseback between January and May 1755. Although the Quartermaster Department received augmentation once Braddock's regiments arrived, St. Clair was saddled with grave and serious responsibilities and a formidable work load throughout the entire campaign. To his great credit, he performed his tasks with considerable energy, and to the best of his abilities.

The great accomplishments of Edward Braddock, John St. Clair, and the soldiers that worked underneath their leadership were entirely erased as a result of the debacle of the Battle of Monongahela. However, until approximately 1:30 p.m. on July 9, 1755, the Braddock campaign had been one of the most incredible feats in military history. Starting from absolutely nothing, Braddock and St. Clair had assembled an entire military expedition between January and April, and then moved it from Alexandria, Virginia, to the Forks of the Ohio in less than three months. This was a journey of approximately 250 miles, of which 150 miles of entirely new roads across the Allegheny Mountains had to be sited, designed, constructed and maintained through raw virgin wilderness. Braddock and St. Clair had moved an army of 2,000 men accompanied by a substantial artillery train in approximately four months once the army had landed on the shores of Virginia, and this army crossed the Monongahela River entirely ready and capable of besieging the French Fort Duquesne upon their arrival. This ranks as a remarkable achievement, for which Braddock and St. Clair should have received great commendation that remains absent over 250 years following the event.

Quartermaster Sir John St. Clair was humorless, serious, haughty, ambitious, imperious and dour. His two surviving portraits, both rendered by accomplished and skilled artists, support this assessment. In the man's defense, during the course of the Braddock campaign, St. Clair was toiling under considerable stress and tension, and carrying an extremely demanding work load. The toll this stress and tension took upon him, and the attendant physical and mental exhaustion he experienced, must have been significant if not overwhelming. His response to these travails was to become extremely short-tempered, brisk and untactful in conversation, harsh and coarse in demeanor, with an argumentative disposition. Such a response to constant stress, tension and workload is all too human. However, St. Clair's demeanor during the Braddock campaign placed him at odds with the colony of Pennsylvania including the prominent Lieutenant Governor Morris and George Croghan, whose support was critical to achieving success for British Arms. St. Clair's personality clearly degraded his relationship with Braddock and the British Officers accompanying him.

St. Clair repeatedly experienced similar personality clashes, in 1756 with the mayor of Albany, Colonel John Bradstreet and Governor William Shirley, and he was effectively removed from his position during the Forbes Campaign of 1758 because of his failure to cooperate with Pennsylvania and Virginia officers against the direct guidance of Brigadier General John Forbes. He repeatedly quarreled with his wife's family, following his marriage at the end of the Seven Years War. In defense of the man, his grievous wound at Monongahela in July 1755 never fully healed, and clearly caused him physical infirmity and pain the remainder of his life, which certainly could not have improved his temperament. Still, the repeated instances of well-documented interpersonal conflict strongly intimate that this was a dominant character trait and more importantly, a great personality flaw of the man. It prevented Sir John St. Clair from ever achieving the military prominence that he desperately yearned to claim for himself, and which his Braddock campaign activities and efforts suggested that he was fully capable of achieving.

Irascible John St. Clair might have been, but he was also indefatigable, hard working, dedicated, committed, and a highly skilled professional soldier. Sadly, all of these other traits and skills were subordinated to his fiery temperament, argumentative tendencies, disposition towards personality conflicts, and abrasive personality. Sir John St. Clair's shortcomings were so severe that, by the conclusion of the Forbes campaign of 1758, the man succeeded in writing himself out of history.

Appendix A

Sir John St. Clair's Braddock Campaign Letterbook

The transcriptions of Sir John's letterbook begins with the first letter in the letterbook, written by St. Clair shortly after his arrival in Williamsburg on January 12.

* * *

p. 1 [St. Clair to Governor Horatio Sharpe of Maryland, Williamsburg, January 12, 1755]

Williamsburgh January 12th 1755

Sir

I should have thought myself extremely happy if I had any prospects of finding you at Willis's Creek for which place I propose setting out from here by the middle of the week, in order to set people to work for Erecting Log houses for the quarters of the two Regiments which are daily expected.[1] [As] as I have no other Method to Accomplish that most Essential part of my Instructions but by Employing a number of the men at that place who are under your Command[.] I must request of you / that no Stop may be put to our Expedition / that you will send in a Letter to Willis's Creek for those then Command'g [Commanding] Officers to give me any number of men wanted for that Service there the troops may not be Oblig'd [obliged] to Continue on board their transports longer than needs must.[2]

When the Work is begun and in a fair way of going on I proposed Returning hither to receive General Braddock's Commands and to see things ready for the Reception of the sick. I am with the greatest Regard and Respect

Sir

P.S. to the other letter of ye [the] 14th It will be of the greatest Consequence to have the proportion of men from your Province in Readiness for Compleat'g [completing] the two Regiments from 500 men each to 700.

His Excellency Governour Sharp

* * *

p. 2 [St. Clair to James Pitcher, Williamsburg, January 14, 1755]

Williamsburgh Jan: 14th: 1755

Sir

I should have thought myself Extremely lucky if I had arrived in England before you embark'd [embarked] for America, that I might have had the pleasure of your Acquaintance. I take the Opportunity of Colonels Ellison and Mercer[3] / who are going northward from hence to Levy the two Regiments / of giving them a letter for you, to acquaint you of my arrival, and that I have brought with me Duplicates of the letters given to you by Sir Thomas Robenson for the Governours of the Respective Provinces in North America—

Until I got on board I thought you had proceeded directly to America, which made me not ask to see your Instructions before I left London: so that I am entirely Ignorant of your motions this Way.

131

I must entreat of you to send me the State of the independent Companys you have Muster'd, [mustered] that I may have it ready to lay before General Braddock on his Landing, as you have been formerly employ'd [employed] as Commissary you will be better able to Judge how necessary it will be that the Genl [General] should know their numbers in case they should be immediately wanted for Service.

The Governour of this Province desires his Complements to you. I beg you will likewise Accept of those of

Sir

Williamsburgh Jan: 14th: 1755

To James Pitcher

* * *

p. 3 [St. Clair to the governors of various provinces, Williamsburg, January 14, 1755]

Williamsburgh Jan: 14th: 1755

Sir—

I herewith transmit to you two letters from the Secretary of State relating to the present Circumstances of Affairs in America—

As his Majesty has appointed me Deputy Quarter Master General to the Troops to be sent forthwith to Virginia,[4] and those to be Levied in the different Provinces; I have taken the first opportunity of acquainting you with my Arrival in Virginia, in order to make the Necessary Preparations for the Reception of the two Regiments which were to Embark at Cork [Ireland] a few days after my Departure from England, and which we Reasonably may expect will arrive in a very short time.

I shall be glad to know the particulars with Regards to what may [ink smudged fingerprint, one word illegible] lately happened in the province you Command, that I may Acquaint myself accordingly, and have them ready to lay before General Braddock on his Landing that no time may be lost.

As I am an entire Stranger to the ground in America, it is highly Necessary I should get the best information of the Situation that I can, which I have no other way of doing, but requesting of you to send me any Maps or drawings you may have of your province, which I shall return to you after they are Copy'd [copied]. if you have any knowledge of the ground of our back Settlements it will be of use likewise for me to have it [.][T]hese are things that General Braddock will Expect I should have, that I may be exactly informed of the distances of places, for Regulating the marches of the Troops / if necessity Requires it / thro [through] the different provinces

Being Ordered by his Majesty to Correspond with you I am glad of the Opportunity of Expressing the Respect with which I am

Sir

Your Most Obedient & most Humble Servant

To the Governors of Provinces

* * *

p. 5 [St. Clair to General Braddock, Williamsburg, January 15, 1755]

Williamsburgh January 15th 1755

Sir

I was very sorry that I had it not in my power to receive Your Commands before I embark'd for America, least you may find any thing neglected on your arrival, I landed at Hampton on Thursday the 9th Instant and ever since been Endeavouring to Comply with my orders; I shall here send you the heade of them, and shall inform you what steps I have taken in the Execution of them—

- Ye 1st[:] To provide an hospital at Hampton or Williamsburgh for 150 Sick with the Director, 2 Surgeons, 2 Apothecarys and six Mates.
- Ye 2[:] To provide provisions against the landing of the troops and during their stay at Willis's Creek
- Ye 3[:] Bats Horses to be provided for the Officers when they arrive

Ye 4[:] To Consult with the Governour the proper measures for Erecting Loghouses or Barrics [barracks] at Wills's Creek for the following Numbers Vizt. 2 Regts. of 530 men Rank & File each one Sub Director of Ingeniers [Engineers] one Ingenier in Ordinary 12 Ingeniers Extraordinary and 2 Practitioner Ingenier a Detachm't of 110 of the Artillery

Ye 5[:] Floates or Battoes for the Transporting the Artillery and baggage from the falls of the Potomack River to Willis's Creek.

Ye 6[:] To settle with the Govr [Governor] the best and speediest manner to Compleat the two Battns [Battalions] with 200 good men each[.]⁵

The 10th I went to Williamsburgh and delivered my Dispatches to the Governour, the next day I consulted with his Excellency the properest methods of going to work on this urgent piece of service. That day one hundred horses were contracted for, 40 of which were to be delivered the first week in February and the Remaining part the first day of march, each of these horses are to bring with them 200 Weight of Flour to Willis's Creek. the 12th I went with the Governour to Hampton in order to provide an Hospital and Lodgings for the proper Officers.

Next day I went and examined the whole Town of Hampton, but Cou'd [could] not find any one place Sufficient to Contain any number of Sick, all I could get was two very small warehouses, But there are no houses in town which will be shut to us on this Occasion, So how disagreeable it may be to the Surgeons to have their sick Separate there is a Necessity for it at present. There are numbers of indigent people who will take the sick into their houses, and least bedsteads may be wanting I have given directions for 100 Cradles to be built, I have provided two Extreme good lodgings at the Town Clerk's house for two of the principal Officers of the hospital, the others may lodge with those people who keep publick houses until Mr [Mister] Graham leaves his dwelling house, which will be towards the end of February. I should not have hesitated one moment in running up a large hospital of boards, if I cou'd have got a Sufficient Quantity of Deal and Artificiers but both are wanting.

I gave directions to Mr. Hunter / who delivers you this / concerning Stock of Fire wood for the Hospitals and to get as much fresh provisions Collected together for the sick as possible, as likewise to throw on board of the Transports some sheep and fresh pork / and some Beefes if they are to be had/[.]⁶

The Governour has been extremely active and diligent on gathering together all kinds of provisions for Willis's Creek, and to make a Deposite at Fredericksbourgh, and Winchester to be near a hand. The Carriage to the Creek is immensely difficult at this season on account of the scarcity of horses, and if we had them Forages is very scarce—I am in hopes we shall be able to collect 200 horses. If we had more how are they to be fed? I Return'd to Williamsburgh the 13th in the Evening.

Jan 14th I saw some more horses bought for the use of the troops, I wrote Letters to the Governours of all the Provinces and sent my dispatches to them.

I must Sir Refer you to the Governour with regard to Compleating Sir Peter Halketts and Colo [Colonel] Dunbars Regiments, all I shall say that men will not be wanting when you please to call for them.

That part of my Instructions which Regards the building of battoes or Floats on the Potomack at the Falls of Alexa [Alexandria], I am oblig'd to delay executing as I am informed the doing of it would be in vain, for that in winter the Stream is so Raised that there is no Rowing heavy boats against the Current; and that in summer there are many flatts and shoals which will render the Navigation almost impracticable, on the whole I have acted to the best of my Capacity, and whatever difficultys may arise I shall do what I can to Surmount them.

I propose going tomorrow morning from here to Willis's Creek, I shall go one Road and Return the other my Journey will take me at least 12 days going and coming back, being 600 Miles with the same horses, I shall stay there about 6 days which I hope will be sufficient to see our Barrack in a fair way of being built.

Shou'd you arrive with the Troops before my Return, I beg you will send me your orders by an Express that I may know how to Conduct myself.

I have been talking to the Govr Concerning the properest Method of landing the troops, he is of opinion that they should proceed to Alexra in their Transports and march as soon as possible to Willis's Creek, for if they were to land at Hampton and be dispersed about the Country they would have a long march by land, that all the horses and carriages which will be wanted to carry provisions to the deposites wou'd be wanted to attend the Troops on their march to Alexria: and that if they were to march by land they have ferrys to cross which might be attended with a long delay, after examining the Situation of the Country maturely and the quick dispatch that Affairs require, I am of the above opinion with the Governour for we shall at least gain 3 Weeks by going up directly by water. I am in hopes we shall not want either Flour and Salt Pork which is what is convenient to be had in this Country [.] The Gover have wrote to New England for a Cargo of salt fish and if you are of Opinion that rice will do for us and it may be easily had. We may get some Calavances of the pea kind which I believe our people will be fond of.[7] That you may be the best Judge of the difficulty we expect of carriage from Alexria to Wills's Creek the Govr pays Twenty shillings for the Carriage of each barrell of Beef for the 400 Men that have been building a Fort at that place, and who Continue at Work[.]

I think if no unforeseen accident happens to me I shall Return hither the 2d day of February or Sooner if I can do my Business I have the honour of being with the greatest Respect,

Sir

P.S. If a large quantity of Iron is not brought out with the Artillery it will be Necessary that a dozn [dozen] of Quintel[8] should be bought at Hampton for making portable Ovens—

To General Braddock

* * *

p. 9 [St. Clair to Colonel Hunter, Williamsburg, January 15, 1755]

Williamsburgh Jan 15th 1755

Sir

I herewith inclose you a Letter for the Commanding Genl of the Forces which I beg of you to deliver to him with your own hand as soon as possible after he arrives

I make no doubt but that you will Exert yourself in doing what you can for fresh provisions I desire you may buy up what Calavances you can get

I must beg of you to have an Eye to what is doing about the hospital and the making of the Cradles and erecting stoves with a provision of Wood, I am going for Willis's Creek tomorrow morning, and expect to Return the 2d of Feby [February] [.]

I am with great Sincerity

Sir

To Colonel Hunter

* * *

p. 10 [St. Clair to Lord Fairfax, Wills Creek, January 26, 1755]

From the Fort at Willis's Creek Jan. 26th 1755

My Lord

As your Lordship was so good as to promise me that every thing in your power should be done for the goal of the Expedition, it is My duty to Acquaint you on what State I found the Roads in my way hither.

The float on the Shanondoe [Shenandoah River] is now amaking by a Carpenter sent by Your Lop he promised me to have it finished by the 4th Feb. but as I gave him two guineas to employ more hands to work under him I imagine it will be finished by the end of the month. The Roads near the River are very narrow over the Mountains which makes it impossible for Waggons to pass one another and at present a number of Trees lying a cross the Roads[.] there are many small runns of water which requires Trees to be laid over them for the Conveniency of Foot passengers.

The Road from Fort Edwards to the North River is very bad, that River has neither canoes nor floats on it tho' the Ford is deep and at bottom very Stony, the Ford of the Little Capeapon is not near so bad, there is neither canoes nor float over it[.] I shou'd have been glad to have found the new Road marked out, which was only done at the further end 5 miles from Jos. Pearceall's[.]

Your Lords Carpenter is to go to the south branch by the first of the month to build a float over the River which is greatly wanted, it will be likewise good to have a float made over Patterson's Creek in the flow where the new Road that is to be cut is to cross it, I should likewise have been glad to have seen that Road; but no part of it was mark'd. I could pretty well guess where it joined to the Road in the Valley.

When I was two miles on this side of the South branch I had a good view of the ground that runs along the Savage River it seems good for a carriage Road and might be of great Service if your Ldp would order it to be marked out as I shall soon be obliged to visit all that ground.

I must Recommend it to your Lop to give directions that all the new Roads which are to be Cut may be made at least 30 or 35 feet wide and carries along the Ridges of the Mountains as much as possible to avoid the valleys Shou'd the expence of this be too great for the Countys to bear which are only in their Infancy, I shall do my duty to Recommend it to the Governour to have a General Charge made of it[.]

To Lord Fairfax

* * *

p. 12 [Not dated, no address, memorandum for Commissary Walker]

Memorandum for Mr. Commissary Walker

To buy up in Pennnsylvania two hundred thousand weight of flour[9] to be delivd [delivered] At Conogocheag[10] by the 18th day of March the 100 Waggons employ'd for that Service are to proceed to Winchester if Required, and are to be paid for by the Government:

40 Horses are to be at the Fort with 200 Weight of Flour if these horses are according to Contract they are to be sent to Mr. Dick at Winchester to be employ'd in the Governmt Service[.] you are to apprise Mr. Dick of this[,] and let him know that he is to lay in at Winchester provender of all kinds For horses as much as he can, the Church with a little repair will serve for a Magazine[.]

* * *

p. 13 [St. Clair to Commissary Dick, Alexandria, February 2, 1755]

Alex.a February 2d 1755

Sir

As it was impossible for me to be at Fredericksbourgh by the time Appointed, I take the Opportunity of an Officer's going to Winchester to send you this Letter, to acquaint you that I have desired Mr. Walker to send to you to Winchester the 40 horses Contracted for, which were to be delivered at the Fort the first week of Feb: with 200 Weight of Flour on each: These horses you are to Employ in Carrying up provisions to the Camp, and it will be Necessary to have a man hired for each four horses.

It will be Necessary that you buy up all kind of Provendor for horses and lay it up at Winchester, the greater quantity you can get it will be the better to Enable us to Transport our Artillery. Should you want money for that purpose It shall Either be sent you, or you may draw on me for it.

I have desired Mr. Walker to go to Pensylvania to Contract for 200[,]000 Weight of Flour to be delivered at Conogagee the 15th of March, and that the 100 Waggons that Shou'd Carry it were to be taken into the Government's pay if wanted, Which will make it Necessary that you lay in what quantity of Hay and Oats you can at that place.

I shall be glad you will let his Excellency Gover Dinwidee, know from time to time what Success you have had, and what Provisions you have in View. I am

Sir

[To] W. Dick Commissary

* * *

p. 14 [St. Clair to officers in charge of soldiers at Winchester, Fredericksburg, and Alexandria, Alexandria, February 1, 1755]

February 1st 1755

Sir

His Majesty's Service Requiring that Twenty Sawyers and Sixty men that understand the use of Carpenters Tools to be Commandd by a Captain, Two Subalterns, Three Serjeants, Three Corporals, and one Drummer.

You are hereby ordered to draught [draft] from the detachment under your Command all men that are Carpenters by Trade and Sawyers, Boat or Ship Builders and to appoint a Subaltern, or Non Commissioned Officers in proportion to the Number of Draughts with directions to proceed to the next Detachment accordg [according] to their Route till the Number Required shall be Completed, or such a Number as shall be found amongst the Troops, and to proceed after passing the Several detachments to Alexandria where they are to wait for further Orders.

Captain Mercer is appointed to this Command, of which you are to give him the earliest Intelligence that he may Repair to his post at Alexra and must recommend to you in the Strongest manner the choosing of the most trusty Serjeants and Corporals on this detachment.—

P.S. a Copy of this to be sent to the Next detachmt & so on from one detachment to Another.

To The Officer Commanding the Troops at Winchester

To The Officer Commanding a detachmt of Troops on their march from Fredericksbg [Fredericksburg] to Winchester (4 Copies of this to be Made)

To The Officer Commanding the Troops at Fredericksburgh

To The Officer Commanding the Troops at Alexandria

* * *

p. 15 [St. Clair to Major John Carlyle, Alexandria, February 3, 1755][11]

As his Majesty's service requires it that two months Corn and hay be laid in here for four hundred horses for sixty one days you are hereby empowered to buy up at the market price 198[,]400 lb[.] of hay or corn blades, and 4[,]000 bushells of corn or oats, you are to be very secure in making your Contracts, that what is agreed for may be delivered by the time appointed. The sooner the whole is got together it will be the better, and on this being brought to this place you are to prepare proper Magazines for its Reception.

You are from time to time to give me an Account of what provender you have got and what you have in view. Given under my hand at Alexandria 3rd day of February 1755–

To Major Carlisle

* * *

p. 16 [St. Clair to General Braddock, Williamsburg, February 9, 1755]

Williamsburgh February 9th 1755

Sir

I did myself the Honour of Writing to you a Letter of the 15th of January giving you an Account of my Proceedings till that time, least you should have arrived during my absence. I shall now let you know in what manner I have been employ'd [employed] since the date of my last letter, least by duty shou'd [should] call me from this place or from Hampton which might deprive me of the pleasure of Receiving your Commands until my Return.

The 16th Jan I set out for Fredericksburgh and got to that place the 18th being 104 Miles of very good Road. I saw at that place 190 men of the Companys Raised in this Province, I was from the 19th to the 22d in getting to Winchester which is 93 Miles of very bad Road, I saw a Detachment of 70 Men of the same Troops, from the 23d to the 26th. I was on the Road to Willis's Creek this is 85 miles of the worst Road I ever travelled, and greatly Lengthened by the Roads being in the Channels of the Rivers, when they might be shorten'd by Cutting them along the Ridges of the Mountains, which Lord Fairfax promised me shou'd be done about this time, this will shorten that Road about 15 Miles, and avoid the bad Road by Patterson's Creek.

When I had got about two miles on the other side of the South branch I had a full view of the mountains on each side of the Potomack above Willis's Creek, and from what I could see there is a Road easily to be made across the Country to the mouth of Savage River, which will be gaining 30 Miles. If I am not more deceived than I have been of late with Regards to ground, the mouth of Savage River is the place where we ought to cross the Allegany Mountains. I have only been able to find one Woodsman who can give me any distinct Account of that ground, which gives me a great satisfaction. I wrote Lord Fairfax to have the Road mark'd [marked] out to the mouth of Savage River.

I cannot learn what cou'd [could] induce people ever to think of making a Fort or a Deposite for provisions at Willis's Creek; It covers no Country, nor has it the Communication open behind it either by Land or Water, the River not Navigable, and by the last Rains that fall, the River which one has to Cross / some of them five times / were without Floats or Canoes, untill within these few days that they have been set about to be built.

I found the Governour of Maryland at Willis's Creek, who had been at that place but a few days, not long enough to make any considerable Alteration nor to Reconoitre the Country. He had with him at the fort / or more properly a small piece of ground inclosed with a Strong Palisade joined pretty close / three Independent Companys, the one of South Carolina and the other two of New York, the latter seem to be Draughted out of Chelsea, the excuse they make for having so many old men does very little honour to those Companys that are left behind at New York, for they say that they are draughted from them. The Carolina Company is in much better order and Discipline. I likewise saw at Willis's Creek, 80 Men of the Troops Raised in Maryland, they are a good body of men, and if the rest of the Troops raised in that province be as good / which the Governour has reason to Expect / we may get 150 men from that province to enable us to Compleat the Two British Regiments.

Least it should still be more adviseable to pass the Mountains at Willis's Creek, there are a number of Trees cut ready for Erecting Logg houses, and I gave directions for Palisading a house near the Fort for a powder Magazine.

In my last letter to you I acquainted you that Govr Dinwiddie told me that the Navigation of the Potomack is impracticable, this I can now Affirm from Experience[,] because Govr Sharp and I found this for all other Vessels but Canoes cut out of a Single Tree, we attempted to go down the River in this sort of boat, but were obliged to get ashore and walk on foot especially at the Shannondoe Falls: So that the getting of Floats or Battoes made for the transport of the Artillery and the baggage of the Regiments, cou'd serve for no other thing but to throw away the Governments money to no purpose and lose a great deal of Time.

As Govr Sharp expected to have found you arrived he came to this place by Alexandria and Fredericksburgh, at the latter I saw him Review 80 men of the Virginia Troops which amount by this time to 700 or 800 men by what I saw of them I am afraid the Officers who Recruited them have looked more to their Numbers than to the goodness of the men, these 80 were the only ones which Govr Sharp has seen. I make no doubt but that from the Report I made to Govr Dinwiddie of his new Levies, that their numbers will be amended before you arrive. As the nature of the service we are going on will Require a great number of Carpenters, a Company totally compos'd of these is now aforming of 100 Men, from whom we may expect great advantage. I wish we may find people who we may be able to form into two Companys for Rangers.

Whatever Scheme Sir you may think proper out of your prudence to pursue, the first thing to be done at all Events is to have our Artillery, Baggage and provisions carried up to Winchester from Alexanda; for which Reason I have ordered all kinds of provendor for horses to be laid in at these two places, in as great quantity as the Country can afford which is but small. I expect 100 Waggons from Pensylvania with flour at Winchester by the 15th of March which Waggons from will serve for Carrying the Ammunition and Stores up from Alexandria, least the horses of this Country whch [which] are employ'd [employed] before that time shou'd [should] fall off, on this depends the dispatch we shall be able to make, I hope to get as much Oats Hay and Indian Corn blades as will enable us to Transport the whole to Winchester, but I am afraid we shall not be able to Cross the Mountains till the latter end of April when the grass begins to shoot.

During the Transport of the Artillery to Winchester, there will be Sufficient time to Cut the Road to Savage River and to Reconiter the ground towards the head of the Yougangany one Branch of which seems to lock in with the former. As I have seen most of this Country, I shall more freely give my Opinion with Regard to the Disposition of the Troops on their arrival both for the Security of our Magazines, Subsistence of the Troops, Ease of the Inhabitants, and that as few Counter Marches may be made as Possible.

That the Transports which have on board one Regiment may Stop in the River Potomack as near Fredericksburgh as they can, that Regt [Regiment] may be Quartered in the following manner.

3½ Companys at Winchester 6 days march from Fredericksburgh
½ Company at Conogogee 8 days by Winchester
6 Companys at Fredericksburgh and Falmouth
―――――――――
10 Companys

The other Regt

5 Companys at Alexandria, with the Complt [complement] of Artillery and Stores of all kind
1 Compy [Company] at Dumfries 2 days March from Alex.a
1 Compy at Upper Marlbro 2 days March in Maryland
1 Compy at Blandensburgh 1 day March in Maryland
2 at Frederick, 2 days March in Maryland

By this disposition the other Companys which are quartered at Winchester, Conagogoee and Fredrick [Frederick, Maryland] form the Chain to Cover our Magazines, and will be near at hand to advance either to Willis's Creek or Savage River as you shall judge most proper.[12]

I have pressed the Governour of Pennsylvania to have his Country Reconoitred towards the head of the Yougahangany and to have the Road leading to it marked out Ready to be Cut or if there is any nearer way to the French Forts, to have all these Roads marked out; for that when we Cross the Mountains we must depend a great deal on the Supplys of provisions from that Province. I am with the greatest Respect.

Sir

Your Most Obedient & Most Humble Servant—

To Major General Braddock

* * *

p. 20 [St. Clair to Colonel Napier, Williamsburg, February 10, 1755][13]

Williamsburgh February 10th 1755

Sir

I know no better way of giving you an Account of my proceedings in this Country, then to Transcribe two Letters I wrote to General Braddock, the one of the 15 of January and the other of the 9th of February which I hope will be Satisfactory.

[Extract of St. Clair Letter to Braddock]

Williamsburgh Jan 15th 1755

Sir

I was very sorry &c.

To Major Genl Braddock

[Extract of 2nd St. Clair Letter to Braddock]

Williamsburgh Feb. 9th 1755

Sir

I do myself the Honour &c.

To Maj. Genl Braddock.

[St. Clair resumes his letter]

I am in hopes this will give you some light into our present Situation, if I have not been full enough great allowances is to be given for one Coming into a Country where he is an Entire Stranger, and I may say where the Inhabitants are totally Ignorant of Military Affairs; their Sloth and Indolence is not to be described. I wish Genl Braddock may be able to make them shake it off. I shall undertake to talk to the Germans here in the language they have been brought up under in Germany; there is no persuading any of them to enlist in the Virginia Companys.

I have not had time to make myself master of the Indian Affairs, so shall only say in general terms that I am afraid the French have drawn more of them over to their Interests, especially the 6 Nations, we may expect to see a great number of them but never to feel them. Since I left Willis's Creek there are some letters come to Govr Dinwiddie & Sharp of the 3d Febry which makes them apprehensive of being attacked as the French are making great quantity of Indian shoes at their Fort,[14] that the first column of the Indians are arrived[,] And two more on their march. The Comg Officer at the Fort has orders to be on the defensive, but that is not Necessary for 2 of his Companys have neither Legs to get upon the heights nor to run away thro [through] the Valleys.

I am in great hopes this advice is true, and that they will make their Attacks in different parts[.] if so they are already in a pannick [panic], but on the Contrary if they are lying quiet and Relieving their out posts often and at regular houses, then their Attacks will follow and may succeed, I should be pleased to hear that they were making Incursions in the Country for the above Reason; this is the only thing that will awaken the Sleepy headed Mortals of this and the Neighboring provinces, I shall now Acquaint you in what manner I am to be employ'd for some time to come if General Braddock with the Troops do not Arrive.

Govr Sharp goes to morrow for Maryland, being Oblig'd to meet his Assembly the 20th. He takes his Road thro Fredericksburgh and Alexandria, at the Former he is to Review the Virginia department, & discharge the bad men / which are too numerous / and choose all those who are fit to fill up our Regt at the latter he is to form the Company of Carpenters to be ready on our Troops landing.

I will carry this letter down to Hampton with my other letters on the 14th / for the 16th is fixed for Captain Sprye sailing / and shall see the hospitals and every thing in order for the sick. I shall Return to Williamsburgh the 16th and the 18th set out for Winchester where I shall Execute the same thing as Govr Sharp does at Fredericksburgh on 600 of the Virginia troops, and see that forage is laid up, this may take me up some days then I go to Alexandria either to wait General Braddock's Arrival or to go where the Service Requires me most, I wish I have not tired your patience with my long letter, but if you find I have been too particular I am sorry for it, I thought it was erring in the safe side I am with great Sincerity

Sir

Your Most Obedient and Most Oblig'd [Obliged] & Humble Servant,

To Colonel Napier[15]

P.S. In Jeffereys map[16] Winchester is marked Frederick. Willis's Creek marked Caicuchick Creek. The Road to Savage River I mention runs from a small River which Runs in from the West into the South Branch. I send you an account of the Strength of the French which I look upon to be genuine, and an Uncorrect map of the Country of the other side of the Alleghany Mountains.[17]

* * *

p. 22 [St. Clair to Henry Fox, Williamsburg, February 11, 1755][18]

Williamsburgh February 11th 1755

Sir

It was not in my power until now to get Ready for the sailing of the Gibraltar Man of War.[19] Ever since I landed in Virginia which was on the 9th Janury I have been employ'd in Endeavouring to execute his Majestys Commands the particulars of which I shall inform you of, in the order that I set about them.

I have no better way of acquainting you what I have done, but by Transcribing two Letters I have prepared for General Braddock, on his arrival both as a Report of what I have done and in what light things appear to me in this Country. This long delay may be too Circumstantial but for my own Justification I am Obliged to write very fully. The 1st Letter is dated the 15th of Janry and the Second the 9th of Febry.

[Extract of St. Clair Letter to Braddock]

Williamsburgh Jan: 15th 1755

To Major General Braddock

[Extract of 2nd St. Clair letter to Braddock]

Williamsburgh Febry. 9th 1755

To Major General Braddock

[St. Clair resumes his letter]

I have had no time to inform myself about the different Interest of the Indian Nations but from what I here I am afraid that the French have drawn from us the 6 Nations; their way of fighting I do not apprehend to be formidable, they might have been of use to us in supplying us with Provisions in the Season. I have taken the Liberty of sending you a proposal which may plague the Indians and not be of any Service to the French, who I am sure deserve all the mischief we can do them.

I am in hopes that the Numerous Train of Small Mortars[20] which I mentioned to Coll Napier are sent out with their Shells, we shall reap Infinite benefit from 'em[.] I beg Sir that you will take it into your Consideration, if Fuzees for the Officers and Serjeants be not proper to be sent out as Spontoons and halberts are of no use in this Woody Country.[21]

The Reports of the Strength of the French on the Ohio are various, I herewith Transmit you the most probable Account I can get which I am apt to believe is genuine.

Nothing will give me greater pleasure than to hear that my proceedings have met with your approbation & I shall act in every Respect for the good of the Service and with as much frugallity as possible. I am with the greatest respect—

Sir

Your Most Obedient and Most Oblig'd Humble Servant—

To The Rt Honble [Right Honorable] Henry Fox

* * *

p. 24 [St. Clair's Proposal for a Settlement on the Ohio, February 12, 1755][22]

A proposal for making a Settlement on the Ohio.

That Mr. Keith our Minister at Vienna has made application to Marechal Batiany who is Vice Roy of Croatia for the embarking 200 or 300 Croates or Warasdines at Tenga. Those men may embark as the Palatines do without giving the least umbrage to the Court of France.

That Their Officers shou'd enlist the men to serve for the term of three years it required to serve so long, and afterwards to have lands allotted to them and their Officers & if they Choose to settle [.] if not, that they shall be sent back to their own Country at the Expense of the Government

That they shou'd have liberty to build Forts for their own Security & be free from all Taxes.

That during the time they are Carrying on War, they are to have bread and Pork, over and above their pay, and that their Wives and Children are to be allowed the same Provisions.

That their Chaplains of the Greek Church will be Paid for by the Government.

February 12th 1755.

* * *

p. 25 [St. Clair to Sir Thomas Robinson, Williamsburg, February 12, 1755]

Williamsbourg in Virginia Febry 12th 1755

I have the Honour of Acquainting you that I arrived in this Country the 9th of January and after delivering your Dispatches to Governour Dinwiddie, I sent those for the Governours of the Northern Provinces by Lieutenant Col. Ellison & those for the Southern provinces were sent by an Express.

I have been constantly employ'd in making the Necessary Dispositions for the Reception of our

Troops on their landing of which I have transmitted a full Account to the Secretary of War. Be assured sir that I have done and shall do every thing I can for the Success of our Expedition in which I hope to find no difficultys but what a little care and Activity may Surmount which shall not be Wanting.

On my part nothing can give me greater pleasure than to hear that my Conduct has your Approbation I shall endeavour to follow the schemes I saw Count Brown lay down when he was in the apperenes,[23] which is much the same Country we are to March throu [.] I am with the greatest respect—

Sir

To the Right Honble Sir Thomas Robinson

* * *

p. 26 [St. Clair to Governor Sharpe, Williamsburg, February 12, 1755]

Williamsburgh February 12th 1755

Sir

As I find that the Companys of the Virginia Regiment which I had an order to Review at Winchester are now on their march to Wills's Creek; that the Service may not Suffer, or any blame laid on me, I beg you may send me a letter to be left at Mr. Gordon's at Fredericksburgh where I shall be the 19th that I may know if I am to make the same Review at Willis's Creek. And if I have any thing to do with the Independent Companys of Carolina and Now York, and if I am to see which men of the Maryland detachments will do for our Troops. I am with great Respect,

Sir

P.S. Shou'd I go to Willis's Creek please to let me know if all the Virginia Troops are to be continued thereby the inconveniencies of which will Certainly occur to you.

to Governor Sharpe of Maryland

* * *

p. 27 [St. Clair to Governor Morris of Pennsylvania, Williamsburg, February 14, 1755]

Williamsburgh Feb: 14th 1755

Sir,

I did myself the honour of Writing a Letter to your Exy [Excellency], of the 14 January in which I Requested of you to send me any Maps or Drawings that you might have of Pennsylvania. It has given me a good deal of uneasiness that I have not Received your answer which I expected before now in order to have been informed of the Situation of your Province, I am here alone without any assistance otherwise I should have sent an Engineer to have Reconoitered your Frontiers, and if I could have been spared from the urgent Service I am on here I should have visited your Country myself. I have sent a messenger with this to Philadelphia that your Excly may be the better informed of our Situation and what part is expected that you should Act for the Common good[.] The B. [British] Troops are daily expected and as the Season is far advanced, they have no time to Loose before they begin their opperations, I have done every thing in my power to facilitate their march from their landing place to the Allegany Mountains which will be a very great trouble and Expence as I make no doubt, but that the French will unite all their Strength together to make a Stand before we can get on the Ohio which will Oblige us to have the assistance of and all of the regiments now Raising in the Northern provinces, this Step must confuse the French a good deal as they will expect an Attack from all quarters. You must be very sensible what a great detour these Troops must make by marchg thro' Philad [Philadelphia] Frederick in Myld [Maryland]. Crossing the Potomack at the mouth of the Monocasey and joining us at Wincher [Winchester]. This wou'd restrain all our Motions. For this reason I must press your Excly in the most earnest Manner to open a Communication by Cutting or repairing the Roads towards the head of the Yougheagany or any other way that is nearer to the French Forts, by the Map I have of yr province there appears to me to be a Road from Phila which Crosses the Susquena a little below the junctn [junction] of the River Juniata, and that there are two paths from your place leading to the black log [sic] which is at no very great distance from the Youghangany / called the Turkeys Foot / where we are to Cross. Shd the Roads not be wanted for this purpose I may venture to assure your Excy that no General will Advance with an Army without having a Communication open to the provinces in his Rear both for the Security of his Retreat and to facilitate the transport of Provisions the Supplying of which we must greatly depend on your province. I have sent a Commissary to Pennsylva to Contract for 100 Waggon Loads of Flour to be delivered at Conogogoea by the 20th of March and yt [that] the Waggons if wanted are to be taken into the Service to Carry up our Stores[.] I beg of you to give what assistance you can to Mr. Walker who is charged with that Commission[.] Yr Excly may expect to have the French / or rather Canadians / with some Indians making an appearance on your Frontier. You may make whatever of these Movemts you please to your Assembly, but you may take my word for it that if such movemts are made they have no other View in it but to distract us in our Councils and endeavour to harass the Inhabitants a sure sign that they are in a panick. On the Contrary if they lie quiet in their Forts they apprehend no danger and are to be dreaded. I hope your people will not look on the Road to ye Ohio as an Inlet to our Enemies but lay aside all Animositys and act for the good of their Country. Shou'd any small Rivers be to Cross when the Roads are amaking, I must Recommend to have Floats made on them for the Crossing a waggon, and that the Roads be made wide at Least 30 Feet and Carryd along the Ridges of the Mountns to avoid the Channel of the Runns of Water. I have been a good deal employ'd about this kind of work since I arrived but it is now almost Finishd [finished].[24]

I am with the greatest Respect,

Yr Excys

Most Ob: and Most Humb: Servant [Most Obedient and Most Humble Servant]

To the Governour of Pennsylvania—

* * *

p. 29 [St. Clair to Colonel Napier, Hampton, February 15, 1755]

Hampton Virginia February 15th 1755

Sir,

After writing to you a Letter of four or five sheets of paper I thought I should have done, at least until another opportunity shou'd offer. In my last Letter to you I acquainted you that the Troops at Willis's Creek were apprehensive of a visit from the French, on this Rumor all the Virginia Troops who were at Winchester have marched thither / I suppose to show their Alertness / this step has been taken without any orders from Govenors Dinwiddie or Sharp. I am Concerned for it as there is no possibility of their Staying there, for their Numbers must Consume the provisions and what vexes me, is that it will give a pleasure to the French to see us weak enough to swallow such a Bait[.] it is [as] easy for the Fort to contain 10,000 men as the Number that is there at present, I have sent an Express to Govr Sharp to acquaint him of this march as it was agreed that I shou'd put the new Levies in some form & order, and been desired of him to know if I am to go to Willis's Creek the 18th and that I shall wait his answer at Fredericksburgh.

I offered my Service to both the Govrs who were together when they Received the news of the French intending to attack them, to go and take Command at the Fort but they did not think it Necessary, had I gone I / in the place of calling for more Troops / wou'd [would] have sent two thirds away of those that were there, exclusive of the new Levies[.] Shou'd I go to the Fort and by the movements of the French find it Necessary to stay I shall make the best disposition I can to save us from insults.

Let me have your opinion about the New York independent Companys enlisting men for a term of Years, had they any Toleration for it?

The Virginia Troops are at a great loss for officers which makes me recommend to be sent out to us Lieutenant James Dabrel on the half pay in the detach Service he is a good Officer as I am told, and I know him to be a brisk Young man[.] he was on the Expedition to Surinam. If he is in London you may see him and I dare say you'll find him answer the Character I give of him[.] if he is not in London Coll York, who knows him[,] may soon send him over from the Hague.

Mr. Pitcher is here who I dare say has made no favourable Report of the New York Companies in New York.

If fuzees be not sent out for the Serjeants and Officers I beg you may consider if they will not be of more use than Spontoons and Halberts in this Woody Country.

I have sent you inclosed the Map Mentioned in my last[,] and in my Former Letter is a proposal for getting some Croates to Settle on the Ohio[.]

To Colonel Napier

* * *

p. 31 [St. Clair to General Braddock, Williamsburg, February 17, 1755]

Williamsburgh Feb. 17th 1755

Sir,

As the Carrying up of our Provisions will Require my being at Fredericskburgh[,] Winchestr and Alexa I am Obliged to set out from this to morrow morning that no time may be lost after your arrival.

The Governs of Virginia and Maryland have agreed that I shall be employ'd in Reviewing the new Raised Troops but as they are marched to Willis's Creek since Gvr Shapr left this place, I have wrote to Annapolis for his further Instructions which I shall Receive at Fredericksburgh, and know if I am to go to the Creek or that the Troops are to Return to Winchester.

As the Nature of the Service I am going upon is so uncertain it is impossible for me to fix any time for my Return at all Events I shall be able to Join the Troops at their landing at Alexandria.

Shou'd you think it more Adviseable to encamp the 2 Troops than to Quarter them in the manner I proposed in my last there is a good Camp Close to the Town of Alexandria, all I can say of the encamping the Troops is that I have felt no Weather in this Country since my arrival but what a Soldier might be very comfortable in his Tent[.] if you approve of this method it will get our new men easily disciplined[,] and detachments may be sent up to Cover our Magazines.

Shou'd it not be in my power to be at Hampton on your arrival I take the liberty of Recommending Capt. Mackellar an Enginier to you[,][25] who will do anything better than I can pretend to[.] I have lived with great Intimacy with him these 20 Years and can answer for him being a good Officer in every Respects. I am with the greatest Respect,

Sir,

P.S. I have Just received the inclosed from the Gover of North Carolina

To the Honble General Braddock

* * *

p. 32 [St. Clair to Governor Arthur Dobbs of North Carolina, Williamsburg, February 17, 1755][26]

Williamsburgh Feb 18th 1755

Sir,

I Received your Excys most obliging Letter of the 10th Instant for which I return you my most hearty thanks. As I am just going to undertake my second Journey to Willis's Creek I really have not time to Write so fully as I wou'd incline but must refer you to Govr Dinwiddie.

I am thoroughly sensible of the great pains you have taken, in exerting yourself at this Juncture. If all the Governrs follow your Example, we certainly cannot fail of success. I am highly pleased with the choice you have made of the Captain to Command the Company you are to send us[.] General Braddock will expect them with impatience.

I shall be glad to have from you the Maps that you mention but if you cou'd send me as early as possible a draught of the Ground between the Potomack and Lake Erie, it would be of great Service to me as I must go and Reconoitre part of that Situation so soon as the Troops arrive. I have the honour of being with the greatest Respect,

Sir,

To Gover Dobbs of North Carolina—

* * *

p. 33 [St. Clair to various commanding officers, Fredericksburg, February 21, 1755]

Frederisksburgh February 21st 1755

Sir,

Having Received Orders to Review the Troops at Winchester, Willis's Creek of the Virginia and Maryland detachments I herewith Transmit to you a Copy of the Returns that I beg you will have Ruled and filled up for me.

I shall be at your quarters so soon as I can settle some things of the service that will take me up a couple of days in this place.

I have directed Adjt Frazier to proceed to Willis's Creek to prepare the same returns for me.

Three Duplicates of each will be wanted. I am,

Sir,

Your Most Obedt Hm.

To the Commg Officer at Winchester and Wills's Creek of the Virginia Troops

To the Independent Companys of New York, South Carolina and the My'ld. Detachment.

* * *

p. 34 [St. Clair to Colonel Innes, Fredericksburg, February 21, 1755]

Fredericksburgh February 21st 1755

Sir,

As I have Received order to Review all the Troops at Willis's Creek and Winchester, I have sent Adjt Frazier to both the Places in order to prepare things for that Service,

I have in form inclosed you Letters for the Commadg Officers of the Corps that I am to re–View, that I may be oglig'd to stay longer than needs must with you as I shall see you so soon and have a great deal to say to you I shall add nothing more than to assure you that I am always with Truth

Sir

Yours truly,

To Colonel Innes

* * *

p. 35 [St. Clair to Lord Fairfax, Fredericksburg, February 21, 1755]

Fredericksburgh Febry 21st 1755

Sir,

I did myself the Honour of Writing to your Lop when I was at Willis's Creek Concerning the Cutting the Roads for the intended Expedition, which I am very sorry to hear are not in the forwardness I had Reason to Expect. I therefore write this to your Lop. To know if I am to expect any assistance from the Country of which your Lop. Is Proprietor, if not I must attend myself with a large detachment of what Troops we have and cutt the proper Roads which I am ordered to do by his Majesty. And as I have no proper Convenience for want of Roads for the Subsistence of those men which will be employ'd for the safety of the Country. I have Reason to Expect that the Country will furnish them with Provisions.

The Reporting My Lord, at home that the Roads are not finish'd by any frivolous disputes that may happen at your Courts of the Diffirent Countys can be of no excuse to me no excuse to me in doing my duty, I shou'd with Regret be oblig'd to Report to my Royal Master that it wou'd be <u>much</u> easier to Carry on War from an Enemys Country than to protect his just Rights to one of his most Loyal provinces in America—[27]

I shall be at Winchester in order to give directions about the Roads at Wednesday the 26th when I shall be glad of Receiving your Lop. Answer that I may take the proper steps in Securing our Communication which if not done must retard all our operations. I have the honour of being with the Greatest Regard

My Lord

Yours truly,

To Lord Fairfax

* * *

p. 36 [St. Clair to Governor Sharpe, Fredericksburg, February 22, 1755]

Fredericksburgh February 22d 1755

Sir,

I Received your Excys Letter of the 17th Instant and was just going to Willis's Creek to Execute your Commands, when I received the Inclosed which obliges me to Return to Williamsburgh. I have take upon me to move the Troops from hence to Port Royal in order to make Room here for the British Forces. I have the honour of being—with the greatest respect

Your Excellency's Most Ob: Hum Servt.

[P.S.] As the Maryland Forces will be wanted to Compleat the English Regiments I have sent an Order by Mr. Pitcher to Willis's Creek, that the detachment of Maryland Forces now at that place may forthwith march to Frederick to join the rest, they will be then at home to be incorporated with the British Regts.

* * *

p. 36 [St. Clair to Major John Carlyle, Fredericksburg, February 22, 1755]

Sir—

As Genl Braddock, with the British Forces is arrived. You are hereby ordered to get together all the Fresh provisions you possibly can and compleat every thing in the best manner for their reception as soon as may be, if any Carpenters should be wanting I have directed Captain Mercer to give you what number may be necessary.

Mr. Pitcher the Commissary of Musters is going to Willis's Creek, and will go from thence to Alexandria You are ordered to provide quarters for himself, Servt. And two Horses.

To Govr Sharp and Major Carlisle

* * *

p. 37 [General Braddock to St. Clair, Williamsburg, February 26, 1755][28]

Sir John St Clair

As the good of his Majestys Service Requires that a Review should be made of the three Independent Companys now at Willis's Creek, as well as of the Forces newly raised in the Provinces of Virginia and Maryland, and as the Circumstances of Affairs puts it out of my power to make that whole Review myself.

I therefore order you to make the Review of such troops as you shall find at Winchester, Willis's Creek, Frederick, or else where, and to make a report to me of the State you find them in you are likewise required and directed to order all such men of the Independent Companies from Carolina and New York, of the Virginia and Maryland Forces, as you shall find unfitt for his Majestys Service / giving the Reasons why they are so / to be forthwith discharged, whether formed into Companies, detachmts or Recruits.

You are likewise to mark down such men as you shall think proper for Compleating the two British Regiments daily expected, that they may be in readiness for them on their Landing, and to order them with proper officers forthwith to repair to Alexandria and Fredericksbourg, and to remain there till further orders. All Blacks or Molattoes / except the young and Strong / to be discharg'd [discharged]. the others to be sent to the Commissaries with their discharges inclos'd / Mr Dicks or Mr Walker / least they shou'd not Choose to employ them. And You are hereby orderd [ordered] to give such directions with Regard to the Quartering the Virginia Troops as shall be found most Convenient for the service, should you think Winchester or Willis's Creek inconvenient.

I am

Sir Your Most Humble and Obedient Servant

E. Braddock

Williamsburgh Feb: 26th 1755

* * *

p. 38 [General Braddock to St. Clair, Williamsburg, February 26, 1755]

By his Excellency Edward Braddock Esqr

Commander in Chief of all his Majesty's Forces in North America

On the forming the Virginian Levies into Companies for which you have my Order; you are hereby directed and Required to Administer / as Commissary / to the Officers and men of these Companies the Oath of Allegiance; for so doing this shall be your Sufficient Warrant and Authority.

E. Braddock

Given at Williamsburgh
This 26th day of February 1755

By his Excellency's Command
W. Shirley Secretary

To
Sir John St. Clair, Bart
Quarter Master General of his
Majesty's Forces in N. America

* * *

p. 39 [General Braddock to St. Clair, Williamsburg, February 27, 1755]

By his Excellency Edward Braddock Esqr General and
Commander in Chief of his Majesty's Forces in North America

Sir,

These are to order and direct you when you take the Review of the Troops in Virginia and Maryland to make such dispositions of the Forces as shall appear to you to be most Convenient for his Majesty's Service at this time by moving the Troops from one place to another as well the independent Companies of New York and South Carolina, as the Virginia and Maryland Forces. For so doing this shall be your sufficient Warrant and Authority.

Given under my hand at Williamsburgh this 27th day of February 1755

E. Braddock

To
Sir John St. Clair
Quarter Master General of his
Majesty's Forces in N. America

* * *

p. 40 [General Braddock, Orders, Williamsburg, February 26, 1755]

By his Excellency Edward Braddock Esqr General and
Commander in Chief of his Majesty's Forces in North America

Whereas an Act of Parliament was passed in England the last Session Subjecting all Troops rais'd in the Colonies to the Regulations and orders of the Articles of War I therefore think it expedient and hereby order that upon forming the four Companies of Rangers, Company of Carpenters, and the Troop of light horse, and whatsoever Troops are or shall be rais'd for the service of the present expedition, that the Articles of War be publickly read to the officers and men, and that every man Severally shall take the Oaths of Allegiance, and Supremacy, and in Consequence of these Articles they are to obey from time to time any orders they shall receive from me or any of their Superior Officers.[29]

E. Braddock
By his Excellency's Command
W. Shirley, Secretary
Williamsburgh Feb: 26th 1755

* * *

p. 41 [General Braddock to St. Clair, Williamsburg, February 28, 1755]
Williamsburgh February 28th 1755
Sir

I have laid before Gover Dinwiddie a scheme to form two Companies of Carpenters[,] four or more Companies of Rangers if men can be found. And also one troop of light horse; and I have Received his honour's answer, desiring I will Establish them as I think most conducive to his Majesty's Service.

I Therefore order you in the Review you are now making to form the Companys above mentioned conformable to the establishment you will Receive with this and for so doing this shall be your Authority.

I am
Sir
Your Most Humble Servant &c.
E. Braddock
To
Sir John St. Clair, Bart
Quarter Master General of his
Majesty's Forces in N. America

* * *

p. 42 [General Braddock, Orders, not dated, not addressed]
Establishment of Two Companies of Carpenters

	First Company		*Subsistance*
	Captain George Mercer		0.12.6
	1st Lieutenant William Bromaugh[30]		0.6.0
	2nd Lieutenant Thomas Bulleeks[31]		0.5.0
	Sergeants—3	Pay 2.4	0.2.0
	Corporals—3	Pay 1.8	0.1.4
	Drum—1		
	Private Men—50	Pay 1.2	0.1.0
	Bat Man—3	Pay 0.8	0.0.6
	Second Company		
	Captain William Polson[32]		
	1st Lieutenant John Hamilton[33]		
	2nd Lieutt Joshua Lewis[34]		
	Serjeants—3	Pay as above	
	Corporals—3		
	Drum—1		
	Private men—50		
	Bat Man—3		

Cloathing expected daily and will be sent to them as soon as it arrives—

Tools and Aprons will be provided by the Quarter Mastr General

Every Officer will Receive a Soldiers Tent, and a Tent will be delivered to every Eight men.

No Servants will be allow'd from the Companys, each Capt Will be allow'd £ 24 to purchase two horses for his own and Companies Tents.

The two Subalterns of each Company will be allow'd Twelve £ between them for the purchase of one horse for their own Tents and baggage.

The bat men to have no arms[,] to be provided with Frocks.[35]

* * *

p. 43 [General Braddock, Orders, not dated, not addressed]

Establishment for Four Companies of Rangers

First Company   *Subsistance*

Captain Adam Steven		0.10.0
1st Lieutenant John Savage[36]		0.5.0
2nd Lieutenant Edmond Waggonor[37]		0.4.0
Sergeants—3	Pay 1.4	0.1.0
Corporals—3	Pay 1.0	
Drum—1	Pay 0.10	
Private Men—50	Pay 0.8	
Bat Man—3	Pay 0.8	

Second Company—Pay as above

Captain Andrew Lewis[38]
1st Lieutenant James McNeal
2nd Lieutt William Wright
Serjeants—3
Corporals—3
Drum—1
Private men—50
Bat Man—3

Third Company—Pay as above

Captain Thomas Waggoner[39]
1st Lieutenant Henry Woodward
2nd Lieut Walter Stewart
Serjeants—3
Corporals—3
Drum—1
Private men—50
Bat Man—3

Fourth Company—Pay as above

Captain William Peyronie[40]
1st Lieutenant John Wright[41]
2nd Lieut. Edmd Waggener[42]
Serjeants—3
Corporals—3
Drum—1
Private men—50
Bat Man—3

Whatever further Companies of Rangers are Rais'd are to be upon the same Establishment.

The Staff Officers for the two Companies of Carpenters and Companys of Rangers

Adjutant	4 s Subsistance	Simon Frazer
Quartermaster	4 s Subsistance	
Surgeon	5 s Subsistance	

Cloathing for the Rangers will be sent as soon as it Arrives.

Arms and Accoutrements are already at Alexandria and Fredericksburg.

Every Officer, Serjeant, Corporal and private man to be arm'd with a Firelock with a Sling and Bayonet, Cartouch Box.

Every Captain to Receive £ 24 and the two Subalterns of each Company 12 £ to Supply them with Bat Horses.

No Officer is to take more horses than the number above mentioned.

Every Officer is to be furnished with a private Man's Tent and a Tent to be delivered to every 8 Men.

The Bat Man per Company allowed above the Compliment to carry no Arms.

* * *

p. 44 [General Braddock, Orders, not dated, not addressed]
Establishment for the Troop of horse Rangers

		Subsistance
Captain Robert Stewart		0.12.6
1st Lieutenant John Mercer[43]		0.6.0
2nd Lieut. Car. Gustavius deSplitdolph[44]		0.6.0
2 Sergeants	Pay 2.6	0.1.10
2 Corporals	Pay 2.0	0.1.4
30 Privates	Pay 1.6	0.1.0
4 Bat Man	Pay 0.8	0.0.6

The Captain is to be allowed £ 48 for the purchase of Four horses he is to carry all the Tents.

The two Lieutenants to be allowed £ 24 each, for the purchase of two horses each.

The Serjeants Corporals and private men to be allowed one horse each.

Four Bat Men to be allowed to the Companies above the Compliment two to the Captain and one to each of the Subaltern Officers.

Every Officer, Serjeant, Corporal and Private to be arm'd with a Short Carbine, Case of pistols and Cutting Sword.

The Captain is to Look out for horses and to take care his men are all well Mounted; he will Receive money for the Purchase of them from Governour Dinwiddie.

E. Braddock

By his Excellencys Command

W. Shirley Secretary

* * *

p. 46 [Acting Governor DeLancey of New York to St. Clair, New York, February 3, 1755][45]

New York February 3d 1755

Sir,

I had the honour of your Letter of the 14th January by Lieut. Colonels Ellison and Mercer; whom I have provided with horses in in [sic] pursuance of his Majesty's Expectations Signified to me by Letter from Sir Thomas Robinson of the 26th of October. I take this Opportunity to Congratulate you on your safe arrival at Virginia

The intelligence I have lately received from Oswego of the 1st of January, is that the Indians who

Returned from Montreal Report that an Officer was arrived there from the Ohio, who was to Return back this Winter with a Reinforcement Sufficient to Rout all the English from thence; My opinion is that the French will not be able to pass in the Winter, for the Lakes are not hard enough Frozen to bear them and they dare not Venture by water in this season for one night's hard frost might leath 'em [leave them] where they may Possibly perish.

In august last a party of French Indians of St Francois and Recancourt near Trois Rivieres a place on St. Lawrence River between Quebeck and Montreal came thro' the Lakes Champlain and St Sacrament[46] into this province and destroyed a Settlement Called Hooseek, which is about 18 Miles east from that part of Hudson's River which is 9 Miles above Albany and Carry'd off the small Remains of an Indian Nation which was Settled near that place.

As to maps of this Country, we have none, there is one preparing by Mr. Evans I am told, which will soon be published. I use those in Charlevoise. As to the knowledge I have of the Country, I shall give it you in a few words as I can: the City of New York is Seated on Hudson's River, about 21 Miles from the Ocean, from New York to the City of Albany is about 144 Miles the Course of the River is North a little easterly, Navigable for small Sloops. Albany is on the West side of the Hudson's River thence to Schenectady is 16 Miles, a Town on the Mohawk River which empties itself into Hudson's River, from Schenectady you go up the Mohawk River in Canoes or Battoes to near the head thereof, Meeting with only one small Carrying place; from the head of the Mohawk River you cross 4 Miles by land into the Wood Creek, which carries you down into the Oneida Lake and so through the lake into the River that leads to Oswego a Fort belonging to his Majesty on the side of the lake Ontario. The distance between Albany and Oswego is computed to be 27 Miles; It takes 8 days to come up the River St. Lawrence from Montreal to Oswego; from Oswego to the French Fort at Niagara its computed to be about 160 Miles; I think it is not so much, the great fall of Niagara is perhaps the most important pass in all No [North] America, the French Forces pass this way going to the Ohio, What the distances are from Niagara to the Peninsula on the Lake Erie and thence across to the Ohio, and down to Monogehala you will have been better inform'd where you are; than I can. I wish you health and Success in this Service and am,

Sir

Your Most Obedient and Most Humble Servant

James DeLancey

Sir John St Clair

* * *

p. 48 [Major John Carlyle to St. Clair, Alexandria, February 18, 1755]

Alexandria February 17th 1755

Sir,

Since you left this I have taken every Method I cou'd think of to purchase the Hay and Corn fodder you desired, but have not been able to buy above Ten Thousand Weight I have not yet had any Accot [account] from Mr Diggs of his success in Maryland; I am doubtful he we no be able to [sic] purchase much, the people that make quantitys not knowing of a Certain Market have given the most and best to their Horses, and cattle. I have purchased and Stor'd about Twelve hundred bushells of Oats and have agreed for a Thousand bushells more; I have secured any quantity of Indian Corn, and have an Offer made me of a Quantity of Hay and Corn that will be delivered if wanted at a place on the Road to Winchester near halfway, and have mentioned it to Col. Sharpe and he seems to think it very proper, as by that means the Waggons need take less provendor from here as they will be sure of a Supply at their middle Stage.

I have had Workmen at Work upon the Kitchen and the Owner of the house is fitting up his Ball Room that on the arrival of the Forces may depend on every assistance in our power. Any Commands you may please to lay upon me may depend on my Utmost Endeavour to Execute, and am;

Sir

Your Most Obedt Humb Servt

John Carlyle

* * *

p. 49 [Governor Sharpe to St. Clair, Alexandria, February 17, 1755]

Sir,

As the good of his Majesty's service Requires that a Review be made of the three independent Companies now at Willis's Creek, as well as of the Forces newly raised in the Provinces of Virginia and Maryland and as the Circumstances of Affairs puts it out of my power to make that Whole review myself.

I therefore Order you to make the Review of such Troops as you shall find at Winchester, Willis's Creek, Frederick or Else where; and to make a Report to me of the State you find them in, you are likewise Required and directed to order all such men of the independent Companys from Carolina and New York of the Virginia and Maryland Forces as you shall find unfit for his Majestys Service / giving the Reasons why they are so / to be forthwith discharg'd whether formed into Companys, detachments or Recruits.

You are likewise to mark down such men as you shall think proper for Compleating the two British Regiments daily expected that they may be in readiness for them on their landing and to order with proper Officers forthwith to Repair to Alexandria and Fredericksburgh and to Remain there 'till further Orders; All Blacks and Molattoes / except the Young and Strong / to be discharg'd the others to be sent to the Commissaries with their discharges inclosed / to Mr Dick or Mr Walker / least they should not Chuse to employ them—

I am with great Truth

Sir

Your Most Obedt and Most Humble Servant

Horo [Horatio] Sharpe

P.S. You are hereby ordered to give Such directions with Regard to the Quartering the Virginia Forces as Shall be found most Convenient for the service. Should you think Willis's Creek or Winchester inconvenient.

Alexandria February 17th 1755

To Sir John St Clair—

* * *

p. 50 [Governor Dinwiddie to St. Clair, Williamsburg, February 18, 1755]

Williamsburgh February 18th 1755

Sir

As you are going to Fredericksburgh, Winchester & the Camp, I desire you will please Review the Recruits rais'd in this Colony and those that you think not fit for Service. Pray discharge them.

Those from the eastern shore, if not arrived at Fredericksburgh, have orders when they arrive to remain there[,] or to march for Alexandria.

Write Mr Carlyle to press Waggons agreeable to Act of Assembly to carry up 400 brls [barrels] of pork that will very soon be sent to Alexandria.

I think it proper to send an express to Genl Sharpe as Commander in Chief in regard to returning the men from Willis's Creek, as you think there are too many there.

Those you think fit for the British Forces will be / I think / proper to send to Alexandria, with any one of the Captains you may appoint. And those you intend for Rangers, am of Opinion they shou'd be at Winchester but I leave the whole to your own Judgement.

And I think those of the Maryland Company fit for Rangers will be properly disposed of at Frederick.

No doubt your employing the Company of Carpenters in such Necessary Works you see proper will be of Essential Service in short as you Command in the absence of Gov. Sharpe; every thing you direct will meet with Approbation.

I wish you a pleasant Journey and Safe Return from [Note: This is left blank] [.]

Sir

Your Most Humble Servt

Robt [Robert]Dinwiddie

P.S.
Guns at Alexandria Virg.
Those Remain of the Former Troops 150
Sent Up 500
At Fredericksburgh
Sent from Hampton—Firelocks 150
Sent from Wilmsbg.—200
To Sir John St Clair Bart

* * *

p. 51 [Governor Dinwiddie to St. Clair, not addressed, not dated]

Sir John

I give you the trouble of some Letters which I beg you to deliver as directed. When you come to Shanandoe Ferry, order your guide to conduct you to Lord Fairfax's who I doubt not will be glad to see you.

I appointed Messrs Dick & Walker Commissaries of Stores and Provisions[.] They have my orders to build boats over the Runns between Winchester & Willis's Creek Which I hope e'er this air in good Forwardness.[47] Col. James Innes has had the Command at Willis's Creek and the direction in building a Fort, Magazine and Barrack. He is a very Worthy Man. You may freely confide in him for Account of what has been done, and Assistance for what you may think proper to do. I shall be glad if You Return by the New Road, the North side of Potomack; that you may the better Judge the most proper way for Carrying up the Artillery, and other heavy Stores.

I wish you health a pleasant Journey, and a happy Return & I Remain in great Truth

Sir

Your Most Obligd & Humble Servant

Robt. Dinwiddie

To the Honble Sir John St Clair Bart

* * *

p. 52 [Governor Sharpe to St. Clair, Alexandria, February 17, 1755]

Sir

I herewith send for your perusal / under cover to Govr Dinwiddie / the perticular Return made out upon my Review which be pleased to seal and deliver to Mr Frazier who has my Orders to Carry it to Williamsburgh unless you should want his Attendance.

The Company of Carpenters I have formed into Six Squads and the Workmen According to their knowledge in the different Professions are Equally distributed and found myself Obliged to keep some indifferent men that understand their Business. However shall give Orders to Capt Mercer to discharge such men, when other can be had in their Stead[.] A Return of the Company is herewith sent you,

From the Several Complaints made by Mr. Finnions [Note: name may not be correct] Recruits I have great Reason to Imagine that those horses exhibited by him at Wimsbg [Williamsburg] were such only as he Forcibly and illegally took away from the Complainants, if true so scandalous an Act deserves to be discovered; to which end I must beg of You to make a perticular Enquiry of [Name I cannot make out] Beasley in Capt Stewarts Compy that was constantly employed as a Messenger who has had several horses taken from him by that hand.

I find that Captain Stephens has Eight or Ten Servants enlisted as Soldiers, whereof Edward Evans is a Drummer and one James Ferrile a Convict; that he has lately appointed a Serjt altho scandalously broke and rendered incapable by the sentence of a Court Martial.

I am with the greatest Respect,

Sir

Your Most Obedt & Most Hble Servt

Horo [Horatio] Sharpe

Alexandria February 17th 1755

P.S. Captain Mercer has Orders from me to obey any Orders, he shall at any time Receive from You or the Governour.

To Sir John Sinclair—

* * *

p. 53 [Governor Jonathan Belcher of New Jersey to St. Clair, Elizabethtown, New Jersey, February 3, 1755][48]

Sir,

I have Received by Col. Ellison your favour of the 14th of last Month, as also the two Letters from Sir Thomas Robinson one of his Majesty's principal Secretaries of State, and in that of the 4 of November past, as well as by yours, I find his Majesty has appointed You Deputy Quarter Master General of his Forces in North America; and that you were soon expecting the arrival of General Braddock, and of the two Regiments from Ireland; and that it wou'd be of the greatest Consequences, to take the proportion of men from this Province, in readiness for Compleating the two Regiments, from 500 men each to 700, and I am sorry in answer to this Article, to say, that Not withstanding I have for near twelve months past been urging two Several Assemblies, to their duty to their King, as well as to their own Interest, in granting all the Aid and Assistance they Possibly Cou'd for Repelling the Incroachments of the French upon the King's Territories in these parts. Yet they have not to this day raised an Men or Money, but the Most I cou'd bring them to in their Session of October last was to grant for the King's Use, near about the sum of Six Thousand Pounds Sterling provided his Majesty allow'd of the raising it in the way and Manner projected in a bill they sent to me, with a Petition to the King for his Approbation of the said Bills, and till there comes an Answer to this, I have no Expectation that this Assembly will do anything in the present exigency of Affaires.

I am Sensible Sir, you must be much a Stranger to the grounds in these Parts, and that it is very Necessary you should get the best information you can of the Situation and Circumstances of the Colonies, and wish I cou'd furnish you with any maps or drawings of this, but I have never seen any such thing since my arrival here; that has been deem'd Authentic, or of any Value, and I have very little knowledge of the ground in the back of this, and the Neighbouring Colonies, yet as this is a very material article I shall endeavour to make the best Enquiry I can in it, and if I learn anything Worth Your Notice I shall loose no time in transmitting it to you under Cover to Mr. Dinwiddie, The Governour of Virginia, but I shou'd think that the Indians in Friendship with us, and such English Traders and hunters as are conversant in the Parts, whither the King's Troops may be destin'd[,] wou'd be the best, and most able Informer you can get in this Matter.

In Obedience to his Majesty's Commands, I shall very Chearfully be Aiding and Assisting to you to the utmost of my power, for the King's Honour and Interest.

And it wou'd give me great pleasure if you cou'd possibly point out to me any way or Manner of doing you any personal Acceptable Service in these parts, for I am with much Esteem, and Respect,

Sir

Your Most Obedient & Most Humble Servant

J. Belcher

Elizth. [Elizabeth] Town (in New Jersey)

Febry 3d 1755.

* * *

p. 55 [Governor Morris of Pennsylvania to St. Clair, Philadelphia, February 17, 1755]

Sir,

Captain Rutherford will deliver to you with this a Map of this Province, and of part of the Country back of It, including part of the Lake Erie and of the River Ohio a Considerable way below the Monongahela I have not been able to get any other Maps Coppy'd than What I now send but I have a Person at Work, and will send some others as I can get them finish'd. Capt Rutherford who has been a Considerable Way back in the Province of New York will explain to you not only this but the others that I shall have the honour to send You. You will find him a man of sense and extremely well Acquainted with American Affairs in general and those of the Indians in Particular. I have the Honour to be.—

Sir

Your Most Obedt And Most Humble Servant,

Robt H. Morris

Philadelphia February 17th 1755.

* * *

p. 56 [Governor Sharpe to St. Clair, Williamsburg, February 9, 1755]

Williamsburgh February 9th 1755

Sir

As the good of his Majesty's Service requires that a Review shou'd be made of the Forces newly Raised in the Province of Virginian and as the Circumstances of Affairs puts it out of my power to make that Whole Review myself.

I am under a Necessity of desiring you / as you propose going up the Country soon / to make a Review of the Troops at Winchester and to make a Report to me and to the Governour of the Province of the State you find them in. You are Likewise Required and directed to order all such men as you shall find unfit for Service / giving the Reasons why they are so / to be forthwith discharg'd from the Companys they are now in, shou'd you be in doubt about any of the men, You are in that Case to Report them for my Orders thereon[.]

You are likewise to mark out such men as you shall think proper for Compleating the two British Regiments daily expected that they may be in Readiness for them on their Landing.

I am

Sir

Your Humb: Servant

Horo Sharpe

To Sir John St Clair
Quarter Master General of the Forces in America

* * *

p. 57 [St. Clair to Captain Cocke, Fredericksburg, March 1, 1755]

Fredericksburgh March 1st 1755

Sir

I herewith inclose you a Letter to Lieutenant Hamilton which I desire you will immediately send to him by an Express as the Service Requires his being at Alexandria early on Tuesday Morning in order to March on Wednesday with the Company he belongs to to [sic] Winchester.

I expect to be with you at Port Royal in a fortnight hence & shou'd be glad you wou'd Continue at Quarters till I see you that you may be in the way of Receiving any Occasional Orders I may have for you. Ensn [Ensign] Frazier is likewise to stay at Quarters.

You will receive some Recruits who I have directed to Lieut. Woodward / Who is to stay here / to forward to you, these men are to be Victualled as your ane.[49] I am

Sir

Your Most Humbl Servt

P.S. If Mr. Savage is with you with his Recruits, they are to remain there till further orders from Genl Braddock or from me.

* * *

p. 58 [St. Clair to Lieutenant John Hamilton, Fredericksburg, March 1, 1755. Note: this is presumably the letter forwarded by p. 57 to Captain Cocke]

Fredericksburgh March 1st 1755

Sir

You are hereby Required and Directed to repair forthwith to your Post at Alexandria; in order to March with the Company you now belong to, who take the Road for Winchester on Wednesday next so that as being the Oldest Lieutt [Lieutenant] of that Company, you will have the Command of it on the March; and it will be very proper for you to be at your Post by Tuesday morning to Receive my Orders.

I am

Sir Your Most Humble Servt

* * *

p. 59 [St. Clair to Lieutenant Henry Woodward, Fredericksburg, March 1, 1755]

As the good of his Majesty's Service Requires that an Officer Shou'd Continue at this Place, I therefore order you for that service that you may be in the way to Receive any Artillery and Stores sent you from Hampton, and see them forwarded to Winchester for which Mr. Commissary Dick has my Directions.

You are to go in ten days to Colel [Colonel] Baites and see in what Forwardness the Wheels are, which I bespoke and to make me a Report in Writing directed at Alexandria.

Shou'd any Officer come to this place with Recruits you are to let them know that it is my orders that they Conduct them to Port Royal and Remain there under the Command of Capt Cocke Until I come to that Quarter to Review them.

Fredericskburgh March 1st 1755

* * *

p. 60 [St. Clair to Ensign Hector Neil, Fredericksburg, March 1, 1755]

As the service Requires that an Officer shou'd Remain here to have an Eye to the Sick[,] You are hereby ordered to Remain here, and Visit the Hospitals every day to see that the sick men have firing[50] and proper Victuals delivered to them; shou'd You find that any of the Sick sells their provisions for Rum or Strong Liquor you are in that case to send them to Jail the proper Place for such Delinquents[.]

Fredericksburgh March 1st 1755

* * *

p. 61 [St. Clair to General Braddock, Fredericksburg, March 1, 1755]

Fredericksburgh March 1st 1755

Sir

I have the Honour of acquainting your Excellency that I arrived at this Place this day and have taken such Steps as will make the carriage of the four 12 Pdrs [Pounder Cannon] Very easy, I have given directions for four setts and two Spare wheels to be made with the Axel Trees, and have prepared wood for the Bodys of the Train Cause,[51] so that when the Train arrives it will be necessary that a Detachmt of a dozen of them with an Officer be sent to this place to give the Directions for Constructing these Machines, which may be done in two days after the Wheels are finish'd.

I wish your Ex. wou'd send the guns to this place with the Train of Small Mortars and their Shells that we may be handing them up to Winchester. I have appointed Lieutt Woodward for that service to whom they may be Consign'd. It will be a difficult matter for the Commodore to spare 400 Shotts for each gun if this is the case your Excellency has only to send up one twelve pound shott with a Letter from Capt. Orde to Lieut. Woodward and he will get the number Required made at this place. As they may not be very expert in Casting Ball, it may be good to have the Pattern Shott to be of a Little Less size than usual as those guns will only serve for sparing the Breach [breech of the cannon].[52]

When the Troops arrive I beg that the Inventory and Ordnance Stores may be laid before the Officer of the train to see if there will be powder sufficient, which I am in doubt about, if there is not the Commodore will be able to spare us some, if so what we get from the ships will be better in half barrells than whole ones. I spoke to Captain Orme to desire that your Excellency would send up Mr McKellar the Engineer if he comes to Capt. Canesby's he will provide them with horses that will carry him to Fredericksburg. Mr. McKellar is an Officer who will see the Roads finished, which I will set about on my going to Winchester. I herewith transmitt a Letter which I Received from Lord Fairfax it is worthy of his Lop. The other directed to Govr Sharpe I likewise transmit as it properly belongs to your Excellency. I have taken a Copy of the Weekly Return. The above Letters I received since I began to Wister[53] this Letter by the Common Post which makes it unnecessary for me to send an Express. I beg my Complimts to the Govr and his Family. Be assured that I always am with the greatest Respect

Your Exy's [Excellency's]

Most Obedient & Most Hble. Servt

To His Excellency General Braddock

* * *

p. 63 [St. Clair to Governor Sharpe, Alexandria, March 3, 1755]

Alexandria March 3d 1755

Sir

The arrival of General Braddock hindered me Coming to Alexa Sooner to put in Execution much the same plan which was laid down by You.

I have sent you of this by an express to know if your Affairs can Possibly Permit you to come down to Alexanda, my Instructions are so very positive that they put it out of my power to come to You. I have so many things to Communicate and to Consult with you that it will be scarce possible for me to put them into Writing. If I find by the Return of the Express that you are not able to come, I shall send you the most Carefull Officer I can find to communicate several things to you, and to have your concurrence in the Modelling [sic] and disposing of all your Maryland Forces, who are all by this at Frederick.

If Capt. Dagworthy[54] is not at his post, I beg you'll send him to it; My duty will Require my Staying at Alexandria till Thursday Morning. I more Willingly flatter myself with the hopes of seeing you, as it may be the means of saving you a Journey to Williamsburgh, which you may not have / at present / time to make, on Account of the Affairs of Your Assembly. The Troops I hope are in by this time, every thing seems to go well Towards the success of our Expedition. I am

Your Excellcy's Most Obedient and Most Humble Servant

P.S. Lord Albermarle dead of an Apoplexy.[55]

To Horatio Sharpe Esqr Govr Md

* * *

p. 64 [St. Clair's Orders for Company of Carpenters, Alexandria, March 3, 1755]

Alexandria March 3d 1755

Orders.

The Company of Carpenters to be under Arms to morrow morning at Seven o Clock in order for a Review, no one to be Absent but the Sick, a Return of them and their Names to be Given in.

The Officers who have their Recruits at this place to have them ready to morrow morning at 7 o'Clock that they may be passed.

The annexed being a form of the Return that each Recruiting Officer is to give in & Ready filled up.

* * *

p. 65 [St. Clair Orders for 2nd company of artificers, Alexandria, March 5, 1755]

Orders for the 2d Company of Artificiers

You are hereby Required and directed to march from this with the second Company of Artificiers to Winchester and there to execute such Orders as I shall leave for you at that place. You are to provide your men with Necessarys as soon as you possibly can that you may begin your march[.]

During your stay at this place Mr. Carlile [sic] will furnish you with provisions for your Effective men, and will furnish you with 5 days Provisions which your men are to Carry with them for their March.

You are to Remain at Winches. till further orders, and on Your Arrival at Quarters you are to Apply to Mr. Dick or his Clerk who will Furnish you with Provisions for your Effectives.

You are to Observe on your march, and in Quarters good order and Discipline and Conform your self in every Respect to the Rules and Articles of War.

Given at Alexandria this 5th day of March 1755

* * *

p. 66 [St. Clair Orders for Virginia troops at Alexandria, Alexandria, March 5, 1755]

Orders for the Virginia Troops at Alexandria March 5th 1755

A List of the Companys of Artificiers and the two Detachments Commandd by Captain Hogg and Lieutt Savage to be made According to the annexed form, three copies of each to be made.

A Return to be given of the Arms and Accoutrements of each Company and detachmts. The swords to be given in to Mr. Carlile, who will sign receipts for them.[56]

The Officers commanding the Companies of Artificiers are to provide the non Commission'd Officers and private men each with a Haversack of Osnabrig[57] large enough to carry five days provisions. The men are to pay for these necessaries by a Stoppage out of their pay which the Officers are directed to make.

Each Officer Commanding a Company or detachmt is to keep each Man's Accott [account] Stated Debm and Credm and they are directed to Supply their men with all Necessaries without taking any profit from the men.

Each man of the Artificiers to be provided with the following Necessaries as soon as possible Vizt. 3 shirts & Stocks[.] 3 pr yarn stocgs [stockings], 2 pair of shoes, shoe and Garter Buckles, Indian spatterdashers, and a pair of brown marching Spatterdashers.

If any man sell their Arms, Accoutrements, Ammunition, or Cloathing, he will be severely punish'd.

The Commanding Officer at Quarters is to Order an Officer to visit the hospitals every day and to make a report to him.

Orders for Captain Mercer

You are hereby ordered to Remain at this place with the Company of Artificiers under your Command, you are to observe good Order and Discipline in your Quarters. You are to Receive provisions for your Effective men from Major Carlyle for which you are to give him a Weekly Receipt for his Voucher.

Given at Alexandria this 5th day of March 1755

* * *

p. 67 [St. Clair to Governor Dinwiddie, Alexandria, March 6, 1755]

Alexandria March 6th 1755

Sir

I have enclosed this letter to General Braddock who will deliver it to your Excellency, I am under a Necessity of sending it by express that I may receive your answer on my Return to this place. You may easily believe that I must have met with many things in this review and new Modelling of the Virginia Forces which I cou'd not foresee when I Received my Orders and Instructions done at Williamsburgh. I shall therefore lay before you in what Condition I found those I have Reviewed and what I have Reason to expect from those at Winchester, and Willis's Creek.

Capt Cocke is at Port Royal with upwards of 60 men, which have been Reviewed, he is now joined by a number of Recruits raised by Ens Smith and Mr Cuslache [?]. I sent the former from Fredericksburgh to take charge of those men till they are Reviewed. I have desired Lieut. Woodward to Stay at Fredericksburgh to see any Artillery or Stores landed and forwarded to Winchester.

I have formed the 2 Companys of Artificiers, the First is a very good one and Compleat, the second wants 11 men which I shall get some way or other and send to them at Winchester where they are to march on Saturday. I have Formed a Detachmt of rangers of 47 men and have given the Command of them to Lt Savage till your pleasure is known in what Manner they are to be disposed of. I have given Capt Hog the care of 21 Men that I have draughted for the British Batts and they march to Fredericksburgh on Saturday where he will be joined by the others as soon as I Review them. I have destin'd Alexandria for the Maryland Draughts, you are greatly Oblig'd to Lt Savage for the good Recruits he has rais'd that Officer has done his duty and deserves your countenance.

I expect to be able to Compleat Capt Lewis's Company / including the 18 at Jackson's River / with the men he Marched to Winchester, and with those Recruited by the man you paid 10 Pistoles[58] to: and hope to have half a dozn [dozen] of men for the British Regiments.

I find by a Letter from Col. Innes that he has dicharg'd some of Captn Waggener's and some of Capt Pysoneces people, that there Remains at the fort of the former's 65 Men and of the latter's 58 out of which I am in hopes to form the two Companys for those two Captains.

Capt Stephens and Capt Stewarts Companys are much more numerous at Winchester, you have certainly Reason to expect two Companys formed from them, which if these Officers has not put it in my power, they are greatly to blame.

This is the state of your forces at present, as near as I can guess; and from what I have seen I hope to be able to make out 6 Companies of Rangers, if I am not deceived by building too much on Capt Stewart who I am afraid has not as yet discharg'd the number of bad men I saw at Fredericksburgh.

Lieut Savage is here with 47 Rangers mostly of his own raising[.] These men are desirous to serve with him; I did not care to appoint Capt Stephens to that Company least the men of his Company might be averse[,] especially as I saw a great probability of forming six companies which would employ all your captains: If the scheme of forming the 6 Companys of Rangers meets with approbation Capt Hog may be posted to the Company here, and Captn Cooke to the other when formed at Port Royal. This will be attended with some little inconveniency with Regard to the posting the Subaltern officers. Lieut Savage will be to Capt Hogg's Company. I shou'd wish'd [sic] the subaltern officers had not been named to Companys, on account that few of them understand that point of the service, which is that if they had a Commission from his Majesty, naming them to a particular Company it is in the power of the Commanding Officer to change them. In case I do not get above 20 men of Capt Stewart's recruits fit for service, and to give him his Commission—for the Troop of light Horse before he has his Complimt of men Compleat.

I beg your Excellency may Explain to me what I have requested, Shou'd you Compleat the Rangers to 6 Companys. I take on me to beg all the Commissions may be of the same date. I shall act in every respect for the good of the service and shall lay before you any abuses that have been committed that they may be remedied for the future, I must repeat to you that if I find any difficulty in forming the 6th Company of Rangers the whole blame will be on Capt Stewart whose Company I saw the first time I was at Fredericksburg.

There is a pay Mr p [Pay Master] Wanting for the Troops, I am not able to lay down an Establishmt for one, which Capt Orme will put you in a way of doing, a Lieut is the proper Officer for Such an employment; and I may venture to say that Mr Savage has done a great deal for the service, and in deserving of that Office, for want of such an Officer I declare the thing to be almost next to an impossibility of getting the past accounts Settled.

No manner of Care has been taken about the Arms, I wish I cou'd fix the Neglect on any one Person, I shou'd Lay hold of him. I am afraid I shall be under a Necessity of Convincing some of your young Gent how Necessary it is to follow Military Orders.

Be so good as desire Capt Orme to see if there is any Stuff to make Tents of, those that have been made hither to are of no manner of use in the Field, the Officers Small tents when wet are a load for a Waggon being made of sail Cloath. They will be of great service for Magazine tents if we Entrench a Camp at Savage River. I expect Gover Sharpe here every moment; and shall let you know by postscript what steps we agree on for the Modelling the Maryland Forces. On the whole the men of the Virginia Forces are much better than I had Reason to Expect. I am with the greatest Respect,

Your Exy's

[P.S.] I must Refer you to Genl Braddock with Regard to Gover Sharpe.

* * *

p. 70 [St. Clair to General Braddock, Alexandria, March 6, 1755]

Alexandria March 6th 1755

To His Excy. General Braddock

I find myself under a Necessity of sending an Express to your Excellency, that I may Receive further directions on my Return hither for the forming the Virginia Forces, I enclose you a letter for the Governour which ought to have been sent to you / at least the substance of it / but there is no one in this place who I cou'd employ to write for me.

I did myself the honour of writing to your Excellency from Fredericksburg and gave you an Account of what I had been doing at that place, I cou'd not possibly get hither till Monday noon, and am afraid I shall be detained some days longer on account of the great fall of snow, and a Drift which has filled up the roads, the Magistrates are to go with me that I may give them directions concerning the Roads as far as Winchester; for that Reason I wou'd be glad to have the snow melted before I leave this, I have this for it, that the weather changes in this Climate every 24 hours.

Since being at this place, I have formed two Companys of Carpenters Your Excellency will by the Returns I have sent Capt Orme see that the first is Compleat and that the second wants eleven men which I shall get them as soon as I can; these latter are under marching Orders, and will begin their march on Saturday for Winches. I have picked out twenty one good men for the British Battns they march to Fredericksburgh on Saturday under the Command of Capt Hogg. I have formed a Detachment of Rangers under the Command of Lieut Savage. They are near Compleat, but I am unwilling to form them till my return; and that I Receive an answer to the inclosed Letter.

Your Excellency will easily Imagine what a difficult thing I am now about I shall think myself Lucky if I can have my Conduct Approv'd of. I have given the Soldiers warning of what will happen to them if they come under the lash of the Military law, and I dread I shall be obliged to do what will be disagreeable to some of the Officers.—

I sent an express to Gover Sharpe to know if his Affairs wou'd permit him to come to this place, I shall keep this Letter open until the express Returns if he cannot come hither, I shall send him an Officer Concerning the forming the Maryland Forces, after I have draughted them at Frederick at which place I shall receive his answer.

The Company of Artificiers and 47 Rangers that are here in Quarters are very much at a loss for a Surgeon, and when the Maryland Forces arrive there may be more use for one; this is the Reason I have hurried away the 2d Company of Carpenters to Winchester and the draughted to Fredericksburgh, it wou'd be of great benefit for the Service if your Excellency wou'd get one of the Surgeons or Mates of the Man of War sent hither until the Troops land, what makes me the more desirous of having a Surgeon is that a very Ugly fever is raging in these parts, which I am afraid some of our men have got[.]

I hope this Letter will find you employ'd with the arrival of the of the Forces from Ireland, if you have not time to write to me, with Regard to any Article of my Letter to the Gover I beg to have directions to inable [sic] me to put in Execution what the Gover wills me on account of the Forces of the Colony I am with the greatest Respect.

Your Exys &ca.

March 7th

P.S. Since writing the above Gover Sharpe has adjourn'd his assembly for a Couple of days, and is come to this place, I shall get 150 of his Maryland Forces for the British Battns and he proposes to me to Raise 2 Companys of Rangers on the footing of the Virginia ones on Condition that I wou'd pay the 150 men or more after I draughted them for the British Battns which I think is but Reasonable, and I have agreed to it, it will be 12 days before I can get to Frederick, the Roads are I am afraid unpassable [sic.], on the Account of the heavy Rain that is now falling.

I beg your Excellency will consider if the frame of the Vessels is for Lake Erie or Lake Ontario if for the latter it ought to be sent to New York.[59]

I beg the express may not be sent back soon as I do not think I can Return hither in less than 14 days.

Gover Sharpe has promised to give me all the assistance possible in the Recruiting Capt. Rutherford's Company, I shall order him on the Recruiting service, but I can follow no Expedient for Compleating Capt Clarkes. Capt Dumore of the South Carolina Company will command at the Fort. If I can get a few spare men for that Company they shall have them if the people will enlist Voluntarily in it.

* * *

p. 73 [St. Clair to Major John Carlyle, Alexandria, March 6, 1755]

Alexandria March 6th 1755

Sir

I must desire that you will take Receipts from the Commanding officer of Companys and Detachments for the Quantity of Provis: you deliver out to them those Receipts are to be signed every Monday for the weeks provision before, and will serve you for your proper Vouchers. I am,

Sir

Your humble Servant

To Major John Carlyle

* * *

p. 74 [St. Clair Orders to Captain Hogg of the Virginia Forces, Alexandria, March 7, 1755]

Orders for Capt. Hogg at Alexandria March 7th 1755

You are hereby Required and directed to march from this with a Detachment of men for the British Regiments to Fredericksburg and to Continue at that Place till further Orders[.] if you find an Opportunity of going by Water to the nearest landing place to Fredericksburgh you are to take it.

During your Stay at this place Mr Carlyle will furnish you with Provisions for your Effectives[,] and will furnish you with Provisions for Your march.

On your arrival at Quarters, you are to Apply to Mr Dick or his Clerk who will furnish you with provisions for your Effectives, and you are to sign a Receipt every Monday for the Quantity you have had taking care not to Exceed the numbers on your weekly Return.

You are to Observe on your March and In Quarters good order and Discipline and Composing yourself in every Respect to the Rules and Articles of War

Given under my hand at Alexandria this 7th day of March 1755

John St Clair

* * *

p. 75 [St. Clair to Lieutenant Savage, Alexandria, March 7, 1755]

Sir

You are hereby Required and directed to Remain at this place with a Detachment of rangers under your Command[.] you are to Observe good order and Discipline in Quarters. You are to Receive Provisions for your Effective men from Mr Carlyle for which you are to Give a Weekly Receipt for his Voucher. Given under my hand at Alexandria this 7th day of March 1755

John St Clair

To Lieut Savage

* * *

p. 76 [Captain Orme to St. Clair, Hampton, March 6, 1755]

Sir

As the Transports are not yet arrived and as the Season must Necessarily be broke up before the Companies can be Settled in their several Cantonments many Inconveniencies seeming also to arise from the separation of the Troops, it being impossible to dispose, cloath & arm and Discipline the Service in the short time that will be allow'd for it His Excellency therefore orders me to let you know he thinks a Camp at Alexandria will much better answer all these purposes and the General therefore intends to Order all the Ships to Proceed to Alexa and the whole to disembark there, and that their own Quarter Masters shall mark out an encampment till you can arrive, which he desires may be as soon as possible, and that all the Virginia and Maryland Recruits may be ordered to Alexandria with what Provisions &c. you may judge necessary, and to Obviate any inconveniences from the Cold his Excellency will direct all the Soldier's Bedding to be landed with them.[60] I am

Sir

Your Most Obedt Sevt

Robt Orme Aid de camp

Hampton March 6th 1755

To Sir John St Clair, Bart

* * *

p. 77 [St. Clair to Captain Cocke, commanding officer of detachment of Virginia forces at Port Royal, Winchester, March 12, 1755]

By Sir John St Clair Bart Quarter Master General to the British Forces in America

You are hereby Required and directed to March from Port Royal to Alexandria with the detachment of Virginia Forces under your Command in order that they may be formed into Companys. You are to begin your March two days after your Receive this order, and you are not to march thro Maryland.

Mr. Commissary Duke [Dick] will furnish you with Provisions for your March, which you men are to Carry, he will likewise furnish you with Osnaburg Stuff to make Haversacks[61] for the men who have been Reviewed which the men are to pay for.

During your Stay at Alexandria Mr. Carlyle will furnish you with provisions for your Effective men for which you are to give a Receipt.

You are to Observe on your march and in Quarters good order and Discipline, and Conform yourself in every respect to the Rules & Articles of War, the Officers not to Quit their men on their march.

Given under my Hand at Winchester this 12th day of March 1755

The Recruits which are not reviewed are included in this Order.

To Capt Cocke Commanding a Detachmt of Virginia Forces at Port Royal

* * *

p. 78 [St. Clair to General Braddock, Great Cacecapon, March 12, 1755]

Great Capecapon March 12th 1755

To General Braddock

On my being at Winchester I Received a Letter from Capt. Orme Acquainting me that our Excellency had come to a Resolution that the Troops shou'd proceed to Alexandria, and Encamp at that place, as the season is so far Advanced we shall certainly gain time by keeping our people together.

The People of Fairfax County have promised me that the road leading from Alexandria to the top of the Blue Ridge shall be cut. I carried the Overseers with me and pointed out to them what I wou'd have done[,] on my arrival at Winchester I sent expresses for the Overseers of the Roads / between the Blue Ridge and Winchester / from Alexandria and Fredericksburgh, they all say they will Compleat them Immediately; as I am going up I shall take the same steps.

I found the Virginia Troops at Winchester in much the same Condition as I expected, and have discharg'd 124 of them. I have got 24 Men for the British Battns which was more than I had reason to Expect, by Capt. Lewis not Coming to Winchester with his Company I shall be Oblig'd to Return that way to form his Company and give him Orders for Augusta County. I may say no Officer ever had such a Review as this has been, what with detecting Irish Papists and examining sore shins I had my hands full, but we have got rid of both the One and the Other.[62]

I shou'd have wrote this Letter from Winchester but I was willing to see Mr Commissary Dick, who I met at this house; I herewith Transmit to your Excellency what he tells me of Mr Commissary Walker's Success at Pennsylvania.

I am now making a Disposition for my seeing Youghangany River before I Return to Alexandria[,] this may take me up three days, but it will put me past all doubts with Regard to our passing the Potomack.

I shall return to Alexandria as soon as I possibly can[,] the preparations that I am making are absolutely Necessary for our Expedition. I hope 28th of the month; and sooner if possible[.] I have got some setts of wheels in this Country for our heavy Guns, they shall be sent to Fredericksburgh.

On the Receipt of Capt Ormes Letter I have ordered Capt Cocke to march from Port Royal to Alexandria, that the Company of Rangers may be form'd at that place, and his men draughted for the British Battalions, those at Fredericksburgh, are already draughted and we may have them at Alexnda in three or four days after the Troops arrive. I shall take care to have the Latter with you, as soon as the Maryland Forces.

I am with the greatest Respect

Your Excellency's Most Obedient and Most Humble Servant.

* * *

p. 80 [St. Clair to Captain Thomas Clarke, commanding independent company of New York, Wills Creek, March 18, 1755]

Agreeable to the Receiving Instructions given unto me by his Excy General Braddock Commander in Chief of his Majesty's Forces in North America. It is expected that a Report shou'd be made, that all the Troops in his Majesty's pay shou'd be compleat and fit for service by the 25 of March. And Whereas, in making the Review of the two independent Companys of New York, the Company Comand'd by Capt Clarke is in a great measure found unfit for service, on account of a deficiency in their Numbers, and a great number of old men so that the Company wants more than half to Compleat it.

That his Majesty's service may suffer as Little as Possible by this great Neglect, I hereby order that the independent Company Comand'd by Capt Clarke do march from this to Frederick in Maryland and then the Subaltern Officers, are to go from thence on the Recruiting Service so that the Company may be Completed with good able Bodied men, to Its Establishment by the 25 day of April.

Capt Clarke is hereby Ordered to provide his Company with Camp Equippage and all other Necessarys According to the annexed List to be ready to take the Field by the 25 of April. Given under my hand at the Fort at Willis's Creek this 18th day of March 1755.

To Capt Thoms [Thomas] Clarke Commandr [Commander] of an Indept [Independent] Company of New York

* * *

p. 81 [St. Clair to Captain Waggoner of Virginia Forces, Wills Creek, March 18, 1755]

By Sir John St Clair Baronet, Quarter Master General to the British Forces in North America

You are hereby Required and Directed to March from this on Wednesday the 10th Instant and to proceed to Winchester with the men of the Virginia Forces to be discharg'd[.] on your arrival at that place You will Receive 8 days provisions for your men, and you are to Discharge them.

Orders will be left for you at Winchester for your Return to the Fort. You are to take Lieut. Speidolf under your Command as Far as Winchester.

The Officers are not to quit their men on their march[,] and to preserve good order and Discipline conformable to the Articles of War.

Given under my hand at the Fort at Willis's Creek this 18th day of March 1755

To Capt Waggoner of the Virginia Forces

* * *

p. 82 [St. Clair to Captain Thomas Clarke, commanding independent company of New York, Wills Creek, March 18, 1755]

By Sir John St Clair Baront Quarter Master General of the British Forces in North America

Conform to the Instructions unto me given by his Excellency Edward Braddock Esqr General and Commander in Chief of his Majesty's Forces in North America. You are hereby Required and directed to March from this on Thursday 20th Instant, and to proceed to Frederick in Maryland. You are there to discharge such men as have been mark'd down as unfit for service.

The Officers are not to quit their men on their March and Discipline and Conform yourselves in every Respect to the Rules and Articles of War.

Given under my hand at the Fort at Willis's Creek this 18th day of March 1755

To Capt Thomas Clarke Command'g Independent Company at New York

* * *

p. 83 [St. Clair to Mr. Perkins, Winchester, March 21, 1755]

Mr. Perkins

Sir

At your Request as a Civil Magistrate, I have delivered over John May to you in order to be prosecuted at Civil Law Concerning a Rifle which was lost in a scuffle said May had with some of the Inhabitants. You cannot be ignorant that the said May was offered up to the Civil Magistrate on this Fray happening, but on their declining the prosecution he was try'd by a Regimental Court Martial and Severely Punished.

To avoid having any Misunderstanding between the Civil and Military Powers, I have ordered him to be discharg'd and my duty Obliges me to inform you that if this man Receives any further punishment or Confinement, that I shall lay the thing before his Majesty's Attorney Genl that his Majesty may not be stripped of his Soldiers on such Frivolous account as these.

I am.

Sir

Your Humble Servant

Winchester March 21st 1755

* * *

p. 84 [St. Clair Order to company of rangers, Winchester, March 21, 1755]

By Sir John St Clair Bart Quarter Master General of his Majesty's Forces in America

You are hereby Required and Directed to March with the first Company of Rangers under your Command, and make the Roads passable for all kind of Carriages from Winchester to Enoch Enoch's[63]

on the Capecapon, when you have cut the Roads that far, You are to Consult with Henry Enoch the proper place for crossing on a Flatt. You are to Cut the Roads down to that place, and Level the banks of the River for that purpose, Shou'd I not be able to join you before you have Cut the Roads this far, you are to pass the River and Cut the Road blaz'd out by Henry Enoch to the Mouth of the South Branch, he will attend you on this service[.] and has directions from me that all the inhabitants within Eight Miles of the Road that is to be Cut shall attend on this important piece of service for the good of their Country. You are to march from hence so soon as you can get Tools, and you are to work with 20 men of your Company each Day who shall be paid six pence British Sterling for their Work which the Commissary shall have my Orders to pay. The Commissary has my directions to furnish you with provisions. If this work can be finish'd before my Return, You are to pass the Potomack to Col. Crisip's and march from that to the Fort at Willis's Creek, You are on your March and when Encamp'd to Observe good Order and Discipline and Conform yourself in every Respect to the Rules and Articles of War.

Given under my hand at Winchester this 21st day of March 1755

* * *

p. 85 [Governor Sharpe to St. Clair, Annapolis, March 15, 1755]

Annapolis March 15th 1755

Sir

I had writ to Captain Dagworthy, directing him in case you chose to draught his Company into the British Regiments to preserve and take care of the Men's Arms, Blankets, Kittles, Cantines apprehending they will be supplied with those Articles as soon as they Join the Regiments. If you approve not of his following these Orders You will be pleased to direct Otherwise, and you will find Capt Dagworthy Ready to Obey you. I have just Received a Letter from Mr Carlyle at Alexandria, Advising me that three Transports with Col. Burton and some other Officers, and Part of Dunbar's regiment were just come up to that place, where they proposed to disembark as Yesterday. He also tells me that the General had order'd all the Troops to land there and as the Season is Already far Advance'd to encamp at their arrival in that case pray what must be done with the Beeves and flour, that have been purchased, and Order'd to Bladensburgh, Rocks Creek, Conagoga, Frederick Town, and Marlbro. Govr Dinwiddie intimates to me that I might expect the pleasure of of seeing the General here soon, as he proposed to do me the honour of having an Interview with Gover Shirley at my house, as soon as I hear of the General's arrival at Alexandria I shall wait on him. Our Assembly is yet setting, but I dispair of persuading them to grant any supplies. The Gent who presents you this is one of the three I mentioned to you were desirious of going Volunteers. I have desir'd them to Return again hither before they wait on Col. Halkett and if you approve thereof be pleased to Order Capt. Dagworthy hither to go Recruiting.

I am with the greatest Esteem.

Your Most Humble and Most Obedt Servt

Horo Sharpe

P.S. the gun Carriage did not answer my Expectations but I have sent it to Alexandria.

* * *

p. 86 [Braddock to St. Clair, Williamsburg, March 15, 1755]

To Sir John St Clair, Baront

Dear Sir

Upon Lieut. Col. Burton's[64] Coming to Virginia, he having but two Companys with him[.] at his Request, and that of the Officers with him I consented he shou'd go no further than Alexandria and encamp there[65] upon a Supposition as every body here agreed that the bad Weather was broke up, but as I find it is as cold as ever it was, and may probably continue, I wou'd desire you to Cantone them according to the Plan we agreed upon, but if possible not so far distant, and not less than a Company in a place, and that the Draughts be sent to their immediately, that they may have time to drill them. The Transports are all arrived but two and are Dispatch'd away to Alexandria, as Col. Dunbar's Regiments is also arrived, you may if you think it necessary send some Body to Stop them at the Landing place on this side, and from thence make them proceed to their Quarters, they tell me the well Water at Alexandria is apt to give the Flux[.] if so, the men shou'd be cautioned not to drink it, as the River is at hand.[66] there are not on the whole number of men already come over two sick. I propose to be at Alexandria the twenty second or twenty third instant.

I am with great Regard,

Your Most Huml and Most Obedt Servant

Edward Braddock

Williamsburgh March 15th 1755

* * *

p. 87 [St. Clair Memorandum for General Braddock, Williamsburg, March 28, 1755]

Memorandum for General Braddock

That a proper person of the Artillery shou'd be sent to Rock Creek to Receive the Stores sent thither by water, and lodge them in the Storehouse provided by Mr. Beal, that he is to see these stores loaded on Waggons for Conogagee, for which he is to take Receipts from the Waggoners, for the Quantity loaded, and that he is to give a ticket Specifying their load which the Waggoner is to deliver to the person who is appointed to Receive the Stores at said place, and on that persons signing a Receipt for the load, the Waggoner will be paid by the Comy of Stores at the Rate of 16 pence of Maryland money a mile, as the law of Maryland directs, Care is to be taken that they load 2000 Weight. Mr. Cresap will provide Storehouses at Conogagee.

That a Proper Person of the Artillery shou'd be sent to Conogagee to Receive the Stores sent thither by land from Rock Creek, he is to see that the stores are according to the List sent him from Rock Creek, and give the Waggoner a Receipt on the back of their Ticketts, for their payment. He is to see the Stores put on board Cannoes, and sent to the Fort at Willis's Creek, and to Consign them to the Officer at the Fort, who will Receive them, and Mr. Commissary Walker will pay the Water Carriage.

That an Officer of the Artillery shou'd be sent Eight days hence to Willis's Creek, to Receive all stores sent thither, for which there are proper Magazines.

That a proper Person of the Artillery shou'd be sent to Winchester, to Receive and forward all Stores by land in the same manner as the one at Rock Creek.

It is recommended that the Commissary of Stores for the Artillery shou'd Consult with Mr Commissary Dick, that he may know what Waggonage he is to state to him for the Ordnance of Stores.

Alexandria, March 28th 1755

* * *

p. 88 [Braddock to St. Clair, Williamsburg, April 1, 1755][67]

By his Excellency Edward Braddock Esqr General and Comander [sic] in chief of his Majesties Forces in North America

To Sir John St Clair, Deputy Quarter Mastr Genl

In case of Your meeting no Field Officer at Willis's Creek, of Superior Rank to yourself. I do hereby empower and direct You, as soon as you shall get thither, if you shall think it Necessary for his Majesty's service to take upon you the Command of all the Forces there, and all Officers and other whom it may Concern, are in such case hereby Required, and directed to Obey you Accordingly. Given at the Camp at Alexandria the first day of April 1755.

E. Braddock

By his Excellency's Command

W. Shirley

* * *

p. 89 [St. Clair memorandum for commissaries, not addressed, not dated]

Memorandum for the Commissaries.

As the Army will be able to take the field by the 10th day of May, the Commissaries are directed to Assemble two Hundred Waggons, and two Thousand Horses, at the Camp of the British Army at Willis's Creek by that day, that they are to take all Necessary precaution in providing pack saddles and halters for the Horses. That they shall first hire as many Waggons with Horses as they can, and as many as are short of the above number are to be purchased at the best terms Possible, and to be in Readiness at the time mentioned, but the horses not to be delivered till the 8th or 9th of May.

* * *

p. 90 [St. Clair Proposal for advancing army from Winchester and Frederick, Winchester, April 3, 1755]

Winchester April 3d 1755

Proposals for a Disposition for Advancing the Army from Winchester and Frederick in Maryland.

1st   The two Brigades being Advanc'd to Winchester and Frederick and the Artillery to Winche. A detachment of the Winchester Brigade is to march up with it to Willis's Creek to strengthen the Convoy and to Cover it but if the road to be cut from the Bridge on the Opikan [Opequan River] to Bear Garden, proves passable for the Artillery then the Artillery shall March along that Road, without Coming to Winchester, which will save them nine miles, and the detachment from Winchester shall march and join them at Henry Enoch's, and Convoy them to Wills's Creek, As that Road is to be Reconoitered soon, a Report of it shall be made to the Officer Commanding the Brigade at Winchester.

A detachment to be sent from the Brigade at Frederick to Canogogee, to Cover our Flour Magazines, and to Assist in embarking the Stores; this Detachment to be made as soon as may be.

As the removal of the Brigades from Winchester and Frederick to Wills's Creek, must depend upon the Quantity of Flour that is to be sent from Pensylvania; the time for their Removal from the said place can be fixed, when a proper quantity of that Flour is arriv'd at Conogogee from whence it may at any time be carried by water up to Willis's Creek, and of this timely notice shall be given to the Commander in Chief, and to the Commdg Officer of said Brigades, that they may march immediately.

2nd   When the Troops are Assembled, and the whole got together in Readiness to March from Willis's Creek to Fort Duquesne; the march must be Fixed for one of the two following Routes, viz.

One through the Meadows, and Across the River Yohiogane, being the Route taken by Col. Washington last Year, and the other must be by turning the head of that River, if found practicable, the latter seems most Eligible, since by taking the Former, the French may dispute our passage, in crossing the River, and give us the trouble of laying Bridges, and making Works to Cover them. The Reconoitring of the latter Route, shall be set about with the utmost Expedition, and if Found practicable, the Troops now at Willis's Creek, may be employ'd in Cutting the Road Open. They may venture to Cut the length of 25 Miles before the other Troops arrive.

The disposition of marching the Army from Willis's Creek, may be better deferred until the above Route Round the head of the Yohoganie is Reconoitred, then a disposition shall be made, and sent with the Report of that Route.

The Commissaries have directions to Assemble horses and Waggons by the 10th day of May; which is the soonest that horses can have grass, and if we Cannot March by that time, the horses and Waggons may be employ'd in bringing such Provisions as may be Wanting.

* * *

p. 92 [St. Clair to General Braddock, Winchester, April 6, 1755]

Winchester April 6th 1755

To General Braddock

I herewith transmit to your Excellency the disposition for advancing the Troops to Wills's Creek, which Mr. Mackellar and I hope will meet with your approbation. I have taken all the Necessary Steps with Regard to putting it in Execution by giving Instructions to the Commissaries for the Assembling together 200 Waggons and 2000 Horses by the 10th of May.

I have sent to Alexandria a Waggon Master for the Regts. He is a young man well Recommended; and was to have gone a Volunteer with the Army, this may give encouragement to the Inhabitants to go with us, there will be two more wanting, which the Commissaries named to me, the one to go to Maryland, and the Other to Pennsylvania to assemble the Carriages, These may serve for Waggon Masters to the Train if the Officers think proper to employ them, if not they may be paid off when they have done their Works. Mr Commissary Walker is gone to Augusta County for those men and to send down Waggons, he returns in ten days to Wills's Creek.

Mr Commissary Dick goes from this tomorrow for Fredericksburg to hasten up the Guns, the Cohorns with most of the stores are already arrived, we have got the powder safely lodged in a very proper place and are preparing a Place for the Ordnance Stores which I hope will be finished by tomorrow Night, and an Account taken of the stores.

I hope that Govr Dinwiddie will excuse me for taking the float of Rowland's ferry on the Potomack, and sending it to Goose Creek for the passage of our Waggons.

We found a great many more things to do here, than I had Reason to Expect, which has detain'd us a day or two longer from going to see the Roads Cut. I am in hopes to find them in great forwardness. You Shall have the Report of them sent to Frederick in Maryland. I am a good deal uneasy that there is no Troops at Conogogee. I beg a Detachment may be sent to that place from Frederick to Cover our Magazines, in the mean time I shall Stop Capt Dagworthy with half his Company who ought to be on their March by this time from Frederick. The other half will be wanted at Col. Cresaps for Repairing a Road.

Fifteen waggons go from hence tomorrow for Alexandria which will serve for the march of the first Brigade. In case your Excellency shou'd not be Return'd from Annapolis, when the Messenger Arrives at Alexandria, I have wrote to Sir Peter Halkett about this[.] Whatever Steps are taken I shall Acquaint you of it, from time to time, and shall make your stay at Frederick as short as I can, Whatever Commands you may have for me, I beg they may be sent to Wills's Creek.

I need not put your Excellency in mind that money is Wanted for everything. If nothing else can be done, paper money of Maryland must be had, otherwise all our Carriages will be at a Stop, please to send up as much as is to be had of it, to Mr Commissary Walker at the Fort. I have the honour of being with the greatest Respect.

Your Excy's

Most Obedient, and Most Huml Servant,

* * *

p. 94 [St. Clair to General Braddock, Cacecapon, April 13, 1755][68]

From Enoch's House on Caperaphon River April 10th 1755

To General Braddock

I am Obliged to send your Excellency an Express to Acquaint you that Mr Mackellar and I have viewed the Road leading from the Ridge on the Opekan to this place, and we find it passable for all sorts of Carriages. I have directed that 34 Teams of horses shou'd be at Alexandria the 18th for transporting the Artillery directly to Wills's Creek for if they were to stop at Winchester it might Occasion Fresh Delays. The Artillery may stop a day on the Road at Mr Commissary Dick's plantation to Refresh their horses, this is on the Road 7 Miles on this side Shannandeau Ferry.

I have not heard anything of the proper persons of the Artillery either being sent to Winchester or Conogagee, by that Neglect of Capt. Hind[69] I was detain'd two days at Winchester, and was I to go from hence to Conogagee Which is 50 miles; the same thing must happen to me, as I make no Doubt but that the Commanding Officer of the Artillery has very sufficient reason for Neglecting your Orders, I do not apprehend it any business of mine to Repair his Neglects, especially when I am now making this Road passable for the Carriages and which I expect will be in Order for the Artillery to pass by the 14th having only 14 miles now to Cut.

I shall Execute your Excellency's Command in Reconoitering the Road to Fort Duquesne but to fix on a time for the Accomplishing thereof is not in my power, I had given a Meeting to one of the Commissioners of Pennsylvania on Tuesday for a Night, the Reason of it your Excellency will see by the letters I inclose; there is no flour arrived as yet from Pennsylvania, Mr Cresop Advises me that he Expects part of it this week.

The Road from Frederick to Wills's Creek, as I have Cut it is as Near as going all the way thro Maryland, but I shall do all that lies in my Power to get the Latter Road opened that we may be able to use the Maryland Waggons, in case the Water Carriages shou'd fail us. I must entreat Your Excellency to send up a Detachment to Conagagee for the Embarking our Stores; and that you will be pleased to Order the Artillery to be Ready by the time mentioned above.

I Shou'd be extremely glad to have the Return of the messenger by Tuesday at the Fort, for I hope the next day to be able to go to Reconoitre.[70] I have the honour of being with the greatest Respect,

Your Excellency's

[P.S.] A great No. of the Pieces of Eight brought up by Mr. Dick have a Very bad look, some of them were brought to me in Change Which I did not Refuse or else no one wou'd have taken them. If they are bad as I apprehend it is a most horrid imposition.[71]

* * *

p. 96 [St. Clair to captains Cocke and Jones, Cacecapon, April 13, 1755]

Camp on Cacapehon Creek April 13th 1755

Messiers Cocke & Jones

Sir

I have this moment Received an Express from his Excellency General Braddock Complaining that the Country people are very Dilatory in sending their Waggons and Teams of horses for our Artillery & Stores which are lying at Alexandria[.] this is the only thing that Retards all our Operations. I hope you have sent down the Waggons for their 2d Loading but I am very sorry to Acquaint you that the numbers which were to bring me down last week are far short of what I expected.

I am now to Acquaint you that 58 Waggons are immediately Wanted to be at Alexandria and 24 Teams of horses with their Harness besides the 34 Teams of Horses I Ordered Mr Dick to send down[.] I wou'd not have the Country people Plead that they have their ground to plough, the Service of the King and Country must be first done, and the People who have the Waggons employ'd will soon earn money enough to purchase horses for Labour.

You are therefore to warn all the Waggons in the Country for his Majesty's Service, the numbers mentioned above to be sent to Alexandria and the others are to load stores at Winchester for the Fort taking the Road by H. Enoch's and Crossing the Potomack at the mouth of the south Branch. Shou'd any of the Inhabitants Refuse to go on this Service, You are to let me know their names that I may apply to Sir Peter Halkett for a Detachment of our Soldiers to be Quartered on them; and you may take my word for it, that if those people do not go on this service with their Waggons and horses, I shall Convince them that they had better draw up our Artillery gratis from Alexandria, and been Yoked in place of their horses.[72]

I am

[salutations not transcribed]

* * *

p. 97 [St. Clair to Captain Orme, Cacecapon, April 13, 1755]

Camp West Side of Cacapehon April 13th 1755

To Captain Orme

I have this moment Received yours by an Express Concerning Waggons and horses for transporting the Artillery &c. In a letter I wrote to General Braddock of the 10th I told him that I had done upon that head, but I now find the demands encrease, and all I can do for this is to pursue the Steps I have already taken with diligence and Perserverance. I was very well aware of the difficulty we shou'd labour under in Regard to the Artillery, and therefore took my Measures Accordingly, but if the Commanding Officers of that Corps and the Commissary, expect to have their Artillery and Stores march together, I think they must be disappointed, unless they stay until the grass Grows up, for I am very Well informed that one fourth part of the horses in the Country are not assayed fit for Service, I thereupon think the most Expeditious Method will be to take the Waggons as they can get them to Willis's Creek. It may indeed be Attended with the Inconveniency of Misplacing a few things, or perhaps losing a few, but this I think cannot come in Competition with the dispatch Required, I shall however use my Endeavours to get as many at a time as I can.

I shall Order down twenty four teams with harness, and as many Waggons as can be got; When they March they are to Proceed by the new Road from Opeckan Ridge straight to Willis's Creek and not to go to Winchester.

I told General Braddock the Road between this Place and the South Branch wou'd be finished by tomorrow Night, but I find it will Require three or four days more / Which is the Reason of my having stay'd here so long / but even that time will be soon enough for their March; the directions in your Letter with Regards to Sir Peter Halkett, and the Rangers, I shall take care to follow

I shall be at Willis's Creek on Tuesday next to keep my Appointment with the Commissioners from Pennsylvania, which was for that or that day Fornight,[73] Receive their Report with Regard to the Road to be Cut over Laurel Ridge; this Report must determine the time of my Waiting upon the General at Frederick, and if it proves favourable, I shall venture to wait upon him, and Mr Mackellar and Gordon will undertake to Recoinoitre that Road; and I shall order them a proper Party for their Escort on the Road to Fort duQuesne, which I meant to Reconoitre before; and save our Crossing the Monongahela and Yohogany[.] if his Excellency does not Approve of this, You'll please to let me know by Express. I am &c.

P.S. Please to employ all the Smiths at Frederick to make the following Particulars

Felling axes ... 100
Horses shoes, hundredweights ... 10
Whip Saws ... 12
Miner's Tools ... 3 Sets for breaking and blowing Rock

* * *

p. 99 [St. Clair to Sir Peter Halkett, Cacecapon, April 13, 1755]

Camp West Side of Cocapehon 13th April 1755

Sir

As the Road from Opeckon Ridge to Willis's Creek / Without going to Winchester / will be Open in 2 or 3 days, You are to send a Detachment of the Brigade under your Comand [sic] to Henry Enoch's at that place, and to Remain here until the Artillery arrives from Alexandria, and upon their arrival they are to join and Escort them to Willis's Creek. Your detachment may March upon the 22d Instant, their first days march to Patton's and the 2d to sd Place, Fifteen days Provisions besides the 5 days provisions which they carry will probably be Necessary to bring them to Willis's Creek. You shall be Acquainted when things are in Readiness at that place for marching the Remainder of Your Brigade.

There are some Arms belonging to this Country in Store at Winchesr which will Probably be taken for the use of Yours and Col. Dunbar's Regiments those that are here are in very bad Repair and if you will be so good as to employ Your Armourers while you Remain at Winchester to put them in Order it will be an Acceptable Service, and they shall be thankfully paid for their trouble. I am with the Greatest Regards

Sir Your

[P.S.] April 14th I am informed that some of the Country people upon goose Creek and Broad Run have not sent their Waggons to Alexandria According to Orders, this You can be informed of at

Davis's 4 miles beyond Quaker Thompson', and if it is true, I shou'd be glad I you wou'd send Orders to your next Division to Quarter some Soldiers on them at free Cost, until the whole are past.

I am sir
Sir Peter Halkett or Officer Comandg the Brigade at Winchester

* * *

p. 100 [St. Clair to officer commanding the artillery, Cacecapon, April 13, 1755]

Camp on Cocapheon April 13th 1755

Sir

As the Road from the Ridge on the Opekon for Willis's Creek will be Open before you can Receive this, You are to take that Road with the Artillery without touching at Winchester, the Wagons with Stores are to proceed directly to Willis's Creek in the same manner.

You will find a Detachment of Sir Peter Halkett's Regiment at that place, who will Strengthen your Convoys and Escort them at Willis's Creek. I am

Sir

To the Officer Commanding the Artillery

* * *

p. 101 [Sir Peter Halkett to St. Clair, Winchester, April 16, 1755]

Winchester the 16th April 1755

Sir

Yesterday about Eleven I Received your Letter one Mile on this side of the Bridge they are making, your letter Concerning the Waggons who have not gone down to Alexandria I sent forward to the Officer Commanding the Second Division of my Regiment.

Let me know if one Capt and two Subalterns with fifty men will be a Sufficient Escort for the Artillery, or if I shou'd Order a Stronger party, the Number of the Artillery you expect I have not heard and cannot judge exactly what the Escort shou'd be, if the Artillery is to be in Brigades different Escorts will be proper[.] Agreeable to the Advice I have from you, It shall be directed, all parties shall have fifteen days provisions besides those that they shall carry.

Upon Tuesday, I shall send off the Company of the Virginia Rangers, who are under Order to March, and they shall have the above provisions with them, upon the 22nd the Escort shall march.

The Arms you Mention, I shall have examined if there are people Amongst us who can Repair them, I shall set them to Work, after I have had some of my own arms Repaired.

I have Received orders from Britain to Augments my Regt with ten Sergeants, ten Corporals, and three hundred men, if I can Raise them I shall have ten Additional Officers, I wish that you would pick me up a few Recruits I have [en]listed five to day at one Pistole and a Dollar and half a Dollar to the Man who brings a man.[74]

Capt Stewart hears that you have brought up a Considerable number of horses, out of which his Troop is to be Mounted; he wants to know if it is so, and if he Shou'd or Shou'd not buy up horses. Capt Stewart wants to know Who he is to Apply to for harness.

That Troop has only got Swords, let me know how they are to be Provided with other Arms and Accoutrements fit for a Troop, here and at Alexandria there is no leather proper to make Bucketts of. Directions must be Given for having it from some other place, if he must Order the buying of it, he wants to know what will be a proper Quantity, by this Express let me have your Answer to the above particulars, and favour me with what besides may Occur to you. Col. Walgrave has got Genl Sir Georges Dragoons, the Seventh & Ninth Regiments of Foot are Ordered to Britain and are to be Augmented to the British Establishment.[75] I am

Sir

Your Most Obedt Humble Servt

Peter Halkett

[P.S.] Let me know if the Officers must have Forrage here, or must buy in the Country.

To Sir John St Clair, Quarter Mast. Genl at the Camp West Side of Cacapehon

* * *

p. 103 [Captain Orme to St. John, not addressed, not dated]

Dear Sir John

We have a general want of Wagons but particularly on this side[.] The Train demands besides the Wagons already sent to Winchester 53 for that place and 212 horses Eighty of which must be furnish'd with harness for the Conveyance of their own Carriages and ordinance. 12 more are wanted for the Remainder of Sir Peter Halketts Regiment and baggage [sic] and for the Cloathing of the Rangers, as the whole service is Obstructed thro this Deficiency, the General Orders me to inform you of it and directs you will find out some Expedient to Supply them, and with the greatest Expedition.

Sturdy Wagons are absolutely Necessary on the Maryland side. I have applied by the General's directions to Governour Sharp who has imprest [sic-impressed] some but very short of the Compliment[.] he is expected here tomorrow, and his Excellency will again urge him to use every method to procure more, the General has order'd the march of Col. Dunbar's Regiment on Saturday next and a party of a Captain and fifty to Conogage agreeable to your desires, this Officer has his Excellency's Instructions to Retain all the Pennsylvania Teams to Assist us in our March to Wills's Creek, if you have already secured a Sufficient Number for that purpose, please to contradict this Order.

The Rangers foot and horses are gone for Winchester, two Wagons set out to day with part of their Cloaths, the General begs of you to give your Orders for Arming and Cloathing them and to hasten Capt Stewart in the purchase of his horses that they may be all Ready to Join us at Wills's Creek, and also to provide the Serjeants of Sir Peter Halkett's with Firelocks and to send a quantity of Arms to Wills's Creek for Col. Dunbar's Serjeants, and to furnish those Recruits which are order'd to be brought to Wills's Creek with an intent to Compleat the two Regiments to a Thousand each in pursuance of some instructions the General has lately Received.

Sir Peter Halkett has Received from his Excellency March Routes According to Your Letter and Sir Peter is ordered to Remain at Winchester till he Receives directions to Continue his March, this you will Please to Recollect and also to inform him if the Road is Cut from the Bridge on the Opekan that he May Regulate his detachment Accordingly.

For God's Sake my dear Sir John prepare every thing as fast as possible for our march Soon[.] Spare nothing but the want of horses and Forrage, I wish you may be able to Provide Sufficient numbers, I am Convinced if there is any Deficiency we shall owe it to the impossibility of procuring horses & Forrage.

The General proposes leaving this place on Tuesday next. I hope you will let us see you very soon at Frederick many measures of Consequence Remaining yet to be Settled

His Excy desires his compliments and I am.

Your Most Obt Humble Servant

Robt Orme

Mr Shirley desires his Complimts.[76]

* * *

p. 105 [St. Clair to Colonel Halkett, Wills Creek, April 17, 1755]

Fort at Wills's Creek April 17th 1755

Sir

Last night I arrived at this place after having been on the Roads a Week to make them passable[.] on my coming to this Place I found every thing in the Situation I left it, that is to say not any one thing done which I had Ordered, and what is worse the Pennsylvanians have disappointed us in Cutting their Roads and sending in their flour.

I am under a Necessity of going to Frederick in Maryland to General Braddock to see if he will march a party of the 2d Brigade into that province to press Wagons loaded with Flour, otherwise our expedition must be at a stop.[77] I am able to do but little without some of Your Regt. at this place. I have now Ordered 100 men to Cut the Road which I expected wou'd have been finish'd before now, and shall want a great many men to work on the two Bridges that are to be Laid[,] and must have a Strong detachment to go with the Ingeneers to Reconoiter the Road to Fort Duquesne. All his I cannot Affect without a Strong detachment from you, and if I had men enough of the Independent Companys and Virginia Forces[.] I have no one Officer I cou'd depend on for seeing any orders executed in my absence. You see Dear Sir Peter on what a dismal Situation I am which you can only Remedy by coming up here with the Corps leaving a detachment at Winchester[,] or by your Remaining at Winchester, and sending up your Lieutenant Col. With a Large Detachment to this place.

The Route is to Henry Enoch's 2 days March as before
From Henry Enoch's to the Spring 2 Miles
From the Spring to Col. Cresops 18 Miles, at the mould of the South branch you pass the Potomack.
From Col. Cressop's to the Camp at Will's Creek 14 Miles

I must Remain here until I receive the Return of the Express From General Braddock which I expect to morow. I shall leave my Opinion in Writing of what Steps I think ought to be taken for Carrying on our Expedition. I found this place both destitute of Charcoal and Plank[.] People seem to be surprised that I stand in need of the Latter.

I am

P.S. I beg you wou'd get your Armourers to Cut a Sufficient Quantity of Virginia Arms for the horse Rangers and give out Firelocks and Bayonets of those Arms in Store for your Serjeants[.][78]

To Sir Peter Halkett

* * *

p. 107 [St. Clair memorandum on marching troops from Winchester to Wills Creek, Winchester, April 21, 1755]

Winchester April 21st 1755
Of the marching of the Troops from Winchester to Wills's Creek
The Shortest Road Cut for the Artillery

1st From Winchester to Potts, good Camp	12 Miles
2d From Potts to Henry Enoch's	16
3. From Henry Enoch's to Cox's at the Mouth of Little Cacapehon	12
4 From Cox's to Col. Cresops	8
5 From Col. Cresap's to the Fort	16
Total	64

Remarks on the above Road

1st days march, the Road is good, no Runns of Water to pass of any Consequence.

2d days march, Shou'd a great body of Troops march together they may not be able to pass the River of Cacapehon a Quarter of a mile from their Camp, in that case the Troops may camp on this side of Cacapehon at Enoch Enoch's [sic.], in this case they are only to March 7 Miles next day to the head of the mountain where there is a good Spring. The Float will be finish'd by Tuesday next, shou'd the Troops choose to foard off great Cacapehon which will not take them knee deep they like this Road to the Right, that Straight Forward did not Answer. If the Float be ready it will be better to use it.

3d days march, it will be best to encamp opposite to Cox's especially if the water of little Cacapehon is high.

4th days march, The Officer leading the division of Troops may send to Col. Crysops who can send them down by water what provisions they want[,] there being a Deposite of Provisions at Col Cresop's. At the mouth of little Capacehon the Troops pass the Potomack in a Float[.] four miles from that is Town Creek where the Float is building, if it is not Ready they may pass it in canoes, this day's march being only 8 Miles, the house where the Troops encamp belongs to Col. Cresop but inhabited by Mr Jackson who keeps an Inn.

5th days march, the Comanding Officer leading the Division is to send to the officer Commanding at Wills's creek to send his Wagons to the two creeks to Carry them over least the Bridge be not Ready. The First Creek is three miles from the Fort, and the second just by it—

* * *

p. 109 [St. Clair description of the second and longest road to Wills Creek, not addressed, not dated]

A Discription of the 2d and longest Road to Wills's Creek

It being impossible to Give a Route by that Road.

From Winchester to Jos. Edward's 25 Miles at this place the great River of Cacapehon is to be Crossed in a Float, a good camp at Edward's. From Joseph Edwards to the North River of Cacapehon 2 miles, here is a stony Foard [Ford] without Float or canoe. 12 miles further is the Foard of Little Cacapehon without a Float or Canoe; but no so deep [sic] as the former. The wagon with provisions may unload on the Far side of those Rivers and return for the Soldiers. Ten miles further is Joseph Pearcell's a Tolerable Camp.

At Jos. Pearcell's the south Branch of Potomack is to be crossed in a Float the best Road is along the Middle Ridge and to cross Patterson's Creek at Mr. Crackone's where is a Canoe, this Route has no water on it for 10 miles, but it saves crossing that Creek 5 times at bad Foards where there is no Canoe nor Float. From Joseph Pearcell's to John Walkers on the Potomack 23 Miles, shou'd the Potomack not be passable for wagons and the float not made the Officer Comanding the Detachment is to send to the Comand Officer at the Fort for a Wagon to carry up his Tents and to Carry his men over the two Creeks near the Fort.

From Walkers to the Fort 8 Miles in all 88[.]

* * *

p. 110 [St. Clair to Mr. Hoight on the south branch of the Potomack River, Winchester, April 21, 1755][79]

By Sir John St. Clair Quarter Master General to his Majesty's Forces in America

You are hereby Required and Directed to warn or cause to be warned all the Wagons on the South Branch and in the Neighborhood about to Repair immediately to Winchester, to carry up the Artillery and Stores to the Fort, in case any of the Inhabitants Refuse to go on this Service for the safety of the Country, you are to apply to Lieut Reinhard Baily of the Sir Peter Halkett's Regiment, who is sent to encamp at Jos. Pearsall's who will send partys of Troops to be Quartered on the Inhabitants at Free cost, for their disobedience to these his Majesty's orders delivered to them by me.

Given under my hand at Winchester

The 21st Day of April 1755

John St Clair

To Mr. Hoight on the South Branch

* * *

p. 111 [St. Clair instructions to Captain Polson, commanding 2nd company of artificers, Winchester, April 21, 1755]

Instructions for Capt Polson Comanding the 2d Company of Artificers in Consequence of the Orders you have Received from Sir Peter Halkett to March with what Remains of your Company at Winchester, You are instructed to join the detachment of your Company now building a Float on great Cacapehon at Henry Enoch's, which Float you are to see Finished with all possible dispatch, that done you are to march with that part of your Company to the Mouth of Little Cacapehon and with the Assistance of Mr Byonce you are to have Oars made for the Float at That Place, and have it Tarr'd for which Mr Byonce has my directions, Shou'd you want any provisions for your men you are to Apply to Col. Crysop for it, the Rope sent for the Float on the Potomack is not to be us'd.

You are to Cross the Potomack and go to Town Creek where you will find one of the Ingeniers, who will direct you whether you are to Stop at this place to build a Float or proceed to the Fort to Build Bridges.

Lieut. Hamilton with the Detachment of your Company now at the Opekan is to remain to Escort up the Artillery to the Fort.

Route

To Pott's 1st day march
To Henry Enoch's 2d days march
To Cox's at the Mouth of the Little Cacapehon 3d days March
To Town Creek 4th days March
Lieut. McNeil is to go on the Recruiting Service
Given under my hand at Winchester this 21st day of April 1755
John St Clair, Depy Qr Mr General

* * *

p. 112 [St. Clair instructions to Lieutenant Hamilton the 2nd company of artificers, Winchester, April 21, 1755]

Instructions for Lieut. Hamilton of the 2d Company of Artificiers. In consequence of the Orders given to You by Sir Peter Halkett to take upon you the Command of the detachment of the Compy You belong to who are now making a Bridge over the Opekan. You are to see that Bridge Finished with all expedition that done you are to wait for the Artillery and march your party to the Fort with it, in Order to Repair their Carriages on the Road, shou'd the Artillery not march all together you are in that case to divide your people into small Squads of which you are to apply to the Commanding Officer of the Artillery to Receive his Directions Concerning the number of men you are to march with each Brigade.

Given under my hand at Winchester

This 21st Day of April 1755

* * *

p. 113 [St. Clair to Lieutenant Lewis, Winchester, April 21, 1755]

Winchester April the 21st 1755

Sir

I did not Receive your Letter of the 1st of this month till Yesterday. I am sorry that my not getting it in due time, has put it out of my power to grant your Request with Regards to leave of Absence for a few days. Lieut. Hamilton goes to Relieve you on your Command in Order that You may join your Company who you will find within a few miles of the Fort.[80] The service will Require your joining it Immediately, as Captain Steven only waits for you that he may go a Recruiting by General Braddock's Orders. I am with great Truth.

Sir Your Most Humble Servant

To Lieut. Lewis

* * *

p. 114 [St. Clair instructions to Lieutenant Richard Bailey of Sir Peter Halkett's regiment, Winchester, April 21, 1755]

Instructions for Lieut. Richard Bailey of Sir Peter Halkett's Regiment

Winchester April 21st 1755

As you have Received Orders from Sir Peter Halkett to March with a Detachment to encamp at Jo. Pearcell's on the South Branch, when you arrive at that place, or on your march, if Application shou'd be made to you by Mr. Hoight for any parties of men to be quartered on the Inhabitants for Refusing to send their wagons to Winchester in Order to Carry up the Artillery stores to the Camp, you are hereby directed to Furnish such partys to be quartered on the Inhabitants, and you are to take care that they demand no more provisions but the Quantity allowed to them from the Country.

Given under my hand at Winchester April 21st 1755
John St. Clair, Depy Quar Mr General
To Lieut. Richard Bailey of Sir Peter Halkett's Regiment

* * *

p. 115 [Captain Orme to St. Clair, Alexandria, April 13, 1755]
Dear Sir John

The General Received your Express at 4 o'Clock to day and has directed me to inform you it gives him much Satisfaction some horses are ordered to come to this place, tho the numbers mentioned in Yours is insufficient for the Conveyance of the train, in a Letter I dispatch'd to you dated the 11th I have laid before you the state of Wagons and horses, which it is desired you will supply with all Expedition as it Retards the service very much not being able to Remove the Artillery from this Town, and care must be taken to provide Carriage for the Removal of those Stores already sent to Winchester, and also those from Frederick. A proper Person is sent to Winchester from the Artillery and one was ordered to Conogogee, who fell ill upon the Road but is now proceeding. I beg you will Remember to inform Sir Peter Halkett of your resolution to march the Train wide of Winchester, I am.

Dear Sir
Your Most Humble & Obedt Servt
Robt Orme Aid de Camp
Alexandria April 13th 1755
My Compliments to Mr Mackellar
To Sir John St Clair

* * *

p. 116 [Governor William Shirley of Massachusetts to St. Clair, Boston, March 18, 1755]
Boston New England March 18th 1755
Sir

I had the honour of your letter, dated January 14th by Lieut. Col. Ellison, at which time it was uncertain whether the plan of Operations lately determined upon, in this and the Neighboring Colonies wou'd take Effect; wch [which] Occasioned my waiting so long before I answer'd it, and as the prosecution of my part of it at least is still uncertain, until I shall know the Result of General Braddock's Judgmts upon it for which purpose (Among others) I am to meet him at Annapolis in about 10 days, I shall defer answering you in that Particular until my arrival there.

I have been inquiring after such Charts of Drawings as may be of use, and will bring with me what I shall be able to Collect that may be useful to you.

I shall be very proud to Receive your Commands if I may be of any service to you here; in a private way as well as of a Correspd with you, for his Majesty's Service, being with great Regard

Sir
Your most Humble & Most Obedt Servt
W. Shirley
To Sir John St Clair Baronet

* * *

p. 117 [Governor Reynolds of Georgia to St. Clair, Georgia, March 13, 1755]
Georgia the 13th March 1755
Sir

I have Received your Letter / with two others from the Secretary of State, Relating to the present Circumstances of Affairs in America / and in Return am to Acquaint you that nothing has lately happened in his Majesty's Province of Georgia under my Government, that Requires your Attention.

As I am but lately arrived in this Country I cannot pretend any knowledge of the ground at the back of our Settlements, which is but little known to any Body hereabouts, nor have I been able to procure any Maps or Drawings of this province of which there has never yet been a good Survey taken.

This Colony is in a State of Infancy, and can contribute neither men nor money at present to the general service, but I shall very gladly Obey to the utmost of my power the orders I have Received to be Aiding and Assisting to Sir John St Clair in the Execution of his duty, and to give him the best Advice I can upon all Occasions Relating to the King's service in every Respect, as I shall also upon all other Occasions be glad to assure you that I am.

Sir

Your Most Obedt and Most Huml Servt.

J. Reynolds

To Sir John St Clair

* * *

p. 118 [St. Clair to General Braddock, Fort Cumberland, May 2, 1755]

Fort Cumberland May the 2d 1755

Sir

As Govr Dinwiddie made a Contract with the bearer of this / Robt Callendar / for 100 horses, fifty one of which he delivered to Mr. Commissary Walker as will appear by his Receipts, so that there is due to Mr. Callendar £ 536/12/4 ½ for horses saddles and flour; which I am under the Necessity of applying to your Excellency to direct the Com'y at Winchester to pay for notwithstanding the Contract was made by the Govr it was at my Request.

Mr Callendar has likewise at Winchester a Number of horses more to fulfill his Contract, which your Excellency may take on the Service that the persons appointed to Examine them shall think proper, as I shall send you an Express the 4th I have nothing further to add but that I am with great Respect,

Your Excellency's Most Obedt Humble Servt

J St

To General Braddock

* * *

p. 119 [Governor Dinwiddie to St. Clair, Williamsburg, May 1, 1755]

Williamsburgh May the 1st 1755

Dear Sir

I received your letter by the bearer Mr Lyons, I have paid him his Wages to this day, our People do not incline to be at any more expenses than what was established at Alexandria, therefore I must Recommend Mr Lyon to your Favour.

Col. Hunter gives me an Account of Sundry Necessaries Supply'd you which I shall pay him, your Relation does not yet Appear, when he does I shall take the Necessary care of him.

I am sorry you had hurt your hand, but hope you have Recovered it, and that you are in perfect health. Captain Dobbs / son to Govr Dobbs / Joins the Army with a Company from North Carolina. I Recommend him to your Friendship.

The Season of the Year far advanced, I shall be glad to hear of your March over the Alleghany Mountains, and sincerely wish a Successful Campaign, which from the Force &c. I have no great doubt of.

That God may Protect you is the sincere wish of

Worthy Sir

Your Affectionate Humbl Servt

Robt Dinwiddie

Sir John St Clair

* * *

p. 120 [Governor Dinwiddie to St. Clair, Williamsburg, May 10, 1755]

Williamsburgh May 10th 1755

Sir

Your favour of the 2d I Received, and observe the great Trouble you have had, and good Judgement in Fixing the Roads.

I shall lay your Letter before the Assembly, and I do not doubt but they will give the Necessary directions in keeping the Roads clear that belong to this Dominion.

I am glad the Forces begin to Join at Wills's creek, and I wish to have a Letter from you from the Ohio, the season of the Year Advances very fast, I hope you will be able to give an Agreeable Account of the Ground you have been Reconoitering, and I hope the divine success will attend the Operations of this Campaign.

I am much hurried and must therefore leave off, only assuring you that I am with great Regard and Respect,

Sir

Your Most Obedt Huml Servt

Robt Dinwiddie

[P.S.] Your Cousin not yet arriv'd when he comes be assured I shall take particular Notice of him—

* * *

p. 133 [General Braddock, instructions to St. Clair, Fort Cumberland, May 28, 1755. Note that letters p. 132 through p. 140 have been moved to their proper chronological sequence in the letterbook.]

Instructions to Sir John St. Clair Deputy Quarter Master General

1. You will proceed with a detachment of Six Hundred men, Order'd for that purpose under the Command of Major Russell Chapman, to Open & Repair a Road over the Allegany Mountains, towards the great meadows to a distance not exceeding forty Miles.[81]

2. You will Acquaint Major Chapman, whom I have directed to Consult You in the execution of his Orders, what part of the detachment you Shall think necessary to be employ'd in Opening and Repairing the Road, and you will also give him your opinion with Regard to the disposition of the Remainder, for the defense of the Working party, and the Convoy under his Escort.

3. You will cease opening and Repairing the Road, at the end of seven days, or sooner if it shall be thought Adviseable, and fix upon such a Spot as shall appear proper to yourself, and the Engineers Order'd upon this Service for Constructing a place of Defence for the party, and the provision order'd to be lodged there.

4. Upon Major Champman's leaving you, You will employ the Remaining part of the detachment, which will be left under your Command, in Compleatg the place of defence, and you will make such dispositions, and preserve such discipline as the service shall Require.

Edward Braddock

Camp at Fort Cumberland May 28th 1755

* * *

p. 132 [General Braddock to St. Clair, not addressed, May 31, 1755. Note: this letter has been moved to its proper chronological sequence.]

Sir

It was very far from my intention that your Detachment shou'd be seven day march from me. I propos'd that the Road you shou'd make in seven days. I might be able to March it in three or Four at Farthest, but According to the Account I hear of it I must be much longer marching it than you as my Carriages are heavier and more Numerous which is by no means what I propos'd[.] I must therefore desire you to make no more haste than good Speed let me have your answer pr Bearer; and believe me to be

Your Most Obedt Huml Sert

Edward Braddock

May 31st 1755

* * *

p. 134 [St. Clair to Braddock, camp at George's Creek, June 1, 1755]

Camp near George's Creek June the 1st 1755

Sir

I received your Excellency's Letter by Capt. Orme and wou'd have answer'd, had he not Return'd to your head Quarters, as he cou'd Acquaint you more fully of our Situation having seen it on the Spot.

It never was my intention to go on and leave any Road to be cut by the Body of the Army, unless it is the five miles next to the Fort, which may be easily repaired by the Troops before they March. I carried out with me ys Morning 150 Men to Savage River which Road will be Completed this Evening so that we may move our Camp tomorrow to that place. I have sent back a working party of 200 Men five miles towards the Camp to Repair the Damages done by our Carriages, which I dare say they will Compleat this Afternoon, I shall Report its situation in a postscript to the Letter.

Your Excellency need not be Apprehensive of us getting too far ahead, I wish with all my Heart that the Ground wou'd permit it. I believe with much difficulty we shall be able to get to the little Meadows the 7th day but shou'd be sorry to stop at that place / for Fear of destroying your Forrage / more than one night. Cou'd we get on ten miles farther to Bear Camp, and Stop at that place until the whole Comes up to the Little Meadows, I shou'd think it Adviseable, and have the Little Meadows for the Rendezvous of the Army: for Shou'd your Excellency ever attempt to March your whole Convoy in one Body, you will be under an absolute Necessity of falling into Divisions, so that it appears to me that it will be the best manner to march in three divisions and Join the whole at the Little Meadows—the Van Guard excepted.

I shall be glad to know your Excellency's sentiments on this head that I may guide Myself Accordingly. I shall undertake nothing which will put it out of our power to send back the Empty Waggons by the time Appointed for their Arrival at the Fort. Shou'd the whole Number of Guides not have join'd the Brigades, the bearer of this Grymes is Recommended to me as a person who knows the Country very well. I have the Honour of being with the Greatest Respect.

Your Excellency's Most Obedt and Most Huml Servt

To General Braddock

* * *

p. 136 [Captain Orme to St. Clair, not addressed, June 2, 1755]

Sir

The General received your Letter, and has ordered me to inform you that he does not Choose to have you advance more than the seven days as he is very desirous of getting from this place as soon as possible and that his Excellency intends a junction of the whole Convoy at Georges Creek, instead of the Little Meadows, and he would have the Road Repair'd as much as it will Admit of.

I am

Sir

Your Most Humble Obedt Servt

Robt Orme, Aid de camp

June 2d

* * *

p. 137 [St. Clair to General Braddock, camp at Savage River, June 2, 1755]

Camp at Savage River June the 2d 1755

Sir,

I am this Moment favoured with your Excellency's Comands [sic] by Capt Orme and beg leave to inform you that I by no means intended to march beyond the 7th days march at any Rate, and such time I hope will carry us to the Little Meadows, or very near their, and as we shall, I think, have no reason to Fortify ourselves there, the Convoy of Waggons Shall be return'd the next day after our arrival which will shorten the time of your Excellcy's Stay at Cumberland Fort.

Our present Convoy has this day got over the hill on this side George's Creek, and with as little trouble as we cou'd hope for. We have taken a great deal of pains upon the Road over it, but some Parts of it cannot be made very good in so short a time, we shall likewise Continue to make it from here to the Little Meadows, as well as the Nature of the ground, and the time will Admit off. I hope we shall get there on Wednesday Night for there is no nearer place to encamp at[.]

I beg leave to inform your Excellency that if you Rendezvous the whole at George's Creek you will find it difficult to pass the Rear of your Convoy from there till late the 2d day or perhaps the 3rd.

If your Excelly disapproves of our marching forward to the Little Meadows you'll please to inform me tomorrow and we shall Stop at Laurel Run and only Cut the road forward.

Monocahukas arriv'd with the Indians but wants to go to the Fort unless Monture comes to them to Morrow, therefore beg your Excellency may please to send him. I am,

&c.

To General Braddock

* * *

p. 138 [St. Clair to General Braddock, Camp at Little Meadows, June 10, 1755]

Camp at the Little Meadows June 10th Six at Night

Sir,

Monocatus son is this moment arrived from Fort Duquesne, he left it on Sunday afternoon, and brings Accounts that he saw at that place in all 70 Indians and 100 French who were preparing to set out at yesterday morning to harass us in our March. That they were daily in expectation of a Reinforcement of 200 more but were detain'd by the water being low.

I wou'd have sent this young Indian to your Excellency this Evening, but he is inclinable to go early in the morning to apprise his Father at the great meadows least he shou'd be in any danger from the Enemy.

He further says that the Delawares have sent to the Shanaus [Shawnees] and the Mohawks in the French interest to withdraw from the French and hold Councils with them, and that the French are now mounting Six 4 pounders which they have lately received[.] the French had an Account of our being ready to march by a Deserter of the Independent Companys who deserted from our van Guard, I am

Your Excellency's

* * *

p. 140 [Captain Orme to St. Clair, not addressed, June 11, 1755. Note: this letter was written in response to the letter from St. Clair on p. 138 and has been moved to its proper chronological sequence.]

Sir

The General has ordered me to return you his thanks for the intelligence you have sent him he is now encamp'd at the Foot of the First Hill and proposes marching forward tomorrow. The General disires you will use any methods to procure further Information, and immediately advise him of it. I am.

Sir

Your Most Humble and Obedt Servant

Robt Orme, Aid de camp

June the 11th 1755

* * *

p. 139 [Captain Orme to St. Clair, not addressed, June 12, 1755]

Sir

The General has received your letter by Lieutenant Woodward and orders me to inform you he proposes to march from the camp tomorrow and will be at the Little Meadows on Sunday, his Excellency disires you will not proceed upon any farther work upon the Road and only employ them on the business of securing the camp till he can relieve your party, and would not have you fatigue your men by too much Labour. The general has retrenched very much the Number of Waggons and encreas'd by many means the pack loads

I am Sir Your Humble & Obedt Servt

Robert Orme

Aid de camp

June 12th 1755

* * *

p. 121 [St. Clair note explaining that letters from May 27 to July 9 fell into enemy hands, not addressed, not dated]

The Copies of my Letters from the 27th of May to the 9th of July fell into the Enemies hands, there was none of them of Consequence excepting one to Col Napier of the 19th of June in which I represented to him the absolute Necessity of making a Stop near Fort Duquesne by throwing up an Entrenchment for our Security, and bringing up a second Convoy, and Opening the Communications behind us to Pennsylvania

The French also got an original letter of mine which I wrote to the Earl of Hindford, which I had no Opportunity of sending back it was to the same purpose as that of Col Napier.

* * *

As transcribed in Stanley Pargellis, Editor, *Military Affairs in North America, 1748-1765, Selected Documents from the Cumberland Papers in Windsor Castle* (Archon Books; 1969) 93-95.

[Sir John St. Clair to Colonel Robert Napier, aide to the Duke of Cumberland]

Camp of the Van Guard of the Army at the little Meadows, June 13th, 1755

Sir,

Since General Braddocks arrival about the 20th of Febry I have not wrote to you, I delayed it from time to time expecting to be able to give you a full account of our Situation: I certainly shou'd have wrote to you on the arrival of all our Troops at Wills's Creek, but I was so employed about cutting the Roads, that I had not one moment to spare.

In my last letter to you I acquainted you that I was to review the Independent Companys and to form the Provincial Troops of Virginia and Maryland in which Service I was employd till the 24th of March, they being scattered all about the Country. On my coming that day to Alexandria I found the British troops disembarked and beginning to land their Stores. The 26th General Braddock and Governour Dinwiddie arrived. I left Alexandria the 2d of April, in order to foreward the Transport of our Artillery & Stores to Wills's Creek, bt did not get to the fort till the 16th being obliged to repair old Roads and cut new ones, in which I made very great progress considering that we had Snow in the Mountains till the 15th of April. The Roads leading to the Fort were not cleared till the 1st of May; the next Day the first Division of our Troops arrived and the 10th the last Division; the first Division of the Artillery the 16th of May & the last the Day following: from that Day till the End of the Month, things were preparing for the march of the whole.

The Situation I am in at present puts it out of my power to give you a full discription of this Country; I shall content myself with telling you that from Winchester to this place is one continued track of Mountains, and like to continue so for fifty Miles further. Tho our Motions may appear to you to have been slow, yet I may venture to assure you that not an Hour has been lost; considering that no Magistrate in Virginia or I believe in Maryland gave themselves the least trouble to assist in collecting the Country People to work upon the Roads, and to provide us with Carriages; But on the Contrary every body laid themselves out to put what money they cou'd in their Pocketts, without forwarding our Expedition. In this Situation we never cou'd have subsisted our little Army at Wills's Creek, far less carried on our Expedition had not General Braddock contracted with the People in Pennsylvania for a number of Waggons, which they have fulfilled; by their Assistance we are in motion, but must move slowly untill we get over the Mountains. I cou'd very easily foresee the difficultys we were to labour under from having the Communication open only to Virginia, which made me Anxious of having a Road cut from Pennsylvania to the Yaugheaugany; I wrote to Govr Morris the 14th of Febry on this Head, notwithstanding of which, that Road has not been set about till very lately. The last Report that I had of it, was, that it wou'd be finished in three Weeks hence; the two Communications will join about forty Miles from hence, but it is not fixed on which side of the Yaugheogany.

The little knowledge that our People at home have of carrying on War in a Mountaneoius Country will make the Expence of our Carriages appear very great to them, that one Article will amount near to 40,000 Pounds Stir [Sterling].

Thus far I do affirm that no time has been lost in pursuing the Scheme laid down in England for our Expedition; had it been undertaken at the beginning from Pennsylvania it might not have been carried on with great Dispatch and less expence: I am not at all surprized that we are ignorant of the Situation of this Country in England, when no one except a few Hunters knows it on the Spot; and their Knowledge extends no further than in following their Game. It is certain that the ground is not easy to be reconoitred for one may go twenty Miles without seeing before him ten yards.

The Commanding General pursues his Schemes with a great deal of vigour and Vivacity; the Dispositions he makes will be subject to be changed in this vast tract of Mountains, I mean instead of marching the whole together (the Van Guard excepted) in one body, he will be obliged to march in three Divisions over the Mountains and join about the great Meadows, fifty two Miles from the fort. The General is bent on marching directly to Fort du Quesne, he is certainly in the right in making his Dispositions for it: But it is my opinion he will be obliged to make a Halt on the Monongahela or Yaughanagany untill he gets up a second Convoy, and untill the Road is open from Pennsylvania, which the Inhabitants will not finish unless they are covered by our Troops.

I have not as yet talked to the General of this, nor shall I, untill we get over the Mountains, for then things may appear in another light, and I am unwilling to propose any thing which might lok like starting Difficultys The marching to the french fort is certainly practicable with this present Convoy; but in which light must we appear if we are obliged to abandon our Conquests for want of Sustenance. What was looked on at home as easy is our most difficult point to surmount, I mean the passage of this vast tract of Mountains; Had we a Country we coud subsist in after we get over them, the thing wou'd be easy.

I am at this place with 400 men as a Van Guard, and to cut the Roads, I was not able to reach this Ground till the 8th Day, 'tho only 20 Miles from Wills's Creek, it is certain I might have made more dispatch but I was charged with a Convoy of 50 Waggons. The Roads are either Rocky or full of Boggs, we are obliged to blow the Rocks and lay Bridges every day: What an happiness it is said to have wood at hamd for the latter!

One of our Indians who left the french Fort the 8th Inst, tells me that there are only 100 french & 70 Indians at that place; that they were preparing to set out the Day after to dispute the passage of the Mountains. I have seen nothing of them as yet, nor do I expect th[at] they will come so far from home. They have lately received Six 4 pounders which they were busy mounting when the Indian came away. I shoud be glad to have a Visit from them at this Camp, it is a very good one Surrounded with an Abattis.

I expect the General with the Army will be at this Camp the 15th and that I shall receive his Orders to move on the same Day. I shall take care to let you know every thing that happens amongst us which I dare say will be to your Satisfaction. I am with the greatest Regard, Sir, Your most obedient and most humble Servant,

John St. Clair

[Endorsed] 1755 Journal from Sir Jn. St. Clair. June 13. Recd Augst 29th.

* * *

p. 122 [St. Clair to Commodore Keppel, Wills Creek, July 18, 1755]

Sir

The present Situation that I am in puts it out of my power to Transmit to you in order to be forwarded to England the previous Steps to our unlucky defeat, I hope by the time Col. Dunbar[,] who now Commands[,] comes here which will be in three days hence that I may have strength and Spirit enough to dictate the Necessary letters on this melancholy subject.

I cannot help Requesting of you not to send any ship of War to England unless you Receive our Commanding Officers Letters for the better information of his Majesty[.] I have escaped much better than many of my Brother Officers, though I was shot through the Body amongst the first that were wounded or Shot dead upon the Spot.

&c. &c.

Fort at Wills's Creek

July 18th 1755

* * *

p. 123 [St. Clair to Colonel Napier, Wills Creek, July 22, 1755][82]

Fort at Wills's Creek 22d July 1755

Sir,

I wrote to you a letter of the 12th of June which I hope you have Received by this time, that Letter gave you an Account of the Obstructions we was like to meet with on our March, on account of Carriages[.] a few days after writing that Letter, General Braddock with the Army arrived at the Little Meadows about the 17th of June[.] General Braddock sent for me and told me he laid down a Scheme of his own for marching on, which before that time had been given to the Brigade Major in Orders. The Scheme was that a detachment shou'd be formed of those of the British Battalions which came from Ireland, and that those shou'd March with the Artillery together with three Companies of the Virginia Forces under the Command of General Braddock. The Remaining part of the Army under the Command of Col. Dunbar, was to follow with the great Convoy, this Step I look'd upon to be a prelude to marching in divisions which was the only way we cou'd have brought up our Convoy.

This Strong detachment march'd on and arriv'd at the Strong Camp of the great Lick, which is Twenty one miles on the other side of Youchagani and 80 miles from this Fort. The great Advantage of this strong ground made me propose to the Genl to halt with the detachment, and bring up Col. Dunbar with his Convoy, this proposal was Rejected with great indignation. We march'd on till the Seventh of July, Twenty three Miles Further, I then objected to our marching any further in that Order of March with a Convoy, and proposed since this small body must march to the French Fort that we shou'd march part of our small numbers and take post before the Fort leaving our Convoy to come up, I urg'd strongly that no General had hitherto march'd up at Midday to the Gates of the Town he was to besiege leading his Convoy, and if General Braddock attemptd [attempted] it he must look to the Consequences. Tuesday the 8th we march'd to a Rising Ground within three Quarters of a mile of the Monogahela and Encamp'd there. Wednesday the 9th Col. Gage with about 300 men march'd at daylight past and Repast [sic] the Monongahela where he took post. The Workmen and Coverers[83] immediately followed, and then the rest of the detachment, so that the whole had pass'd by half an hour after 12 o'Clock being three miles, the Reason of Passing the Monogahela Twice was to avoid the narrows which is a road on the banks of said River Commanded by a high hill which Road wou'd have taken a day's work in making passable. After Col. Gage and I had pass'd the River we Received Orders from Capt. Morris Aid de Camp to March.[84] The underwood continued very thick for a quarter of a Mile beyond the Monogahela then we came into an open wood free from underwood, with some gradual Risings this wood was so open that Carriages cou'd have been driven in any part of it[.] about a mile on the other side of the last Crossing of the Monongahela we began to feel the Enemies Fire and hear their Shouts, those who were under my Command immediately form'd[.] on those in my front, falling back up on me, I ran to the front to see what the Matter was when I Received a Shot thro' the Body. I then returned to my own people posted Captain Polson's Company of Artificers and Capt. Porniers Company of Rangers to Cover my two Cannon, I then went up to General Braddock who was then at the head of his own guns and beg'd of him for God's sake to gain the rising ground on our Right to prevent us being totally surrounded. I know no further of this unlucky Affair to my knowledge being Afterwards insensible.

It will be needless for me to give you any particular Account by hearsay, our Affairs are as bad here as bad can make them[.] with Regard to my self in particular I was fully Resolved if we had met with success to desire to have been recalled finding I could be of little use being never Listened to[.] but as our Affairs stand at present it is a thing I shall not thing [A spelling error, St. Clair intended "think."] off, and shou'd be glad of having Another Opportunity of making use of the knowledge I have of the Country and its Inhabitants. By the time I shall have your Answer I hope to be in a Condition of doing my duty, therefore Shou'd be glad you wou'd point it out to me whether it is to be here or in New England under General Shirley. I am with the greatest Respect.

Sir

Your Most Obedt and Most Humble Servant

To Colonel Napier

* * *

p. 126 [St. Clair to Henry Fox, Wills Creek, July 22, 1755][85]

Fort at Wills's Creek the 22d July 1755

Sir

I wish with all my heart that the Situation I am in at Present wou'd permit me to give you a detail of all our Affairs since the landing of our British Battalions, our Operations to the 17th of June deserve to have met with better fate, but some infatuation or other since that day has led us all astray, were one to say such an One or such were Culpable must at length fall on the General who is dead and gone. The Dividing of the Army in two at the little Meadows, and not Waiting for the Junction of Col. Dunbar with the other half at the strong Camp of the great lick 30 miles from Fort Cumberland was a thing that I never cou'd Advise, and I Remonstrated strongly against it, and when the General was bent on marching to Fort duQuesne, I advised him when twenty miles from the Fort, to march on a Detachment, to take post near the Fort in the night, and then to bring up his Convoy for that no General had ever led up his Convoy at noon day to the place he was to besiege, my Advice was rejected with great indignation, all that I cou'd say to the General, that a few days wou'd show who were his good and who his bad Councillors.

Wednesday the 9th of July Col. Gage with about 300 men March'd at day light, past and Repast the Monongahela where he took post, the Workmen and Coverers immediately follow'd, and then the Rest of the detachmt so that the whole had pass'd by half an hour after Twelve being 3 miles the reason of Passing the Monongahela twice was to avoid the narrows which is a Road on the banks of the River Comanded [sic] by a high hill which Road would have taken a days work in making it passable. After Col. Gage and I had pass'd the River we Received Orders from Capt. Morris Aid de Camp to march[.] the underwood Continued very thick for a quarter of a mile beyond the Monongahela then we Came into an Open wood free from underwood, with some gradual Risings, this wood was so Open that Carriages Cou'd have been drove in any part of it, about a mile on the other side of the last Crossing of the Monongahela we began to see the Enemies Fire and hear their shouts. Those who were under my Command immediately forg [forming.] on those in my Front falling back upon me I ran to the Front to see what the matter was when I Received a Shot thro the Body, I then Returned to my own people, posted Capt. Polson's Company of Artificers and Capt. Porince's Company of Rangers to Cover my two Cannon, I then went up to General Braddock who was then at the head of his own Guns and beg'd of him for God's sake to gain the Rising ground on our Right to prevent our being totally Surrounded. I know no further of this unlucky Affair to my knowledge as I was afterwards insensible.

By the time I shall be able to Receive your Commands I shall be able to undertake any duty. If you Judge I can be of any service to my country in this part of the world no man shall do it with greater pleasure, tho' I was fully Resolv'd after this Campaign was over to have beg'd to have been recalled on Account of the Channel [sic] in which our Military Operations were Carry'd on. I have the honour of being with the greatest Respect.

Sir

Your Most Obedt Most Oblig'd Humble Servant

To the Right Honourable Henry Fox

* * *

p. 128 [Commodore Keppel to St. Clair, Hampton, July 22, 1755]

Hampton July the 25th 1755

Sir

I Condole with you sincerely upon the Unhappy defeat of his Majesty's Arms, and on your being wounded, I hope you will soon be able to Execute your talents again, and Endeavour to make some use of the Troops that are left.

I have wrote to Col. Dunbar, and he will inform you that I sail myself for England to Morrow Morning on the seahorse and no other Ship with me but I leave a Sloop who will take Col. Dunbar's letters to Adml Boscawen and who I suppose will on Course dispatch them for England if the Col. asks it of him. I wish you a speedy Recovery, and am Dear Sir John

Your very Humble Servant

H.   Keppel

P.S. I hope the sea part did their duty. Any Letter from you to me will find me by its being directed to Mr. Clealand at the Admy [Admiralty] On his Majesty's Service.

* * *

p. 129 [Letter of March 24, 1755, from William Greene of Rhode Island to St. Clair]

Not Transcribed, no campaign interest.

* * *

p. 130 [Letter of May 17, 1755, from Duke of Richmond to St. Clair]

Not Transcribed, no campaign interest.

* * *

p. 142 [Earl of Hundford to St. Clair, from Carmichael House near Lanack, November 24, 1754]

Not Transcribed, no campaign interest.

* * *

p. 142 [St. Clair to Governor Dinwiddie, Fort Cumberland, July 23, 1755]

Fort Cumberland 23d July 1755

Dear Sir

The anxiety of mind and the pain of Body, must be the Occasion of this Letter being very unconnected, tho I have no reason to Reproach myself for being the least instrumental of any of the evils that have befallen us, yet its Consequences appears to me to be very terrible for the Southern Provinces.

As all General Braddock's papers are lost, everybody at this place is at a loss what to do, all that I can recommend to you, for the good of Your Province is to compleat Your Troops with the greatest diligence Those Companys of Paulson's Wagoners and Poraney's who were under my command the 9th suffered greatly so that Captain Waggoner, Lieut Stewart, Lieut Woodard, and Lieut McNeil were the only surviving Officers, and some of those wounded so that there Companys will require a great deal of repair both Officers and men.

The first Company of Artificiers has been long upon the decline their feare before they left this

Fort was they should not have fighting enough, they gave out that they were much readier to fight than to work, this kind of Spirit Rose at the head and Communicated downwards: so that it will be the ruin of the late Capt Poulson's Company to incorporate them with the first Company of Artificiers, Poulsones people did their work better than any people I ever saw and on all Occassions was the first Form'd for Action. You certainly will want one Company of Artificiers and shou'd you turn the first Company of them into Rangers I believe the Officers will be pleased with it; Allen is among the number of the dead, which is the Reason I don't send you a Return of your troops, I wou'd willingly recommend people to succeed Poulson and Perone; Mr. Woodward being as I am told with a great deal of Spirit, and Lieut Savage was not in the Action, I think has some kind of promise from you.

Your Excellency need not spare me if you think I can be of any use in reestablishing your troops, or in any thing else you think me Capable of. I believe I shall be under a Necessity of waiting upon you so soon as I am able in Order that I may Compleat my Accts. I have the Honour of being with the greatest Regard

Your Excellencys Most Obedt

To Governour Dinwiddie

* * *

p. 144 [Governor Dinwiddie to St. Clair, July 4, 1755]

Not transcribed, no campaign interest.

* * *

p. 146 [Governor Dinwiddie to St. Clair, July 26, 1755]

Not transcribed, no campaign interest.

* * *

p. 147 [St. Clair to Governor Dinwiddie, Fort Cumberland, August 1, 1755]

Fort Cumberland August 1st 1755

Sir,

Yesterday I had the honour of Receiving your Excellency's Letter of the 26th of July for which I Return you my most sincere thanks for your kind wishes and Expressions of Friendship. I wrote to you a short letter of the 23rd of last month by Major Campbell which I hope you have Received before this time, I have very little else to say to you at present, but to Recommend to you in a more particular manner what I wrote to you in my former Letter. I mean that of Compleating the provincial Troops, and keeping them in Repair. Governor Innes has sent you the Returns by which you will see the numbers that are deficient, and that it will be much more Conducive to his Majesty's service, that those be Completed, than that a Number of more men shou'd be rais'd who must of Necessity be Officered with men not so well experienced as those now on the Provincial Service as I had a thorough knowledge of your men before they were modelled to the present establishment[.] I can easily give you my Opinion from whence the evils arose, that caused such a number of them to be discharg'd, and the needless expense that brought upon your province, the first thing that your Assembly did was to pass a Vagrant Act, which included no less than three hundred men who were Rendered incapable of gaining their Bread, by old sores, and whom I was obliged to discharge for the good of the service, whether the Gentm of your Assembly will think proper to Continue that Act will depend upon them. If they do it to save money they had much better disband the Troops they now have and throw themselves at the mercy of the Indians. Your Excellency can expect no man will Continue in your service, who visibly sees he has no provision made for him after he is disabled in the service of his Country nor has he Cloaths to defend himself from the Inclemency of the weather during the Winter. This latter part you cou'd not Possibly avoid, for we are in the same Situation for those Recruits that were new Cloathed, are now all in Raggs, for which Reason no Troops Ought to be new Cloathed until they enter their Winter Quarters, but this we cou'd not avoid.

Your Excellency will therefore Consider whether you think the men will be able to get over the

Winter without Blanketts, of which they have a few or none at all, and indeed it is worthy your Assembly's Notice to think of granting something to the few surviving Officers of their Troops, who were at the Action the ninth of last month, who lost all their Equipage. Whatever fault you may have to find with the behavior [of the] British Troops, I assure you I have to lay to the Courage of the Forces of your Province, during the few Minutes I was able to stay with them in the Action.

I speak more feelingly of the Officers who have lost their Equipage and I am in the same situation myself. I saw your Excellency's letter to Col. Dunbar but to put its Contents in execution is morally impossible.

The British Troops and independent Companys move towards Pensylvania [sic] tomorrow, as for my own part, I must stay here untill [sic] I get well which I've now a fair prospect of. My Complimts [compliments] to your Lady and family and believe me to be,

Your Excellency's

Most Obedt and Most Humb Servt.

To Governor Dinwiddie

* * *

p. 149 [Governor Dinwiddie to St. Clair, Williamsburg, August 1, 1755]

Williamsburgh August the 11th 1755

Sir,

Your letter of the 1st of this month I received, and am very glad you are in a fair way of recovery, which I wish may be soon and when able to travel I shall be glad to see You here.

Our Assembly now Sitting, and have voted £ 40,000 on which as soon as they rise I propose Compleating our Forces as for the Numbers you discharg'd &c. I shall not trouble you on that head till I have the pleasure to see you. The Officers who suffered in the late Action I have recommended to the Assembly, and hope they will be considered.

Probably the Scheme I propose in my Letter to Col. Dunbar may appear to some impracticable, but as I could Reinforce him now with 1000 men I think they might have made a Second attempt if the panick that seiz'd the private men of the Regulars could have been dispell'd. But as that was not thought proper, Pray Sir John is it eligible that Col. Dunar shou'd march into Winter Quarters in the middle of Summer? The service the Regulars have done is that they have open'd the Road from Fort Cumberland to the Ohio, which will facilitate the Invasion of the Enemy on our Frontiers which are left to be defended by 400 sick & Woundd [wounded] and the Remains of our provincial Troops. I think his leaving us in so distress'd Condition is without Precedent, and do not You think when the Enemy hears that the Regulars are march'd for Philadelphia upward of 200 miles from Fort Cumberland. May they not take the Advantage of this Step & Rob and Plunder our people burn the Habitations and murder all that may venture to Resist them. I do not know the Rules of the Army but I expected Col. Dunbar cou'd not Leave our Frontiers without Orders from General Shirley, to whom I sent an Express ten days ago. I Cannot but say its an unexpected thing and has Rais'd great Uneasiness among our people that after his Majesty's great favour in sending over these Forces for our protection, that they have actually been a great disservice to us by opening the Road to the Ohio and leaving us to defend the Frontiers.

As I cannot assign any Reason for Col. Dunbar's Sudden March to Winter Quarters I suspend saying anything till I see You. Pray take care of your health and I Hope from your good Spirits you will soon recover. My wife and Girls Join me in kind Respects, I am.

Sir

Your Most Humble Servant

Robt Dinwiddie

[P.S.] His Majesty's poor Subjects on the Frontiers of this Domins [Dominionsk] are left to the Mercy of an inhuman Enemy A dismal Situation indeed.

To Sir John St Clair, Bart

* * *

p. 155 [St. Clair to Colonel Napier, Fort Cumberland, August 15, 1755]

Fort Cumberland August the 15th 1755

Sir

My Letter of the 22d of July gave you an Account of the unhappy Action of the 9th of that month with the French and Indians, the Severity of my wounds at that time prevented my writing to you in as full a manner as I inclined, and as I am now a little recovered I shall be more particular. We have learnt nothing from the French Fort since the action that can be depended upon with any Certainty but in general that there numbers were much greater than we imagin'd, and indeed we had no Certain intelligence of their numbers nor of any thing they did for some Considerable time before the Action, We have likewise heard that the reason of their not pursuing us was their being apprehensive of Colo. Dunbar's party being at hand and expected that we shou'd return and Reingage them next morning. The second day after the action, we arrived at Colo. Dunbar's Camp, and that evening and the next day were taken up in destroying some of our provisions and almost all our military stores, which I think gave the finishing stroke to all further Attempts for this year, this I believe was one of Mr. Braddock's last orders, and if it had been left to himself I think he wou'd not have give it, the intention of it was to make waggon Room for the wounded, and to facilitate our Retreat, but I think all this might have been effected with great security and the stores saved likewise, with only taking a little more time.

Colonel Dunbar march'd from here the 2d Instant with the Remains of the two British Battalions, and the three Independent Companys of New York and So Carolina to go to Winter Quarters in Philadelphia and left this place garrison'd with the Country Troops only those number'd with all the sick and wounded who were not able to march with him. A longer stay wou'd have been very Acceptable to the Country, for they are under daily apprehension of some Incursions from the Indians, and the Country Troops desert Continually, and seem to be no less intimidated than the Country people themselves, so that there is very little dependence upon them, this misfortune has been represented to Colo. Dunbar since his march he is now at Shippensburgh, but seems to decline making any movements back this way without General Shirley's Orders, and whether they may come [in] time enough to prevent the impending danger is a matter of uncertainty. I am now tolerably recovered of my wound, and hope I shall be able to go soon to Williamsburgh to concert with Mr. Dinwiddie about the security of the Frontiers, and settle some other particulars with Regards to the Establishment of the Provincial Troops.

Experience convinces us now that this Country was not well Chosen for carrying on our Expedition, the Representations that have been made at home with regard to the Advantage of water Carriage and so much much [sic] Waggon Road, have either been very partial or extremely injudicious; the water Carriage at the best of time is very tedious and liable to abundance of Accidents, through the smallness of the bottoms and Scarcity, unskillfulness, and Villany of the water men, in dry Weather it is quite impracticable. The Land Carriage is long, the Country very mountainous, many of the Mountains high, Steep, Rocky and Stony, the Plains between are Swampy, generally full of Close thick woods, and troublesome runns of water. The best of years there is a scarcity of Forrage, Cattle and Carriages, and the Country People are the least Adapted for Military Service of any that I have seen, they are both delicate and Timirous [timorous], we shou'd have avoided most of the disadvantages to the northward, where the Country is plentiful the roads much better and the people of a bold Warlike Genious [Genius] besides that Road wou'd lead us thro a Country well peopled with Indians that would be ready to Join us if we made any Shew [show] amongst them.

Notwithstanding these oposite Circumstances I am still of Opinion that an Expedition might be carryed on to the Ohio even from this Country and with a moral certainty of success, but we must follow different methods from what we observed in our last, particularly building small Forts in well Chosen places and at proper distances, this I proposed frequently before, but was as often laughed at on account of the time and Expence they must take up, but we went then upon an unhappy supposition of Certain success, and that it depended upon our presence only, without the formality of observing Military precautions and the Dictates of Common Sense. If a thing of this kind was to be Carryed on again, there is one place which I wou'd particularly Recommend I mean the Camp at the great Lick Creek (mentioned in my last) the ground is naturally strong, the woods very open, the soil rich and abounding with good pasture, and the distance from the french Fort Commodious being only about thirty miles. After saying so much about publick business, I must now beg leave to speak a few words with regard to my own affairs. <u>You know I came here Deputy Quarter Master General with Majors Rank only</u>.[86] I have Spared no pains to forward his Majesty's service, I have no Chance or prospect of making money nor shou'd I mind that if I saw any likelyhood of Acquring a little military Skills tho at the risk of my bones, I have lost all my baggage and about a hundred and thirty £ worth of horses, and to sum all up I have lost my Commission, and so the last loss is the only retrievable one, I must beg the favour of you to get a Copy of it out of the War Office if you can mend it a Step I shall think it a good Recompence for my other losses, and I shall use my Endeavours, not to let his Majesty's service suffer by it. I am &c.

To Colo. Napier.

* * *

p. 158 [St. Clair to Henry Fox, Fort Cumberland, August 16, 1755]

Fort Cumberland August the 16th 1755

Sir,

In a letter of the 22d last I gave you an Account of our unhappy affair of the 9th the subject is to disagreeable to say more upon it, and I believe it had by this time been handled by several besides myself, all I think Necessary to tell you further about it is, that next day after our arrival at Colo. Dunbar's Camp, the greatest part of our Military Stores, and a good deal of provision were destroyed to facilitate the dispatch of our Retreat and to make wagon room for the wounded men of which as you may see by the Lists, we had a great number. This I believe was one of the last orders given by General Braddock, and I must say that I wish it had not been given for I think the greatest part or indeed all these valuable Stores might have been saved by taking a little more time to Transport them.

Colonel Dunbar's March from hence the 2d Instant, with the Remains of the two British Battalions and the three Independent Companies of New York and South Carolina in order to go to Winter Quarters to Pennsylvania, he left this place Garrison'd only with some of the Country Troops, and I believe his presence here for some time longer wou'd have been Acceptable to the Country as they are under daily apprehension of some incursions from the Indians, and the Provincial Troops are daily deserting, and seem no less intimidated than the Country people themselves, these Circumstances have been Represented to Colonel Dunbar since he has been gone as well as before, he is now at Shippenburgh, and seems not disposed to take much notice of Affairs in this Country, nor to make any Movement until he hears from General Shirley.

We have had no Advice from the French Fort since the Action, that can be depended upon, one of their Prisoners who has been carry'd off from this Country two months ago, made his escape from them, a few days after the Action, but his Accounts are so full of Contradictions and impossibilities that they are not worth Relating, nor do we know whether some of our people may be Prisoners with them or which is most likely all destroyed.

I still remain here under cure of my wounds with a good many more, Several of the men have died & Captain Floyer an Officer of Warburton's who served as a Volunteer in the Action, I am in a fair way of Recovering and believe I shall soon go to Williamsburgh to settle some Affairs with Governor Dinwiddie Relating to the Country Toops, and measures to be taken for the time to Come.

Had this Country been known as well as it is now I think it wou'd not have been made use off to Carry on an Expedition; besides the want of Cattle Carriages and Forrrage, the roads are exceedingly bad, and not to be made tolerable without a great deal of Labour and expence, we have done great deal to them, but they still want a great deal more, they are Rocky, Stony, and Mountainous and some parts swampy; to this I may add that the Genius of the Inhabitants does not seem to be cut out for Military Exploits, they have the least of that turn of any people I have ever seen, and the worst adapted to it. I shall not from here infer that it may not be made use off to Carry on future projects but hope our successes to the Northward will throw them into a better Channel. The most likely means that occur to me of securing a Settlement, upon the Ohio must be by entrenching, or fortifying some strong posts in the Neighborhoods of it, from whence we may have it in our power to make Descents upon them where they are weak or oblige them to keep a greater Garrison than they can possibly maintain. Great Lick

Creek mentioned in my last is one of the properest places that I know of for this purpose both on account of its Strength and distance from the Fort.

I shall shall [sic] always make it my Study to forward every part of his Majesty's service that depends upon me; and to make my Conduct agreeable to you, and all my Superiors. I am with the greatest Respect

Sir

To the Right Honble Henry Fox

* * *

p. 160 [St. Clair to General Shirley, Fort Cumberland, August 18, 1755]

Not transcribed, no campaign interest

* * *

p. 161 [Duke of Richmond to St. Clair, from Venice, January 6, 1755]

Not transcribed, no campaign interest

* * *

p. 163 [St. Clair to Sir Thomas Robinson, Williamsburg, September 3, 1755]

Williamsburgh September the 3d 1755

Sir

I shou'd have done myself the honour of Writing to you since our unlucky defeat of the 9th of July, had not the severity of my wounds prevented my writing, nor indeed was my head well settled to dictate a Letter, as the Account of our Action must have been handled by a great number, it will be disagreeable to say more upon it, had any of the previous dispositions been made by my Advice, I shou'd have looked upon myself Oblig'd in my own Justification to give you the Reasons why such dispositions were followed. All I shall trouble you with Sir at present is to tell you that I equally found fault with, and Objected to our dispositions before they were put in execution, even as much as I can do at present.

The numbers we had in the Field were reckon'd but small; it must then be an infatuation that misled us to divide these small Numbers into equal parts, and with the one half to march up to Fort Duquesne Clogg'd with a Convoy.

All I cou'd say to General Braddock cou'd not make him stop within 30 miles of the French Fort and bring up his second Convoy, which cou'd have only been the difference to us of six days, and the ground we had to halt on was so advantageous that all the Force in Canada cou'd not have turn'd us off of it, the General and his Advisors were so much prepossess'd that nothing was wanting at Fort Duquesne, for the Reduction of it, but his presence, that he went on with this unlucky Supposition, when he had march'd within 16 miles of the Fort, I begg'd of him to send 400 men to take post before it in the Night to hinder any Sortie to be made on the Convoy. These men I pray'd he wou'd give me the Comand [sic] of. It is impossible for me to give you a Circumstantial Account of the Action as I got one of the first shots that was fired thro my Body. I had no more Strength left than to go to the General and beg him to Occupy a Rising ground on the right, to save us from being totally surrounded.

I find since the Attack on our Convoy, that our Miscarriage was laid to the Cowardice of our British Soldiers. I hope never to live to see that Argument made good against our men unless some previous Steps were taken to make them dilatory in doing their duty.

So soon as I was able I got myself Carried down from Fort Cumberland to this place to Concert with Governor Dinwiddie in what manner the Provincial Troops shou'd be rais'd for the defence of this Province. I am now going to follow Colo. Dunbar, who is on his March to Albany, with the two British Battalions, and three Independent Companys, and I hope to be able to Join him before he can come to any place of Action. It is my duty Sir, to Acquaint You that a Notion prevails here, that Colo. Dunbar ordered all the provisions and Stores that were with the Convoy he had Charge of to be destroyed on General Braddock's arrival at his Camp after his defeat. in Justice to Colo. Dunbar, I Apprehended, when I saw the Stores destroy'd that it was done by General Braddock's Orders who was then alive, and

Colo Dunbar at that time told me he was surprised that General Braddock wou'd take the Comand [sic] upon him, he being so dangerously wounded, all that I can say of the Matter is that all the Officers that I talked with looked on this as done by General Braddock's Orders. The Governour of the Province, I find, finds great fault with this Step for it absolutely puts it out of our power, to make a Settlement on the ground I mentioned in the former part of my Letter 30 miles from the French Fort, and 80 miles from Fort Cumberland, I am extremely sorry that the severe wound I received, which broke my shoulder blade and Collar bone, has hinder'd me from being with General Shirley by this time. The passage of the ball is not quite shut, nor am I able to walk 100 yards nor have I the use of my Arm. However in the circumstances that I am I shall do every thing that I can to forward his Majesty's service. I have the Honour of being with the greatest Respect,

    Sir

    Your Most Obt andMost Humble Servant

    To the Right Honble Sir Thomas Robinson

* * *

p. 165 [St. Clair to Colonel Napier, from Williamsburg, September 3, 1755]

Not transcribed, no campaign interest

* * *

p. 167 [St. Clair to Lord Woodhale, Williamsburg, September 3, 1755]

Williamsburgh September 3d 1755

My Dear Lord

I must Conclude that your Lordships Letters to me of late have met with the usual Fate, that is to say, being six months in coming to my hand; for it is not long since I received one from your Lordsp dated in November last. I look upon it as a great disapointment [sic] to me that your Nephew did not come out to me, by this time he wou'd have been a Lieut in Sir Peter Halkett's Regiment, I have by the same Opportunity wrote to Mr. Stewart, to know if he is either on his passage or coming out, As I still believe I shall be able to get him kept on the muster Rolls, altho' his Commission was taken by the French it being wrapt up in mine.

I hope your Lordship will give great Allowances for my not being so regular a Corespondent as I ought to be; since the 9th of July I have been just able but to write my name, from the severity of the wounds I recd in our late Action.

The Situation of our Affairs on this Continent Obliged me to be Carried down from Wills's Creek to this place to Consult matters with the Governour for the Safety of this Province.

Our British Battalions are on their March to Albany, to which Place I shall set out in a few days. The wound that I received which broke my Shoulder Blade and Collar bone is almost Closed, but I am afraid that I will break out more violently, as I feel a great pain within me about two inches below the passage of the ball, if so I shall be Oblig'd to quit the Active part of our Business, which I have been so much accustomed ... [remainder of letter not transcribed...]

* * *

p. 169 [St. Clair to Earl of Hyndford, Williamsburg, September 3, 1755]

Williamsburgh September the 3rd 1755

My Lord,

The Letter which you Lordship did me the honour to write me of the 25th of Novemr. did not Reach me till about the 13th of June. I wrote an answer to it, but unluckily did not find an Opportunity of forwarding it to you, until the fatal day the French and Indians attacked our Convoy that letter contained a full Account of our Proceedings <u>till the 17th day of June which unluckily was the time General Braddock separated the Army, and seem'd only to think that his presence alone was sufficient for the reduction of Fort Duquesne.</u>[87]

I make no doubt but an enquiry will be made into the reasons of our Miscarriage which at last must fall on the General who is dead and gone, his advisors having only to say that he wou'd have it so, for my own part I do solemnly declare that so far as giving my Consent to his rank proceeding, <u>I gave him open warning what must happen to him</u>,[88] and shou'd my Conduct be called in question on this Occasion I will show to the publick my sentiments on Military Affairs, which wou'd Otherwise be Conceal'd.

I cannot pretend to give your Lordship a detail of our unlucky defeat, as I was the first Officer wounded in the Action. It was not in my power to do any duty that day having had my Shoulder Blade and Collar Bone broke. I shall only make this Observation to your Lordship once a Military Man, <u>that something besides Cowardice must be Attributed to a Body of men, who will suffer the one half to be diminished by Fire without being pursued in their Retreat</u>.[89] I believe this is the first Instance in this or any other age, and that General Braddock was the first Officer who march'd up a Convoy at noon day to the gates of the Town he was to besiege, without either having invested it or taken post before it some hours before.

Our British Battalions are march'd towards Albany where I Shall follow them, as fast as my Shatter'd Constitution will permit me. I am afraid it will not do for a Winter Campaign. On my seeing General Shirley I shall do all that lies in my power to be of service to Ensign Cook had he been with me in this Army. He wou'd probably have shared the Common fate of those that were with me.

<u>The Province of Virginia have given 40,000 £ for the Support of 1[,]000 men the Comand of which is given to Colo. Washington</u>,[90] the other Provinces of Maryland and Pensylvania seem little inclinable to do any thing for their own security. I make no doubt but they will soon be awaken'd out of their Lethargy by the Incursions of the French and Indians which they will Certainly make upon the back settlements.

I must entreat your lordships Assistance in putting his Royal Highness in mind of Advancing me a Step higher; as I am a Rank lower than any other of the Quarter Masters, and have Completed about 300 miles of Roads in this Country, lost all my Equipage, and got my Bones broke into the Bargain; I think I have a just Claim to what all others have had.

It wou'd be a great Presumption in me to Offer your Lordship my Service in these parts, for you know you always Comand him who is with great Regard,

My Lord

To the Earl of Hyndford

* * *

Appendix B

Sir John St. Clair's Chronology, October 1754–September 1755

Date	Event	Location	Remarks
7 October 1754	St. Clair commissioned a major in the 22nd Foot		22nd Foot, then an Irish establishment, St. Clair probably absent from regiment in England or Scotland
15 October 1754	Appointed deputy quartermaster general for North America		
mid–October to early November, 1754	Works on campaign plans with Braddock and Duke of Cumberland	London, England	
Early November, 1754	Embarks aboard HMS *Gibraltar* for Virginia	London	
Early November 1754–8 January 1755	Onboard HMS *Gibraltar*, en route to North America	North Atlantic	
9 January 1755	Arrives in Virginia onboard HMS *Gibraltar*	Hampton, Va.	
10 January 1755	Travels from Hampton to Williamsburg	Williamsburg, Va.	Delivers dispatches to Governor Dinwiddie upon arrival
11 January 1755	Meets with Governor Dinwiddie	Williamsburg	
12 January 1755	First letter is written from Williamsburg	Williamsburg	
12 January 1755	Travels to Hampton with Governor Dinwiddie	Hampton	
13 January 1755	St. Clair and Governor Dinwiddie review general hospital arrangements	Hampton	
Evening, 13 January 1755	St. Clair and Governor Dinwiddie return to Williamsburg	Williamsburg	
14–15 January 1755	Works on contracts and correspondence	Williamsburg	
Morning, 16 January 1755	Departs for Fort Cumberland	From Williamsburg	
16 January 1755–1 February 1755	Trip to Fort Cumberland		

Date	Event	Location	Remarks
16–18 January 1755	Travels from Williamsburg to Frederick, Md.		
19–22 January 1755	Travels from Frederick to Winchester		
23–26 January 1755	Travels from Winchester to Fort Cumberland		
27 January–1 February 1755	Returns from Fort Cumberland to Alexandria, Va.		
1 February 1755	Works on contracts and correspondence	Alexandria, Va.	
	Travels from Alexandria to Williamsburg		Date unknown
9–13 February 1755	Works on contracts and correspondence	Williamsburg	
14 February 1755	Travels to Hampton to dispatch correspondence for England	Hampton	HMS *Gibraltar* sails for England from Hampton on 16 February 1755
15 February 1755	Reviews general hospital arrangements	Hampton	
16 February 1755	Travels to Williamsburg	Williamsburg	
16–17 February 1755	Works on contracts and correspondence	Williamsburg	
18 February 1755	Planned trip to Winchester, Virginia	From Williamsburg	
18–21 February 1755	Travels from Williamsburg to Frederick		
21–22 February 1755	Works on contracts and correspondence	Frederick, Md.	
22 February 1755	Returns to Williamsburg		In response to General Braddock's arrival in Virginia
22 February 1755–1 March 1755	Works on contracts and correspondence, meetings with General Braddock	Williamsburg	
	Travels from Williamsburg to Frederick		Dates unknown
1 March 1755	Works on contracts and correspondence	Frederick	
1–3 March 1755	Travels from Frederick to Alexandria		
3–7 March 1755	Works on issuing contracts and correspondence	Alexandria	
	Travels from Alexandria to Winchester		Dates unknown
12 March 1755	Works on issuing contracts and correspondence	Winchester	
12 March 1755	Travels to Great Cacecapon River	Crossing of Great Cacecapon	
	Travels from Great Cacecapon River to Fort Cumberland		Dates unknown

Appendix B

Date	Event	Location	Remarks
18 March 1755	Works on issuing contracts and correspondence	Fort Cumberland	
	Travels from Fort Cumberland to Winchester		Dates unknown
21 March 1755	Works on issuing contracts and correspondence	Winchester	
	Travels from Winchester to Alexandria		Dates unknown
28 March 1755	Works on issuing contracts and correspondence	Alexandria	
	Travels from Alexandria to Winchester		Dates unknown
3 April–2 May 1755	Works on road west of Great Philadelphia Wagon Road, between Winchester and Fort Cumberland, and on movement of Braddock's army from Alexandria to Fort Cumberland		
6 April 1755		Winchester	
13 April 1755		Henry Enoch House on Cacecapon River	
16 April 1755	Meets with Pennsylvania representatives, including George Croghan	Fort Cumberland	
21 April 1755		Winchester	
21 April 1755	Meets with Braddock and Benjamin Franklin on wagon and horse availability	Frederick	This suggests a very long, and perhaps impossible, day's ride from Winchester to Frederick
22–27 April 1755	With Braddock, works on wagon and horse availability	Frederick	
27 April–2 May 1755	Travels from Frederick to Fort Cumberland		Dates unknown
2–28 May 1755	Performs quartermaster duties	Fort Cumberland	
10 May 1755	44th Foot, 48th Foot, and royal artillery complete march from Alexandria to Fort Cumberland	Fort Cumberland	
18 May, 20 May, 25 May 1755	Surveys road routes west of Fort Cumberland	Fort Cumberland and west	Surveying documented for these dates, likely performed on other dates also
"Late May" 1755	Attends two councils of war with General Braddock and field officers	Fort Cumberland	Precise dates not known
Morning, May 29, 1755	With Major Chapman of the 44th Foot leads advanced party from Fort Cumberland to construct road to west	Depart Fort Cumberland	

Sir John St. Clair Chronology, October 1754–September 1755

Date	Event	Location	Remarks
29 May–2 June 1755	Supervises road construction across Will's Mountain west of Fort Cumberland	Will's Mountain	
2 June 1755	Lieutenant Spendelow reports new route discovered, avoiding Will's Mountain	Will's Mountain	
2–6 June 1755	Supervises road construction along Spendelow's alternate route	North and west of Will's Mountain	
2 June 1755	Surveys road route and road construction	Savage River Camp	
4 June 1755	Surveys road route and road construction	Mudlick Creek Camp	
5 June 1755	Surveys road route and road construction	Little Meadows Camp	
5–16 June 1755	Surveys road route and construction of Little Meadows Camp	Little Meadows camp	
13 June 1755	First Working Party begins construction of road west of Little Meadows under St. Clair	Little Meadows Camp	
13 June 1755	Deposits his letterbook to 12 June 1755 with baggage train of army	Little Meadows Camp	Letterbook from 12 June to 9 July 1755 subsequently lost
15 or 16 June 1755	Council of war with General Braddock and field officers	Little Meadows Camp	
19 June 1755	British main column departs Little Meadows camp		
21–24 June 1755	Surveys road route and crossing of Youghiogheny River	Great Crossings, Youghiogheny River	
24 June 1755	Surveys road route and road construction	Camp East of the Great Meadows	
25 June	British main column marches through Great Meadows	Orchard Camp	
26 June	British main column marches up Chestnut Ridge	Rocky Fort Camp (Jumonville)	
27 June	British main column marches down Chestnut Ridge	Plantation of Christopher Gist	
28 June	British main column marches north to Youghiogheny River	Robinson's Falls Camp	
29–30 June	St. Clair working party works on Stewart's Crossing of Youghiogheny River and road "two days forward"	Robinson's Falls Camp	

Appendix B

Date	Event	Location	Remarks
30 June	British main column marches across Stewart's Crossing of Youghiogheny River	Unnamed Camp East of Stewart's Crossing	
1 July	British main column marches north	Unnamed Camp	
2 July	British main column marches north	Jacob's Cabin Camp	
3 July	British main column marches north	Salt Lick Creek	
3 July	Council of war with General Braddock and field officers, at St. Clair's request	Salt Lick Creek	
4 July	British main column marches northwest	Thicketty Run Camp	
5 July	British main column remains in camp, St. Clair leads survey party forward	Thicketty Run Camp	
6 July	British main column marches northwest	Monacatootha's Camp	
7 July	Performs scout of ridge north of Turtle Creek	Blunder Camp	
8 July	British main column marches west; St. Clair works on road to Monongahela River	Unnamed Camp	
9 July	Battle of the Monongahela		
1:00 p.m. 10 July	St. Clair (badly wounded) and servant reach Colonel Dunbar's column	Rocky Fort Camp (Jumonville)	
10–18 July	Convalesces at Rocky Fort camp		
10–18 July	Evacuated from Rocky Fort camp to Fort Cumberland		Actual dates unknown
18 July	Writes short note (first documented activity after Battle of the Monongahela)	Fort Cumberland	St. Clair Letterbook resumes
18 July–18 August	Convalesces at Fort Cumberland	Fort Cumberland	
18 August 1775	Last known letter from Fort Cumberland	Fort Cumberland	
Mid to Late August	Evacuated from Fort Cumberland to Williamsburg		Actual dates unknown
September 1755	Convalescing in Williamsburg		

Appendix C

Catalogue of Sir John St. Clair's Letterbook during the Braddock Expedition

Letterbook Page	Description
p. 1	St. Clair to Governor Horatio Sharpe of Maryland, Williamsburg, January 12, 1755
p. 2	St. Clair to James Pitcher, Williamsburg, January 14, 1755
p. 3	St. Clair to the governors of various provinces, Williamsburg, January 14, 1755
p. 5	St. Clair to General Braddock, Williamsburg, January 15, 1755
p. 9	St. Clair to Colonel Hunter, Williamsburg, January 15, 1755
p. 10	St. Clair to Lord Fairfax, Wills Creek, January 26, 1755
p. 12	Not dated, no address, Memorandum for Commissary Walker
p. 13	St. Clair to Commissary Dick, Alexandria, February 2, 1755
p. 14	St. Clair to officers in charge of soldiers at Winchester, Fredericksburg, and Alexandria, February 1, 1755
p. 15	St. Clair to Major John Carlyle, Alexandria, February 3, 1755
p. 16	St. Clair to General Braddock, Williamsburg, February 9, 1755
p. 20	St. Clair to Colonel Napier, Williamsburg, February 10, 1755
p. 22	St. Clair to Henry Fox, Williamsburg, February 11, 1755
p. 24	St. Clair's proposal for a settlement on the Ohio, February 12, 1755
p. 25	St. Clair to Sir Thomas Robinson, Williamsburg, February 12, 1755
p. 26	St. Clair to Governor Sharpe, Williamsburg, February 12, 1755
p. 27	St. Clair to Deputy Governor Morris of Pennsylvania, Williamsburg, February 14, 1755
p. 29	St. Clair to Colonel Napier, Hampton, February 15, 1755
p. 31	St. Clair to General Braddock, Williamsburg, February 17, 1755
p. 32	St. Clair to Governor Arthur Dobbs of North Carolina, Williamsburg, February 17, 1755
p. 33	St. Clair to various commanding officers, Fredericksburg, February 21, 1755
p. 34	St. Clair to Colonel Innes, Fredericksburg, February 21, 1755
p. 35	St. Clair to Lord Fairfax, Fredericksburg, February 21, 1755
p. 36	St. Clair to Governor Sharpe, Fredericksburg, February 22, 1755
p. 36	St. Clair to Major John Carlyle, Fredericksburg, February 22, 1755
p. 37	General Braddock to St. Clair, Williamsburg, February 26, 1755
p. 38	General Braddock to St. Clair, Williamsburg, February 26, 1755
p. 39	General Braddock to St. Clair, Williamsburg, February 27, 1755
p. 40	General Braddock, Orders, Williamsburg, February 26, 1755
p. 41	General Braddock to St. Clair, Williamsburg, February 28, 1755
p. 42	General Braddock, Orders, Not dated, not addressed
p. 43	General Braddock, Orders, Not dated, not addressed

Appendix C

Letterbook Page	Description
p. 44	General Braddock, Orders, Not dated, not addressed
p. 46	Acting Governor DeLancey of New York to St. Clair, New York, February 3, 1755
p. 48	Major John Carlyle to St. Clair, Alexandria, February 18, 1755
p. 49	Governor Sharpe to St. Clair, Alexandria, February 17,1755
p. 50	Lieutenant Governor Dinwiddie to St. Clair, Williamsburg, February 18, 1755
p. 51	Lieutenant Governor Dinwiddie to St. Clair, Not addressed, not dated
p. 52	Governor Sharpe to St. Clair, Alexandria, February 17, 1755
p. 53	Governor Jonathan Belcher of New Jersey to St. Clair, Elizabethtown, New Jersey, February 3, 1755
p. 55	Deputy Governor Morris of Pennsylvania to St. Clair, Philadelphia, February 17, 1755
p. 56	Governor Sharpe to St. Clair, Williamsburg, February 9, 1755
p. 57	St. Clair to Captain Cocke, Fredericksburg, March 1, 1755
p. 58	St. Clair to Lieutenant John Hamilton, Fredericksburg, March 1, 1755 *Note:* This is presumably the letter forwarded by p. 57 to Captain Cocke
p. 59	St. Clair to Lieutenant Henry Woodward, Fredericksburg, March 1, 1755
p. 60	St. Clair to Ensign Hector Neil, Fredericksburg, March 1, 1755
p. 61	St. Clair to General Braddock, Fredericksburg, March 1, 1755
p. 63	St. Clair to Governor Sharpe, Alexandria, March 3, 1755
p. 64	St. Clair's Orders for company of carpenters, Alexandria, March 3, 1755
p. 65	St. Clair Orders for 2nd company of artificers, Alexandria, March 5, 1755
p. 66	St. Clair orders for Virginia troops at Alexandria, Alexandria, March 5, 1755
p. 67	St. Clair to Lieutenant Governor Dinwiddie, Alexandria, March 6, 1755
p. 70	St. Clair to General Braddock, Alexandria, March 6, 1755
p. 73	St. Clair to Major John Carlyle, Alexandria, March 6, 1755
p. 74	St. Clair Orders to Captain Hogg of the Virginia forces, Alexandria, March 7, 1755
p. 75	St. Clair to Lieutenant Savage, Alexandria, March 7, 1755
p. 76	Captain Orme to St. Clair, Hampton, March 6, 1755
p. 77	St. Clair to Captain Cocke, commanding officer of detachment of Virginia forces at Port Royal, Winchester, March 12, 1755
p. 78	St. Clair to General Braddock, Great Cacecapon, March 12, 1755
p. 80	St. Clair to Captain Thomas Clarke, commanding independent company of New York, Wills Creek, March 18, 1755
p. 81	St. Clair to Captain Waggoner of Virginia forces, Wills Creek, March 18, 1755
p. 82	St. Clair to Captain Thomas Clarke, commanding independent company of New York, Wills Creek, March 18, 1755
p. 83	St. Clair to Mr. Perkins, Winchester, March 21, 1755
p. 84	St. Clair Order to company of rangers, Winchester, March 21, 1755
p. 85	Governor Sharpe to St. Clair, Annapolis, March 15, 1755
p. 86	Braddock to St. Clair, Williamsburg, March 15, 1755
p. 87	St. Clair memorandum for General Braddock, Williamsburg, March 28, 1755
p. 88	Braddock to St. Clair, Williamsburg, April 1, 1755
p. 89	St. Clair memorandum for commissaries, not addressed, not dated
p. 90	St. Clair proposal for advancing army from Winchester and Frederick, Winchester, April 3, 1755
p. 92	St. Clair to General Braddock, Winchester, April 6, 1755
p. 94	St. Clair to General Braddock, Cacecapon, April 13, 1755
p. 96	St. Clair to captains Cocke and Jones, Cacecapon, April 13, 1755
p. 97	St. Clair to Captain Orme, Cacecapon, April 13, 1755
p. 99	St. Clair to Sir Peter Halkett, Cacecapon, April 13, 1755
p. 100	St. Clair to officer commanding the artillery, Cacecapon, April 13, 1755

Letterbook Page	Description
p. 101	Sir Peter Halkett to St. Clair, Winchester, April 16, 1755
p. 103	Captain Orme to St. John, not addressed, not dated
p. 105	St. Clair to Colonel Halkett, Wills Creek, April 17, 1755
p. 107	St. Clair memorandum on marching troops from Winchester to Wills Creek, Winchester, April 21, 1755
p. 109	St. Clair description of the second and longest road to Wills Creek, not addressed, not dated
p. 110	St. Clair to Mr. Hoight on the south branch of the Potomack River, Winchester, April 21, 1755
p. 111	St. Clair Instructions to Captain Polson, commanding 2nd company of artificers, Winchester, April 21, 1755
p. 112	St. Clair instructions to Lieutenant Hamilton the 2nd company of artificers, Winchester, April 21, 1755
p. 113	St. Clair to Lieutenant Lewis, Winchester, April 21, 1755
p. 114	St. Clair instructions to Lieutenant Richard Bailey of Sir Peter Halkett's Regiment, Winchester, April 21, 1755
p. 115	Captain Orme to St. Clair, Alexandria, April 13, 1755
p. 116	Governor William Shirley of Massachusetts to St. Clair, Boston, March 18, 1755
p. 117	Governor Reynolds of Georgia to St. Clair, Georgia, March 13, 1755
p. 118	St. Clair to General Braddock, Fort Cumberland, May 2, 1755
p. 119	Lieutenant Governor Dinwiddie to St. Clair, Williamsburg, May 1, 1755
p. 120	Lieutenant Governor Dinwiddie to St. Clair, Williamsburg, May 10, 1755
p. 133	General Braddock, instructions to St. Clair, Fort Cumberland, May 28, 1755 *Note:* Letters p. 132 through p. 140 have been moved to their proper chronological sequence in the letterbook.
p. 132	General Braddock to St. Clair, not addressed, May 31, 1755 *Note:* This Letter has been moved to its proper chronological sequence.
p. 134	St. Clair to Braddock, Camp at George's Creek, June 1, 1755
p. 136	Captain Orme to St. Clair, not addressed, June 2, 1755
p. 137	St. Clair to General Braddock, Camp at Savage River, June 2, 1755
p. 138	St. Clair to General Braddock, camp at Little Meadows, June 10, 1755
p. 140	Captain Orme to St. Clair, not addressed, June 11, 1755 *Note:* this letter was written in response to the letter from St. Clair on p. 138, and has been moved to its proper chronological sequence.
p. 139	June 12, 1755, Captain Orme to St. Clair, not addressed, June 12, 1755
p. 121	St. Clair note explaining that letters from May 27 to July 9 fell into enemy hands, not addressed, not dated
p. 122	St. Clair to Commodore Keppel, Wills Creek, July 18, 1755
p. 123	St. Clair to Colonel Napier, Wills Creek, July 22, 1755 *Note:* This account of St. Clair's of the battle is re-printed in Stanley Pargellis, ed. *Military Affairs in North America, 1748–1765* (New York: Appleton-Century, 1936), 102–103.
p. 126	St. Clair to Henry Fox, Wills Creek, July 22, 1755 *Note:* This account of the engagement is all but identical to the more widely reprinted account sent to Napier on the same day.
p. 128	Commodore Keppel to St. Clair, Hampton, July 22, 1755
p. 129	Letter of March 24, 1755 from William Greene of Rhode Island to St. Clair *Note:* not transcribed, no campaign interest.
p. 130	Letter of May 17, 1755 from Duke of Richmond[1] to St. Clair *Note:* not transcribed, no campaign interest.

Appendix C

Letterbook Page	Description
p. 142	Earl of Hyndford[2] to St. Clair, from Carmichael House near Lanark, November 24, 1754
	Note: not transcribed, no campaign interest.
p. 142	St. Clair to Governor Dinwiddie, Fort Cumberland, July 23, 1755
p. 144	Governor Dinwiddie to St. Clair, July 4, 1755
	Note: not transcribed, no campaign interest.
p. 146	Governor Dinwiddie to St. Clair, July 26, 1755
	Note: not transcribed, no campaign interest.
p. 147	St. Clair to Governor Dinwiddie, Fort Cumberland, August 1, 1755
p. 149	Governor Dinwiddie to St. Clair, Williamsburg, August 1, 1755
p. 155	St. Clair to Colonel Napier, Fort Cumberland, August 15, 1755
p. 158	St. Clair to Henry Fox, Fort Cumberland, August 16, 1755
p. 160	St. Clair to General Shirley, Fort Cumberland, August 18, 1755
	Note: not transcribed, no campaign interest.
p. 161	Duke of Richmond to St. Clair, from Venice, January 6, 1755
	Note: not transcribed, no campaign interest.
p. 163	St. Clair to Sir Thomas Robinson, Williamsburg, September 3, 1755
p. 165	St. Clair to Colonel Napier, from Williamsburg, September 3, 1755
	Note: not transcribed, no campaign interest.
p. 167	St.Clair to Lord Woodhale, Williamsburg, September 3, 1755
p. 169	St. Clair to Earl of Hyndford, Williamsburg, September 3, 1755

Chapter Notes

Introduction

1. Robert Dinwiddie (1693–July 27, 1770) was the British lieutenant governor of the colony of Virginia from 1751 to 1758, first under Governor Willem Anne van Keppel, 2nd Earl of Albemarle, and then, from July 1756 to January 1758, as deputy for John Campbell, 4th Earl of Loudoun. Dinwiddie was from an old Scottish family, was born in Glasgow and educated at the University of Glasgow. Before he entered public service and politics he was a successful Scottish merchant and businessman. Since both governors of Virginia were exclusively absentee (the governor of Virginia was a post distributed by the king as a lucrative patronage), Dinwiddie was the actual governor of the colony. Dinwiddie was a stockholder in the Ohio Company who stood to gain considerable land and wealth if the Ohio Country became an English, and Virginian, possession. He was a strong proponent of British and Virginia ownership of the Ohio Country, had sent the young George Washington to the French to protest their occupation of the Ohio River Valley in 1753, had instigated military action against the French in 1754, and had played an eminent role in encouraging the dispatch of a regular British military force against Fort Duquesne in 1755. He dominated Colonial politics in Virginia for much of the Seven Years War.

2. In 1755, regiments were still known by their commanding officers' names. In this study, the more commonly used and readily recognizable regimental numberical designations will be utilized.

3. John Kennedy Lacock, "Braddock Road," *The Pennsylvania Magazine of History and Biography* XXXVII (1) (1914): 1–2.

4. As an example, two recent histories repeat and endorse these poorly documented allegations regarding Braddock: James M. Perry, *Arrogant Armies, Great Military Disasters and the Generals Behind Them* (New York: John Wiley & Sons, 1996), 4–30; and Geoffrey Regan, *Great Military Disasters, A Historical Survey of Military Incompetence* (New York: M. Evans, 1987), 180–191.

Chapter 1

1. Martin West, transcriber, *George Washington Remembers, Reflections on the French & Indian War* (Lanham, MD: Rowman & Littlefield, 2004), 41.

2. Charles R. Hildeburn, "Sir John St. Clair, Baronet, Quarter Master General in America, 1755 to 1767," *The Pennsylvania Magazine of History and Biography* 9, no. 1 (1885), 1–14.

3. William Nelson, ed., *Documents Relating to the Colonial History of the State of New Jersey* XXV, "Extracts from American Newspapers, Relating to New Jersey, 1766–1767" (Paterson, NJ: The Call Printing and Publishing Company, 1903), 503.

4. For this, refer to Pargellis, *Military Affairs in North America*, 58.

5. Christopher Duffy, *The Wild Goose and the Eagle, A Life of Marshal von Browne, 1705–1757* (London: Chatto & Windus, 1964), 130, 148–149, 152.

6. Alfred Procter James, ed., *Writings of General John Forbes, Relating to his Service in North America* (Menashga, WI: The Collegiate Press, 1938; reprint, New York: Arno Press, 1971), 1.

Chapter 2

1. *A Military Dictionary Explaining and Describing the Technical Terms, Works and Machines, Used in the Science of War with an Introduction to Fortification* (Dublin: C. Jackson, 1780).

2. George Smith, *An Universal Military Dictionary* (London: J. Millan, 1779). Quoted in Arthur S. Lefkowitz, *George Washington's Indispensable Men* (Harrisburg: Stackpole Books, 2003), 6.

3. Mr. de Jeney, *The Partisan: Or, The Art of Making War in Detachment with Plans proper to facilitate the understanding of the several Dispositions and Movements necessary to Light Troops, in order to accomplish their Marches, Ambuscades, Attacks and Retreats with Success*, trans. from the French of Mr. de Jeney By an Officer in the Army (London, 1760), 29.

4. Will H. Lowdermilk, ed., "Major General Edward Braddock's Orderly Books, From February 26 to June 17, 1755," *History of Cumberland, Maryland* (1878; reprint, Baltimore: Regional Publishing Company, 1976).

5. Abbott, ed., *The Papers of George Washington*, 1:241–245.

6. George Smith, *An Universal Military Dictionary* (London: J. Millan, 1779). Quoted in Lefkowitz, *George Washington's Indispensable Men*, 4–5.

7. Forbes headquarters papers, "Memorandum of Brigade Major Halkett [undated]."

8. Will H. Lowdermilk, ed., "Major General Edward Braddock's Orderly Books, From February 26 to June 17, 1755," *History of Cumberland, Maryland* (1878).

9. *The Partisan*, 16.

10. *General Wolfe's Instructions to Young Officers* (London: J. Millan, 1780), v–vi.

11. Hamilton, *Braddock's Defeat*, 55, 61–63.

12. Nichols, "Organization of Braddock's Army," 126.

13. *General Braddock's Orderly Book*, ix.

14. *General Braddock's Orderly Book*, x.

15. A Society of Gentlemen in Scotland, *Encyclopedia Britannica, or a Dictionary of Arts and Sciences* (Edinburgh: A. Bell and C. Macfarquhar, 1768–1771), 2:240.

16. *A Military Dictionary*.

17. Thomas Robinson I, 1st Baron Grantham (1695–1770). Sir Thomas Robinson was a prominent British politician and diplomat. In 1755, he was serving as British secretary of state for the southern department. Robinson had primary responsibility for the North American colonies. Robinson was somewhat detracted from these duties by an additional responsibility for the Newcastle ministry, leader of the House of Commons, a position in which he served without particular distinction or accomplishment.

18. Dominick Graham, "The Planning of the Beauséjour Operation and the Approaches to War in 1755," *The New England Quarterly* 41.4 (December 1968), 557.

19. Simes, *Treatise on Military Science* (1780), 73.

20. Simes, *Treatise on Military Science* (1780), 73–76.

21. Simes, *Treatise on Military Science* (1780), 73.

22. Sargent, *Expedition to Fort Duquesne*, 360.

23. Pargellis, *Military Affairs in North America*, 112.

24. Simes, *The Military Guide for Young Officers* (1776), 146.

25. Hamilton, *Braddock's Defeat*, 55.

26. E. Ralph Bates, *Captain Thomas Webb, Anglo-American Methodist Hero* (World Methodist Historical Society, 1975). Webb would go on to become one of the Methodist Church's most influential early ministers, and he played a significant and prominent role in establishing the Methodist Church in North America during the 18th century.

27. Lucy S. Sutherland and J. Binney, "Henry Fox as Paymaster General," in Rosalind Mitchison, ed., *Essays in Eighteenth-Century History, from the English Historical Review* (New York: Barnes & Noble), 232.

28. T.H. McGuffie, "A Deputy Paymaster's Fortune: The Case of George Durant, Deputy Paymaster to the Havana Expedition, 1762," *Journal of the Society for Army Historical Research* XXXII: 132 (Winter 1954), 145.

29. *Benjamin Franklin Papers*, 6:224.

30. Pargellis, *Military Affairs in North America*, 81.

31. J. Cook Wilson, ed., "The Campaign of General Braddock," *English Historical Review* 1:1 (January 1886), 149–152.

32. Gordon Kershaw, "The Legend of Braddock's Gold Reconsidered," *Maryland Historical Magazine* 96:1 (Spring 2001), 107.

33. "Halkett's Orderly Book," in Hamilton, ed., *Braddock's Defeat*, 67.

34. Gordon Kershaw, "The Legend of Braddock's Gold Reconsidered," *Maryland Historical Magazine* 96, no. 1 (Spring 2001), 96.

35. Douglas R. Cubbison, "The Coins of the British Private Soldier in the American Revolution," *The Petit Guerre, Newsletter of Captain Fraser's Company of Select Marksmen, British Brigade and Brigade of the American Revolution* (Winter 2004); and Douglas R. Cubbison, "Eight Pence a Day, Pay of the British Private Soldier During the American Revolution," *The Petit Guerre, Newsletter of Captain Fraser's Company of Select Marksmen, British Brigade and Brigade of the American Revolution* (Winter 2004), Online at www.csmid.com.

36. Kershaw, "The Legend of Braddock's Gold Reconsidered," 94.

37. Pargellis, *Military Affairs in North America*, 81.

38. Kershaw, "The Legend of Braddock's Gold Reconsidered," 96, 98–99.

39. *Washington Papers*, 1:281.

40. Washington's journey is documented in *Ibid.*, 1: 281–293.

41. Edward E. Curtis, *The British Army in the American Revolution* (1926; reprint, Gansevoort, NY: Corner House Historical Publications, 1998), 177–179.

42. Ross Netherton, *Braddock's Campaign and the Potomac Route to the West* (Winchester, VA: Winchester-Frederick County Historical Society, 1989), 20.

43. Kenneth H. Tuggle, "Dr. Thomas Walker Bicentennial Celebration," *Filson Club Historical Quarterly* 24 (July 1950), 276–279.

44. Sargent, *The Braddock Expedition to Fort Duquesne*, 179.

45. Hamilton, *Braddock's Defeat*, 93, 96, 102, 123; *Braddock's Orderly Book*, xxxviii, xlviii, Li.

46. McCardell, *Ill-Starred General*, 213–214.

47. *Braddock's Orderly Book*, xxxviii.

48. James D. Munson, *Colonel John Carlyle, Gentleman, A True and Just Account of the Man and His House* (Northern Virginia Regional Park Authority, 1986), 66.

49. Curtis, *The British Army in the Revolution*, 134–139.

50. *General Braddock's Orderly Book*, lv.

51. *Benjamin Franklin Papers*, 6:244.

52. *A Military Dictionary* (1780).

53. Houston, "Benjamin Franklin and the Wagon Affair of 1755," 270; and *Benjamin Franklin Papers*, 6:221–222.

54. E.G.W. Bill, "A Cadet at the Royal Military Academy, 1778–1780," *The Journal of the Royal Artillery* 84 (October 1957), 311.

55. Simes, *The Military Guide for Young Officers* (1776).

56. Douglas W. Marshall, "The British Engineers in America, 1755–1783," *Journal of the Society for Army Historical Research* LI: 207 (Autumn 1973), 155.

57. Kopperman, *Braddock at the Monongahela*, 38.

58. Ness, "The Braddock Campaign, 1755," *The Military Engineer* (January–February 1959), 20.
59. Pargellis, *Military Affairs in North America*, 484–485.
60. General W. H. Askwith, *List of Officers of the Royal Regiment of Artillery, The Year 1716 to the Year 1899* (London: Royal Artillery Institution, 1900), 24.
61. Hamilton, *Braddock's Defeat*, 57.
62. Lieutenant Colonel M.E.S. Laws, "R.N. and R.A. in Virginia [Royal Artillery and Royal Navy] in 1755," *Journal of the Society for Army Historical Research* LVII: 232 (Winter 1979), 194–195.
63. Edward G. Williams, "Treasure Hunt in the Forest," *Western Pennsylvania History* 44:4 (December 1961), 383–396.
64. "A List of Officers, Engineers, Ministers and Others Appointed to Attend His Majesty's Forces Ordered on an Expedition to North America under the Command of Major General Braddock," War Office Records, Board of Ordnance Miscellaneous Records, 1754, Public Records Office.
65. "A List of Officers, Engineers, Ministers and Others Appointed to Attend His Majesty's Forces Ordered on an Expedition to North America under the Command of Major General Braddock," War Office Records, Board of Ordnance Miscellaneous Records, 1754, Public Records Office.
66. *A Military Dictionary* (1780).
67. Simes, *Treatise on Military Science*, 82–84.
68. Hamilton, *Braddock's Defeat*, 69. Webbster's rank cannot be determined.
69. Hamilton, *Braddock's Defeat*, 73–74; 79; 91.
70. de Jeney, *The Partisan*, 31.
71. Amherst papers, printed in Ian McCulloch, "Highland Chaplaincy in the French & Indian War, 1756–1763." Available at http://www.electricscotland.com/history/scotreg/mcculloch/story3.htm (accessed on 15 September 2009).
72. The most comprehensive analysis of the role of the chaplain in the British 18th century army is Paul E. Kopperman, "Religion and Religious Policy in the British Army, c. 1700–96," *The Journal of Religious History* 15 (1987), 390–405.
73. *Advice to the Officers of the British Army, with the Addition of Some Hints to the Drummer and Private Soldier* (London: W. Richardson, 1783), 64–70.
74. Fairfax Harrison, "With Braddock's Army, Mrs. Browne's Diary in Virginia and Maryland," *Virginia Magazine of History and Biography* XXXII: 4 (October 1924); quoted in Paul E. Kopperman, "Religion and Religious Policy in the British Army, c. 1700–96," *The Journal of Religious History* 15 (1987), 395.
75. "The Journal of Captain Robert Cholmley's Batman," in Hamilton, ed., *Braddock's Defeat*, 34.
76. *General Braddock's Orderly Book*, xi.
77. "Captain Orme's Journal," in Sargent, *The History of an Expedition Against Fort Duquesne in 1755*, 377.
78. Wahll, *Braddock Road Chronicles*, 389–390,
79. N. Darnell Davis, "British Newspaper Accounts of Braddock's Defeat," *The Pennsylvania Magazine of History and Biography* 23 (1899), 324.
80. R.E. Barnsley, "The Life of an 18th Century Army Surgeon," *The Journal of the Society of Army Historical Research* XLIV, no. 179 (September 1966), 130.
81. Sargent, *History of an Expedition Against Fort Duquesne in 1755*, 136.
82. Abbott, ed., *George Washington's Papers*, I:315, 316, 325.
83. Paul E. Kopperman, "The Medical Aspect of The Braddock and Forbes Expedition," *Pennsylvania History* 71:3 (2004), 265.
84. Hamilton, *Braddock's Defeat*, 54–58.
85. Kopperman, "Medical Aspect," 279. Mrs. Browne noted her brother being treated by "Mr. Tuton" at Fort Cumberland on July 13, 1755. Calder, ed., "The Journal of Charlotte Brown," 184. Presumably, this was Surgeon's Mate George Tuting.
86. Kopperman, "Medical Aspect," 265.
87. Calder, ed., "The Journal of Charlotte Brown," 169.
88. Harrison, ed., "With Braddock's Army," 310.
89. Hamilton, *Braddock's Defeat*, 57.
90. Captain Joseph Otway, *An Essay on the Art of War, Translated from the French of Count Turpin, In Two Volumes* (London: A. Hamilton, 1761), I: 155–162.
91. Jodie Gilmore, "Washington's Spies: General George Washington's Intelligence Network during the American War for Independence Contributed Largely to His Success," *The New American* 21 (March 7, 2005); and Alexander Rose, *Washington's Spies: The Story of America's First Spy Ring* (New York: Bantam, 2007).

Chapter 3

1. Houlding, *Fit For Service*, 20, 54–55.
2. James, ed., *Writings of Brigadier General John Forbes*, 1.
3. Hildeburn, "Sir John St. Clair," 2.
4. Maryland governor Horatio Sharpe (1718–1790). Sharpe served as the governor for Proprietor Lord Baltimore. He was commissioned as a captain in the Royal Marines in 1745, and served for several years as a lieutenant colonel in the West Indies. Sharpe was appointed governor of Maryland in 1753, and was consistently regarded as an excellent governor. Because of his prior military service, he worked particularly well with British military officers, particularly Braddock and Brigadier General John Forbes. Sharpe served as governor until 1768, and returned to England shortly before the outbreak of the American Revolution. Edward C. Papenfuse, et al., *A Biographical Dictionary of the Maryland Legislature, 1635–1789* (Baltimore: Johns Hopkins University Press, 1985), II: 726–8; and Paul H. Giddens, "Governor Horatio Sharpe and His Maryland Government," *Maryland Historical Magazine* XXXII (June 1937), 156–74.
5. Deal was a "thin kind of fir planks, of great use in carpentry." *Encyclopedia Britannica*, 2:309.
6. "Journal of Charlotte Brown" in Calder, *Colonial Captivities, Marches and Journeys*, 174–175.
7. "Journal of Charlotte Brown," in Calder, *Colonial Captivities, Marches and Journeys*, 174–175.

8. Pargellis, *Military Affairs in North America*, 77.
9. Munson, *Colonel John Carlyle, Gentleman*, 70.
10. Cubbison, *The British Defeat of the French in Pennsylvania*, 63–64.
11. Pargellis, *Military Affairs in North America*, 84–85.
12. Franklin, *The Autobiography of Benjamin Franklin* (New Haven: Yale University Press, 1964), 216–217.
13. Alan Houston, "Benjamin Franklin and the Wagon Affair of 1755," *William and Mary Quarterly* 3rd Series, LXVI:2 (April 2009), 251–252.
14. J. Bell Whitfield, Jr., and Leonard W. Labaree, "Franklin and the Wagon Affair, 1755," *Proceedings of the American Philosophical Society* 101:6 (1957), 552.
15. Houston, "Benjamin Franklin and the Wagon Affair of 1755," 257, 274.
16. Pargellis, *Military Affairs in North America*, 85.
17. Ross Netherton, *Braddock's Campaign and the Potomac Route to the West* (Winchester-Frederick County Historical Society, reprint, 1989), 5.
18. Alan Guy, "A Whole Army Absolutely Ruined in Ireland, Aspects of the Irish Establishment, 1715–1773," *Report—National Army Museum* (1978–1979), 30, 32; and Neal Garnham, "Military Desertion and Deserters in Eighteenth-Century Ireland," *Eighteenth-Century Ireland* 20 (2005), 91–97, 103.
19. An excellent discussion of the situation of these two regiments is J.A. Houlding, *Fit for Service: The Training of the British Army, 1715–1795* (Oxford: Clarendon Press, 1981), 49–50.
20. Before the Seven Years War was concluded, the British army was regularly enlisting men "for terms of years."
21. Nichols, "The Organization of Braddock's Army," 131, 138.
22. The independent companies have received scant attention from historians. The only scholarship on them was performed by the renowned historian Stanley M. Pargellis, "The Four Independent Companies of New York," in *Essays in Colonial History Presented to Charles McLean Andrews by His Students* (1931; reprint Freeport, NY: Essay Index Reprint Series, Books for Libraries Press, 1966), 96–123.
23. Stephen Brumwell, "Home From the Wars, Attitudes Towards Veterans in mid–Georgian Britain, and the Provisions Made for Them," *History Today* 52, no. 3 (March 2002), 41–47.
24. Max M. Mintz, *The Generals of Saratoga, John Burgoyne & Horatio Gates* (New Haven and London: Yale University Press, 1990), 37.
25. Pargellis, *Military Affairs in North America*, 79.
26. Pargellis, *Military Affairs in North America*, 86–87.
27. Mercer has received little attention from historians, and is well deserving of a full biography. Alfred P. James, "George Mercer of the Ohio Company, A Study in Frustration," *The Western Pennsylvania Historical Magazine* 46: 1 (January 1963), 2, 11–19.
28. The Emmanuel Episcopal Church of Cumberland, Maryland, is constructed upon the foundations of Fort Cumberland, and there is interpretation both within the church and on the church grounds. Underneath the Church the foundations of the fort, portions of the magazine, and the tunnel to Wills Creek all survive.
29. *Captivities, Marches and Journeys*, 182–183.
30. Laws, "R.A. and R.N. in Virginia," 198–199.
31. Pargellis, *Military Affairs in North America*, 108.
32. "A Seaman's Journal," in Hulburt, *Braddock's Road*, 90.
33. "The Journal of Captain Robert Chilmley's Batman," in Hamilton, ed., *Braddock's Defeat*, 14.
34. Elaine G. Breslaw, ed.,"A Dismal Tragedy: Doctors Alexander and John Hamilton Comment on Braddock's Defeat," *Maryland Historical Magazine* 75:2 (June 1980), 132.
35. Thomas Anburey, *Travels Through the Interior Parts of America* (1923; reprint, ed. Bedford, MA: Applewood Books), 208–209, 227–229; and Evelyn M. Acomb, ed., *The Revolutionary Journal of Varon Ludwin Von Closen, 1780–1783* (Chapel Hill: University of North Carolina Press, 1958), 177–178.
36. The Philadelphia economic and transportation system is well characterized in John Flexer Walzer, *Transportation in the Philadelphia Trading Area, 1740–1775*, University of Wisconsin, Madison, M.A. thesis, 1968; and Thomas M. Doerflinger, "Farmers and Dry Goods in the Philadelphia Market Area, 1750–1800," in Ronald Hoffman, John J. McCusker, Russell R. Menard and Peter J. Albert, eds., *The Economy of Early America, The Revolutionary Period, 1763–1790* (Charlottesville: University Press of Virginia, 1988), 166–195.
37. Walzer, "Transportation in the Philadelphia Trading Area," 254.
38. The home of Joseph Edwards, an early settler of western Virginia. His home was located on the Cacapon River, and was subsequently fortified in 1756. It site is twenty miles west of modern Winchester, Virginia, in the state of West Virginia.
39. Walzer, "Transportation in the Philadelphia Trading Area, 1740–1775," 150, 152; and Philip L. Lord, *War Over Walloomscoick: Land Use and Settlement Pattern on the Bennington Battlefield, 1777* (Albany: University of the State of New York, State Education Dept., 1989), 25. For contemporary length of a rod refer to Society of Gentlemen in Scotland. *Encyclopedia Britannica*, III: 553. Charles Fisher and Lois M. Feister, *Archaeology of the Colonial Road at the John Ellison House, Knox's Headquarters State Historic Site, Vail's Gate, New York* (Albany: Bureau of Historic Sites, 2000), 13.
40. Deputy Governor Robert Hunter Morris (1700–1764). Morris served as deputy governor to the proprietory colony of Pennsylvania from 1754 to 1756, throughout the entirety of the Braddock campaign. Because the proprietory governor of Pennsylvania lived in England throughout this period, the deputy governor was the effective governor of the colony. Morris had an extremely challenging position, serving as the go-between for the Penn family who were determined to eke out every possible pound from the colony, and the equally stingy assembly who challenged the proprietory authority at every possible opportunity. Compounding

Morris' challenge was obtaining funding or approval for any military service or commitment from the predominantly Quaker assembly.

41. Burd had reached the top of Allegheny Mountain when the news reached him on July 17 that Braddock had been defeated. Accordingly, Burd and his party abandoned work on the road and retreated east, burying their work tools at the top of the ridge. Archer Butler Hulbert, *Historic Highways of America, Volume 5: The Old Glade (Forbes) Road* (Cleveland: The Arthur H. Clark Company, 1903), 15–33.

42. Underlined in original.

43. Presumably this is a transcription error, and should have read "Henry Enoch."

44. Williamson, *Treatise on Military Finance*, 60–61; and Glenn A. Steppler, *The Common Soldier in the Reign of George III, 1760–1793*, Ph.D. thesis, University of Oxford, 1984 (typescript at the David Library of the American Revolution, Washington's Crossing, Pennsylvania), 91.

45. *The Papers of George Washington*, I: 262–264.

46. *The Papers of George Washington*, I: 274.

47. "Captain Orme's Journal," in Sargent, *The History of An Expedition Against Fort Duquesne*, 296–297.

48. The previously described underground magazines at Fort Cumberland, which still survive.

Chapter 4

1. The standard, and indeed the only, biography for Governor General Thomas Gage is John R. Alden, *General Gage in America, Being Principally A History of His Role in the American Revolution* (New York: Greenwood Press, 1948). Unfortunately, this biography is focused upon Gage's role as royal governor and commander-in-chief in Boston, Massachusetts, prior to the American War for Independence, and its coverage on Gage's participation in the Seven Years War is relatively succinct.

2. Munson, *Colonel John Carlyle, Gentleman*, 72.

3. Sargent, *History of an Expedition Against Fort Duquesne*, 395–396.

4. Ross D. Netherton, "The Carlyle House Conference: An Episode in the Politics of Colonial Union," in James Allen Braden, ed., *Proceedings of Northern Virginia Studies Conference, 1983, Alexandria: Empire to Commonwealth* (Alexandria: Northern Virginia Community College, 1984), 57–84.

5. The best scholarship on this Conference, which the author highly recommends, is Ross D. Netherton, "The Carlyle House Conference: An Episode in the Politics of Colonial Union," in James Allen Braden, ed., *Proceedings of Northern Virginia Studies Conference, 1983, Alexandria: Empire to Commonwealth* (Alexandria: Northern Virginia Community College, 1984).

6. Orme Journal in Sargent, *Expedition to Fort Duquesne*, 306.

7. Charles Scarlett, Jr., "Governor Horatio Sharpe's Whitehall," *Maryland Historical Magazine* XLVI (1951), 11.

8. Colonial Williamsburg owns and operates an original early 19th century chariot. Office of Communications, the Colonial Williamsburg Foundation, "Colonial Williamsburg's Coaches," http://www.history.org/Foundation/newsroom/2012PressKit/releases/2012%20Coaches%20of%20Colonial%20Williamsburg.pdf, 2 June 2012.

9. Pargellis, *Military Affairs in North America*, 31.

10. Sargent, *Expedition to Fort Duquesne*, 296.

11. Sargent, *The History of An Expedition Against Fort Duquesne*, 158–160.

12. McCardell, *Ill-Starred General*, 169–170.

13. *General Braddock's Orderly Book*, xxiii.

14. Fairfax County Park Authority, "Fairfax County, Virginia, An Historical Tour Map & Guide to Places of Interest" (1986, revised).

15. Netherton, *Braddock's Campaign and the Potomac Route to the West*, 9, 21.

16. Marcus Benjamin, "Braddock's Rock, A Study in Local History," speech to National Society of Colonial Dames in the District of Columbia (April 12, 1899), 12. Available at http://www.archive.org/details/braddocksrockstu00benj on June 15, 2009.

17. "The Journal of Captain Robert Cholmley's Batman," in Hamilton, *Braddock's Defeat*, 10.

18. The so-called "Seaman's Journal" has been printed in three sources: Sargent, *An Expedition to Fort Duquesne*, 366–389; Archer Butler Hulbert, *Historic Highways of America, Volume 4, Braddock's Road and Three Relative Papers* (Cleveland: The Arthur H. Clark Company, 1903), 79–107; and most recently by M.E.S. Laws, "R.N. and R.A. [Royal Navy and Royal Artillery] in Virginia, 1755," *Journal of the Society for Army Historical Research* 57 (Winter 1979), 193–205. The author of this journal is unidentified, and remains unknown. Its formal title is "A Journal of the Proceedings of the Detachment of Seamen, Ordered by Commodore Keppel, to Assist on the late Expedition to the Ohio with an impartial Account of the late Action on the Banks of the Monongahela the 9th of July 1755 as related by some of the Principal Officers that day in the Field." Historian Archer Butler Hulbert felt that this journal was authored by Engineer Harry Gordon. Hulbert, *Braddock's Road*, 79–82. However, modern historian Paul Kopperman believes that this journal was rather maintained by a naval midshipman who fell ill at Fort Cumberland on June 10, and did not proceed any farther. Kopperman notes that a known account of Gordon's differs materially from this Journal. Kopperman, *Braddock at the Monongahela*, 243–245. The author believes that Dr. Kopperman makes the more compelling argument. This specific citation is from Laws, "RN. and R.A. in Virginia," 196–197; and Hulbert, *Braddocks' Road*, 85.

19. "The Journal of Captain Robert Cholmley's Batman," in Hamilton, *Braddock's Defeat*, 10.

20. Laws, "RN. and R.A. in Virginia," 196–197; and Hulbert, *Braddocks' Road*, 85.

21. Tara L. Tetrault and Mary Gallagher, "Archaeological Testing at the Dowden's Ordinary Site" (July 29, 2005); and Don Housley, Montgomery County Parks and Planning Department, e-mail to Douglas R. Cubbison, June 26, 2009.

22. Laws, "RN. and R.A. in Virginia," 196–197; and Hulbert, *Braddocks' Road*, 85.

23. "The Journal of Captain Robert Cholmley's Batman," in Hamilton, *Braddock's Defeat*, 10–11.

24. Joy Beasley, cultural resources manager, Monocacy National Battlefield, e-mail to Douglas R. Cubbison, June 16, 2009.

25. Laws, "R.N. and R.A. in Virginia," 197; and Hulbert, *Braddocks' Road*, 85–86.

26. Robert Kozak, *"Shelter from the Storm": Frederick, Maryland in the Seven Years War* (Bowie, MD: Heritage Books, 2008), 16, 81–83.

27. "A Seaman's Journal," in Hulbert, *Braddocks' Road*, 86.

28. "The Journal of Captain Robert Cholmley's Batman," in Hamilton, *Braddock's Defeat*, 12.

29. Laws, "RN. and R.A. in Virginia," 197.

30. Abbott, ed., *The Papers of George Washington*, I:263.

31. Abbott, ed., *The Papers of George Washington*, I:266.

32. Laws, "RN. and R.A. in Virginia," 197.

33. "The Journal of Captain Robert Cholmley's Batman," in Hamilton, *Braddock's Defeat*, 12.

34. "The Journal of Captain Robert Cholmley's Batman," in Hamilton, *Braddock's Defeat*, 12–13.

35. Laws, "RN. and R.A. in Virginia," 197.

36. Laws, "RN. and R.A. in Virginia," 197.

37. Laws, "RN. and R.A. in Virginia," 197–198.

38. "The Journal of Captain Robert Cholmley's Batman," in Hamilton, ed., *Braddock's Defeat*, 13.

39. Calder, ed., "The Journal of Charlotte Brown," 181.

40. Laws, "RN. and R.A. in Virginia," 198.

41. "The Journal of Captain Robert Cholmley's Batman," in Hamilton, *Braddock's Defeat*, 13.

42. Laws, "RN. and R.A. in Virginia," 198.

43. "The Journal of Captain Robert Cholmley's Batman," in Hamilton, *Braddock's Defeat*, 13.

44. Laws, "RN. and R.A. in Virginia," 198. A British traditional stone weighs 14 pounds, so the horses were carrying no more than 196 pounds including the rider and saddle.

45. "The Journal of Captain Robert Cholmley's Batman," in Hamilton, *Braddock's Defeat*, 13.

46. Laws, "RN. and R.A. in Virginia," 198.

47. Calder, ed., "The Journal of Charlotte Brown," 181–182.

48. "The Journal of Captain Robert Cholmley's Batman," in Hamilton, *Braddock's Defeat*, 13.

49. Quoted in McCardell, *Ill-Starred General*, 180.

50. Laws, "RN. and R.A. in Virginia," 198.

51. The question has generated some minor historical discussion, but the author believes that the true meaning of "rattlesnake colonel" continues to somewhat elude modern historians. "Rattlesnake Colonel," *Notes and Queries* 10–XI (March 6, 1909), 191–192; and Albert Matthews, "Rattlesnake Colonel," *The New England Quarterly* 10:2 (June 1937), 341–345.

52. Calder, ed., "The Journal of Charlotte Brown," 182.

53. Sargent, *Expedition to Fort Duquesne*, 312–313.

54. "The Journal of Captain Robert Cholmley's Batman," in Hamilton, *Braddock's Defeat*, 14.

Chapter 5

1. "Halkett's Orderly Book," in Hamilton, ed., *Braddock's Defeat*, 93.

2. "Halkett's Orderly Book," in Hamilton, ed., *Braddock's Defeat*, 93.

3. Thomas Simes, *The Military Guide for Young Officers, Containing a System for the Art of War, Parade, Camp, Field Duty, Manoeuvres, Standing and General Orders, Warrants, Regulations, Returns, Tables, Forms, Extracts from Military Acts, Battles, Sieges, Forts, Posts, Military Dictionary* (1776; reprint, Uckfield, East Sussex: The Naval & Military Press in association with the Royal Armouries, 2006), 7–8.

4. "Halkett's Orderly Book," in Hamilton, ed., *Braddock's Defeat*, 68.

5. "Halkett's Orderly Book," in Hamilton, ed., *Braddock's Defeat*, 88–89.

6. Laws, "RN. and R.A. in Virginia," 201.

7. "Orme Journals," in Sergeant, *Expedition to Fort Duquesne*, 317.

8. Thomas Simes, *The Military Guide for Young Officers, Containing a System for the Art of War, Parade, Camp, Field Duty, Manoeuvres, Standing and General Orders, Warrants, Regulations, Returns, Tables, Forms, Extracts from Military Acts, Battles, Sieges, Forts, Posts, Military Dictionary* (1776; reprint, Uckfield, East Sussex: The Naval & Military Press in association with the Royal Armouries, 2006).

9. "Orme Journals," in Sergeant, *Expedition to Fort Duquesne*, 318–320, Plate III, Plate IV.

10. "Orme Journals," in Sergeant, *Expedition to Fort Duquesne*, 321.

11. Nichols, "Organization of Braddock's Army," 125.

12. Laws, "R.N. and R.A. in Virginia," 201.

13. "The Journal of Captain Robert Cholmley's Batman," in Hamilton, ed., *Braddock's Defeat*, 17–19.

14. "Halkett's Orderly Book," in Hamilton, ed., *Braddock's Defeat*, 96–97.

15. Thomas E. Crocker, *Braddock's March: How the Man Sent to Seize a Continent Changed American History* (Yardley, PA: Westholme, 2009), 161–162.

16. "Orme Journals," in Sergeant, *Expedition to Fort Duquesne*, 323–324.

17. Laws, "RN. and R.A. in Virginia," 201–202.

18. The author wishes to acknowledge the immense contribution that the study of Mr. Robert "Bob" Bantz of the Braddock Road's route in Western Maryland has made to the scholarship of the Braddock campaign, and wishes to thank Mr. Bantz for generously making his extensive research available.

19. Philip L. Lord, *War Over Walloomscoick: Land Use and Settlement Pattern on the Bennington Battlefield, 1777* (Albany: University of the State of New York, State Education Dept., 1989), 21–31.

20. Dr. Walter L. Powell, ed., *The Braddock Road by*

John Kennedy Lacock (The Braddock Road Preservation Association, 2010), introduction.

21. John Kennedy Lacock, "Braddock Road," *The Pennsylvania Magazine of History and Biography* 38:1 (1914), 16.

22. Laws, "R.N. and R.A. in Virginia," 202.

23. Abbott, ed., *The Papers of George Washington*, 1:293, 307, 310.

24. Abbott, ed., *The Papers of George Washington*, 1:322.

25. "The Journal of Captain Robert Cholmley's Batman," in Hamilton, ed., *Braddock's Defeat*, 19.

26. "Orme Journal," in Sergeant, *Expedition to Fort Duquesne*, 335.

27. "The Journal of Captain Robert Cholmley's Batman," in Hamilton, ed., *Braddock's Defeat*, 19–21.

28. "The Journal of Captain Robert Cholmley's Batman," in Hamilton, ed., *Braddock's Defeat*, 21.

29. "Orme Journal," in Sergeant, *Expedition to Fort Duquesne*, 331.

30. "Orme Journal," in Sergeant, *Expedition to Fort Duquesne*, 331–332.

31. Abbott, ed., *The Papers of George Washington*, 1:321; and "Captain Orme's Journal," in Sargent, *The History of an Expedition Against Fort Duquesne*, 336.

32. McCardell, *Ill-Starred General*, 223–224.

33. Abbott, ed., *The Papers of George Washington*, 1:321.

34. Pargellis, *Military Affairs in North America*, 96–97.

35. "Captain Orme's Journal," in Sargent, *The History of an Expedition Against Fort Duquesne*, 336.

36. Abbott, ed., *The Papers of George Washington*, 1:322.

37. "Captain Orme's Journal," in Sargent, *The History of an Expedition Against Fort Duquesne*, 335.

38. "General Braddock's Orderly Book," lv.

39. "Captain Orme's Journal," in Sargent, *The History of an Expedition Against Fort Duquesne*, 338.

40. Sargent, *Expedition to Fort Duquesne*, 203.

41. Quoted in Paul A. W. Wallace, "Blunder Camp": A Note on the Braddock Road," *Pennsylvania Magazine of History and Biography* 87:1 (January 1963), 22.

42. J. Cook Wilson, ed., "The Campaign of General Braddock," *English Historical Review* 1:1 (January 1886), 150.

43. "The Journal of Captain Robert Cholmley's Batman," in Hamilton, ed., *Braddock's Defeat*, 22.

44. Lacock, "Braddock Road," 22.

45. "Captain Orme's Journal," in Sargent, *The History of an Expedition Against Fort Duquesne*, 340.

46. Cynthia Kral and John Boback, *Report on the Location and Status of the Extant Segments of Braddock Road, Fayette County, Pennsylvania* (2003), 8–29.

47. "Captain Orme's Journal," in Sargent, *The History of an Expedition Against Fort Duquesne*, 341.

48. "The Journal of a British Officer," in Hamilton, ed., *Braddock's Defeat*, 45.

49. "The Journal of Captain Robert Cholmley's Batman," in Hamilton, ed., *Braddock's Defeat*, 23.

50. Kral and Boback, *Report on the Location and Status of the Extant Segments of Braddock Road, Fayette County*, 30–38.

51. "Captain Orme's Journal," in Sargent, *The History of an Expedition Against Fort Duquesne*, 343; and "Halkett's Orderly Book" in Hamilton, *Braddock's Defeat*, ed., 112.

52. Pargellis, *Military Affairs in North America*, 94.

53. Elaine G. Breslaw, ed., "A Dismal Tragedy: Doctors Alexander and John Hamilton Comment on Braddock's Defeat," *Maryland Historical Magazine* 75:2 (June 1980), 132.

54. Stanley Pargellis, "Braddock's Defeat," *American Historical Review* XLI:2 (January 1936), 266–267.

55. Kopperman, *Braddock at the Monogahela*, 166–167.

56. McCardell, *Ill Fated General*, 213–214, 224.

57. "The Journal of Captain Robert Cholmley's Batman," in Hamilton,ed., *Braddock's Defeat*, 24.

58. "Captain Orme's Journal," in Sargent, *The History of an Expedition Against Fort Duquesne*, 344.

59. Kral and Boback, *Report on the Location and Status of the Extant Segments of Braddock Road, Fayette County*, 53–57.

60. "The Journal of a British Officer," in Hamilton, ed., *Braddock's Defeat*, 46.

61. "Halkett's Orderly Book," in Hamilton, ed., *Braddock's Defeat*, 114.

62. "The Journal of Captain Robert Cholmley's Batman," in Hamilton, ed., *Braddock's Defeat*, 24.

63. "The Journal of a British Officer," in Hamilton, ed., *Braddock's Defeat*, 46.

64. "Captain Orme's Journal" in Sargent, *The History of an Expedition Against Fort Duquesne*, 345.

65. Lacock, "Braddock Road," 27.

66. "Captain Orme's Journal," in Sargent, *The History of an Expedition Against Fort Duquesne*, 345.

67. "The Journal of a British Officer," in Hamilton, ed., *Braddock's Defeat*, 46–47.

68. "Captain Orme's Journal," in Sargent, *The History of an Expedition Against Fort Duquesne*, 346.

69. Kral and Boback, *Report on the Location and Status of the Extant Segments of Braddock Road, Fayette County*, 65–69.

70. "Captain Orme's Journal," in Sargent, *The History of an Expedition Against Fort Duquesne*, 346.

71. Wallace, "Blunder Camp," 26.

72. Lacock, "Braddock Road," 31–32.

73. "Captain Orme's Journal," in Sargent, *The History of an Expedition Against Fort Duquesne*, 346–348.

74. "Captain Orme's Journal," in Sargent, *The History of an Expedition Against Fort Duquesne*, 349.

75. "The Journal of a British Officer," in Hamilton, ed., *Braddock's Defeat*, 47.

76. As described in "The Journal of a British Officer," Hamilton, ed., *Braddock's Defeat*, 47–48; "The Journal of Captain Robert Cholmley's Batman," in Hamilton, ed., *Braddock's Defeat*, 25–26; and "Captain Orme's Journal," in Sargent, *The History of an Expedition Against Fort Duquesne*, 350.

77. "Captain Orme's Journal," in Sargent, *The History of an Expedition Against Fort Duquesne*, 351–352.

78. "The Journal of a British Officer," in Hamilton, ed., *Braddock's Defeat*, 48.
79. Wallace, "A Note on the Braddock Road," 29–30.
80. "Captain Orme's Journal," in Sargent, *The History of an Expedition Against Fort Duquesne*, 352.
81. "The Journal of Captain Robert Cholmley's Batman," in Hamilton, ed., *Braddock's Defeat*, 26.
82. Wallace, "A Note on the Braddock Road," 30.
83. Frank A. Cassell, "The Last Days of General Braddock: The March Through Westmoreland and Allegheny Counties," *Westmoreland History* 7:2 (September 2002), 3–15; and Frank A. and Elizabeth W. Cassell. "A Tour of Braddock's Road from Fort Necessity to Pittsburgh," *Westmoreland History* 7:2 (September 2002), 16–22.
84. "Captain Orme's Journal" in Sargent, *The History of an Expedition Against Fort Duquesne*, 353.
85. Paul E. Kopperman, *Braddock at the Monongahela* (Pittsburgh: University of Pittsburg Press, 1977), 18.

Chapter 6

1. John Muller, *A Treatise of Artillery, 1780* (1780; reprint, Bloomfield, Ontario: Museum Restoration Service, 1977), 127, 128.
2. Sargent, *Expedition to Fort Duquesne*, 185.
3. Elaine G. Breslaw, ed., "A Dismal Tragedy: Doctors Alexander and John Hamilton Comment on Braddock's Defeat," *Maryland Historical Magazine* 75:2 (June 1980), 134.
4. "British B Eyewitness Account," in Kopperman, *Braddock at the Monongahela*, 166–174.
5. Breslaw, "A Dismal Tragedy," 131–140.
6. Breslaw, "A Dismal Tragedy," 131.
7. "The Journal of Captain Robert Cholmley's Batman," in Hamilton, ed., *Braddock's Defeat*, 27.
8. "The Journal of a British Officer," in Hamilton, ed., *Braddock's Defeat*, 49.
9. "The Journal of Captain Robert Cholmley's Batman," in Hamilton, ed., *Braddock's Defeat*, 28; and Kopperman, *Braddock at the Monongahela*, 50–51.
10. Breslaw, "A Dismal Tragedy," 134.
11. Kopperman, *Braddock at the Monongahela*, 31.
12. Breslaw, "A Dismal Tragedy," 134.
13. "Harry Gordon Account," in Kopperman, *Braddock at the Monongahela*, 199.
14. "Captain Orme's Journal," in Sargent, *The History of an Expedition Against Fort Duquesne*, 355.
15. Harry Gordon, "A Letter from Will's Creek: Harry Gordon's Account of Braddock's Defeat," ed. Charles M. Stotz, *Western Pennsylvania Historical Magazine* XLIV (June 1961), 133.
16. "William Dunbar Account," in Kopperman, *Braddock at the Monongahela*, 187.
17. Kopperman, *Braddock at the Monongahela*, 50.
18. Sheldon S. Cohen, ed., "Major William Sparke Along the Monongahela: A New Historical Account of Braddock's Defeat," *Pennsylvania History* 62 (October 1955), 551.
19. Hulbert, *Braddock's Road*, 103.
20. "Captain Orme's Journal," in Sargent, *The History of an Expedition Against Fort Duquesne*, 355.
21. The distance is variously reported, approximately half a mile seems to be the most generally accepted. "After we had marched 800 yards from ye river," "The Journal of a British Officer," in Hamilton, editor, *Braddock's Defeat*, 49; "We had not marched above 800 yards from the River," in "William Dunbar Account" in Kopperman, *Braddock at the Monongahela*, 187; "Our front had not Got above half a Mile from the Banks of the River," in "Harry Gordon Account" in Kopperman, *Braddock at the Monongahela*, 199. Lieutenant Colonel Gage reported the fight to have occurred closer to the Monongahela: "We had scarcely marched a quarter of a mile from the river," in "Thomas Gage Account," in Kopperman, *Braddock at the Monongahela*, 191.
22. "It was now near two o'clock," according to Captain Orme, "Captain Orme's Journal," in Sargent, *The History of an Expedition Against Fort Duquesne*, 353. Lieutenant William Dunbar recorded the time as "near one o'Clock" in "William Dunbar Account," in Kopperman, *Braddock at the Monongahela*, 187. An unidentified British officer remembered it as "between 12 and One" in "British Account A," in Kopperman, *Braddock at the Monongahela*, 163. Captain Adam Stephen with the Virgina provincials remembered it as "about two o'clock in the afternoon" in "Adam Stephen Account" in Kopperman, *Braddock at the Monongahela*, 226.
23. "Mr. James Furnis Account" in Kopperman, *Braddock at the Monongahela*, 189.
24. Carl Von Clausewitz, *On War*, ed. and trans. Michael Howard and Peter Paret (New York: Alfred A. Knopf, 1993), 97.
25. Leroy V. Eid, "'A Kind of Running Fight': Indian Battlefield Tactics in the Late Eighteenth Century," *The Western Pennsylvania Historical Magazine* 71, no. 2 (April 1988), 147–171.
26. Breslaw, "A Dismal Tragedy," 134.
27. "The Journal of Captain Robert Cholmley's Batman," in Hamilton, ed., *Braddock's Defeat*, 28.
28. "Harry Gordon Account" in Kopperman, *Braddock at the Monongahela*, 99.
29. Breslaw, "A Dismal Tragedy," 136.
30. Governor Sharpe of Maryland reported that St. Clair "was shot thro the Body under the right Pap [nipple]" but this is probably not accurate. Given the medical capabilities of the era, a shot through the body would almost certainly have proven fatal, and St. Clair himself and his attending physician both described his wounds differently. Quoted in Abbott, ed., *The Papers of George Washington*, I:341.
31. Abbott, ed., *The Papers of George Washington*, I:339.
32. Harry Gordon, "A Letter from Will's Creek: Harry Gordon's Account of Braddock's Defeat," ed. Charles M. Stotz, *Western Pennsylvania Historical Magazine* XLIV (June 1961) 133.
33. Laws, "R.N. and R.A. in Virginia," 203.
34. "Thomas Gage Account," in Kopperman, *Braddock at the Monongahela*, 192.

35. Ibid.
36. Lieutenant General Humphrey Bland, *A Treatise of Military Discipline, In Which is Laid down and Explained The Duty of the Officer and Soldier, Through the several Branches of the Service* (London: 1727; rev. ed., 1759), 138, 145–146.
37. Gage would serve, without any real distinction or accomplishment, in North America throughout the Seven Years War. In his first independent command in 1759, he failed miserably. He would become British commander in chief in North America, and retire in disgrace having been soundly defeated by the Americans in Boston in 1775. Gage rose to the highest military rank in the British army without ever displaying any real military skills or acumen. His single biography, John R. Alden, *General Gage in America* (New York: Greenwood Press, 1948), is predominantly focused upon his role in the American Revolution. Gage's Papers remain at the William L. Clements Library, University of Michigan, Ann Arbor. Among the most significant of 18th century military papers, they unfortunately remain un-transcribed, un-edited, and un-published. For his service in the 1759 Campaign, refer to Douglas R. Cubbison, *"All Canada in the Hands of the British": General Jeffery Amherst and the 1760 Campaign to Conquer New France* (Norman: University of Oklahoma Press, 2013), 152–154.
38. N. Darnell Davis, "British Newspaper Accounts of Braddock's Defeat," *The Pennsylvania Magazine of History and Biography* 23 (1899).
39. "Horatio Gates Account," in Kopperman, *Braddock at the Monongahela*, 196.
40. As articulated in "Captain Orme's Journal" in Sargent, *Expedition to Fort Duquesne*, 319–320 and Plate IV.
41. Breslaw, "A Dismal Tragedy," 135–136.
42. Breslaw, "A Dismal Tragedy," 136.
43. Pargellis, *Military Affairs in North America*, 110.
44. "The Journal of a British Officer," in Hamilton, ed., *Braddock's Defeat*, 50.
45. "William Dunbar Account," in Kopperman, *Braddock at the Monongahela*, 187.
46. "Harry Gordon Account," in Kopperman, *Braddock at the Monongahela*, 200.
47. "George Washington Account," in Kopperman, *Braddock at the Monongahela*, 231.
48. "Captain Orme's Journal," in Sargent, *Expedition to Fort Duquesne*, 355–356.
49. "The Journal of Captain Robert Cholmley's Batman," in Hamilton, ed., *Braddock's Defeat*, 30.
50. "John Campbell Account," in Kopperman, *Braddock at the Monongahela*, 180.
51. "William Dunbar Account," in Kopperman, *Braddock at the Monongahela*, 187–188.
52. "The Journal of a British Officer," in Hamilton, ed., *Braddock's Defeat*, 52.
53. Williams, "Treasure Hunt in the Forest," 391. To the authors' knowledge this order has never been located in the archives of the Board of Ordnance. If this letter survives somewhere in the recesses of the Public Records Office of the United Kingdom, it would be the last ever signed by Braddock.
54. Quoted in Hildeburn, "Sir John St. Clair," 7.
55. Underlined in the original in a very dark, thick line.
56. McCardell, *Ill-Starred General*, 261.

Chapter 7

1. Adam Stephen to St. Clair, camp at Fort Cumberland, September 3, 1755; and St. Clair to Adam Stephen, Albany, October 24, 1755, St. Clair letterbook.
2. St. Clair to Colonel Napier, November 27, 1755, Ibid.
3. St. Clair to Colonel Napier, Duke of Richmond, and Earl of Hyndford, November 18, 1755; St. Clair to Colonel Napier, November 27, 1755, Ibid.
4. St. Clair to Sir Charles Hardy, Albany, March 29, 1756; St. Clair to Govenor Shirley, Albany, April 1, 1756; St. Clair to Sir Charles Hardy, Albany, April 5, 1756, Ibid.
5. *William Johnson Papers*, III:43.
6. St. Clair to Govenor Shirley, Albany, April 1, 1756; Governor Shirley to St. Clair, Boston, April 10, 1756, Ibid.
7. St. Clair to Major General Napier, Albany, August 30, 1756, Ibid; and Hildeburn, "Sir John St. Clair," 8.
8. Some limited St. Clair correspondence regarding the supply of Fort Ontario can be found in the Sir William Johnson Papers.
9. St. Clair to Colonel Napier, New York, December 22, 1755, Ibid.
10. Memorial, St. Clair to Governor Shirley, Albany, May 10, 1756, Ibid.
11. St. Clair to Major General Napier, Albany, November 4, 1756, Ibid.
12. St.Clair to Governor Shirley, New York, March 2, 1756, March 8, 1756 and March 16, 1756, Ibid.
13. St. Clair to Agent John Calcraft, Agent for Royal American Regiment, Albany, August 10, 1756, Ibid. St. Clair's commission was dated January 6, 1756. Hildeburn, "Sir John St. Clair," 9.
14. "Governor Denny to Forbes, Philadelphia, 4 April 1758"; "Sir John St. Clair to Forbes, Philadelphia, April 6, 1758"; and "Sir John St. Clair to Forbes, Philadelphia, April 9, 1758," Forbes Headquarters Papers, University of Virginia, Charlottesville, Virginia.
15. Forbes Headquarters Papers, "Instructions for the Quarter Master General in the Southern Provinces, 1758" [undated].
16. *Writings of General John Forbes*, 168–169; and Cubbison, *The British Defeat of the French in Pennsylvania, 1758*, 64.
17. *Writings of General John Forbes*, 174.
18. *The Papers of Henry Bouquet*, I: 371.
19. *The Papers of Henry Bouquet*, II: 163–164.
20. Cubbison, *The British Defeat of the French in Pennsylvania, 1758*, 93.
21. Erna Risch, *Quartermaster Support of the Army: A History of the Corps, 1775–1939* (Washington, D.C.: Center of Military History, U.S. Army, 1989), 379. Horses had not materially changed between 1755 and 1861.

22. *Writings of General John Forbes*, 157–158.
23. E.L. McAdam, Jr. and George Milne, eds., *Johnson's Dictionary, A Modern Selection* (New York: Pantheon, 1963), 351.
24. *The Papers of Henry Bouquet*, II: 282.
25. *Writings of General John Forbes*, 198.
26. Forbes Headquarters Papers, "Letter from St. Clair to Forbes, dated Winchester, May 21, 1758."
27. Simes, *The Military Guide for Young Officers*, 7–8.
28. Forbes Headquarters Papers, "Letter, Forbes to St. Clair, dated Philadelphia, May 25, 1758."
29. *Pennsylvania Archives*, III: 446–447.
30. *The Writings of General Forbes*, 114.
31. Forbes Headquarters Papers, "Letter, St. Clair to Forbes, dated Carlisle, June 17, 1758."
32. *The Papers of Henry Bouquet*, II: 360.
33. The whiskey topic is addressed at length in Cubbison, *The British Defeat of the French in Pennsylvania, 1758*, 58.
34. *The Papers of Henry Bouquet*, II: 492.
35. *The Papers of Henry Bouquet*, II: 373.
36. Forbes Headquarters Papers, "Letter from Governor Glen to Forbes, Ray's Town, August 8, 1758."
37. *Writings of General John Forbes*, 168.
38. *The Papers of Henry Bouquet*, II: 436.
39. *The Papers of Henry Bouquet*, II: 434.
40. Cubbison, *The British Defeat of the French in Pennslvania, 1758*, 104–105.
41. Ibid., II: 430–436.
42. Ibid., II; 496.
43. *The Writings of General Forbes*, 128.
44. *Writings of General John Forbes*, 146.
45. *Colonial Records of Pennsylvania*, VIII: 167–169.
46. The entire St. Clair-Stephen affair is comprehensively described in Cubbison, *The British Defeat of the French in Pennsylvania, 1758*, 107–108.
47. Ibid., 151–152.
48. *The Writings of General Forbes*, 139.
49. *The Writings of General John Forbes*, 199.

Chapter 8

1. *Writings of General John Forbes*, 287–288.
2. *The Papers of Henry Bouquet* III: 122–124.
3. Ibid., III: 186, 196.
4. There is considerable Amherst-St. Clair correspondence regarding these accounts in General Jeffery Amherst Papers, WO 34/59, microfilm copy at David Library of the American Revolution, Washington Crossing, Pennsylvania, Microfilm Reel 35. Additional correspondence is in Marion Tinling, ed., *The Correspondence of the Three William Byrds of Westover, Virginia, 1684–1776*, 2 vols. (Charlottesville: Virginia Historical Society, 1977), I: 760–762; and George Reese, ed., *The Official Papers of Francis Fauquier, Lieutenant Governor of Virginia, 1758–1768*, 3 vols. (Charlottesville: University Press of Virginia, 1980–1981), I: 14–18, 438–439; II: 464, 473–474.
5. St. Clair to Amherst, Trenton, Colony of New Jersey, August 6, 1761, Amherst Papers.
6. St. Clair to Amherst, Trenton, March 13, 1762, Amherst Papers.
7. Amherst to St. Clair, New York, June 25, 1763, Amherst Papers.
8. St. Clair to Amherst, Carlisle, July 19, 1763; St. Clair to Amherst, Philadelphia, July 24, 1763; St. Clair to Amherst, Trenton, August 22, 1763, Amherst Papers.
9. Amherst to St. Clair, New York, September 7, 1736, Amherst Papers.
10. The 18th century church was replaced in 1846–1854, "St. Mary's Episcopal Church," accessed at http://www.stmarysburlington.org/index.php?option=com_content&view=article&id=57:history&catid=34:about-us&Itemid=64, May 2, 2014; and Hildeburn, "Sir John St. Clair," 11–12.
11. The author appreciates the assistance of professional colleagues Don Hagist and John Houlding for confirming St. Clair's commision details.
12. Elizabeth St. Clair to sister Hannah Moland, Belleville, February 25, 1763, MS 379, Logan Family Papers, Subseries H, Dickinson Family Papers, Box 40, Moland Family Estate, Historical Society of Pennsylvania, Philadelphia, Pennsylvania.
13. Catherine Moland to John Dickinson, Ibid.
14. Hildeburn, "Sir John St. Clair," 12.
15. St. Clair wrote a letter to John Dickinson from Trenton on December 23, 1765, Dickinson Papers.
16. Lady St. Clair to John Dickinson, February 7, 1767, Ibid.
17. Sir John St. Clair, "Will, October 26, 1767, Essex County, New Jersey," New Jersey State Archives. His will was proved November 30, 1767. A. Van Doren Honeyman, ed., *Documents Relating to the Colonial History of the State of New Jersey, Volume XXXIII, Calendar of New Jersey Wills, Administrations, Etc.,Volume IV, 1761–1770* (Somerville, NJ: The Unionist-Gazette Association, Printers, 1928), 370.
18. William Nelson, ed., *Documents Relating to the Colonial History of the State of New Jersey, Volume XXV, Extracts from American Newspapers Relating to New Jersey, Volume VI, 1766–1767* (Paterson, NJ: The Call Printing and Publishing Company, 1903), 502–503.
19. Quoted in David T. Shannon, "Quartermaster General Sir John St. Clair and the Moland Family" courtesy of the Moland House Museum, Warwick Townshp Historical Society, Hartsville, Pennsylvania.
20. Elizabeth St. Clair to John Dickinson, Elizabeth Town, May 10, 1769, Moland Papers, Historical Society of Pennsylvania; and British army lists, 1768, 1769.
21. Records of the American Loyalist Claims Commission, 1776–1831, Great Britain Audit Office, microfilm copy at the David Library of the American Revolution, Volume 99, File 58; British army lists, 1779–1784.

Appendix A

1. St. Clair consistently uses this spelling for Wills Creek.
2. Note first use of forward slashes, per transcription note 3.
3. Lieutenant Colonel Robert Ellison was scheduled

to become lieutenant colonel of the regiment that William Shirley was to raise in North America (the 50th Foot). Lieutenant Colonel James Mercer would similarly become the lieutenant colonel of the 51st Regiment of Foot (Pepperrell's regiment). Both officers accompanied St. Clair to Virginia on the *Gibraltar*. Upon debarkation they proceeded to the north to raise their two regiments. Mercer commanded Fort Ontario at Oswego during the winter of 1755–1756, and was killed at the siege of Fort Ontario by a French cannon shot on August 14, 1756.

4. Underlined for emphasis in original.

5. Battalions or regiments, the terms were used interchangeably in the mid–18th century.

6. Properly "beeves," live cattle driven along with the army, that would be butchered to provide the army with fresh beef.

7. Beans, peas and other pulses, particularly chickpeas. An English bastardization of the Spanish garbanzo. The *Oxford English Dictionary* gives the first (printed) use in 1620.

8. "Quintal" or English hundred weights (112 pounds). In other words St. Clair is saying that a dozen English hundred weights of iron (1,344 total pounds) should be bought in Hampton.

9. This would be 200,000 daily rations of flour, which would bake about 250,000 pounds of bread. This is a substantial quantity of flour, approximately 100 days' rations (subtracting some for loss) for 2,000 soldiers. John Williamson, *A Treatise on Military Finance, Containing the Pay, Subsistence, Deductions and Arrears of the Forces on the British and Irish Establishments, And All the Allowances in Camp, Garrison and Quarters, With An Enquiry into the Method of Clothing and Recruiting the Army, And An Extract from the Report of the Commissioners of Public Accounts Relating to the Office of the Pay Master General* (London: T. Egerton, 1782). Microfilm copy at U.S. Military Academy Library, West Point, New York).

10. St. Clair found the correct spelling of Conocoheague extremely challenging, he rarely spelled it the same twice, not even in the same letter or even the same paragraph.

11. John Carlyle's home survives today as a prominent tourist attraction in Alexandria, Virginia. The author enjoyed an extremely productive and illuminating visit to the house in August 2009.

12. St. Clair's proposed approach would subsequently be overruled by Braddock. Because of the several drafts from other regiments to bring the 44th and 48th Foot up to strength, and the numerous new (and thus untrained) provincial enlistees, Braddock was determined to keep the regiments together as long as possible so that they could be drilled to a high standard, and that normal discipline could be established within the newly expanded regiments.

13. Colonel Robert Napier, adjutant general, and the Duke of Cumberland's secretary for military affairs (c. 1700–1766). St. Clair had apparently obtained dispensation to correspond directly with Napier, and thus through Napier directly to William Augustus the Duke of Cumberland, younger son of King George II and the politically prominent captain general of the British army. Stanley Pargellis, ed., *Military Affairs in North America, 1748–1765, Selected Documents from the Cumberland Papers in Windsor Castle* (Archon Books, 1969), 8.

14. It cannot be determined if St. Clair is describing moccasins, leather "Indian" shoes used for active summer campaigning or snowshoes to be employed in winter or spring campaigns over the Allegheny Mountains. Possibly, at this time, St. Clair himself did not know that there was a difference.

15. The original of this letter as received by Napier and the Duke of Cumberland is transcribed in its entirety in Pargellis, *Military Affairs in North America*, 66.

16. A map of "North America from the French of Mr. D'Anville Improved with the Back Settlements of Virginia and Course of Ohio Illustrated with Geographical and Historical Remarks" published in London by Thomas Jefferys, 1755.

17. St. Clair is advising Napier, and the Duke of Cumberland, that the maps utilized in England to plan the campaign were badly flawed.

18. Henry Fox, 1st baron Holland, secretary of state for the Southern Department (1705–1774). Not particularly well regarded, Fox was mostly renowned for the success with which he exploited public office for private gain. Fox had previously served as secretary of war, and later served as paymaster to the forces for most of the Seven Years War. Needless to say, Fox was quite well placed politically, and St. Clair would have been eager to court his favor.

19. In other words, St. Clair is writing by the *HMS Gibraltar* on its return trip to England.

20. Most likely referring to the 4.2" coehorn mortars, an extremely light and easily carried mortar.

21. Note that St. Clair is already recommending that the British regiments adapt their armament for the actual conditions that they would encounter in America. A fusee is a lightweight musket of relatively high quality, privately purchased by an officer to augment the sword and replace the spontoon with which officers were habitually armed.

22. Needless to say, this is a ludicrously fanciful proposal, which was never to be implemented.

23. St. Clair's rather quaint spelling refers to the Pyrrenes Mountains of Spain.

24. Needless to say, St. Clair was nowhere "finished" with road construction in February 1755. In fact, he had barely begun to construct roads!

25. Patrick Mackellar was the principal engineering officer with Braddock's army. Born in 1717, Mackellar had served his initial service at the royal arsenal and military school in Woolwich, and had gone on to progressively more demanding Engineering assignments where he had demonstrated skills in architecture, military engineering, and construction. George T. Ness, Jr., "The Braddock Campaign, 1755," *The Military Engineer* 339 (January–February 1959), 20.

26. Governor Arthur Dobbs (1689–1765) of North Carolina. Sheriff (1720), surveyor general (1730), and

member of Parliament (1727–1730) in his native Ireland, he became one of the five royal colonial governors of North Carolina in 1754. Dobbs was a land speculator and owned large tracts of land in the newly formed colony of North Carolina, which he manipulated into arriving as royal governor of North Carolina on October 31, 1754. He was an effective wartime governor, and in particular gave Brigadier General John Forbes strong support from the colony during the 1758 campaign.

27. Underlined in original.

28. First letter from Braddock to St. Clair. Braddock arrived in Virginia on February 20, 1755.

29. The "Articles of War" established the orders and regulations issued under royal authority for the management, administration and discipline of the British army. The Articles of War were to be read regularly to the soldiers, to ensure that they understood their contents. One documented regimental orders specified that the five (of twenty total) articles that elaborated discipline of the private soldier were to be read to the men at the time of enlistment, and subsequently every two months. Glenn A. Steppler, "British Military Law, Discipline and the Conduct of Regimental Courts Martial in the later Eighteenth Century," *English Historical Review* 102 (1987), 862–863. Steppler is the best source on British military law of the 18th century.

30. William Bromaugh, a first cousin of the distinguished attorney and diplomat George Mason of Virginia, had served as an ensign with Washington in 1754. He was promoted to captain after the Braddock campaign, and remained with the Virginia regiment from 1756 to 1757. Abbot, ed., *Washington Papers*, 210.

31. Most likely Thomas Bullitt (1730–1778), who had served as an ensign with Washington in 1754. His name is spelled variously. A highly experienced provincial officer, he would later be promoted to captain, and Bullitt would render particularly valuable service wth Washington's First Virginia Regiment of provincials in the Forbes campaign of 1758. He also fought with the Continental army in the American Revolution, and founded Louisville, Kentucky. Thomas W. Bullitt, *My Life at Oxmoor, Life on a Farm in Kentucky Before the War* (1911; reprint edition privately printed, 1995), 119–121.

32. Polson, a fellow Scotsman, would be killed at the Battle of the Monogahela on July 9, 1755. W.W. Abbot, ed., *The Papers of George Washington, Colonial Series* (Charlottesville: University Press of Virginia, 1983), I:79.

33. Lieutenant Hamilton would be killed at the Monongahela. Ibid., I:342.

34. Possibly a younger brother of Captain Andrew Lewis.

35. Presumably this means linen work frocks to protect their uniforms when doing fatigue duties such as caring for their officer's horses, unpacking and packing their baggage, and erecting their tents.

36. Served with Washington in 1754, survived the Braddock campaign and would subsequently serve as a lieutenant and captain in Washington's 1st Virginia Regiment. Abbot, Ed., *Washington Papers*, 210.

37. Younger brother of Thomas Waggener, he would be killed at the Monongahela.

38. Lewis would be promoted to major of the 1st Virginia Regiment, and would distinguish himself in the Forbes campaign before being captured at Grant's defeat before Fort Duquesne in September 1758. He would survive and become a prominent citizen of West Virginia and serve in both Lord Dunmore's War and the American Revolution. Abbot, ed., *Washington's Papers*, 139–140.

39. Waggoner subsequently served throughout 1756–1757 with Washington's Virginia regiment and participated as a company commander in the Forbes campaign of 1758. Abbot, ed., *Washington's Papers*, 79–80.

40. Killed at the Battle of the Monongahela. Abbot, ed., *Washington's Papers*, 115, 342.

41. Killed at the Battle of the Monongahela. Abbot, ed., *Washington's Papers*, 342.

42. Presumably a younger brother of Thomas Waggener. Killed at the Battle of the Monongahela. Abbot, ed., *Washington's Papers*, 342.

43. John Fenton Mercer (1735–1756), brother of George Mercer. Abot, ed., *Washington Papers*, 79.

44. Also spelled "Splitdorf." Washington referred to him as a "Swedish Gentleman, who was a Volunteer." He fought with Washington during the 1754 campaign, and was killed at the Battle of the Monongahela. Abot, ed., *Washington Papers*, 115, 342.

45. James DeLancey (1703–1760) was acting governor of the colony of New York from 1753 to 1755. DeLancey, a native born New Yorker, studied law and was admitted to the bar in London before he returned to New York City in 1725. DeLancey was a member of one of the most prominent families in New York, and was quite well placed politically. His sister was the wife of renowned and wealthy British admiral Sir Peter Warren. DeLancey served as chief justice from 1733 until his death in 1760. A political rival of governor George Clinton, he used his influence in England to obtain Clinton's recall in 1753, and served as acting governor until he was replaced by the arrival of Sir Charles Hardy in September 1755 to become permanent governor. DeLancey served as governor during the entirety of the Braddock campaign.

46. Shortly to be re-named Lake George by William Johnson.

47. Governor Dinwiddie, a Scotsman, is writing to St. Clair, a fellow Scotman. The phrase "e'er this air" is a Scottish colloquialism for "by this time are."

48. Governor Jonathan Belcher of New Jersey (1682–1757). Belcher served as the governor of Massachusetts from 1730 to 1741, and governor of New Jersey from 1746 until his death in 1757. Belcher is best known as the founder of Princeton University. Born in Massachusetts, Belcher was a graduate of Harvard, earned a fortune as a merchant, and then turned to colonial politics.

49. In other words, "as your own." Here, St. Clair's Scottish heritage shows.

50. "Firing" in military verbiage of the 18th century

refers to firewood or coal. British soldiers were to be issued twelve pounds of firewood for every four days, with those in hospital drawing a double allowance. John Williamson, *A Treatise on Military Finance, Containing the Pay, Subsistence, Deductions and Arrears of the Forces on the British and Irish Establishments, And All the Allowances in Camp, Garrison and Quarters, With An Enquiry into the Method of Clothing and Recruiting the Army, And An Extract from the Report of the Commissioners of Public Accounts Relating to the Office of the Pay Master General* (London: T. Egerton, 1782). Microfilm copy at U.S. Military Academy Library, West Point, New York, 53–54.

51. What St. Clair means by a "train cause" cannot be determined. It is not a standard artillery or wagon term, but in the letterbook the words "train" and "cause" seem to be linked, rather than forming a separate sentence.

52. Because casting of shot was not a precise science in the 18th century, a certain amount of "windage" was tolerated for round shot. Here, St. Clair is suggesting that the shot should be made smaller rather than larger, as if the shot were larger it would strain the cannon barrels when fired. St. Clair's suggestion makes little sense, as if the shot were manufactured within acceptable windage this would not be a concern. Normally a shot gauge, or gunners' calipers, would be employed to ensure that the shells were acceptable. The diameter of a 12-pounder round shot was 4.4" and acceptable windage was 0.223." Adrian B. Caruana, *British Artillery Ammunition, 1780* (Bloomfield, Ontario: Museum Restoration Service, 1979), 14.

53. Apparently an abbreviation for "Winchester." The corrected spelling is used throughout the remainder of the transcription, to avoid confusion.

54. Captain John Dagworthy (1721–1784) started as a New Jersey shopkeeper then moved to Maryland in the 1740s and prospered. He had seen some decidedly limited service in King George's War in the 1740s. He would serve as commander of the Maryland troops not only in the Braddock campaign of 1755, but also the Forbes campaign of 1758. Dagworthy had quarreled with Washington during the 1754 campaign, when he tried to assume Washington's command on a rather spurious claim. Dagworthy was a commander of Maryland militia during the American Revolution, his efforts at higher command being blocked by Washington.

55. Lieutenant-General Willem Anne van Keppel, 2nd earl of Albemarle, died on 22 December 1754. He was a distinguished soldier, and governor of Virginia in absentia.

56. Note that St. Clair is directing that the Virginia provincials turn in their swords for storage, rather than carrying them on the campaign.

57. Osnaburg linen.

58. A Spanish pistole, a gold coin worth two escudos in Spanish value, the equivalent of four Spanish dollars or approximately seventeen shillings (slightly less than the twenty-one shillings in a British gold guinea).

59. A perfectly reasonable request, as it would save Braddock and St. Clair the difficulty of hauling parts of boats across the Allegheny Mountains, which would be of no possible utility until the Monongahela River was reached, and could not proceed beyond Fort Le Boeuf at the northern end of French Creek in any event. The fact that boats were even sent with Braddock to enable him to operate on Lake Erie and Lake Ontario suggests an utter lack of knowledge regarding North American geography behind the planning of this expedition in London in 1754.

60. Note here Braddock's instructions that additional bedding be landed to take care of his soldiers in the unseasonably cold spring weather.

61. Haversacks were linen bags with shoulder slings, which were issued to soldiers during field operations to carry their rations and mess gear within. In accordance with British army procedures in 1755, British soldiers were not routinely issued haversacks as part of their annual equipment and clothing issue. These were a piece of field equipment that would only be provided under extraordinary circumstances that required them to be issued. In this case, the soldiers would pay for them out of "stoppages" from their pay, that is, money withheld from their pay for lost, worn-out or damaged equipment, or extraordinary equipment above their annual authorization.

62. At this time, Catholics were not permitted to enlist into the crown forces.

63. Presumably this is a transcription error, and should have read, "Henry Enoch."

64. Lieutenant Colonel Ralph Burton of Dunbar's 48th Foot. Burton, a close acquaintance of Braddock, had exchanged a majority in the horse guards to go on the expedition. Burton enjoyed a distinguished military career, being promoted to Major General in 1762. Franklin Thayer Nichols, "The Organization of Braddock's Army," *William and Mary Quarterly*, Third Series 4:2 (April 1947), 125–126.

65. As can be deduced from this, the transports carrying the 44th and 48th Regiments of Foot began arriving at Hampton on March 2, 1755. The last transport arrived on March 18. McCardell, *Ill-Starred General*, 150–152.

66. Again, another incident of Braddocks' concern for the well being of his soldiers.

67. The day before, Braddock had issued pay to all of his soldiers, with the intent that (as in Europe) they would use their pay to purchase necessary items such as tobacco, clothing, shirts, stockings, and hair dressing for the march to Fort Duquesne. Since none of these supplies were actually available in Alexandria, and since the soldiers had just spent long weeks trapped aboard transport ships, the soldiers proceeded to spend their money upon the very few commodities that were available in relatively large supply in Alexandria, these apparently being limited to hard cider, peach brandy and whiskey. The result was one of the single most spectacular drunks in American history. McCardell, *Ill-Starred General*, 156; and Gordon Kershaw, "The Legend of Braddock's Gold Reconsidered," *Maryland Historical Magazine* 96, no. 1 (Spring 2001), 95.

68. On this date, while St. Clair was pre-occupied

constructing the new road from Winchester to Wills Creek, General Braddock was meeting with the royal governors of Massachusetts, Virginia, Maryland, New York and Pennsylvania along with Colonel William Johnson of New York as superintendent to the Six Nations (Iroquois Confederation) at John Carlyle's House in Alexandria. Ross D. Netherton, "The Carlyle House Conference: An Episode in the Politics of Colonial Union" in James Allen Braden, ed., *Proceedings of Northern Virginia Studies Conference, 1983, Alexandria: Empire to Commonwealth* (Alexandria: Northern Virginia Community College, 1984), 61–62.

69. Captain Lieutenant R. Hind, a senior officer of the royal artillery on Braddock's expedition.

70. St. Clair is alluding here to problems with the postal service, which was irregular and undependable. Because of challenges with this postal system, in March 1755 Braddock requested that Mr. Benjamin Franklin of Philadelphia, then serving as joint postmaster general of the colonies for the crown, a post he had held since 1753, establish a regular post between Winchester and Philadelphia. Franklin traveled to Winchester in early April 1755 to establish just such a route, and met both St. Clair and Braddock on this trip to the great benefit of the campaign. Leonard W. Labaree, "Benjamin Franklin and the Defense of Pennsylvania, 1754–1757," *Pennsylvania History* 29 (January 1962), 11–12.

71. St. Clair is encountering here counterfeited specie, a common and recurring problem in not only the American colonies, but Great Britain itself.

72. St. Clair was not known for having a calm temper and controlled demeanor, much less any real tact and diplomacy. This letter certainly displays St. Clair's ability to antagonize American colonists in particular.

73. It is not certain what St. Clair means by this. Presumably they were supposed to meet on this date, or this date in a fortnight (or fourteen days).

74. It is unclear from the letter if the soldier recruiting another soldier was to be paid 1 1/2 dollars (approximately six shillings), or ½ dollar (approximately 2 shillings).

75. This last sentence is news regarding regiments and officers with the army in England and Ireland.

76. William Shirley, Jr., eldest son of Governor William Shirley of Massachusetts, military secretary to Braddock.

77. St. Clair here makes a strong remonstrance regarding the incessant problems that he had obtaining wagons.

78. In other words to reduce the barrel and stock length, thus turning muskets into carbines, more appropriate for horse mounted soldiers. Again, note that St. Clair is adapting inappropriate weapons for use under frontier conditions.

79. These letters must have been written early in the morning, or were misdated. On this date, General Braddock, captains Orme and Morris, Secretary Shirley, and St. Clair are recorded to have arrived at Colonel Dunbar's headquarters at Frederick, Maryland. Laws, "R.N. and R.A. in Virginia," 197.

80. Refer to letter p. 112, of the same date.

81. This detachment departed from Fort Cumberland on May 29. Laws, "R.N. and R.A. in Virginia," 201.

82. This account of St. Clair's of the battle is reprinted in Stanley Pargellis, ed., *Military Affairs in North America, 1748–1765* (New York: Appleton-Century, 1936), 102–103. The letter transcribed in Pargellis is Napier's original as received in England. The letter transcribed here is St. Clair's copy. It is important to note that there are no discernable differences between the two versions.

83. Presumably this means the covering party, including two artillery pieces, for St. Clair's party working on the road.

84. Captain Robert Morris, Braddock's second aide-de-camp.

85. Note that this account of the engagement is all but identical to the more widely reprinted account sent to Napier on the same day.

86. Underlined in original in a very thick, dark line.

87. Underlined in the original in a very dark, thick line.

88. Underlined in the original in a very dark, thick line.

89. Underlined in the original in a very dark, thick line.

90. Underlined in the original in a very dark, thick line.

Appendix C

1. Charles Lennox, 3rd Duke of Richmond and Lennox (1735–1806). He succeeded his father to the peerage in 1750 and was admitted to the prestigious royal society (a learned society for science) in 1755. The Duke of Richmond would serve as colonel of the 33rd Regiment of Foot from 1756 to 1758 and would subsequently serve as a prominent English politician. The duke of Richmond was well placed politically and socially, and it is important to note that St. Clair was writing to him as a contemporary, a peer, and a friend.

2. James Carmichael, 3rd earl of Hyndford (1701–1767). An extremely prominent Scottish peer, the Earl of Hyndford served as one of the lord bedchambers to George II. Again, the earl of Hyndford was well placed politically and socially, and it is important to note that he was writing to St. Clair as a contemporary, a peer, and a friend.

Bibliography

Braddock Campaign Sources

Abbott, Raymond B. "Braddock's War Supplies and Dunbar's Camp" *Western Pennsylvania Historical Magazine* XVII (March 1934), 49–52.

Abbot, W.W., ed. "General Edward Braddock in Alexandria, John Carlyle to George Carlyle, 15 August 1755." *Virginia Magazine of History and Biography* 97:2 (April 1989), 205–214.

Abbot, W.W., ed. *The Papers of George Washington, Colonial Series*. Charlottesville: University Press of Virginia, 1983.

Appleman, Roy E. "Historical Report on Fort Necessity, Braddock's Grave, Jumonville's Grave and Braddock's Trail." National Park Service, U.S. Department of the Interior, 1935.

Appleman, Roy E. "Preliminary Report on the Braddock Trail from Fort Necessity to Dunbar's Camp." National Park Service, U.S. Department of the Interior, 1935.

Appleman, Roy E. "Report on Expedition Over Old Braddock Road from Fort Necessity to Rock Spring Camp." National Park Service, U.S. Department of the Interior, 1949.

Baker, Norman L. *Braddock's Road, The Final Thrust, Fort Cumberland to the Monongahela, A Definitive Mapping of Braddock's Route*. Jumonville, PA: Braddock Road Preservation Association, 4 November 2011.

Benjamin, Marcus. "Braddock's Rock, A Study in Local History." Speech to National Society of Colonial Dames in the District of Columbia, April 12, 1899. Available at http://www.archive.org/details/braddocksrockstu00benj, June 15, 2009.

Berkehile, Don H. "Conestoga Wagons in Braddock's Campaign, 1755." *Bulletin 218: Contributions from the Museum of History and Technology*. Washington, D.C.: Smithsonian Institute, 1959, 142–153.

Bolling, John. "A Private Report of General Braddock's Defeat." Ed. John A. Schutz. *Pennsylvania Magazine of History and Biography* LXXIX (July 1955), 374–377.

"Braddock Road Accounts, 1755–1756." Records of the Proprietary Government, Provincial Council, 1682–1776, Record Group 21, Pennsylvania State Archives. Bureau of Archives and History, Pennsylvania Historical and Museum Commission. These records solely consist of payments to individuals involved in the abortive Burd's Road construction.

Breslaw, Elaine G., ed. "A Dismal Tragedy: Doctors Alexander and John Hamilton Comment on Braddock's Defeat." *Maryland Historical Magazine* 75:2 (June 1980), 118–144.

Campbell, J. Duncan. "Survey of the Braddock Road Through Fort Necessity National Battlefield Site." Fort Necessity National Battlefield, National Park Service, U.S. Department of the Interior, April 1964.

Cassell, Frank A. "The Last Days of General Braddock: The March Through Westmoreland and Allegheny Counties." *Westmoreland History* 7:2 (September 2002), 3–15.

Cassell, Frank A. and Elizabeth W. Cassell. "A Tour of Braddock's Road from Fort Necessity to Pittsburgh." *Westmoreland History* 7:2 (September 2002), 16–22.

Chartrand, René. *Monongahela, 1754–55, Washington's Defeat, Braddock's Disaster*. Oxford: Osprey, 2004.

Clark, Dr. Dora Mae. "The British Treasury and the Administration of Military Affairs in America, 1754–1774." *Pennsylvania History* II:4 (October 1935), 197–204.

Clary, David A. *George Washington's First War: His Early Military Adventures*. New York: Simon & Schuster, 2011.

Cohen, Sheldon S., ed. "Major William Sparke Along the Monongahela: A New Historical Account of Braddock's Defeat." *Pennsylvania History* 62 (October 1955), 546–556.

Cunningham, Colonel Arthur S. "March to Destiny, this being an attempt to reconstruct the Muster Rolls of the Braddock Expedition to Fort Duquesne which ended in disaster 9 July 1755 and to fix the order of March on that ill-fated day." New Oxford, PA: n.p., n.d.

Davis, N. Darnell. "British Newspaper Accounts of Braddock's Defeat." *The Pennsylvania Magazine of History and Biography* 23 (1899), 310–355.

Fleming, Thomas. "Braddock's Defeat." *Military History Quarterly* 3 (Autumn 1990), 84–95.

Franklin, Benjamin. *Autobiography of Benjamin Franklin*. Ed. Leonard W. Labaree, Ralph L. Ketcham, Helen C. Boatfield, and Helene H. Fineman. New Haven: Yale University Press, 1964.

Franklin, Benjamin. *The Papers of Benjamin Franklin*. Volume 6: April 1, 1755 through September 30, 1756. Ed. Leonard W. Labaree, Ralph L. Ketcham, Helen C. Boatfield, and Helene H. Fineman. New Haven: Yale University Press, 1963.

Gilliss, Chas J. "A Buried Treasure." *Historical Society of Fairfax County, Virginia Yearbook* 3 (1954).

Gordon, Harry. "A Letter from Will's Creek: Harry Gordon's Account of Braddock's Defeat." Ed. Charles M. Stotz. *Western Pennsylvania Historical Magazine* XLIV (June 1961), 129–136.

Graeff, Arthur D. "Settling the Wagoners Accounts ... 1755–1756." *Western Pennsylvania Geneaological Society Quarterly* 25:1 (Summer 1998), 26–27.

Hadden, James. *Washington's Expeditions 1753–1754 and Braddocks' Expedition 1755*. Uniontown, PA: 1910; reprint edition, Kessinger, 2009.

Hamilton, Charles, ed. *Braddock's Defeat*. Norman: University of Oklahoma Press, 1959.

Harrison, Fairfax. "With Braddock's Army, Mrs. Browne's Diary in Virginia and Maryland." *Virginia Magazine of History and Biography* XXXII:4 (October 1924), 305–320.

Hildeburn, Charles R. "Sir John St. Clair, Baronet, Quarter Master General in America, 1755 to 1767." *The Pennsylvania Magazine of History and Biography* 9, no. 1 (1885).

Hough, Walter S. *Braddocks' Road Through the Virginia Colony*. Winchester, VA: Winchester-Frederick County Historical Society, 1970.

Houston, Alan. "Benjamin Franklin and the Wagon Affair of 1755." *William and Mary Quarterly* 3rd Series, LXVI:2 (April 2009), 235–286.

Hume, Matthews H. "The History and Construction of Fort Cumberland at Cumberland, Maryland." Paper, Phi Mu Engineering Honor Society, April 8, 1928.

Hulbert, Archer Butler. *Historic Highways of America, Volume 4, Braddock's Road and Three Relative Papers*. Cleveland: The Arthur H. Clark Company, 1903.

Ives, Major Chauncey. "Braddock's Route." *Kittochtinny Historical Society Papers*. Chambersburg, PA: Press of Valley Spirit Publishing Company, 1900.

Jackson, Major Joseph A. *March to Disaster: Major General Edward Braddock and the Monongahela Campaign*. Fort Leavenworth: U.S. Army Command and General Staff College, 2008.

Keppel, Commodore Augustus. "The Keppel Manuscripts Descriptive of the Defeat of Major General Edward Braddock." In Charles Henry Lincoln, *Manuscript Records of the French and Indian War in the Library of the American Antiquarian Society*. 1909; reprint edition, Westminster, MD: Heritage Books, 2007, 171–177.

Kershaw, Gordon. "The Legend of Braddock's Gold Reconsidered." *Maryland Historical Magazine* 96, no. 1 (Spring 2001), 86–110.

Kopperman, Paul E. *Braddock at the Monongahela*. Pittsburgh: University of Pittsburg, 1977.

Kopperman, Paul E. "The Medical Aspect of the Braddock and Forbes Expeditions." *Pennsylvania History* 71:3 (2004), 257–283.

Kral, Cynthia, and John Boback. *Report on the Location and Status of the Extant Segments of Braddock Road, Fayette County, Pennsylvania*. 2003.

Lacock, John Kennedy. "Braddock Road." *The Pennsylvania Magazine of History and Biography* 38:1 (1914), 1–38.

Labaree, Leonard W. "Benjamin Franklin and the Defense of Pennsylvania, 1754–1757." *Pennsylvania History* 29 (January 1962), 7–23.

Laws, M.E.S. "R.N. and R.A. [Royal Navy and Royal Artillery] in Virginia, 1755." *Journal of the Society for Army Historical Research* 57 (Winter 1979), 193–205.

Lenschau, Justus M., Jr. "Braddock's Defeat." *Military Review* 51 (November 1971), 30–40.

"A List of Officers, Engineers, Ministers and Others Appointed to Attend His Majesty's Forces Ordered on an Expedition to North America under the Command of Major General Braddock," War Office Records, Board of Ordnance Miscellaneous Records, 1754, Public Records Office.

Lowdermilk, Will H., ed. "Major General Edward Braddock's Orderly Books, From February 26 to June 17, 1755." *History of Cumberland, Maryland*. 1878; reprint edition, Baltimore: Regional Publishing Company, 1976.

McCardell, Lee. *Ill-Starred General, Braddock of the Coldstream Guard*. Pittsburgh: University of Pittsburgh Press, 1958.

Ness, George T., Jr. "The Braddock Campaign, 1755." *The Military Engineer* 51 (January–February 1959), 18–23; (March–April), 111–117; (May–June), 211–213.

Netherton, Ross D. *Braddock's Campaign and the Potomac Route to the West*. Reprint, Winchester-Frederick County Historical Society, 1989.

Netherton, Ross D. "Building Braddock's Road: Sir John St. Clair and the Beginning of Braddock's March to Fort Duquesne." Paper presented at the Meeting of the Winchester-Frederick County Historical Society, Winchester, Virginia, September 17, 1981.

Netherton, Ross D. "The Carlyle House Conference: An Episode in the Politics of Colonial Union." In James Allen Braden, ed., *Proceedings of Northern*

Virginia Studies Conference, 1983, Alexandria: Empire to Commonwealth. Alexandria: Northern Virginia Community College, 1984, 57–84.

Nichols, Franklin T. "The Organization of Braddock's Army." *William and Mary Quarterly* 3rd Series 4:2 (April 1947), 125–147.

Older, Curtis L. *The Land Tracts of the Battlefield of South Mountain*. Bowie, MD: Heritage Books, 1999.

Pargellis, Stanley. "Braddock's Defeat." *American Historical Review* XLI:2 (January 1936), 253–269.

Pargellis, Stanley, ed. *Military Affairs in North America, 1748–1765, Selected Documents from the Cumberland Papers in Windsor Castle*. Reprint edition, Archon Books, 1969.

Phillips, Douglas, and Barnaby Nygren. "An Inquiry Into the Validity of the Legend of Braddock's Gold in Northern Virginia." Available at http://www.fairfaxhistoricalsociety.org/buried_gold.html (accessed 21 April 2009).

Pulliam, Ted. "A Huge Red Bull's Eye." *American History* 40:3 (August 2005), 50–57.

Riker, Thad W. "The Politics Behind Braddock's Expedition." *American Historical Review* 13:4 (July 1908), 742–752.

Sargent, Winthrop. *The History of An Expedition Against Fort Duquesne in 1755*. 1855; reprint edition, Lewisburg, PA: Wennawoods Publishing, 2005.

Scheel, Eugene. "The History of Loudon County, Virginia—General Braddock's March Through Loudoun in 1755." Accessed online at http://www.loudounhistory.org/history/loudoun-braddock-march-1755.htm, June 15, 2009.

Schultz, John A., ed. "A Private Report of General Braddock's Defeat." *Pennsylvania Magazine of History and Biography* 79:3 (July 1955), 374–377.

Steeley, James V. "A Road Not Lost: Rediscovering Braddock's Road through Westmoreland County." *Westmoreland History* 7:2 (September 2002), 23–29.

Temple, Henry W. *The Battle of Braddock's Field*. Washington, PA: 175th Anniversary Celebration Committee, 1930.

Tilburg, Frederick. "Report on an Expedition Over Braddock Road from Rock Spring Camp to Fort Necessity, April 29, 1950." National Park Service, U.S. Department of the Interior, May 31, 1950.

Tuggle, Kenneth H. "Dr. Thomas Walker Bicentennial Celebration." *Filson Club Historical Quarterly* 24 (July 1950), 276–279.

U.S. Department of the Interior, National Park Service. "A Proposed Trail Along the Braddock Road, A Study of Alternatives Report, Fort Necessity National Battlefield." National Park Service, U.S. Department of the Interior, n.d., ca. 1964.

Wahll, Andrew J., ed. *Braddock Road Chronicles, 1755*. Bowie, MD: Heritage Books, 1999.

Walker, Commissary Thomas. "Hasper Yeates and His Times." Ed. Charles I. Landis. *Pennsylvania Magazine of History and Biography* 46:3 (July 1922), 212–214.

Wallace, Fred C. *Study of the Defeat of General Braddock on July 9, 1755*. Fort Leavenworth: The Command and General Staff School, 1931.

Wallace, Paul A. W. "'Blunder Camp': A Note on the Braddock Road." *Pennsylvania Magazine of History and Biography* 87:1 (January 1963), 21–30.

Walsh, Richard, ed. "Braddock on July 9, 1755." *Maryland Historical Magazine* 60 (December 1965), 421–427.

Williams, Edward G. "Treasure Hunt in the Forest." *Western Pennsylvania History* 44:4 (December 1961), 383–396. Accounts from letterbook of James Furnis, William L. Clements Library, University of Michigan, Ann Arbor, Michigan.

Wilson, J. Cook, ed. "The Campaign of General Braddock." *English Historical Review* 1:1 (January 1886), 149–152. Letter of William Johnson, deputy paymaster general.

Whitfield, J. Bell, Jr., and Leonard W. Labaree. "Franklin and the Wagon Affair, 1755." *Proceedings of the American Philosophical Society* 101:6 (1957), 551–558.

Yaple, Robert L. "Braddock's Defeat: The Theories and a Reconsideration." *Journal of the Society for Army Historical Research* 46 (1968), 194–201.

Primary Sources

Acomb, Evelyn M., ed. *The Revolutionary Journal of Varon Ludwin Von Closen, 1780–1783*. Chapel Hill: University of North Carolina Press, 1958.

Advice to the Officers of the British Army, with the Addition of Some Hints to the Drummer and Private Soldier. London: W. Richardson, 1783.

Amherst, General Jeffery. Papers, WO 34/59. Microfilm copy at David Library of the American Revolution, Washington Crossing, Pennsylvania, microfilm reel 35.

Anburey, Lieutenant Thomas. *Travels Through the Interior Parts of America*. 1923; reprint edition, Bedford, MA: Applewood Books, n.d.

Barnsley, R.E. "The Life of an 18th Century Army Surgeon." *The Journal of the Society of Army Historical Research* XLIV, no. 179 (September 1966), 130–134.

Bland, Lieutenant General Humphrey. *A Treatise of Military Discipline, in Which Is Laid Down and Explained the Duty of the Officer and Soldier, Through the several Branches of the Service*. London: 1727; revised edition, 1759.

Bullitt, Thomas W. *My Life at Oxmoor, Life on a Farm in Kentucky Before the War*. 1911; reprint edition, privately printed, 1995.

Caruana, Adrian B. *British Artillery Ammunition,*

1780. Bloomfield, Ontario: Museum Restoration Service, 1979.

Clausewitz, Carl Von. *On War*. Ed. and trans. by Michael Howard and Peter Paret. New York: Alfred A. Knopf, 1993.

Dickinson Family Papers, Historical Society of Pennsylvania, Philadelphia, Pennsylvania.

Honeyman, A. Van Doren, ed. *Documents Relating to the Colonial History of the State of New Jersey, Volume XXXIII, Calendar of New Jersey Wills, Administrations, Etc.,Volume IV, 1761–1770*. Somerville, NJ: The Unionist-Gazette Association, Printers, 1928.

James, Alfred Procter, ed. *Writings of General John Forbes, Relating to his Service in North America*. Menashga, WI: The Collegiate Press, 1938; reprint edition, Arno Press, 1971.

Jeney, Mr. de. *The Partisan: Or, The Art of Making War in Detachment with Plans proper to facilitate the understanding of the several Dispositions and Movements necessary to Light Troops, in order to accomplish their Marches, Ambuscades, Attacks and Retreats with Success*. Trans. from the French of Mr. de Jeney by an officer in the army. London, 1760.

Muller, John. *A Treatise of Artillery, 1780*. 1780; reprint edition, Bloomfield, Ontario: Museum Restoration Service, 1977.

Nelson, William, ed. *Documents Relating to the Colonial History of the State of New Jersey, Volume XXV, Extracts from American Newspapers Relating to New Jersey, Volume VI, 1766–1767*. Paterson, NJ: The Call Printing and Publishing Company, 1903.

New Jersey Historical Records Survey. *Inventory of the County Archives of New Jersey, No. 19, Sussex County (Newton)*, Newark, NJ: The Historical Records Survey, 1941.

Records of the American Loyalist Claims Commission, 1776–1831, Great Britain Audit Office, microfilm copy at the David Library of the American Revolution.

Reese, George, ed. *The Official Papers of Francis Fauquier, Lieutenant Governor of Virginia, 1758–1768*, 3 vols. Charlottesville: University Press of Virginia, 1980–1981.

St. Clair, Sir John. Will, October 26, 1767, Essex County, New Jersey, New Jersey State Archives.

A Society of Gentlemen in Scotland. *Encyclopedia Britannica, or a Dictionary of Arts and Sciences*. 3 vol. Edinburgh: A. Bell and C. Macfarquhar, 1768–1771.

Tinling, Marion, ed. *The Correspondence of the Three William Byrds of Westover, Virginia, 1684–1776*, 2 vols. Charlottesville: Virginia Historical Society, 1977.

West, Martin, trans., *George Washington Remembers, Reflections on the French & Indian War*. (Lanham, Rowman & Littlefield, 2004

Williamson, John. *A Treatise on Military Finance, Containing the Pay, Subsistence, Deductions and Arrears of the Forces on the British and Irish Establishments, and All the Allowances in Camp, Garrison and Quarters, with an Enquiry into the Method of Clothing and Recruiting the Army, And An Extract from the Report of the Commissioners of Public Accounts Relating to the Office of the Pay Master General*. London: T. Egerton, 1782. Microfilm copy at U.S. Military Academy Library, West Point, New York.

Secondary Sources

Alden, John R. *General Gage in America*. New York: Greenwood Press, 1948.

Bates, E. Ralph. *Captain Thomas Webb, Anglo-American Methodist Hero*. World Methodist Historical Society, 1975.

"Benjamin Franklin in Lancaster County." *Journal of the Lancaster County Historical Society* 61 (January 1957), 3–26.

Bill, E.G.W. "A Cadet at the Royal Military Academy, 1778–1780." *The Journal of the Royal Artillery* 84 (October 1957), 310–312.

Brumwell, Stephen. "Home from the Wars, Attitudes towards Veterans in mid–Georgian Britain, and the Provisions Made for Them." *History Today* 52, no. 3 (March 2002), 41–47.

Chet, Guy. *Conquering the American Wilderness, The Triumph of European Warfare in the Colonial Northeast*. Amherst: University of Massachusetts Press, 2003.

Cleland, Hugh. *George Washington in the Ohio Valley*. Pittsburgh: University of Pittsburgh Press, 1955.

Cubbison, Douglas R. *"All Canada in the Hands of the British": General Jeffery Amherst and the 1760 Campaign to Conquer New France*. Norman: University of Oklahoma Press, 2013).

Cubbison, Douglas R. "The Coins of the British Private Soldier in the American Revolution." *The Petit Guerre, Newsletter of Captain Fraser's Company of Select Marksmen, British Brigade and Brigade of the American Revolution* (Winter 2004), accessed online at www.csmid.com.

Cubbison, Douglas R. "Eight Pence a Day, Pay of the British Private Soldier During the American Revolution" *The Petit Guerre, Newsletter of Captain Fraser's Company of Select Marksmen, British Brigade and Brigade of the American Revolution* (Winter 2004); accessed online at www.csmid.com.

Doerflinger, Thomas M. "Farmers and Dry Goods in the Philadelphia Market Area, 1750–1800." In Ronald Hoffman, John J. McCusker, Russell R. Menard and Peter J. Albert, ed., *The Economy of Early America, The Revolutionary Period, 1763–*

1790. Charlotesville: University Press of Virginia, 1988, 166–195.

Duffy, Christopher. *The Wild Goose and the Eagle: A Life of Marshal von Browne, 1705–1757.* London: Chatto & Windus, 1964.

Eid, Leroy V. "'A Kind of Running Fight': Indian Battlefield Tactics in the Late Eighteenth Century." *The Western Pennsylvania Historical Magazine* 71, no. 2 (April 1988), 147–171.

Fisher, Charles, and Lois M. Feister. *Archaeology of the Colonial Road at the John Ellison House, Knox's Headquarters State Historic Site, Vail's Gate, New York.* Albany: Bureau of Historic Sites, 2000.

Garnham, Neal. "Military Desertion and Deserters in Eighteenth-Century Ireland." *Eighteenth-Century Ireland* 20 (2005), 91–103.

Giddens, Paul H. "Governor Horatio Sharpe and his Maryland Government." *Maryland Historical Magazine* XXXII (June 1937), 156–74.

Graham, Dominick. "The Planning of the Beauséjour Operation and the Approaches to War in 1755." *The New England Quarterly* 41:4 (December 1968), 551–566.

Guy, Alan. "A Whole Army Absolutely Ruined in Ireland, Aspects of the Irish Establishment, 1715–1773." *Report—National Army Museum* (1978–1979), 30–43.

Houlding, J.A. *Fit for Service: The Training of the British Army, 1715–1795.* Oxford: Clarendon Press, 1981.

Hulbert, Archer Butler. *Historic Highways of America, Volume 5: The Old Glade (Forbes) Road.* Cleveland: The Arthur H. Clark Company, 1903.

James, Alfred P. "George Mercer of the Ohio Company, A Study in Frustration." *The Western Pennsylvania Historical Magazine* 46: 1 (January 1963), 2, 11–19.

Kozak, Robert. *"Shelter from the Storm: Frederick, Maryland, A Place of Refuge in the Seven Years War.* Westminster, MD: Heritage Books, 2008.

Lord, Philip L. *War over Walloomscoick: Land Use and Settlement Pattern on the Bennington Battlefield, 1777.* Albany: University of the State of New York, State Education Dept., 1989.

Marshall, Douglas W. "The British Engineers in America, 1755–1783." *Journal of the Society for Army Historical Research* LI: 207 (Autumn 1973), 155–163.

McCulloch, Ian. "Highland Chaplaincy in the French & Indian War, 1756–1763." Available online at http://www.electricscotland.com/history/scotreg/mcculloch/story3.htm (accessed 15 September 2009).

Mintz, Max M. *The Generals of Saratoga, John Burgoyne & Horatio Gates.* New Haven: Yale University Press, 1990.

Munson, James D. *Colo. John Carlyle, Gent., A True and Just Account of the Man and His House.* Northern Virginia Regional Park Authority, 1986.

Office of Communications, the Colonial Williamsburg Foundation."Colonial Williamsburg's Coaches." Available online at http://www.history.org/Foundation/newsroom/2012PressKit/releases/2012%20Coaches%20of%20Colonial%20Williamsburg.pdf (accessed 2 June 2012).

Papenfuse, Edward C., et al. *A Biographical Dictionary of the Maryland Legislature, 1635–1789.* (Baltimore: Johns Hopkins University Press, 1985, II: 726–8.

Pargellis, Stanley M. "The Four Independent Companies of New York." In *Essays in Colonial History Presented to Charles McLean Andrews by His Students.* 1931; reprint edition, Freeport, NY: Essay Index Reprint Series, Books for Libraries Press, 1966, 96–123.

Perry, James M. *Arrogant Armies, Great Military Disasters and the Generals Behind Them.* New York: John Wiley & Sons, 1996.

Powell, Dr. Walter L., ed. *The Braddock Road by John Kennedy Lacock.* The Braddock Road Preservation Association, 2010.

Regan, Geoffrey. *Great Military Disasters, A Historical Survey of Military Incompetence.* New York: M. Evans, 1987.

Scarlett, Charles, Jr. "Governor Horatio Sharpe's Whitehall." *Maryland Historical Magazine* SLVI (1951), 8–26.

Shannon, David T. "Quartermaster General Sir John St. Clair and the Moland Family." Moland House Museum, Warwick Townshp Historical Society, Hartsville, Pennsylvania.

Steppler, Glenn A. "British Military Law, Discipline and the Conduct of Regimental Courts Martial in the later Eighteenth Century." *English Historical Review* 102 (1987), 862–863.

Steppler, Glenn A. *The Common Soldier in the Reign of George III, 1760–1793.* Ph.D. thesis, University of Oxford, 1984 (typescript at The David Library of the American Revolution, Washington's Crossing, Pennsylvania).

Tilberg, Frederick. *Fort Necessity National Battlefield Site, Pennsylvania.* Washington, D.C.: National Park Service, 1954; revised edition, 1956.

Walzer, John Flexer. "Transportation in the Philadelphia Trading Area, 1740–1775." M.A. thesis, University of Wisconsin, 1968.

Index

Albany, New York 112, 130, 150, 189
Alexandria, Virginia 6, 16, 18, 21, 27–28, 30, 34, 36–37, 40–41, 48–49, 51, 53–54, 65, 135–136, 143, 158–159, 161–162, 164, 168, 180; Braddock's encampment 38–39, 46, 60–61, 164–165; King's warehouse 22, 39; movement from 57–66
Allegheny Mountains 3–4, 56, 62–63, 67–68, 70, 74, 116
artificers 25
artillery 24–25, 35, 57–59, 65, 69–70, 140; Pennsylvania Provincial Artillery on Forbes Campaign 114, 121; powder cart 98, *99*; tumbrel *99*; wagon *89*
Amherst, Gen. Jeffery 28, 123–126; correspondence with Sir John St. Clair 210*n*

bakers 21, 72
Balfour, Mr. James (assistant money contractor) 20
bat horses- 39–40, 70, 73, 76, 80, 115, 121–122, 135, 166, 176, 180
Belcher, Gov. Jonathan 153–154
Board of Ordnance 22–23, 209*n*
Bouquet, Col. Henry 39, 116–124
Braddock, Gen. Edward 5–6, *43*, 60–61, 64, 67, 89, 92–93, 102, 107, 132, 136, 143, 145, 147, 155, 158–159, 162, 164, 167–168, 172, 175, 177, 179–180; chariot, English 61, 67; Council of War 75–76, 87–89, 94; death 110; grand conference 61, 67, 80, 97
Braddock Campaign: administrative organization 10–34; artillery train 25, 88–90, 140, 155–156, 165, 167–170, 174; Battle of Monongahela, July 9, 1755 98–110, 182–184, 189–191, 208–209*n*; camp arrangement 75–76, *78, 79*; grand conference decisions 61; line of march *78*; planning phase in London 34, 181, 211*n*; St. Clair's preparations for movement, January–April 1755 34, 132; St. Clair's proposal for movement forward, April 1755 166–167; movement from Alexandria to Fort Cumberland, April–May 1755 34–35, 57–71; movement from Fort Cumberland to Forks of Ohio, June–July 1755 35, 72–97, 177; problems with wagons and horses 39–42, 59, 88–89, 168–173
Bradstreet, Colonel John 111–113, 130
British Army Hospital 29–30, 36–37, 133
British Army staff 10–34, 72–73; agent for the money contractor 18–20; aide-de-camp 10–11; assistant deputy quartermaster general 16; brigade major 13; chaplain 27–29; commissary 21, 166; commissary of musters 15; company adjutant 14; deputy adjutant general 12–13; deputy paymaster general 17; deputy quartermaster general 16, 72–73, 115, 120, 165; military secretary 12; provost marshal 25–27; regimental adjutant 14; regimental quartermaster 17; storekeeper of stores and provisions 21–22; wagon master 22
Browne, Mrs. Charlotte (hospital matron) 28–30, 37, 52, 70
Burd, James 56
Burton, Lt. Col. Dunbar's Regiment of Foot 93–94, 98, 164; biography 213*n*

Carlyle, Mr. John 36, 57, 136, 145, 150–151, 160–161, 164; Braddock at his house 60–61, 89; storekeeper of stores and provisions 21–22, 39, 40
Chapman, Maj. Russel (Halkett's Regiment of Foot) 75–77, 177; biography 77
Chelsea Hospital 47
Clausewitz, Gen. Carl Von (Prussian military theorist) 103
Company of Military Historians 49, *50, 104*
Conococheague, Maryland 39, 57, 68, 114, 135, 142, 167
Craik, Surg. James, Virginia Provincial 29–30, 33
Croghan, George 62–64, 130
Crown Point *see* Fort St. Frederick
Cumberland, Duke of (Prince William) 5

DeLancey, James (acting governor of New York) 149–150; biography 212*n*
Delaware Provincials *see* Lower County Provincials
Dick, Mr. Charles (joint commissary) 21, 36, 135, 145, 151–152, 160, 162, 165, 167–168
Dickinson, Atty. John 127–128
Dinwiddie, Lt. Gov. Robert (Virginia) 4, 5, 21, 44, 46, 48, 61, 110, 137, 140, 143, 151–152, 158, 177, 180, 184–186, 189; biography 201*n*; logistical support for Braddock campaign 36, 40, 53–54, 133, 167, 176
Disney, Lt. Daniel (Halkett's Regiment of Foot) 14
Dobbs, Gov. Arthur (North Carolina) 143, 176; biography 211–212*n*
Dunbar, Col. Thomas 5, 57, 65–71, 75, 90, 93, 108–109, 182, 184–189

engineers 23–24

Fairfax, Lord Thomas 54–57, 62, 73–74, 134–135, 144–145, 152
fascines 81–*82*; knife 83, *84*
Forbes, Brig. Gen. John 6, 9, 34, 113–124, 130
Forbes Campaign Against Fort Duquesne, 1758 54, 113–122, 130
Fort Cumberland 19–20, 28, 34–36, 44, 47, 51–53, 57–58, 61–62, 71–72, 110, 114, 131, 133–134, 137, 144, 146, 151, 163–165, 170–172, 177, 189
Fort Duquesne 4, 35–36, 54, 61, 98–99, 109, 113–122, 140, 179, 181, 188
Fort Ligonier see Loyalhanna Encampment
Fort Ligonier Museum 9, *89*, *99*
Fort Necessity 5, 47, 50–51, 54, 73, 92
Fort Niagara 25, 35, 61, 73, 150
Fort Oswego (on Lake Ontario) 112, 149–150
Fort Pitt 125
Fort St. Frederick (Crown Point) 61
Franklin, Benjamin 22, 41–*43*, 54, 59, 214n
Franklin, William 41–42
Frazier's Cabin 101–103, 107–108
Frederick, Maryland 41–*43*, 47, 54, 57–58, 65–67
Furnis, Mr. James (commissary of stores and provisions to artillery) 25, 103, 109–110, 209n

Gage, Lt. Col. Thomas (44th Regiment of Foot) 75, 94; at Battle of Monongahela 98, 100–101, 102–106, 108; biography 60, 205n, 209n
Gates, Capt. Horatio 47–48, 90, 106
George II (king of England) 5
Gordon, Engineer Henry 24, 53, 74, 77, 104–105, 108, 169
Gordon, Lt. John (Dunbar's Regiment of Foot) 14
Great Crossings 91–92
Great Meadows 92
Great Philadelphia Wagon Road 57, 61–62, 65, 68–69, 194

Halkett, Capt. Francis 13
Halkett, Lt. James 13, 109
Halkett, Col. Sir Peter 5, 13, 53, 57, 63–65, 67, 69–70, 75, 85, 87, 90, 93–94, 164, 167–172, 174–175; at Battle of Monongahela 98–100, 109
Halkett, Mr. Peter 13
Hamilton, Dr. Alexander 53, 92–93, 100, 103, 105, 107, 111
Hamilton, Chaplain John (Dunbar's Regiment of Foot) 27–29
Hampton, Virginia 35–37, 133–134, 139, 143
Haystack Mountain see Wills Mountain
horses see bat horses; wagons
Hughes, Chaplain Philip (Halkett's Regiment of Foot) 27–29
Hunter, Mr. John (money contractor) 18–20, 133–134, 176

Independent Companies of British Regulars 46–48, 59, 131–132, 137, 142, 144–146, 151, 180, 185, 187–188; New York 35, 47–48, 59, 90, 106, 162–163; scholarship on 204n; South Carolina 35, 47
Innes, Col. John (Maryland Provincials) 51, 144, 152, 158

Jacobite Rebellion 13
James, Frederic (artist) 43
Jeffereys, Thomas 42–43, 139, 211n
Johnson, Col. William (Indian supervisor and New York militia officer) 61, 111
Johnson, Mr. William (paymaster) 18, 91

Kennywood Amusement Park 101

Lacock, Prof. John Kennedy 82
Leslie, Lt. Matthew (Halkett's Regiment of Foot) 16, 21
Lewis, Capt. Andrew 51
Little Crossings 87–*88*
Little Meadows 85–87, 90, 178–180
Lower County Provincials on Forbes Campaign, 1758 115
Loyalhanna Encampment 113–122

Macklellar, Engineer Patrick 24, 74, 143, 156, 166, 167, 169; biography 211n
Maryland Provincials 51; Forbes Campaign, 1758 115; recruitment by Sir John St. Clair 51, 145–146, 151–152, 158–160
Mercer, Capt. George- 49–50, 136, 204n
Moland, Elizabeth "Betsey" Moland ("Lady John St. Clair") 125–128
Moland, John House (Warwick Township, Pennsylvania) *126*
Moland Family 125–128
Monongahela River- 1, 3, 7, 14, 16–18, 27–30, 35, 46, 74, 78, 90, 98, 130, 154, 169, 181; crossing, July 9, 1755 96–103, 182–183
Montresor, Engineer John 24
Morris, Capt. Robert 11, 67, 93
Morris, Deputy Gov. Robert (Pennsylvania) 54–55, 63–64, 130, 138, 141, 154, 181; biography 204–205n
Muller, Prof. John 23

Napier, Dr. James (surgeon director) 29
Napier, Col. Robert 42, 46, 48, 90, 92, 112, 139, 142, 180, 182, 187, 190, 211n
Native Americans: Battle of Monongahela 103–109; Braddock Campaign 63–64, 68, 96, 139, 179; Cherokee Indians on Forbes Campaign, 1758 114
New York City 111, 113, 123–124
North Carolina Provincials on Forbes Campaign, 1758 115

Ohio Company 52, 53, 57
Ohio Country 4
Orde [Ord], Capt. Thomas 25, 156
Orme, Lt. Robert 5, 11, 62, 67, 78, 90–96, 103, 108, 156, 159, 161–162, 168, 171, 175, 178–180

pack horses see bat horses
Pennsylvania Provincials 114–116
Philadelphia, Pennsylvania 54, 113–114, 124–125, 204n
Pitcher, Mr. James (commissary of musters) 15, 47, 51, 131–132, 142, 145

Potomac River 58; crossing 65, 68, 70–71, 173–174; transportation 43–44, 48, 54, 59, 133, 137

"Rattlesnake Colonel" 71, 206*n*
Read, John (deputy wagon master) 22
Regiments of Foot 59, 62, 115, 185, 187–188; Col. Sir Peter Halkett's (44th Regiment of Foot) 5, 13, *49, 50,* 57, 60–62, 64–65, 69–70, 75–76, 85, 87, 90, 98, 102, 106–107, 169, 173–175, 190; Col. Thomas Dunbar's (48th Regiment of Foot) 5, 57, 65–71, 75–76, 90, 98, 102, **104,** 106–108, 169, 171; Irish drafts in 44th and 48th Foot, 1755 38, 44–46, 72, 93; provincial drafts for 44th and 48th Foot, 1755 72, 133, 145, 154, 158–162, 164; Royal American Regiment (60th Regiment of Foot) 117, 125; 61st Regiment of Foot 128; 28th Regiment of Foot 125; 29th Regiment of Foot 127
roads 62, 73, 118, 134–137,144–145, 163–164, 167–171, 177; between Winchester and Fort Cumberland, April 1755 60–61, 172–173; construction techniques 54–55, 65, 81–86
Royal Military Academy, Woolwich 23
Royal Navy Detachment on Braddock Campaign 65–72, 74–75

St. Clair, Sir John 67, 69, 92–93, 94, 96; arrival at Hampton, Virginia 36; at Battle of Monongahela, July 9, 1755 98–108, 180, 182–184, 189–191; biography 9; commissary of musters 15, 144–147, 151; correspondence with Gen. Jeffery Amherst 210*n*; Council of War 75; death 127; dispute with Lt. Col. Adam Stephens 119–121; failed crossing of Wills Mountain 80–81; Forbes Campaign, 1758 113–124; grand conference, missed 61–62, 213–214*n*; as "hussar" 42, 121–122; illness 125, 127, 130; initial planning phase in London 34, 181, 211*n*; introduction to his letterbook 6–7; letterbook 1, 2, 131, 180; marriage to Elizabeth "Betsey" Moland 125–127; planning for movement forward, January–April 1755 34, 132; movement from Alexandria to Fort Cumberland, April–May 1755 34–35, 57–71, 129–130; movement from Fort Cumberland to Forks of Ohio, June–July 1755 35, 72–97, 129–130; Pontiac's Rebellion 124–125; Potomac River Transportation 43–44; problems with wagons and horses, 1755 39–42, 76, 115–116, 121–122, 168–173; proposal for movement forward to Fort Duquesne, April 1755 166–167; recruitment of Maryland Provincials 51, 145–146, 151–152, 158–160; recruitment of Virginia Provincials 48–51, 145–147, 152, 154–158, 160–162, 184–185; relationship with Pennsylvania Colony 62–64; at Williamsburg, Virginia 36, 100, 110–111, 131, 189
Sharpe, Horatio (governor of Maryland) 36, 44–46, 48, 51, 61, 116, 131, 137, 139, 141, 143, 145, 151–152, 154, 156, 159–160, 164; biography 203*n*; logistical support for Braddock Campaign 36
Shirley, William (governor of Massachusetts) 12, 61, 111–112, 130, 164, 175, 183, 186–188
Shirley, William, Jr. (secretary to Gen. Braddock) 5, 12, 61, 67, 147, 165, 171
Sparks, Maj. William (Dunbar's Regiment of Foot) 75, 85, 94, 102–103
Specie 18–*19,* 20, 61, 167–168, 213*n*
Spendelow, Lt. Charles, Royal Navy 77; crossing of Wills Mountain 80–81
Stephens, Capt./Lt. Col. Adam (Virginia Provincials) 51, 111, 119–121

Turtle Creek 96–97, 99

Verrant, Ensign Henry (Halkett's Regiment of Foot) 17
Virginia Provincials 93, 115, 171, 172, 184–185; at Battle of Monongahela 98, 105, 110; Forbes Campaign 114–115, 119–121; recruitment by St. Clair, 1755 48–51, 136, 142, 144–147, 151–152, 154–158, 161–162; 1755 Company of Carpenters and Artificers 48- 49, 56–57, 105, 136, 147–148, 151, 156–158, 173–174; 1755 Company of Horse 149, 158, 170; 1755 Company of Rangers 62, 148–149, 158, 161–164, 169–170

wagons 35, 39–41, 53–54, 59, 76, 88–89, 115–116, 121–122, 137, 151, 167–173, 180
Walker, Mr. Thomas (joint commissary) 21, 36, 40, 135, 142, 145, 151–152, 165, 167, 176
Washington, George 57–58, 191; aide-de-camp to Braddock 11, 20, 68, 89, 105, 108–109; 1753 expedition to Ohio Country 4–5, 75; 1754 Fort Necessity Expedition 5, 29–30, 47, 50–51, 54, 73, 75, 80, 92, 95–96; 1755 Fort Duquesne Campaign 85–86
Washington, Townsend (assistant commissary) 21
Webb, Ensign Thomas (Dunbar's Regiment of Foot) 17, 202*n*
Webster, Robert (Halkett's 44th Regiment of Foot; provost marshal) 27
whiskey and rum, on Forbes Campaign, 1758 118, 120
William and Mary College 49
Williamsburg 19–20, 36, 61, 111, 145–147, 164–165
Williamson, Engineer Adam 24
Wills Creek *see* Fort Cumberland
Wills Mountain 80–81
Winchester 20, 30, 33, 36, 38, 40–42, 56–60, 62–69, 83, 114–115, 117, 133, 135–139, 141–146, 150–152, 154–155, 157–159, 161–165, 168–176, 180
Wolfe, Maj. Gen. James 14

Youghiogheny River 74, 91–*95,* 98, 101, 162, 169, 181

www.ingramcontent.com/pod-product-compliance
Lightning Source LLC
Chambersburg PA
CBHW081554300426
44116CB00015B/2877